TRUTH v. JUSTICE

THE UNIVERSITY CENTER FOR
HUMAN VALUES SERIES

AMY GUTMANN, EDITOR

TRUTH v. JUSTICE

THE MORALITY OF
TRUTH COMMISSIONS

Edited by

Robert I. Rotberg and Dennis Thompson

PRINCETON UNIVERSITY PRESS

PRINCETON AND OXFORD

Library of Congress Cataloging-in-Publication Data

Truth v. justice : the morality of truth commissions / edited by
Robert I. Rotberg and Dennis Thompson.
p.   cm.—(University Center for Human Values series)
Includes bibliographical references and index.
ISBN 0-691-05071-6 (cloth : alk. paper)
ISBN 0-691-05072-4 (pbk. : alk. paper)
1. South Africa. Truth and Reconciliation Commission. 2. Apartheid—
South Africa. 3. Human rights—South Africa. 4. Amnesty—South Africa.
5. Human rights. 6. Amnesty. 7. Reconciliation. I. Rotberg, Robert I.
II. Thompson, Dennis. III. Series
DT1945.T78   2000
323′.06—dc21   00-035962   CIP

This book has been composed in Caslon

The paper used in this publication meets the minimum requirements of
ANSI/NISO Z39.48-1992 (R 1997) (*Permanence of Paper*)

www.pup.princeton.edu

Printed in the United States of America

10 9 8 7 6 5 4 3 2 1

10 9 8 7 6 5 4 3 2 1
(Pbk.)

Contents

Acknowledgments

Most of the contributors to this volume presented the drafts of their chapters to the Truth and Reconciliation Commission (TRC), commissioners and staff, at a conference held at Somerset West, Cape province, South Africa, in May 1998. The contributors and the truth commissioners and investigators were joined at the meeting by several South African jurists, sociologists, and physicians. Some of the chapters in this book also emerged from the conference itself, out of what were originally informal presentations.

Thus, this is a book informed by a dialogue between the authors and South African practitioners and interlocutors. It emerges from the raw words of 22,000 testifiers before the TRC, their evaluation by the commissioners and their staff, and intense discussions about the meaning of that evaluation by the conferees.

This book's authors sought and received a critique of their approaches from the commissioners and other South Africans, and revised their chapters in accord with that dialogue. The commissioners and staff of the TRC said that they had received fresh ideas about how to understand their findings and present their conclusions. A summary (not a transcript) of the discussions at Somerset West, prepared by Simon Stacey, is available.

The World Peace Foundation of Cambridge, Massachusetts, in cooperation with the South African Truth and Reconciliation Commission, organized and convened the meeting in Somerset West. In 1996, the Foundation, the Human Rights Program of the Harvard Law School, and the Harvard Center for Ethics and the Professions held an initial discussion of the questions that inform this book. An edited transcript of that meeting was published as Henry Steiner (ed.), *Truth Commissions: A Comparative Assessment* (Cambridge, Mass., 1997).

The editors of this volume gratefully acknowledge the efforts of all their colleagues who wrote and revised, and came together so productively in Somerset West. They also thank the tireless Emily Edson, of the Foundation, and Paddy Clarke, of the TRC, for their unstinting contributions to the smooth running of the Somerset West conference. This book could not have been developed and brought together in its final form without the significant efforts of Dana Francis, Rachel Gisselquist, Stacey Warner, and Maeve McNally of the Foundation, and we thank them as well. Sylvia Coates produced the index.

TRUTH v. JUSTICE

I

Truth Commissions and the Provision of Truth, Justice, and Reconciliation

ROBERT I. ROTBERG

"Never again!" is a central rallying cry of truth commissions, and one about which perpetrators and victims can agree. The notion of "never again" captures the response of societies that are recovering their own equilibria, their own dignity, and their own sense of integrity. Truth commissions are intended to be both preventive and restorative.

But if societies are to prevent recurrences of past atrocities and to cleanse themselves of the corrosive enduring effects of massive injuries to individuals and whole groups, societies must understand—at the deepest possible levels— what occurred and why. In order to come fully to terms with their brutal pasts, they must uncover, in precise detail, who did what to whom, and why, and under whose orders. They must seek, at least, thus to uncover the truth— insofar as this aim is humanly and situationally possible after the fact.

Truth commissions generally are created after a totalitarian/authoritarian regime has been succeeded by a democratic one. Sometimes the transition is preceded by civil and economic war bolstered by world public opinion, some- times by invasion, and sometimes when societal revulsion overwhelms a mili- tary junta, a minority dictatorship, or strong arm pseudodemocrats. Massive human rights violations usually accompany such arrogations of power. The mandate of the successor regime is to establish or revive democracy and to prevent any resumption of human rights abuses. It also seeks to reconcile the old and the new, and to move forward in effective harmony.

Truth commissions thus seek, whatever their mandate from a new govern- ment, to uncover the past in order to answer questions that remain unan- swered: What happened to husbands, sons, wives, and lovers at the hands of the ousted regime? Who gave the orders? Who executed the orders? What was the grand design? Who benefited? Getting the facts provides closure, at least in theory. Making it possible for perpetrators to be confronted by victims and the heirs of victims (as in the South African and Guatemalan cases) can pro- vide further closure. In societies as disparate as Argentina, Bosnia, Cambodia, Cyprus, El Salvador, Guatemala, Haiti, Nigeria, South Africa, and Sri Lanka, and now in Sierra Leone and Kosovo, there is a natural, consuming desire to elicit as complete an accounting as possible of how people disappeared, how they were assassinated, how and why they were flung from airplanes above the Atlantic Ocean, and how and why they were slaughtered in groups and tossed into unmarked graves.

There are the clinical commissions that have tried to discover precisely what happened to persons who vanished during a "dirty war" organized by the defeated regime. They have largely taken testimony behind closed doors and published as accurate a recounting as possible given their constrained circumstances and resources. Sometimes, publication has been delayed or avoided, as in Sri Lanka for some months and in Haiti, for all practical purposes, indefinitely. In several of those cases, especially in the earliest truth commissions, there has been little attempt to go beyond the bare facts—to examine the moral and historical underpinnings of the crimes committed. It has been enough to answer specific questions rather than to affix societal blame. Some, however, have done neither; Haiti's *Si M Pa Rele*, its National Commission for Truth and Justice, is the prime example.

Those more circumscribed and limited commission efforts reflect both the previous paucity of experience with the truth commission method, and also the bargains struck, as in Guatemala and El Salvador, and in adverse or better than adverse circumstances between an outgoing regime and its successor or between modern governments and human rights watchdogs. Most of the commissions that were formed later had broader mandates and extensive goals. They have sought more than an accounting, and something closer to an approximation of a full truth, about the chain of circumstances that resulted in massive human rights violations, and how each individual atrocity fitted into a carefully constructed mosaic of guilt. These more ambitious commissions have tried to apportion that guilt, both to those who attacked others individually and to those who authorized the dastardly acts by direction or indirection. Ultimately, these commissions wanted to understand the structure of previous abuse, and the extent to which it could be articulated.

The Guatemalan three-man Commission on Historical Clarification (1997–1999) was prohibited from naming names and from apportioning blame directly. Yet the nine-volume report of the United Nations–backed Guatemalan commission found the army responsible for more than 200,000 deaths and disappearances during thirty-six years of civil war. It documented 626 massacres perpetuated by the army and 32 by its opponents, and labeled the military actions genocide. By so doing, the commission nullified a 1996 blanket amnesty that banned prosecution for all other crimes.

South Africa's Truth and Reconciliation Commission (TRC) is the prime example of a commission with a mandate much broader than that of Guatemala's, extensive goals, and a comprehensive vision of how such an effort can prevent future conflict and ensure that "never again!" becomes a societal reality. A book examining the nature of truth commissions inevitably must focus largely (but not exclusively) on the new standard-setting model of the practice.

The TRC, though flawed in many ways, has set a high standard for future commissions.

The importance and rationale of the TRC must be understood in the context of apartheid. The rigid, legalized segregation of South African apartheid began in 1948 when the National Party (led and participated in largely by Afrikaners) won a narrow victory and proceeded to legislate against the vast African majority, against Communism, and against all forms of dissent and disagreement with the political aims of Afrikanerdom. Basic human rights were discarded. Terror gradually became perfected as an instrument of state control. For all Africans, coloureds, and Indians, and even for some white liberals, National Party rule was arbitrary and autocratic, obviously discriminatory, and mean. The police state that was created was supported by atrocities and brutalities equal to if not exceeding those on the other side of the Atlantic Ocean.

After the tyranny of apartheid was removed in 1994, and Nelson Mandela, a long-time prisoner, became the new South Africa's first president, Parliament was established, and he appointed (in 1995) the Truth and Reconciliation Commission to discover the dark facts of apartheid, to report them to South Africa and the world, and to trade amnesty, where necessary, for information. The TRC grew out of an elaborate political compromise that rejected the outgoing regime's demand for blanket amnesty and no retribution in exchange for a mechanism (the TRC) that could grant amnesty for political acts. The origins of the commission are discussed more fully below, in chapters in this volume by Alex Boraine and Dumisa Ntsebeza. They are two among the seventeen original members of the TRC, chaired by Anglican Archbishop Desmond Tutu. The TRC's report, published in 1998, is discussed by nearly all of the contributors, but especially by Wilhelm Verwoerd and Charles Villa-Vicencio, two of its authors.

Whereas the first commissions (Uganda, Bolivia, Argentina, Zimbabwe, Uruguay, the Philippines, Chile, and ten or so more) dared not hear testimony in public for fear that it might be too inflammatory or arouse retaliation from the ousted military officers (who were still around) or their patrons, the South African commission not only insisted on public as well as private testimony, and the public interrogation of accused perpetrators by victims as well as prosecutorial figures from the commission's staff, and by the commissioners themselves, but it also went a step further and permitted press and television reports. Widely disseminated verbatim accounts became the content of an ongoing national drama. Rather than having a distilled version of what had occurred in past times summarized in a commission report, and then released, the South Africans were (with very few exceptions) totally transparent. Their activities educated the new society directly, well before its official findings could be presented to parliament and the president.

Truth could thus be affirmed by individuals across the land as well as by commissioners. The story of the past could not therefore be just one story, but a million perceptions of what had been revealed before the commission and argued back and forth between those charged with revealing what and why, and the victims, who wanted nothing but the full truth. The South African version of a commission empowered a popular understanding incrementally, rather than comprehensively by polished summary. Moreover, in this way, the new society was able to begin continuously to reconstruct itself—in terms of what it had gone through and how it was going to cope with its travails. As the South African TRC itself learned more and more, it could peel back layer after layer of apartheid atrocity. The report of the TRC, said a commissioner, could "not tell the story of apartheid as a whole, but only the story of its abuses of bodily integrity."[1] The TRC's hearings could slice closer and closer to the bone of terror and inhumanity in a way that the more limited commissions in El Salvador or Haiti never could.

The South African commission has become the model for all future commissions, which is why the chapters in this book examine the experience of the TRC much more fully than they do commissions elsewhere. But this book is about the theory of truth commissioning as well as its practice. It is about the tensions between truth and justice, about the prevention of future conflict through truth commissions, about reconciliation in postconflict situations, about knowledge as opposed to retribution, about victim's as well as perpetrator's rights, and about societal restoration.

There is a strong sense that a society can move forward only after it comes to terms with its collective angst. In the South African case, that meant dealing with outrages committed by whites against Africans, Africans against Africans, Africans against whites, and the African National Congress (ANC) against its own members, as well as with whites coming to terms with the evils of apartheid, perpetrated over more than forty years, with blacks primarily the victims. Tutu asked whites to apologize and take responsibility for their actions during apartheid. Is there no leader of "some stature and some integrity in the white community," he asked in a statement released to the press, who will admit that the whites "had a bad policy that had evil consequences?"[2]

"Moving forward" and "coming to terms with" are figures of speech that provide the rationale for most truth commissions. There is an assumption that a society emerging from an intrastate cataclysm of violence will remain stable, and prosper, only if the facts of the past are made plain. Critics, including several contributors to this book, question that assumption, suggesting that the "truth" that a commission may uncover can only be tentative. Additional truths, they argue, will emerge by encouraging conflict and controversy, not by establishing one truth and declaring consensus. Continuing moral controversy is desirable in a democracy, and fact-finding in the service of reconciliation must take that goal into account.

The rationale for truth commissions, nevertheless, is that the inexplicable should be understood, that actual murders and murderers will be unmasked, that unmarked graves will be located, and, for example, that the bizarre attempt to poison apartheid's opponents will be revealed. As contributors to this book imply, proper remembrances fulfill the collective needs of badly damaged societies. There is too much injury to individuals and nations. Forgetting reinforces losses of self-esteem among victims and even among victims as a group.

Truth commissions exist because of political compromises, in South Africa's recent case as a substitute for the broad amnesty that the outgoing regime wanted, and could not get.[3] But commissions also exist because society is unwilling to forgive and forget, refusing to move on without confronting the repression of its precursor generation. Those who advocate dispensing with truth commissions and simply moving on after a massive regime change argue that the kinds of confrontation engendered by the commission process only make societal tensions more palpable. Opening the old wounds, they argue, harms rather than helps beneficially to reconstruct a society in transition. By this logic, the truth commission process retards reconciliation. Indeed, a society cannot forgive what it cannot punish.[4] Thus, the prevailing assumption that postconflict reconciliation is both desirable and possible, as well as necessary, may be incorrect. Similarly, some wonder wisely whether the approach to reconciliation that most of the contributors to this book support may be culturally specific; South Africa may have special qualities that differentiate its potential for reconciliation from a society like Sri Lanka, where a bitter seventeen-year civil war continues.

Most commissions have not tried to reconcile the old, which oppressed, with the new, which enshrines democracy. But the Chilean commission did, and the South African version had as its primary mission the seeking of reconciliation through acquiring and displaying the truth, and, in its chairman's religious design, requesting atonement. Thus, for him and for the other commissioners, uncovering the facts—the truth—of the past was a necessary if not sufficient stage that could prepare the new South Africa to be reconciled, and whites and blacks to be reconciled to one another.

Reconciliation may or may not prove possible in the aftermath of an apartheid-riven society. But the TRC operated as if it were, and as if retailing the truth of the deepest machinations of apartheid—the culpability of its highest leaders and its mad-doctor schemes of biological and chemical warfare—would somehow set South Africa free to forge a successful multiracial society. To meet those goals—to encourage the kinds of testimony that would reveal apartheid at its moral worst—the TRC had to find a way to compel the real culprits to come forward and confess. Amnesty was the result, as the postamble to the interim constitution prefigured: perpetrators, black and white, would receive perpetual immunity from prosecution if they testified fully and candidly about their terrible deeds and if they could demonstrate (by the loose standards that the TRC used pragmatically) that their crimes were political; that is, that they served political ends or were motivated by political beliefs.

Because the South African TRC is the latest and the grandest example of postconflict truth seeking, it is critical to inquire to what extent truth can be acquired by such means. Can justice in its several forms be served equally well? Would standard forms of prosecution be preferred? Does the amnesty process satisfy various criteria for justice? Does it distort the trial system that societies usually use to punish transgressors and prevent evildoing? Assuming that reconciliation is both desirable and possible, does the truth commission method, with its transparency and attendant publicity, retard or advance the process? How can commissions achieve these goals through the processes of their constituted endeavors and activities, and through the medium of a published report?

Such questions form the core of this book's combined philosophical and pragmatic inquiry. Gutmann and Thompson's chapter raises a central objection to the truth commission endeavor: truth commissions, they write, "sacrifice the pursuit of justice as usually understood for the sake of promoting some other social purpose such as reconciliation." But "trading criminal justice for a general social benefit . . . is, and should be, morally suspect." Indeed, if the moral case for truth commissions in a democratic society is to be made it must satisfy three critical criteria: It must (1) substitute rights and goods "that are moral" and equivalent (or "comparable") to the justice foregone; (2) be broadly inclusive so as to foster social cooperation among *all* citizens who have legitimate claims on the society being reconstructed; and (3) be "moral in practice," and intimately connected to the democratic ethos of the successor government so that the retribution being sacrificed can be appreciated in terms of the realization of specific, not general, forms of societal benefit.

Gutmann and Thompson assert that the mere stability of a successor government would not satisfy the first criterion, with its emphasis on moral goods. Such social stability only becomes morally relevant when it is part of a new, just dispensation or can be shown to promote justice in the future. Those who defend truth commissions therefore must distinguish moral justifications from the interests of individuals or groups.

The second criterion in their scheme does not mean putting such justifications to a referendum. Rather, there is the test of reason. Gutmann and Thompson want truth commissions to be accessible and inclusive, and they are prepared to take into account the previous history of the country and the conflict, with its critical legacy of injustice. Likewise, the third criterion cannot be satisfied by even a fully moral critique of contemporary violence and injustice for the sake of future peace. The commission is justified best that functions in the democratic spirit of the government which it serves.

Gutmann and Thompson, conscious as they are of the postamble that certified an important political compromise, insist that a political compromise is not necessarily a moral compromise. Providing for amnesty satisfied political needs, not moral ones. What is needed to transform a purely opportunistic, pragmatic political decision into a morally defensible one is the approach that Tutu has articulated so consistently: that criminal justice may be sacrificed for the greater moral justice of enduring societal harmony. This is the restorative justice about which Elizabeth Kiss writes in another chapter of this book.

Tutu also wanted forgiveness and atonement. But those human accomplishments may not be sufficient, morally, to substitute for criminal justice. Forgiveness erases wrongdoing, which has the effect of submitting to evil. According to David Crocker, another chapter's author, "It is morally objectionable as well as impractical for a truth commission . . . to force people to agree about the past, forgive the sins committed against them, or love one another."

Rajeev Bhargava assesses these and other objections to forgiveness. He asks if forgiveness is morally appropriate, and suggests, in any event, that truth commissions cannot bear the burden of bringing about forgiveness by individuals. To forgive is not always appropriate or virtuous. It must, Bhargava concludes, be "consistent with the dignity and self-respect of the victim."

Societal reconciliation is of a different order. Indeed, Gutmann and Thompson claim, "reconciliation is an illiberal aim" if an entire society is expected to embrace one comprehensive moral approach. It is undemocratic, too, for disharmony is desirable and an attribute of a healthy democracy.

A further test of the truth commission method is the extent to which it serves the reciprocal requirements of deliberative democracy. To do so it must practice the democratic principles of the society that a commission is attempting to create. It must share its own views, which the TRC through Tutu has done, with citizens broadly and transparently. Providing a final report that spoke to the entire society also advanced this goal of reciprocity. Unlike a trial, or a series of trials, a truth commission report can express the range of behavior that society needs to judge and condemn, and to which it needs to be reconciled. If it does all that it can do to satisfy such moral criteria, then the goals of societal justice may be satisfied.

The TRC found that the state committed gross violations of human rights, including many of criminal nature. It condoned the extrajudicial killing of political opponents, and colluded with the Inkatha Freedom Party and others. The highest levels of the apartheid regime were responsible for these crimes. Although the "predominant portion" of the gross violations was perpetrated by the state and its agents, the African National Congress (ANC) also blurred the distinction between military and civilian targets. It tortured and killed alleged defectors and collaborators, and thus committed its own gross violations of civil rights. The TRC report named many names, and pulled few punches.[5] It also uncovered evidence of secret biological, chemical, and weapons experiments; the TRC exposed South Africa's Operation Coast, for instance, which tested biological and chemical weapons on troops from Mozambique and tried to invent infertility drugs to give to blacks only.

Bhargava's essay focuses on restoring a society's norms of basic procedural justice. A truth commission does so by discovering grave past injustices and by encouraging perpetrators to confess to their responsibilities. Only through those means, Bhargava suggests, can a defeated barbaric social formation gradually be transformed into a minimally decent society. That is the overriding objective of a truth commission. Morality flows from the restoration of confidence in procedural justice.

Bhargava's essay distinguishes between barbaric social formations that are asymmetric, where a controlling political group generates evil, and symmetric ones, in which social and political evil is produced collectively by an entire society. The second kind of barbaric social formation is profoundly amoral. The first, where a dominant group violates norms and the rest of society seeks to enforce the rules of procedural justice, is much more promising. It is particularly promising when the dominant group, despite its massive system of evil, still honors the intent of procedural justice, if more in the breach than in practice. When the dominant group is ousted, procedural justice needs primarily to be restored, not introduced (as it would be after a period of societal collapse and amorality).

For Bhargava's analysis, it is essential that the distinction between perpetrators and victims is fully acknowledged by truth commissions. If not, truth commissions will find it almost impossible to help transform a traumatized, postconflict society into a minimally decent society. Nor would they be able to help societies stabilize a system of basic procedural justice, which must be a critical objective.

Kiss's chapter affirms truth commissions as a modern instrument capable of strengthening civil society and providing restorative justice. Because they are simultaneously investigative, judicial, political, educational, and therapeutic bodies, they can pursue morally ambitious ends of profound value to a transitional society. Indeed, their moral ambition makes truth commissions politically innovative. At the heart of this innovation is a concept of justice that is survivor or victim centered, not retributive. It has been praised for being "moral, cultural, psychological, and human rather than . . . solely legal or instrumental"; in short, "the creation of a nation."[6]

Restorative justice emerges from this desire to create a new nation—the desire to reconstruct a just society. Punishment alone for perpetrators, in accord with prosecutions and the requirements of an arms-length criminal system, hinders the achievement of restorative justice. The better path, the believers in restorative justice suggest, is forgiveness and reconciliation preceded by an accounting of violations, a confronting of perpetrators by victims, reparations, and a continuing emphasis on personal motivations and transformations. It is the individual-centered approach of the best truth commissions that contributes meaningfully to restorative justice.

Truth commissions, Kiss asserts, provide a mechanism to do justice to and to acknowledge that there were victims and perpetrators on more than one side. Commissions can be used in promising ways to advance beneficent societal goals despite competing narratives of oppression, and bitter, if opposite, memories of evil. If the goal is to reorient a society that has lost its moral way, truth commissions are more supple and constructive than criminal trials or forms of lustration (the banning of perpetrators from public office). There is positive value in what truth commissions seek, especially those like the Argentinean, the Chilean, and the South African versions—where the explicit goal was to restore a just society.

Crocker's transitional justice, like Kiss's restorative justice, is general and expansive. Rather than confining transitional justice to penal or retributive justice, Crocker employs transitional justice to encompass compensatory and distributive justice. Wisely, he suggests that the challenge for a new democracy is to respond effectively to past evils without "undermining the new democracy or jeopardizing prospects for future development."

Crocker judges the extent to which truth commissions actually serve transitional justice by how well they ferret out the truth, provide salutary platforms for victims and their kin, sanction violators effectively (a weakness of Guatemala's Historical Clarification Commission), uphold and strengthen the rule of law (critical if the new society wants to distinguish itself from the authoritarianism and institutionalized bias of the outgoing regime), compensate victims through reparations collectively or individually, contribute to institutional reform and long-term national development, reconcile the defeated with the victorious, and foster public debate leading to publicly acceptable compromises.

André du Toit's concept of transitional justice includes truth as acknowledgment and justice as recognition, together providing a coherent alternative to retributive justice. With victims' hearing as a central focus, du Toit suggests that the TRC's form of transitional justice passed moral tests. Differing with Gutmann and Thompson, du Toit avers that moral determination should depend on context; the compromise that was represented by the TRC was justified by postapartheid needs and circumstances.

Chile's special commission compensated the survivors of human rights abuses and the families of victims. The South African TRC's Reparation and Rehabilitation Committee recommended to Parliament who should be compensated, and by how much. But President Thabo Mbeki said that funds were short, and the provision of financial recompense became unlikely. One of the three Sri Lankan commissions of inquiry devoted almost all of its efforts to deciding whom to compensate, and by how much. The principle, which

Crocker supports, is that the truth commission process is complete only when victims obtain financial redress as well as knowledge ("truth"), and a moral sense of completion. Reparations and compensation strengthen the rule of law, reconciliation, and the overall process of institutional reform. Martha Minow feels even more strongly: no long-term vision of social transformation is possible if the need for reparations (such as monuments, parks, and renamed buildings as well as cash) is ignored.

Crocker examines the contribution of national and international civil society (transnational nongovernmental organizations for the most part) to the effective accomplishment of transitional justice. The experiences of Honduras and Guatemala, where civic groups succeeded only partially in influencing their nations' postconflict attempts to come to terms with human rights abuses, were very mixed, but Crocker argues that a well-informed international or globalized civil society (including agencies of the United Nations, which Crocker assesses) will increasingly reinforce the work of truth commissions in preventing future intrastate conflicts. Never again! will become a greater reality because of the attention of international civil society.

Boraine, the deputy chairman of the TRC and one of those who originally advocated using an elaborated form of the Chilean commission model to deal with South Africa's "unfinished business" in the aftermath of apartheid, argues for a wide-ranging, powerful, and public investigatory commission capable of extraordinary truth-telling and truth-finding. Creating such a body made it possible to contemplate restoring the nation's moral order, profoundly jeopardized as that order had been by abuses of the rule of law and of fundamental human rights. An attempt by the incoming ANC-led government to hold Nuremberg-like trials would have antagonized any hope of a peaceful transition. (Ntsebeza, another member of the TRC and its chief investigator, also develops this argument in his chapter.) Granting the agents of apartheid a blanket amnesty would have infuriated the long-oppressed majority. Establishing a TRC was an available middle course, and one advocated by important sections of civil society; indeed, only such a forum could provide a collection of individual, but carefully investigated, amnesties. No other method could have legitimized the amnesty or forgiveness process that was essential, Boraine and others argue, if South Africa were to move peacefully from war to peace. Hence the postamble (recognizing the political compromise that overcame apartheid) and the adding of reconciliation to truth as the commission's mandate.

Boraine argues that deeply divided societies cannot rely on punishment to heal and reconcile their several communities. He and Ntsebeza explain what the South African Parliament intended by reconciliation and the development of national unity: understanding not vengeance, reparation but not retaliation, and humanness not victimization. The nature of the TRC's hearings were intended to achieve those goals; its final report (as Villa-Vicencio and Verwoerd make clear) was shaped with that same intent in mind. Boraine believes that acquiring a series of individual truths can contribute to the healing process, albeit partially.

In contrast to most other truth commissions, the manner in which the idea of a South African commission was advanced as an alternative to a potentially costly and inconclusive war crimes tribunal, the nature of its mandate and procedures, and the character and composition of its members were decided upon democratically. Other commissions were presidentially appointed and were composed (as in the Chilean case) by leading figures from the old regime as well as the new.

In South Africa, civil society played a large role in composing the commission and its mandate; Parliament, not a president or prime minister, authorized the TRC. Its striking structure and many goals were mandated by an act of Parliament. Its committees—Human Rights (the one that held hearings and made most of the headlines), Reparation and Rehabilitation, and Amnesty—and their functions were laid down in the act. So was its public nature, its powers of subpoena (which the TRC used sparingly), and the procedures by which amnesty could be granted by the committee that subsequently developed into a specialized commission of its own and was not expected to conclude its work until the end of 2000.

Amnesty was never intended to be easily accessible. It was available in South Africa for individuals only; applicants were required to make full disclosure during open hearings. A long list of qualifications limited the consideration of amnesty only to those whose motives and objects were political and subject to the approval of, or were committed at the behest of, a political body. Boraine and others argue that amnesty was the price South Africa had to pay to achieve a peaceful transition and to achieve a "limited" form of justice—to obtain a series of revelatory truths for victims and kin of victims. Ntsebeza says, indeed, that there was no other way. Likewise, in Brazil, Rwanda, and other countries that were at one time overwhelmed by atrocity, it may be impracticable on multiple grounds to prosecute. For retributive justice to have worked for victims, evidence would have been needed, and only through the amnesty procedures could that evidence have been developed.

"The really big maggots are beginning to come out from beneath the stones," exclaimed the husband and father of two victims of apartheid letter bombs in Angola.[7] Like so many relatives of victims, he preferred retribution, but he also appreciated that persons like himself would have been unlikely to have learned how and why their loved ones were killed by agents of the old South African state without the availability of amnesty. In these late 1998 and 1999 hearings before the Amnesty Committee of the TRC, several of the more mendacious South African operatives sought idemnity from prosecution in South Africa and, if they could achieve it, protection from extradition to Britain, Angola, and Mozambique.

Demanding truth for amnesty, as did the TRC, is suspect because the confessed guilty go unpunished, and in the case of the killers of Amy Biehl, an American Fulbright student, go free retrospectively.[8] When the TRC's amnesty committee granted amnesty to four ANC activists who had killed a black Bophuthatswanan policeman in 1986, the committee said that the applicants had fulfilled the two main conditions for amnesty: "telling the truth and proving a political motive." But in the case of the two whites jailed for killing Chris Hani, an ANC leader, in 1993, the committee ruled that they had failed to tell the whole truth and had acted without the authority of their political party. They did not have the necessary "political mandate." Jeffrey Benzien, a confessed apartheid torturer who demonstrated his "wet bag" methods to the TRC, was pardoned for several murders. Eugene de Kock, involved in 107 cases of murder, torture, and fraud, and serving a 262-year sentence in a high-security prison, was among the last to plead for amnesty, and an escape from incarceration and future punishment. Even he was given an amnesty for some of his crimes, but remains imprisoned for many others.

"It stinks to high heaven," said a prominent black editor of the amnesty process. "To imagine that after confessing, these people who committed the more horrendous crimes will then be patted on the shoulder by the TRC," he complained. Indeed, the editor went on, "The TRC is a denial of justice. Without justice, how can the victims feel healed?" For Boraine, forgiveness was preferable to trials that would not only have been costly but could have caused further division in society. "There was no victor and vanquished," he reminded. "Is it not a better alternative," he asked, "to deal with the past through the means of a commission which has a limited life . . . and move forward into the future?"[9] "We know the decisions are going to upset a lot of people," a spokesman for the amnesty committee said about rulings that indemnified torturers and killers of Africans, "but we really don't have a choice. It is part of the process of reconciliation."[10]

Truth for amnesty is said to achieve justice through reconciliation—an "enriched form of justice." But is this special pleading? According to Christian Tomuschat, coordinator of Guatemala's commission, "no one can today insure that [the] immense challenge of reconciliation through truth can be met with success. In order to do so, the historic facts must be recognized and assimilated into each individual consciousness and the collective consciousness."[11] If amnesty is allowed, the common conception of justice is subordinated to future-oriented societal moral considerations. Gutmann and Thompson remind us that whatever the claims for an enriched form of justice (e.g., strengthening democratic institutions), there is a moral cost that is significant. It is a cost that the families of Steve Biko and Griffiths Mxenge, murdered by the apartheid regime, have paid. The justice that comes with punishment of perpetrators has been denied them (despite their strenuous protests). Gutmann and Thompson also suggest that a genuinely moral compromise implies no blanket amnesties, a condition that the TRC's Amnesty Committee breached in one notorious decision that was subsequently overturned by South Africa's High Court.[12]

Ronald C. Slye supports amnesty as a tool for increasing both the quantity and the quality of information available about the past and its abuses. The South African example is unusually important, he says, because of the innovative nature of the amnesty procedure introduced by the TRC; Slye calls it the most sophisticated ever undertaken for violations of fundamental international human rights. Previously, most amnesties were granted to a cohort, and without demanding testimony. The TRC offered amnesty only in exchange for full individual revelations. (However, the TRC could not later revoke that amnesty if new information were discovered.)

In the search for truth and for individual rehabilitation, the TRC process, unlike that of earlier commissions, provided many of the advantages of a criminal trial. Indeed, Slye's examination of the TRC proceedings found more participation by the accused than in a typical trial. He also discovered that despite the absence of the highly developed rules of evidence, procedure, and proof that govern trials in a Western setting, the quality and quantity of information collected by the TRC was comparable or superior to that which might have been produced in a courtroom.

Another advantage of the process pioneered by the TRC, unlike earlier truth commissions, is that it provided accountability, and thus permitted the possibility of reconciliation. Applicants for amnesty (there were more than 7,000) had to describe their acts, and those seeking amnesty for the most heinous violations of human rights had to participate in public hearings and submit to questions from victims and victims' families. Amnesty applicants were compelled to accept responsibility for their actions. In Sri Lanka, families and parliament refused to accept the amnesty for truth trade-off, and hence received limited answers to questions about disappearances.

In his essay in this book, Kent Greenawalt also asks, "Is the granting of amnesty . . . an injustice?" If it is, can the truth commission process justify such an injustice? Or is it primarily that such an injustice prevents other and larger injustices? One answer is that there are gains in justice from identifying offenders, even if some go free. More will be learned that way. Like Slye, Greenawalt suggests that relying on a truth commission will deliver more justice than criminal prosecutions. But Greenawalt would not want readers to assume that every society would experience "more healing" by avoiding criminal prosecutions. Greenawalt concludes that murderers and torturers do not deserve amnesty; indeed, amnesty for them is not moral.

Greenawalt reviews the American history of granting amnesties and executive grants of immunity (mistakenly called pardons), and provides a detailed checklist of different bases for amnesties. Although political expedience is not justice, amnesties may be highly political and still serve the ultimate ends of

justice. Blanket amnesties are not, however, the best ways to proceed. Moreover, he says, amnesty is not a failure to convict. It is something more, with
utilitarian results of importance.

Boraine, along the same line, concludes that the truth commission procedure in South Africa at least "broke" the deathly silence surrounding the grotesque consequences of the apartheid system. The new nation and thousands
of individuals achieved an important catharsis. Bringing forth truth about
what happened helped to create an open society. In addition to knowledge of
specific acts, there was an acknowledgment of individual and group collusion
with apartheid. Part of "never again!" is the impossibility, thanks to the TRC,
of any South African easily ignoring or dismissing the consequences and
atrocities of apartheid. Fortunately, too, the generous amnesty process limited
renewed victimization and favored forgiveness, thus contributing to the peace
of transitional society, or "stable democratization." That is true restorative
justice.

Ntsebeza, in his chapter in this book, also focuses on catharsis. The TRC,
he says, restored to victims of gross human rights violations their civil and
human dignity. The truth did set victims and kin of victims free. It also destroyed a culture of impunity on the part of perpetrators. The public shaming
that came through the open nature of the TRC procedures substituted reasonably well for penal justice. Exposure is punishment. It is a powerful component
of accountability.

If the goal of healing individuals and society in posttraumatic situations is
elevated morally and practically, Minow suggests, the truth commission
method might be better than the prosecutorial. Litigation "is not an ideal form
of social action." Trials have procedural pitfalls. If resisting the dehumanizing
of victims is a societal objective, trials are inadequate. Hence, for public acknowledgement of what happened and who did what to whom, a truth commission provides a safe and effective setting for explicating the truth. In this
context, the trade of amnesty for testimony (with amnesty's ability to encourage the lower-ranking perpetrators to implicate higher-ups) is justifiable.

Trials are assumed to proceed by a strict observance of due process. A serious objection to the truth commission endeavor is its inability to operate according to the canons of that process. The chapter of this book that most fully
addresses that issue is Sanford Levinson's. He cites Chief Justice Earl Warren's majority opinion in *Hannah v. Larche* (1957), which approved the less
than full due process procedures of the U.S. Civil Rights Commission (despite
the dissents of Justices William O. Douglas and Hugo Black, two fierce civil
libertarians), and supported the flexible quality of due process. This resembles
the position advanced by South African Constitutional Court Justices Richard
Goldstone and Albie Sachs at a conference in 1998 in South Africa. They both
agreed with Levinson that truth commissions need not operate like trial courts

since the objectives of the one differ from the other. Trials might deprive individuals of life, liberty, or property; truth commissions seek to piece together the fabric of the past, and thus can operate best—most effectively—with fairness but without the strict requirements of due process. Truth commissions could accept hearsay, even if they evaluated it critically. Courts could not accept it at all.

Levinson also suggests that the granting of amnesties by truth commissions may be considered a special kind of plea bargain. It absolves a perpetrator of legal liability for terrible acts if he or she spells out fully and accurately the extent of the abuse. By waiving their right to a trial, plea bargainers waive their protection against unfounded accusations, which is what the lack of due process does in a truth commission proceeding. They also forfeit their right to counsel, but in that instance as well as one regarding unfounded allegations, the commissioners themselves can attempt effectively to act to protect the accused as well as the victims. (The Chilean and Sri Lankan commissions refused to name names.)

The use of plea bargaining was extended in the twentieth century in part because of numerical burdens on the judicial process. Hence, if the number of persons potentially prosecutable is too high, a commission method of examination is wise. So is a method that gains the most information (the most truth) with the fewest impediments (but still has safeguards). That is the argument that Levinson presents; it was widely discussed by an array of lawyers and jurists at the 1998 meeting.

There is also the question of trauma as a consequence of a truth commission endeavor. After a detailed assessment of how deep and enduring trauma affects individuals in situations like apartheid, and how psychologists of such trauma believe that sufferers can best recover their lives and senses of self, Minow suggests, in chapter XII, that whereas courtrooms carry memories of repression, hearings before the Human Rights Committee of the TRC did not. They created an atmosphere of trust and safety. The absence of adversariality also assisted. So did the TRC's public ability to acknowledge a victim's pain. (Where the TRC failed, many agree, was in its inability to provide sufficient counseling; the need to help victims overwhelmed all the resources available to the TRC.) The TRC proceedings would have failed to provide restorative justice if they had not been seen to be fair, compassionate, and far-ranging.

Minow believes that truth contributes more to reconciliation than does justice. Similarly, she favors final reports that lay out detailed narratives based on the cumulative testimony of perpetrators and victims alike, not a verdict. Commissions can express the complexity of events; tribunals cannot. This process can restore justice through accountability and societal repair, not retribution.

Reports produced by truth commissions follow a process that is less like those of working historians than are criminal trials. Charles Maier, in his chapter, affirms historians' interest in affixing responsibility, which is also the aim of most trials. Truth commissions are less able than either historians or jurists to reach an aggregate judgment about the context of societal responsibility, concentrating as they do on disclosure and contrition. Historians give protagonists their due by exploring their possible choices. Doing justice and doing history, Maier says, are akin because they produce a narrative that is both synthetic and open to conflicting testimony. The narrative is also meant to be coherent, one that interprets, explains, and records. Trials and historians focus on causality, and build a case based on a chain of verifiable events. Judges and historians, at their best, display jurisprudential wisdom.

Truth commissions can also collect materials for a narrative. They may help render what Maier calls weak retributive justice. It may be emancipatory, but a truth commission inevitably produces less than history. Historians, he predicts, will use truth commission revelations of coercion and abuses of power, but will integrate such truth commission findings into a wholly different framework. Historians evaluate issues of complicity and a chain of events that extends both temporally and morally beyond that usually considered by truth commissions. History is rendering justice to the nuanced complexities of different assumptions and divergent views of a chain of events, and all within a single, unified narrative that is much more than a compromise. In that sense, historians have an obligation to render judgment, not to reintegrate a society or attempt to heal victims. It might be harder to satisfy historians than it is victims and kin who want to know what happened, or who did what to whom. Historians want much more.

The legislative act that created the TRC committed the commissioners, in their final report, to "establish as complete a picture as possible—including antecedents, circumstances, factors and context of such violations as well as the perspectives of the victims and the motives and perspectives of the persons responsible for the commission of the violations."[13] But Villa-Vicencio and Verwoerd, who helped to write the report, explain that the TRC could hardly provide a complete picture. A lack of resources limited the commission's staffs' ability fully to investigate a number of barbarities. The TRC was unable to do so in the time available (three years was long enough to open festering sores but too short to have enabled the TRC to follow up all of the potential leads its witnesses and its own investigations suggested). Its mandate also confined the commission to an investigation of a narrow range of violations that had occurred within thirty-four years (not the whole period of apartheid), and to limit it to those who had suffered gross, not everyday, abuses.

Villa-Vicencio and Verwoerd see the report as a road map rather than a comprehensive history. It is less an expansion of the truth than a reduction in the number of lies about apartheid that can be circulated unchallenged.[14] The final report presents decisions in individual cases based on a balance of probability (rather than beyond all reasonable doubt), given the evidence offered to the commission and an honest attempt on the part of the commissioners and their staff to examine that evidence and corroborating material in an unbiased manner. Ultimately, the report balances precariously but precisely between the TRC's responsibility to the public interest and to individuals who may be harmed.

Villa-Vicencio and Verwoerd treat as sacrosanct a commission's obligation to accept what went wrong in the past, without rationalizations, and why. Equally sacrosanct is an obligation to promote national unity on the basis of the full acknowledgment of evil. To fail effectively to acknowledge the extent to which an individual, a state, or a liberation movement violated the rights of others "is to fail to give a full account of the past." It would be immoral and irresponsible to sidestep that challenge.

This book seeks to confront that and many other formidable questions. It does so in multiple iterations, for the contributors accept some but not all of the premises of their colleagues. Where they agree with others' premises, they sometimes argue differently. Since they bring the perspectives and training of political philosophers, political scientists, historians, lawyers, theologians, psychologists, and physicians to bear on the myriad issues that affect conclusions about the truth commission process, it is hardly surprising that they speak with more than one voice. Yet, in composite form, that voice is remarkably supportive of the value of truth commissions for developing truth in postconflict societies. There is less agreement, however, about the possibility of achieving societal reconciliation as a result of truth commission activities. In that regard, several of the authors of this book would not be surprised by the results of public opinion polls: an A. C. Nielsen–Market Research Africa survey reported that two-thirds of the South Africans asked believed that the TRC's investigations had led to a deterioration of race relations. An earlier survey by MarkData found that a majority of whites, coloureds, and Indians, and a third of Africans, believed the TRC to be biased and unfair. The leader of the National Party suggested that the people of South Africa were "further apart than when the Truth Commission started."[15] But the contributors to this book, like their South African colleagues in the meeting at Somerset West, feel that such judgments are premature and situational.

The contributors to this book believe the South African TRC remains the most far-reaching, and the most effective of its genre. Indeed, it is obvious that truth commissions as a whole would have been judged more harshly by this volume's authors if the extraordinary work of the TRC had not been before them. Thus, this volume is about both truth commissions as a genre and the practice of truth commissioning as performed specifically in South

Africa. Its conclusions apply to both the general and the specific, particularly since the South African commission's mandate and procedures will become the starting point for all future truth commissions. It is the prescription for the next commissions, whether in the Balkans, in Cyprus, or elsewhere in Africa.

Notes

1. Mary Burton, in summary (16) of Somerset West meeting between the authors of this book, the TRC, and invited South African jurists and academics, May 1998.

A much more pointed critique of the TRC appeared in mid-1999. Anthea Jeffery, in an analysis of the *Final Report* of the commission, called the work of the TRC fatally flawed. It distorted rather than produced "truth." Her *Truth about the Truth Commission* (Johannesburg, 1999) argues that the TRC relied too heavily on testimony not given under oath and not subject to rigorous cross-examination. Of the more than 22,000 statements by victims, more than 17,000 were based on hearsay. Moreover, when the report was published, only 102 of the 7,000-plus amnesty applications had proceeded through public hearings and thus been subject to cross-examination. In reviewing several instances of massacres and other atrocities, Jeffery also bases her criticisms on the TRC's rejection of official inquest findings, but without convincing explanation.

2. Archbishop Tutu, statement on Truth and Reconciliation, quoted in the *Boston Globe*, 7 August 1998.

3. Albie Sachs and Leon Wessels, speaking at the Truth v. Justice conference in Somerset West, referred specifically to the postamble to the interim South African constitution. It laid out the compromise that resulted in the TRC. See also the chapters in this book by Ntsebeza and Minow.

4. See Martha Minow's chapter in this book for the argument and the context.

5. Excerpts from the *Final Report* of the TRC, *New York Times*, 29 October 1998.

6. Albie Sachs, quoted in Alex Boraine and Janet Levy (eds.), *The Healing of a Nation?* (Cape Town, 1995), 103; Sachs, quoted in Alex Boraine, Janet Levy, and Ronel Scheffer (eds.), *Dealing with the Past: Truth and Reconciliation in South Africa* (Cape Town, 1994), 146.

7. Marius Schoon, quoted in the *New York Times*, 9 September 1998.

8. On July 28, 1999, the TRC freed the four African killers of Amy Biehl. They had served three years of their eighteen-years sentence for murder. But the TRC decided that they deserved amnesty since their crime was politically motivated. *Boston Globe*, 29 July 1998.

9. *Boston Globe*, 9 September 1998; *New York Times*, 8 April 1999; *Christian Science Monitor*, 9 July 1999.

10. Mdu Lembede, quoted in "S. African Amnesties Reopen Old Wounds," *Boston Globe*, 20 February 1999.

11. Quoted in "The Atrocity Findings: The Historic Facts Must Be Recognized," *New York Times*, 26 February 1999. One critic of the TRC saw its effects as an attempt to execute, shape, and correct memory as needed "to serve as backbone to the new

history of the new nation." Breyten Breytenbach, *Dog Heart: A Memoir* (New York, 1999), 21.

12. In late 1997, the Amnesty Committee of the TRC gave blanket immunity to thirty-seven key officials of the ANC. None had appeared before the committee or explained themselves in public. The court overturned the amnesties in May 1998.

13. Promotion of National Unity and Reconciliation Act, no. 34 (1995), Section 3(1)(A). Technically, the *Final Report* is an interim report, with a final *Final Report* meant to be produced in 2000 or 2001, when Amnesty processes conclude.

14. See Michael Ignatieff, "Articles of Faith," *Index on Censorship* V (1996): 113. See also Jeffery's critique, in note 1.

15. The Nielsen–Market Research sample was 2,500 persons. The results were reported and summarized in *Southern African Report*, 31 July 1998, 4.

II

The Moral Foundations of Truth Commissions

AMY GUTMANN AND DENNIS THOMPSON

As South Africa's Truth and Reconciliation Commission (TRC) began its public hearings, the newspaper *The Sowetan* warned, "Reconciliation that is not based on justice can never work."[1] The paper was expressing not only a widely shared doubt about this particular commission, but also the most commonly voiced objection to truth commissions in general. Whether or not the South African effort at reconciliation will work, this commission, like other such institutions in other countries, carries a heavy moral burden. By the terms of their charters, these commissions sacrifice the pursuit of justice as usually understood for the sake of promoting other social purposes, such as historical truth and social reconciliation. The pursuit of justice does not presuppose a retributive view of punishment. It means only bringing individuals to trial who are credibly alleged to have committed crimes and are seeking a legal verdict and an appropriate punishment if they are found guilty. In a democratic society, and especially in a society that is trying to overcome injustices of the past, trading criminal justice for a general social benefit such as social reconciliation requires a moral defense if it is to be acceptable.

Many proponents of truth commissions accept the burden of providing such a defense and try to offer, explicitly or implicitly, moral justifications for these institutions and the practices that they support, such as the granting of amnesty in exchange for full testimony, which the South African commission had the power to grant. However, we shall argue that the three most common justifications of truth commissions are incomplete from a democratic perspective.[2] Each captures one part of the moral case for truth commissions, but only one part. We incorporate these parts into a consistent democratic perspective that offers a more complete set of criteria for justifying truth commissions. A justification for truth commissions is more adequate, according to these criteria, the closer it comes to meeting three moral challenges that justifications of public institutions should try to satisfy in a democracy. And the closer that a truth commission comes to meeting these three moral challenges, the more it can contribute both instrumentally and by its very example to the democratization of its society. We suggest that commissions and citizens can promote this process by practicing an economy of moral disagreement, in which they seek common ground where it exists, and maintain mutual respect where it does not.

First, the justification should be moral in principle: it should explicitly appeal to rights or goods that are moral and therefore are comparable to the justice that is being sacrificed. The stability of a political regime itself is not a moral good or a sufficient reason to sacrifice justice for individuals. A stable regime can be unacceptably repressive. Social stability counts as morally relevant only when it is part of what justice (or some other moral good) either now requires (because justice calls for ending or avoiding a socially devastating civil war), or because social stability is necessary to promote justice in the future, or because social stability is supportive of some equivalent moral good. This challenge calls on those who defend the aims and activities of a truth commission to distinguish a moral justification from a purely prudential or self- or group-interested one. It offers a threshold criterion, asking us to distinguish moral reasons from amoral or immoral.

Second, the justification of a truth commission should be moral in perspective: it should offer reasons that are as far as possible broadly accessible and therefore inclusive of as many people as possible who seek moral terms of social cooperation. The reasons should be accessible not merely to certain groups or individuals within a society but to all citizens who have a legitimate interest in living together in one society. This requirement of inclusiveness does not mean that everyone must actually approve the justification, only that the justification cannot reasonably be dismissed by people who seek moral terms of cooperation. This challenge is created by the need for citizens of a morally pluralistic democracy to work together in seeking fair terms of social cooperation. Because it offers an ideal of accessibility that rarely if ever can be met completely, the justification should not be expected to be accessible to everyone, even to everyone who seeks moral terms of social cooperation. A truth commission should be judged on this criterion by how accessible and inclusive it is, taking into account the social context within which it operates (including the history and therefore the ongoing legacy of injustice).

Third, the justification should be moral in practice: it should offer reasons that are to the extent possible embodied or exemplified by the commission's own proceedings, and are not only intended to be put into practice by other institutions, observers, and future governments. This requirement is all the more important to the extent that the victims of past injustices reasonably perceive that some significant part of justice—such as just punishment for the crimes committed against them, their families, and fellow citizens—is being sacrificed in order to create the truth commission. Some other significant part of justice, therefore, should be realized now in the ongoing activities of the truth commission. This justification goes further than merely suggesting that in some general way the commission will help society move beyond the injustices of the past or will serve as a means to a better democracy in the future (though showing both can be an important part of any adequate justification). The justification of the commission is more fully moral and more adequate to the extent that the means themselves that are used by the commission exemplify the justice that is being pursued. Otherwise, the moral foundation will look dangerously like that which could be offered by any regime that tries to justify current violence and injustice in the name of a promise of future peace and pursuit of the general interest. The more closely connected the practices of the commission are to the character of the democratic government to which citizens aspire, the more adequate its justification.

In analyzing the moral foundations of truth commissions, we use the South African experience as our paradigm. Although the analysis is relevant to many other such commissions, the TRC, we believe, is the most appropriate example because it is the most comprehensive in its purposes and procedures. It was charged with a wide range of responsibilities, including providing an accurate account of atrocities, granting amnesty to those who confessed to their role in political crimes, and making recommendations for reparations. The commission had subpoena power and took testimony in public (unlike some commissions, such as the Chilean one, in which victims and perpetrators testified in private). We cannot offer anything close to a full analysis even of the South African case. A more complete analysis of any single case would require further refinement and quite possibly revision of the more general criteria and arguments that we present here in light of the many relevant particularities of the society. But any more comprehensive analysis that included a moral justification of the commission in question would need to be guided by general standards.

The Moral Burden

The power of the TRC to grant amnesty to political leaders, security officials, and other individuals who confessed to committing political crimes during the apartheid regime was a political compromise between the advocates of total amnesty and the proponents of criminal prosecution. This "truth for amnesty" provision, added in the so-called "postamble" to the interim constitution, is thought by many people, including many victims of apartheid, to be the most morally problematic practice of the TRC. Although only a relatively small proportion of applicants were granted amnesty, some were among the most egregious perpetrators. When amnesty is granted, the guilty not only go unpunished, but even escape trial. When amnesty is not granted, prosecution of the applicants is still possible but has proved difficult.

Some defenders of the TRC deny that this consequence threatens justice. They suggest that the guilty would go unpunished in any case, and that there is therefore no sacrifice of justice. Although they are right to doubt any standard that would suggest that perfect justice could be done without a truth commission, they cannot sustain the claim that the "truth for amnesty" provision entails no sacrifice of justice whatsoever. They cannot be sure that all of the guilty parties would in any case go unpunished. (In fact, not all have gone unpunished in South Africa.) Nor can they escape the moral burden of justifying the trade-off that any proposal entails between various valuable ends of justice in the context of ongoing society in which many crimes against humanity have been committed by members of that society. The moral burden of justifying a truth commission that adopts the "truth for amnesty" provision therefore still remains, even if it is lessened by the recognition that the alternative is not a trial that completely satisfies the ideal of criminal justice.

Other defenders who deny that the "truth for amnesty" provision threatens justice argue that the aim of the commission should be understood as "achieving *justice* through reconciliation."[3] Rather than abandoning justice, the commission actually promotes an "enriched form of justice." By forcing citizens today to "face the horrors of the past," it helps to overcome the "indebtedness" owed to the victims of apartheid. Acknowledging past wrongs and especially repudiating wrongful judicial verdicts certainly may be part, even a necessary part, of achieving justice now.

But these measures are not enough to constitute criminal justice as it is commonly understood, and the defenders of this view do not demonstrate that the common conception of justice should simply be abandoned, rather than outweighed or overridden by more urgent moral considerations. Justice is not achieved when a murderer or rapist publicly acknowledges his crimes but is not brought to trial and suffers no further punishment. (This is true whether one believes that the aim of criminal justice is retribution, deterrence, rehabilitation, or some other purpose.) Even if the victims received financial compensation, the demands of justice (on virtually any theory) would not be satisfied. Nor would the kind of public shaming that perpetrators were said to experience in testifying to the commission count as satisfying justice.[4] It may be true that most victims of apartheid who have testified before the TRC have not sought prosecution of the perpetrators.[5] But it cannot be assumed that the views of the testifiers are representative of the average black South African or even the average victim of apartheid (a category that includes most black South Africans).

Some people who deny that justice is being sacrificed appeal to other moral values, such as a greater need to recognize "systemic and collective evils" rather than individual piecemeal wrongs, and the importance of furthering the "efforts to strengthen democratic institutions."[6] But these arguments are seriously incomplete if they do not come to terms with the moral cost of sacrificing ordinary criminal justice, even while recognizing that it can be realized only imperfectly in a nonideal society. Indeed, in a nonideal society, truth and reconciliation also can be realized only imperfectly. For example, even a simple institutional compromise such as the separation of the Amnesty Committee from the other section of the TRC, causing its final report to be issued long before the Amnesty Committee had finished its work, meant that much of the truth presented to promote reconciliation was not based on truth revealed in exchange for amnesty. If proponents of justice through reconciliation believe that the ordinary conception of criminal justice is completely misguided or inappropriate in a particular context, they need to develop their argument much further than they have done.

The reaction of the families of Steven Biko and Griffiths Mxenge, prominent murdered heroes of the antiapartheid movement, brings out vividly why the moral burden of sacrificing criminal justice should not be ignored. Both families vehemently opposed the creation of the TRC because they believed that it would prevent justice from being done. "[Some people] say that offering amnesty helps the truth come out," says Mhleli Mxenge, Griffiths's brother. Griffiths Mxenge, a human rights lawyer, was brutally assassinated by the counterinsurgency police unit. "But I don't believe that knowing alone makes you happy. Once you know who did it, you want the next thing—you want justice!"[7] The family members believe they are speaking not only for victims and their families but also for other citizens who care about seeing justice done. Furthermore, because the TRC did not observe the customary rules of evidence and the deliberate procedure of criminal process, both victims and perpetrators understandably complained that their due process rights were violated.[8]

The Realist Response

The question remains: Can this sacrifice of justice be justified? A common answer takes what may be called a "realist" approach. Realists do not deny that terrible injustices were committed by many people under apartheid and that they should be condemned. But some realists argue that because the injustices were so widespread and systematic (indeed *because* they were so terrible), it is not practical to prosecute individuals for the crimes. The evidence, they argue, would be difficult if not impossible to discover in many cases; many guilty people would escape, and some innocent people would be punished.[9] The acquittal of former Defense Minister Magnus Malan in 1996 was widely seen as demonstrating that former officials could not be prosecuted successfully. The only hope of finding out what happened in the past would be to encourage the guilty to come forward voluntarily, which they would not do if they faced the prospect of a trial and punishment. The "truth for amnesty" provision itself was a necessary political compromise, without which the new constitution could not have been put into effect. Furthermore, that provision does not rule out prosecution of those who refuse to apply for amnesty or who fail to receive it.

The emphasis of this realist justification seems to suggest that moral considerations are irrelevant, or at least unrealistic. Insofar as a realist response denies the relevance of moral considerations, it fails to meet the first and most basic moral challenge. In addition to its neglect of moral considerations, there is also an internal problem with this realist response. Its emphasis on political necessity itself is not as realistic as it purports to be. It is realistic to suppose that bringing most or all of the perpetrators of political crimes to justice is impossible. But it is not realistic to dismiss as impossible the goal of bringing some perpetrators to justice, at least in societies like South Africa, where extensive records were kept, and where a relatively reliable police force and criminal justice system are now in place.

Shortly after Malan was acquitted, Eugene de Kock, the former head of Vlakplaas, a notorious police hit squad, was convicted on eighty-nine charges, including six counts of murder, and sentenced to two life terms, the maximum allowable under South African law. (In mid-1999, the TRC granted de Kock amnesty for one of his offenses.) Giving up on punishing as many of the perpetrators of political crimes as possible is not an inevitable conclusion; it is a political decision with moral implications, and therefore one that needs to be morally justified. Furthermore, the TRC considered but rejected a less punitive alternative—lustration (denying perpetrators the opportunity to hold public office)—which would have fallen short of satisfying criminal justice but could have gone some way toward fulfilling its underlying aims.[10]

One way to begin morally justifying the decision to forgo prosecution is to argue that even under the relatively favorable conditions of criminal justice that exist today in South Africa, the perpetrators who would most likely be brought to justice would have been lower-level rather than higher-level officials, those who committed lesser crimes under apartheid. Some defenders of the TRC make this argument and suggest that such selective enforcement would itself constitute an injustice of a serious sort. This is a credible starting point for justifying the "truth for amnesty" provision, but it should not be confused with a realist justification. It invokes a moral argument, and suggests that punishing only the lesser crimes of apartheid is worse than punishing no crimes of apartheid at all.

When defenders of the South African commission offer a moral justification for forgoing some prosecutions that would otherwise be possible without the "truth for amnesty" provision, they implicitly recognize the limitations of a realist defense, which relies on necessity rather than morality. To say that bringing any perpetrators of political crimes to justice is impracticable, and that therefore a truth commission is the best available alternative, is an abuse of the argument from necessity; it is also a non sequitur. Even if bringing any perpetrators of political crimes to justice were impossible, it still would not follow that setting up a truth commission would be preferable to other alternatives. The past wrongs could be acknowledged, and society could find many other ways to move forward effectively, without forcing citizens to endure the painful and divisive testimony produced by a truth commission. Many conservative white South Africans and conservative black supporters of the Inkatha Freedom Party voice this view. In the words of an Inkatha politician from Umlazi: "It's just opening old wounds. It makes you hate the person you had forgiven."[11] The view requires a response that goes beyond what the realist offers.

A moral argument is implicit in any defensible claim that a truth commission is the best realistic alternative to seeking justice. If the only goal were to preserve the present political regime and move forward with the practical business of government, a truth commission could be as much an obstacle as an aid to this goal. The beginning of a moral argument is implicit in at least some forms of the realist justification. The incipient argument is that a truth commission should help citizens move ahead together to establish a new society based on commonly shared values (which of course need not be universally shared).

But the goal of creating a society with commonly shared values still lacks moral content and therefore cannot justify the sacrifice of criminal justice. At minimum, the content of the new society's shared values must be incompatible with continuing the morally abhorrent practices of the past. The simple idea of a commonly shared set of values cannot justify anything, certainly not giving up the pursuit of justice. No one should reasonably expect the families of Biko or Mxenge to accept this conclusion if its main justification has so little (if any) moral content. They, along with all victims of apartheid, present strong arguments in favor of pursuing justice against those who committed crimes under apartheid. Their arguments deserve a moral response, one that is more specific than the hope of building a better democracy. Even if some kind of amnesty were necessary to bring the constitutional negotiations to a successful conclusion, this political compromise must itself be shown to be moral compromise. Otherwise, the new democracy will be morally flawed from its inception.

A more specific response is offered by those who argue that a truth commission can help establish not just peace but a decent peace and a minimally decent society.[12] Although this response is sometimes identified as "realist," it runs against the realist response to the extent that decency is identified with specific moral standards such as securing basic liberties and a decent standard of living for all individuals. (To the extent that decency is left undefined, the response suffers from the same problem as holding out the general hope that the commission will build a better democracy.)

Proponents of a decent society generally presume some moral standards, thereby rejecting the realist's morally indifferent response to the critics of truth commissions. The standards, which may be similar to those of deliberative democracy that we defend below, pay homage to the antirealist idea that any adequate justification must assume that seeking shared principles is morally desirable, and further that it is more morally valuable than prosecuting the perpetrators of past political crimes. But these assumptions in turn depend on showing that the principles being sought and the means of seeking them have substantial moral value that was absent from (or less present in) the old society. Otherwise, there is not sufficient moral value to counter the considerable moral cost of granting amnesty to perpetrators of past political crimes.

The realist justification becomes acceptable only if takes on greater moral content. Specifically, what it needs is an account that would show how the process of a truth commission itself can help create a more just society. The shared principles that are being sought for the future must be moral in principle; they must address the legitimate concerns of all members of society; and they must be closely linked to the practices in which the commission is engaged. Insofar as these conditions are satisfied, the realist justification is compatible with the more complete justification we shall suggest below. It provides the missing moral principles, perspective, and practices for a truth commission.

The Compassionate Response

Another common defense of truth commissions adopts the perspective of the victims. Some proponents of this defense follow a therapeutic approach, pointing to the psychological benefits of offering public testimony and receiving public confirmation of injustices.[13] Others take a more theological approach, focusing on the value and meaning of acts of forgiveness and repentance. Archbishop Desmond Tutu, the chair of the TRC, has emphasized Christian forgiveness as a great value of the body's proceedings. He connects this Christian idea to the secular goal of the commission—reconciliation—which is part of its legislative mandate. Other commentators have suggested a similar but more secular version of this idea: the commission enables victims to choose to "fulfill the civic sacrament of forgiving."[14] Taken together, these justifications have been identified, by Tutu and others, as a conception of "restorative justice."[15]

Restorative justice remains relatively undeveloped as a conception of justice, but Archbishop Tutu and other proponents explicitly offer a moral justification for forgoing the conventional justice of holding the perpetrators of apartheid legally responsible for their crimes. The justifications that make up this approach share a compassionate concern for the victims of apartheid and their families, those individuals whose interests were unjustly sacrificed to apartheid.

In caring for the disadvantaged, these justifications certainly live up to the first challenge: they invoke a genuinely moral principle. Yet the question remains as to whether truth commissions actually serve the victims who testify before the commission as well as these justifications claim. If they do, it is also important to ask whether the emphasis of restorative justice on the perspective of the victims who testify before the commission meets the second challenge, which seeks an inclusive perspective that can be shared by all those citizens who are willing to live on fair terms of social cooperation with others. In addition, it is important to ask to what extent these justifications live up to the third challenge: do they link the practice of showing compassion to victims who testified before the TRC with the far more inclusive practices of a democratic government that the country is seeking to build, which will not be oriented primarily toward demonstrating compassion for victims of apartheid?

The TRC heard the testimony of more than 2,000 victims of apartheid-era brutality, and received written submissions from more than 23,000 people. Although the testimony helped establish and publicize the wrongs committed under the previous regime, it also was intended to help the victims and their families find some relief and redemption from their suffering. Many welcomed the chance to testify, and said they experienced some relief and less hostility toward their former oppressors. But in many other cases, testifying reopened old wounds, produced continuing psychological stress, and generated hostility toward the new government and the TRC itself. Officials of the Trauma Center for Victims of Violence and Torture, a nongovernmental group that provides services in the Cape Town area, reported that 50 to 60 percent of the victims they had seen suffered serious difficulties after giving testimony.[16] The TRC was rightly criticized for failing to provide adequate counseling and other concrete support to victims. But such support should be provided to *all* victims, not only those who testified, and therefore should not be considered part of the justification for the distinctive mission of the commission.

The theological version of the compassionate defense does not promise psychological relief, but instead offers the possibility of a deeper kind of spiritual satisfaction that some find in the act of forgiving. The difficulty is that many victims do not share Archbishop Tutu's Christian faith, and even those who do may hold a different view about the appropriateness of forgiveness in such situations. One can grant that on at least some major interpretations of Christian morality, forgiveness may enhance the virtue of granting amnesty and perhaps may even be obligatory. But those who endorse this interpretation should also grant that their interpretation is not shared by many sincere and reasonable Christians. Nor is it shared by many other religious and secular moral understandings that also deserve respect.

Boraine, the deputy chair of the TRC, recounts the reaction of a South African woman to the testimony by the killer of her husband:

> After learning for the first time how her husband had died, she was asked if she could forgive the man who did it. Speaking slowly, in one of the native languages, her message came back through the interpreters: "No government can forgive." Pause. "No commission can forgive." Pause. "Only I can forgive." Pause. "And I am not ready to forgive."[17]

Does anyone have compelling reasons, let alone the authority, to tell this women that she should forgive the man who abducted and killed her husband?

Proponents of forgiveness do not insist that victims should be compelled to forgive their oppressors, only that the TRC provide an opportunity for them to do so. Moreover, most of the perpetrators who confessed probably did not (and should not) have expected their victims to forgive them. Dirk Coetzee, a commander of Vlakplaas, South Africa's counterinsurgency police unit, testified that he ordered the assassination of Mxenge. Speaking to the commission, he said, "I will have to live with my conscience for the rest of my life and with the fact that I killed innocent people." But then he added: "In all honesty, I don't expect the Mxenge family to forgive me."[18]

From the perspective of other citizens and with the aim of the future democratic government in mind, we must ask whether, even if many victims would choose to forgive, it is desirable for them to do so. South Africans of differing perspectives can respect Archbishop Tutu's call for forgiveness without agreeing that they have an obligation to forgive their oppressors, or even that the commission would best serve South Africa by encouraging the victims of apartheid to forgive. Many citizens (including the victims themselves) may reasonably believe that it is morally inappropriate to forgive people who are unwilling to be punished for their crimes or unwilling to offer their victims restitution. Many may also reasonably think that although forgiving does not logically entail forgetting, it makes forgetting much easier, and the crimes of apartheid should not be made easier to forget. Making the memory of the crimes of apartheid less vivid runs the risk of causing similar crimes to be committed in the future, and in itself fails to show the respect for the victims that is their due.

Crimes like those committed under apartheid are acts not only against particular victims but also against society and state. In addition to the victims of crimes having something to forgive, so do society and state. Although forgiveness by a state institution such as a truth commission is logically possible, it is not desirable from a democratic perspective independently of forgiveness by the victims themselves. The crimes of apartheid constitute an affront to the basic democratic principle of treating all adults as free and equal citizens. A postapartheid state that forgave these crimes could not credibly claim to be committed to the most basic democratic principles.

What sense of "restorative justice," if any, can be achieved by a post-apartheid state that (rightly) does not insist on forgiving the crimes of apartheid? Some proponents of restorative justice suggest that the wrongs committed under apartheid can be transcended by the practices associated with a truth commission. But this suggestion is sometimes tied to a far more modest (and credible) claim: by respecting the voices of victims who testify to the crimes committed under the apartheid regime and providing reparations, a truth commission can help restore public recognition of the humanity of apartheid victims. These are worthy moral aims of a commission, but they are not sufficient to support claims of transcendence, upon which the conception of restorative justice seems to be based.

One source of the insufficiency is the failure to address the reasonable claims by some victims that restoration is impossible with amnesty, and that there are alternative ways in which the voices of victims could be heard and reparations granted without offering amnesty to the perpetrators of apartheid. Proponents of restorative justice should recognize that for many victims of apartheid, restoration is incompatible with amnesty, and perhaps unachievable in any case.

Even if restoration is not the best way of justifying the work of a commission, a commission's practice of giving public voice to victims can still be viewed as an important component of a more comprehensive justification. The goals of a commission may be more forward-looking, more political, and more inclusive than those that are conveyed by the restorative notions of forgiveness, therapy, and reparations for the victims who testify.[19] In the South African case, restorative justice seems to elevate these aims above those of establishing a more democratic society for all South Africans who are willing to recognize the reasonable demands of a democracy. The latter aim is more inclusive, even of the perspectives of victims, many of whom can neither forgive nor forget. It is also more inclusive of the perspectives of those perpetrators of apartheid who recognize the heinousness of their crimes and therefore do not (and should not) expect to be forgiven.

The aim of reconciliation, part of the TRC's formal charge, therefore does not have to be understood as requiring forgiveness by either victims or the state. If "the healing of the nation" is taken to mean forgiveness by the victims and repentance by the perpetrators of apartheid crimes, it is a utopian aim, and not even a positive one.[20] The aim of reconciliation should not be seen as seeking some comprehensive social harmony, whether psychological or spiritual. As one commentator on the South African experience observes, "Taken to the extreme, the reconciliation of all with all is a deeply illiberal idea."[21] Reconciliation is an illiberal aim if it means expecting an entire society to subscribe to a single comprehensive moral perspective.

Reconciliation of this comprehensive sort is also deeply undemocratic. A democratic society should still seek reconciliation on some fundamental matters of political morality, such as freedom of speech, press, and religion, equal political liberty, equal protection under the law, and nondiscrimination in the distribution of social offices. But a democratic society that strives for a consensus on such fundamental matters of political morality must still recognize that moral conflict in politics more generally cannot be overcome or avoided. In the democratic politics that the new South Africa seeks, a substantial degree of disharmony is not only inevitable but desirable. It can be both a sign and a condition of a healthy democracy.

The Historicist Response

A third kind of justification takes a more impersonal point of view and finds the value of truth commissions in their contributions to establishing past facts and acknowledging past wrongs. The discovery of historical truth is seen as both an end in itself and a means to a better society. The point is not so much to help the victims but more to create a shared history as a basis for social and political cooperation in the future. Facing unwelcome truths, demonstrating the illegitimacy of apartheid, decriminalizing the resistance movement, forging a collective memory—these are among the many aims embraced by historicist justifications.[22]

Although the historicist justification emphasizes truth, it tries to accommodate the aim of reconciliation. Some writers interpret reconciliation *as* a form of establishing the truth. They suggest that reconciliation should be understood as "a closing of the ledger book of the past . . . like the accountant's job of reconciling conflicting claims."[23] As du Toit puts it: "a conscious and justified settling of accounts with the past."[24]

The collective memory created by settling accounts in this way is partly a culmination of a political struggle. Collective memory, Foucault writes, is a "very important factor in struggle . . . if one controls people's memory, one controls their dynamism. . . . It's vital to have possession of this memory, to control it, administer it, tell it what it must contain."[25] Although Foucault may exaggerate the extent to which collective memory can be created and controlled by any regime, such memory can play an important role in consolidating the power of a newly emerging democracy just as it helps sustain authoritarian regimes.[26] But the more attractive aspect of this justification is its moral condemnation of the past as a way to start developing some common moral standards for the future. The "conscious and justified settling of accounts with the past" becomes a deliberate and worthy way of establishing democratic norms for the future.

On this interpretation, the historicist justification invokes moral principles, in accord with the first requirement. However, some critics may still object that it does not satisfy the second requirement: it fails to support a sufficiently inclusive perspective, because the history on which it relies favors the victors over the vanquished in the recent struggle against the apartheid regime. The violence perpetrated by the previous regime is treated more harshly than violence committed by resistance fighters.

Far from being a weakness of the historicist justification, this asymmetry of criticism of proapartheid and antiapartheid activists is a strength. It is a reasonable response to the challenge of relying on an inclusive moral perspective. An inclusive perspective does not demand neutrality with respect to all sides in a moral conflict. If the cause of one side is more justified than the other, any "settling of accounts" should acknowledge that asymmetry. That the cause of antiapartheid activists was just does not excuse, let alone justify, all their actions, as the TRC explicitly acknowledged.[27] But it does mean that the activists' actions are appropriately judged in a less unfavorable moral light than the actions of the defenders of the apartheid regime. This kind of moral judgment is one that could not reasonably be rejected even by those who once participated in the apartheid regime if they were motivated to find a perspective that could be accepted in principle by their fellow citizens.

The major weakness of the historicist justification is its failure to live up to the third challenge, which asks that the practices of the commission itself exemplify the practices of the democratic government toward which the society is striving. Despite the concessions and qualifications that the historicist defenders may offer (the evidence is imperfect, the conclusions are fallible, and so on), their *aim* is for a truth commission to come as close as possible to a conclusion that expresses the collective, authoritative version of what happened and how it should be judged.[28] The standard historicist justification implies that there is a truth about the past to be finally discovered and authoritatively acknowledged. This truth, moreover, is not merely factual but also evaluative.

The aim of truth-seeking, with its strong intimations of singularity and finality, is not the most appropriate model for political judgment in an emerging democratic society. In most such societies—South Africa perhaps most of all—moral divisions in politics will persist, and deep disagreements about fundamental values will not be resolvable by political processes. The political institutions of a pluralist democracy must find ways to cope with the persistent disagreement in which no side can be shown to be right or wrong in many relevant respects. The practice and culture of such a democracy must make room for a wide range of continuing conflict, even while trying to contain it within the bounds of civility. Civility does not require being friendly or even polite to one's oppressors, but it does call for respecting people as civic equals with whom one has politically deep but reasonable disagreements.

The assumption of ongoing disagreement and continuing conflict differs from the usual model of the aim of most truth commissions, which in this respect behave more like judicial proceedings. A commission typically seeks a historical *verdict*, a final judgment about what happened, intended to be accepted by all citizens. A truth commission that modeled the democratic society it is trying to build would be more welcoming of controversy. It would avoid final judgments where the available evidence or arguments were still uncertain. It would explicitly acknowledge its own limitations, as the South African commission did in a remarkable section of its *Final Report* entitled "The Commission's Shortcomings."[29] A democratically oriented commission most of all would exemplify how people can live with continuing disagreements about what exactly happened in the past and why, and still respect each other as fellow citizens.

Such a commission would not need to assume that truths about the past are impossible to discover, only that many of the truths that we can find now are tentative and many other truths that we are likely to find in the future are better sought by encouraging conflict and controversy, rather than by establishing a politically authoritative consensus. Even some of the defenders of the TRC who emphasize the importance of seeking a consensus on truth recognize the limits of this quest: they describe the primary function of the commission as expressing "unwelcome truths . . . so that inevitable and continuing conflicts and differences stand at least within a single universe of comprehensibility."[30] Comprehensibility of conflicting claims is far less final than reconciliation, and far more accepting of the kind of continuing moral controversy that is not only inevitable but desirable in a democracy.

Democratic Reciprocity

Democracy is the most familiar and now the most justifiable way of dealing with such disagreements in politics. Basic to all moral conceptions of democracy is the idea that people should be treated as free and equal citizens, and should be authorized to share as equals in governing their society. All moral conceptions of democracy therefore defend universal suffrage; free and fair competitive elections; the right to run for public office; freedom of speech, press, and association; and due process and equal protection under the law, along with other civil, political, and socioeconomic rights that are necessary conditions for effective political liberty. Public institutions such as truth commissions must also be morally justified to the citizens on whose behalf they act.

In justifying truth commissions in a democratic context, we rely on a conception of deliberative democracy. Deliberative democracy offers the most promising perspective by which to judge the work of truth commissions that engage in public deliberations because, more than other conceptions of democracy, it defends a deliberative politics that is explicitly designed to deal with ongoing moral controversy.[31] At the core of deliberative democracy is the idea that citizens and officials must justify any demands for collective action by giving reasons that can be accepted by those who are bound by the action. When citizens morally disagree about public policy, they should deliberate with one other, seeking moral agreement when they can, and maintaining mutual respect when they cannot.

The fundamental value underlying this conception is reciprocity, which asks citizens to try to justify their political views to one another, and to treat with respect those who make good-faith efforts to engage in this mutual enterprise even when they cannot resolve their disagreements. Reciprocity also calls for establishing social and economic conditions that enable adults to engage with each other as civic equals. To the extent that those socioeconomic conditions are absent, as they are to varying extents from all existing democracies, a conception of deliberative democracy offers a critical perspective on socioeconomic as well as political institutions.

Even when there is no better alternative to deliberation over ongoing disagreements in nonideal contexts, deliberation does not present itself as a panacea. A deliberative conception of democracy also recognizes the limitations of deliberation in specific contexts. A deliberative conception and deliberation itself can justify using nondeliberative means, for example, when such means are necessary to establish the socioeconomic preconditions for a decent democracy and more deliberative decision making.

Even under the best conditions, deliberation is not a substitute for deciding, and deciding is not a substitute for deliberation. The two go together, and together they are the most morally powerful combination that a democracy can offer to justify its political decisions to the people who are bound by them. A deliberative democracy helps avoid tyranny by recognizing that a vote alone, even that of the vast majority, cannot justify a decision as being substantively correct. But a deliberative democracy also recognizes that deliberation is no substitute for action and that deliberating before deciding is no guarantee that the action will be the right one. But deliberation does encourage attention to relevant values, and to this extent it increases both the legitimacy of democratic decision making and the likelihood that the decision will be a morally reasonable one.

There is certainly a broad scope for reasonable disagreement about how much deliberation is sufficient, whether a particular instance of deliberation is as good as it can be, and whether the ensuing decision is just. But "sufficient," "as good as it can be," and "just" are ideal standards, and failing to meet them does not render a deliberative decision illegitimate. Democratic institutions, practices, and decisions can be judged as more or less legitimate to the extent that they are supported by reciprocal reasons, reasons that can be accepted by those who are bound by them.

To the extent that a truth commission guides itself by reciprocal reasons, it fulfills the requirements for moral justification. First, reciprocity—"making a proportionate return for the good received"—is not only a moral principle but also an important aspect of justice.[32] Moreover, it is a characteristic of justice that has special force in democratic politics, where citizens must cooperate to make their lives go well, individually or collectively. The "good received" is that others make their claims on terms that each can accept in principle. The "proportionate return" is that each makes claims on terms that can be accepted in principle by fellow citizens. Because this kind of exchange is itself a form of justice, a truth commission that strives for reciprocity directly addresses the challenge posed by the sacrifice of other kinds of justice.[33] Even if the question remains as to whether reciprocal justice should take precedence over these other kinds of justice, a justification based on reciprocity engages this moral challenge on its own terms.

The standard of reciprocity also satisfies the second requirement of justification by providing an inclusive perspective. A reciprocal perspective is one that cannot be reasonably rejected by any citizen committed to democracy because it requires only that each person seek terms of cooperation that respect all as free and equal citizens. It does not require that all citizens accept as morally correct the conclusions of any commission or even the laws and policies of any democratic government now or in the future. Reciprocity is a principled perspective that allows for a wide range of reasonable disagreement. South African citizens should be able to agree that apartheid was wrong (because it did not respect all South Africans as free and equal citizens). They should also be able to recognize that many legitimate institutions, such as the legal system, and many professionals, such as lawyers, were implicated to varying degrees in the apartheid regime.[34] But they may reasonably disagree in many cases about the extent to which particular individuals should be held responsible for apartheid's crimes, and about what particular policies would best alleviate its effects.

A commission that accepts reciprocity as a justification also practices what it preaches about the democratic society that it is trying to help create, thus responding to the third challenge of justification. Reciprocity serves as a guide not only for a future democracy, calling on citizens to justify their political views to each other, but also for the commission itself, calling on commissioners and testifiers to practice some of the skills and virtues of the democratic society they are striving to create. The commission thereby applies to its own proceedings one of the most basic principles that any future democratic society should follow. The openly participatory process by which members and staff of the TRC were appointed, and the generally public process in which its proceedings were conducted, demonstrated its own commitment to democratic practices. More generally, sincere efforts on the part of citizens to offer an account of their political past closely resemble the most basic activities in the kind of democratic politics to which a healthy democracy aspires: sharing one's political point of view with one's fellow citizens in an effort to persuade them at least of its reasonableness and potentially of its rightness. The very activity of providing an account that other citizens can be expected to understand as reasonable (even if not right) indicates the willingness of citizens to acknowledge one another's membership in a common democratic enterprise. This is an important part of any ongoing democratic project, and therefore a step toward a democratic future in deeply divided societies.[35]

A truth commission that succeeds in eliciting reasonable accounts of the past from citizens cannot of course claim to have achieved a democratic transformation of society, because reciprocity in its fullest form demands much more than that. But even in this incipient form, a commission that proceeds in this spirit exemplifies the value (and limits) of the democratic virtue of mutual respect among people who deeply but reasonably disagree.

The Economy of Moral Disagreement

One of the most important implications of democratic reciprocity for the conduct of truth commissions, as well as for democratic politics, is what we call the principle of the economy of moral disagreement.[36] This principle calls on citizens to justify their political positions by seeking a rationale that minimizes rejection of the positions they oppose. Following this principle, citizens search for significant points of convergence between their own understandings and those of citizens whose positions, taken in their more comprehensive forms, they must reject. By economizing on their disagreements in this way, citizens manifest mutual respect as they continue to disagree about morally important issues on which they need to reach collective decisions. The meaning of the economy of moral disagreement can be seen more clearly by comparing its demands with those of the three other responses we considered above.

The effort to economize on moral disagreement is no less realistic than the realist's recommendation to set aside justice for the sake of stability and to get on with the business of government. Indeed, the economizing itself can contribute in significant ways to more effective politics, as citizens look for common ground and learn to respect the divisions that remain. Only if citizens economize on their moral disagreements is it realistic to expect the development of minimally decent societies—which eschew systematic violence and repression and secure the most basic liberties and opportunities for their members—in countries such as South Africa.

Furthermore, reciprocity is as realistic as it is moral in that it does not require that citizens seek points of convergence with people who are unwilling to reciprocate. In societies as deeply divided as are South Africa and other countries that have created truth commissions, any absolute demand to economize on moral disagreement regardless of the motivation or actions of one's political adversaries would be not only unrealistic, but also undesirable. Victims of injustice should not be expected to economize on their disagreement with perpetrators of injustice unless the perpetrators of injustice demonstrate a willingness to assume responsibility for their actions. Reciprocity does not require agreement for its own sake. It advocates finding *moral* grounds for agreement. While acknowledging the exigencies of practical politics emphasized by the realists, the principle of the economy of moral disagreement provides a critical standard that adds moral content to political judgments and encourages moral distinctions in the exercise of official discretion.

A commission that seeks to economize on moral disagreement will not grant blanket amnesty. In exercising their discretion, commissioners can demonstrate respect for those who reasonably disagree with them about the relative value of reconciliation and justice by refusing to grant amnesty for the most egregious crimes. A prime example is the case of de Kock, the Vlakplaas commander. Commonly referred to as "Prime Evil," de Kock was convicted of committing crimes, most of which "had little or nothing to do with politics, and others [that] were heinous in the extreme."[37] Unlike some other former apartheid officials, de Kock had done nothing to aid the antiapartheid movement. He seems indeed a fitting candidate for punishment. (His case was pending before the Amnesty Committee in late 1999.)

Archbishop Tutu reminded those who criticized the commission's grants of amnesty that the perpetrators of injustice "are still in the security forces and part of the civil service. These people have the capacity of destroying this land. . . . If there were not the possibility of amnesty, then the option of a military upheaval is a very real one."[38] However true this may be in general, each specific appeal for amnesty needs to be considered on its own merits. Rejecting the request for amnesty of an official like de Kock, who represents an extreme in both his criminal actions and his eagerness to escalate the atrocities of apartheid, is a way that commissioners can demonstrate their respect for critics' desire for justice while maintaining a commission's forward-looking commitment to furthering the cause of democracy in South Africa.

While the principle of economizing on moral disagreement is more demanding than what the realist response requires, it is less demanding than what the compassionate response suggests. It does not require repentance and forgiveness, which seem to ask citizens to learn to love their political adversaries. "[O]nly love has the power to forgive," Arendt wrote. And, "Love, by its very nature, is unworldly, and it is for this reason rather than its rarity that it is not only apolitical but antipolitical."[39] But while reciprocity does not aim at encouraging love among citizens, it does aim at developing some degree of respect among citizens. "[W]hat love is in its own, narrowly circumscribed sphere," Arendt concluded, "respect is in the larger domain of human affairs." Respect is less personal than love. It does not require intimacy or closeness, or even an admiration of a person's achievements or particular qualities. Respect is a civic acknowledgment: the recognition that others are our fellow citizens and that we are willing to treat them as such as long as they demonstrate a willingness to reciprocate. This degree of reconciliation would be a great accomplishment in the South African context, a more political and potentially inclusive achievement than providing psychological or spiritual redemption for some victims. It would also take a great deal of political effort, especially on the part of those South Africans whose past actions have demonstrated disrespect and even contempt for their fellow South Africans.

Although respecting one's fellow citizens does not require repentance or forgiveness, the deliberations of truth commissions encourages citizens both to recognize and to acknowledge the extent to which repentance and forgiveness are valued by their fellow citizens. Deliberation therefore accommodates values that are central to the compassionate response without reducing the aims of a truth commission to those values. Many victims have said that all they want is to tell their story and to have their husband's body exhumed for a decent burial. Having heard the perpetrators testify to horrendous crimes against their loved ones, some of the same victims want something significantly more—reparations and justice in the form of punishment of the perpetrators. An important advantage of a deliberative democratic perspective is that it respects all of these responses, even in the same person. The practice of economizing on moral disagreement does not decide in advance which of many reasonable responses is appropriate. Economizing on moral disagreement also has the potential for accommodating a diverse set of demands, even beyond those that are central to the more compassionate response of restorative justice.

Economizing on moral disagreement does not require that a commission or citizens try to reach consensus on comprehensive conclusions about the past as the historicist response usually does. That principle leaves more questions open to further dispute and discussion than does the project of determining and acknowledging the truth about apartheid and its victims. Citizens who try to economize on moral disagreement may acknowledge the seriousness of judgments of their fellow citizens without necessarily accepting all the judgments as true. They may, for example, regard the judgments as plausible, worthy of further consideration, and even potentially justifiable, without actually endorsing them.

The willingness to testify to crimes committed and to crimes endured, on the one hand, and the willingness to consider seriously the testimony of one's fellow citizens, on the other, constitute an important part of the process of a truth commission that seeks to realize reciprocity. When citizens take each other's testimony seriously, they evaluate the credibility of its content and the credibility of those who are testifying. A fair evaluation requires the open-mindedness to consider the merits of the testimony of those who testify. This kind of open-mindedness is the same quality that makes it possible for citizens of a democracy to respect and to learn from their disagreements.

Unlike a trial that depends on making a definite binary choice between guilt and innocence, a truth commission can encourage accommodation to conflicting views that fall within the range of reasonable disagreement. The justification that we develop here favors such accommodation, a practice that itself is an exercise in democratic politics. It suggests how a truth commission can express respect for differing points of view without either endorsing them as clearly correct or rejecting them as clearly incorrect. It then becomes the responsibility of both the participants and the observers to determine, through ongoing public deliberation, which fall within the range of reasonable disagreement.

This range is not unlimited, and citizens, especially leaders, need not be hesitant about rejecting views that they believe lie outside it. Archbishop Tutu and some senior ANC officials rejected as unreasonable former president de Klerk's written testimony, which accompanied his apology to citizens who had suffered the atrocities of apartheid. In his testimony, de Klerk insisted that he was unaware of a long succession of killings, bombings, and tortures by high-level officials in his own party and government. He claimed that these were "the criminal actions of a handful of operatives of the security forces of which the [National] Party was not aware and which it would never have condoned."[40] Tutu had reasonable grounds to deny this claim, because he had personally told de Klerk at the time about some of these crimes. Although because of a court challenge the commission withheld its conclusion about the individual responsibility of high-level officials, this particular dispute should have been resolved on empirical grounds. Both sides of the controversy had access to the relevant evidence, and both de Klerk and Tutu accepted the moral assumptions about official responsibility that were relevant to resolving this case. This dispute therefore does not lie within the range of reasonable disagreement.

Reciprocity does not demand moral detachment. Economizing on moral disagreement is completely compatible with taking a strong position against apartheid, even raising vigorous objections against individuals and groups that supported the apartheid regime. The economizing that reciprocity recommends is a moral practice, governed by moral principles that would condemn injustices and would judge unjust actions harshly and praise just ones. Nevertheless, a commission inspired by this kind of reciprocity would also call for testimony from the leaders of the resistance to the unjust regime (in South Africa, those who fought apartheid). It would ask these leaders to acknowledge their violations of human rights, as the TRC did, much to its credit, though not without provoking political criticism and legal challenge by the ANC and its supporters. Demanding such an acknowledgment does not entail deciding whether fighting the injustice of apartheid justified the violations of human rights, as in the case of ANC bombings of innocent civilians. The point of the acknowledgment is to demonstrate respect for those innocent individuals who were killed in the antiapartheid cause.

A truth commission economizing on moral disagreement can also encourage attitudes and actions that go beyond mutual respect. It offers the victims of injustice a forum for demonstrating an even stronger form of civic magnanimity, a benevolence that leads to accepting the perpetrators of injustice as civic equals. Because this benevolence is supererogatory, a truth commission cannot expect all or even most victims of injustice to display it. But the TRC was neither foolish nor utopian to think that such benevolence is possible. Its prime model no doubt was President Nelson Mandela himself.

Shortly after he was released from prison, Mandela gave several remarkable speeches in the spirit of reconciliation, none of which showed any signs of bitterness toward his oppressors nor any intention to seek retribution. When asked how he could be so magnanimous toward his oppressors, Mandela replied, "I could not wish what happened to me and my people on anyone." Surely no one should expect such magnanimity from anyone who has suffered the injustices that Mandela and many other South Africans have suffered at the hands of their own countrymen. But to the extent that the TRC not only officially elicited but also publicly recognized the benevolence of citizens who suffered the injustices of apartheid, it secures a better future for South African democracy.

Even the less demanding virtues of democratic reciprocity would, if more fully realized, help build a stronger democracy in South Africa as well as in other countries seeking to overcome the legacy of unjust regimes. Truth commissions alone cannot overcome that legacy. The full realization of deliberative democracy—or for that matter the full realization of a minimally decent democracy—presupposes social and economic conditions that neither South Africa or any other democracy can yet possess. Truth commissions, we have suggested, can constructively contribute to this process of democratization and, as importantly, can help constitute it. Commissions that respect the principles of deliberative democracy provide a cogent response to the moral challenge of their critics, a fruitful guide for their own conduct, and a robust justification for their moral foundation. Neither truth nor justice alone, but a democracy that does its best to promote both, is the bedrock of any worthy truth commission.

Notes

1. "South Africa Looks for Truth and Hopes for Reconciliation," *The Economist*, 20 April 1996, 33.

2. We discuss only some of the most important and most general justifications here. In practice the TRC emphasized different purposes at different stages of its process. (See du Toit's chapter in this volume.) One of the most extensive defenses of the TRC lists fourteen different goals. But virtually all are particular forms of a limited number of the more general justifications, and in fact the authors themselves examine only a few in any detail. See Kadar Asmal, Louise Asmal, and Ronald Suresh Roberts, *Reconciliation through Truth* (Cape Town, 1996), 10–11. The commission itself presented its

primary objective as promoting "national unity and reconciliation," but interpreted it to include various other purposes, such as "promotion of democracy," restoring the "dignity of victims," and encouraging "perpetrators . . . to come to terms with their own past." Truth and Reconciliation Commission, *Final Report* (Cape Town, 29 October 1998), I, ch. 4, "The Mandate," sections 2, 3, and 31.

3. Asmal et al., *Reconciliation*, 12–27 (emphasis added). This argument often takes the form of appealing to a different kind of justice, usually called "restorative." See Archbishop Desmond Tutu's comments in the foreword, TRC, *Final Report*, I, chap. 1, section 36; the TRC's discussion of "concepts and principles" in I, chap. 5, sections 80–100; and the chapters by Kiss and du Toit in this volume. Also see the section of the text in this chapter at notes 15 and 18.

4. Tutu seems to suggest "shaming" may serve as a partial substitute for criminal punishment (*Final Report*, I, chap. 1, section 36).

5. Ibid., 92.

6. Asmal et al., *Reconciliation*, 19, 22.

7. Mark Gevisser, "The Witnesses," *New York Times Magazine*, 22 June 1997, 32.

8. The TRC explicitly acknowledged that in carrying out its function of identifying perpetrators of gross human rights abuses, it gave greater weight to its "truth-seeking role . . . the public interest in the exposure of wrongdoing" than to the "fair treatment of individuals in what was not a court of law." It used a lower burden of proof than that required by the criminal justice system (*Final Report*, I, chap. 4, 153–155). However, the amnesty hearings followed more closely the adversarial and judicial procedures. On some limitations of any appeal to due process, see the chapter by Levinson in this volume.

9. For a statement of this aspect of the "realist" position, see the chapter by Ntsebeza in this volume.

10. *Final Report*, I, chap. 1, section 11.

11. Tina Rosenberg, "Recovering from Apartheid," *New Yorker*, 18 November 1996, 91.

12. See Bhargava's chapter in this volume.

13. For the strengths and weaknesses of the therapeutic approach, see the chapter by Minow in this volume.

14. Asmal et al., *Reconciliation*, 49.

15. See citations in note 3 above.

16. Suzanne Daley, "In Apartheid Inquiry, Agony Is Relived but Not Put to Rest," *New York Times*, 17 July 1997, A10.

17. Timothy Garton Ash, "True Confessions," *New York Review of Books*, 17 July 1997, 36–37.

18. Rosenberg, "Recovering," 95.

19. Some forward-looking, political, and inclusive goals for the South African Commission are articulated by Boraine in his contribution to this volume.

20. The phrase is from a statement made by Tutu during the hearings, quoted in Ash, "True," 37. For a different perspective, see Boraine's chapter in this volume.

21. Ash, "True," 37.

22. See Asmal et al., *Reconciliation*, 46, and the titles of chaps. 4, 7; Mark Osiel, *Mass Atrocity, Collective Memory and the Law* (New Brunswick, N.J., 1997), 210–211.

23. Asmal et al., *Reconciliation*, 47.

24. Ibid.

25. Michel Foucault, "Film and Popular Memory," *Radical Philosophy* XI (1975): 24, 25.

26. For a discussion of the difficulties in deliberately creating collective memory, see Osiel, *Atrocity*, 209–212.

27. See *Final Report*, IV, sections 60–81.

28. The National Unity and Reconciliation Act that created the TRC set this goal: "Establishing as complete a picture as possible of the causes, nature and extent of the gross violations of human rights which were committed during the period from March 1960 to the cut-off date, including the antecedents, circumstances, factors and context of such violations, as well as the perspectives of the victims and the motives and perspectives of the persons responsible for the commission of the violations . . ." (*Final Report*, I, chap. 4, section 31). The commission in the end did not claim that it had succeeded in presenting a "complete picture," and in its "perpetrator findings" (V, chap. 6, sections 77–150) it followed a more cautious, judicial approach. But many of the general conclusions of the report have the character of an authoritative historical verdict (see, e.g., I, chap. 2; II, chaps. 1, 3–5).

29. *Final Report*, V, chap. 6, sections 52–62, "The Commission's Shortcomings." At the conference at which an earlier version of this article was presented to members of the commission and staff, the authors suggested that the final report might include a candid discussion of its own limitations.

30. Asmal et al., *Reconciliation*, 46. For a description of "contrapuntal history," which is consistent with this approach, see the chapter by Maier in this volume.

31. This conception of democracy including the value of reciprocity and the idea of an economy of moral disagreement that we present here is developed more systematically in our *Democracy and Disagreement* (Cambridge, Mass., 1996).

32. Lawrence C. Becker, *Reciprocity* (London, 1986), 73–144.

33. Although the commission apparently adopted a notion of restorative justice, it went to some length to try to justify giving priority to this value over ordinary criminal justice. See the *Final Report*, I, chap. 5, sections 53–100.

34. For a valuable discussion of the commission's hearings on the role of judges and lawyers, see David Dyzenhaus, *Judging the Judges, Judging Ourselves: Truth, Reconciliation and the Apartheid Legal Order* (Oxford, 1998). Also, see the discussion of the institutional hearings, especially on business and labor, the legal community, the health sector, and the media, in the *Final Report*, IV, chaps. 2, 4–6.

35. For a complementary perspective on the value of deliberation by truth commissions, see Crocker's contribution to this volume.

36. See Gutmann and Thompson, *Democracy and Disagreement*, 84–94.

37. Rosenberg, "Recovering," 90.

38. Ibid., 89–90.

39. Hannah Arendt, *The Human Condition* (New York, 1959), 217–218.

40. Second Submission of the National Party to the Truth and Reconciliation Commission, May 1997, "General Comments," 8 (available on the official TRC website [*www.truth.org.za*] under Human Rights Violations Committee, Submissions, National Party).

III

Restoring Decency to Barbaric Societies

RAJEEV BHARGAVA[1]

THE *first* claim of this chapter is that the primary function of a truth commission is to help a barbaric society become minimally decent and, in the aftermath of evil, to reinstate confidence in norms of what Stuart Hampshire calls basic procedural justice, a term that connotes fair procedures of negotiation.

The distinction between symmetrically and asymmetrically barbaric societies forms the basis of my *second* claim: when a society moves away from symmetric barbarism, then, all things considered, some mechanism to deal with gross injustice of the past, such as a truth commission, is necessary and sufficient for achieving minimal decency. However, when a society moves toward minimal decency from asymmetric barbarism, it is more or less imperative to have a truth commission, although not enough. In such contexts, a truth commission is necessary but not sufficient.

In a minimally decent society, former victims are not reconciled with their former oppressors, nor are groups with inherited hostilities toward one another reunited. If so—and this is my *third*, entirely negative, claim—it cannot be the primary objective of a truth commission to achieve reconciliation between victims and perpetrators.[2] A future cancellation of estrangement is not ruled out, however. Indeed, though not immediately apparent, a truth commission creates conditions for future reconciliation. When this happens, a truth commission may also be seen as a facilitating mechanism of forgiveness.

Truth Commissions for Minimally Decent Societies

A minimally decent society is governed by minimally moral rules. A complete breakdown of such rules characterizes a barbaric society.[3] In this context, what makes these rules moral is their capacity to prevent excessive wrongdoing or evil and not their ability to promote a particular conception of the good life, including a substantive conception of justice. Such moral rules include negative injunctions against killing, or maiming or ill-treating others, and also a system of basic procedural justice.

Nagel has urged us to develop secular theories of evil consistent with universal claims of positive morality and has emphasized the need for a conception of human beings that accommodates their capacity not only for morality but also for monstrosity.[4] Hampshire has given us such a conception, and his idea of basic procedural justice is part precisely of a minimum morality to deal with this capacity for monstrosity and evil.[5] World War II and, in particular, the horror of the Nazi regime provided the occasion for Hampshire to recognize it: "I learnt how easy it had been to organise the vast enterprises of torture and of murder, and to enrol willing workers in this field, once all moral barriers had been removed by the authorities. . . . Once notions of fairness and justice are eliminated from public life and from people's minds and a 'bombed and flattened moral landscape' is created, there is nothing that is forbidden or off limits, and the way is fully open to natural violence and domination."[6] One now witnesses Evil: "a force not only contrary to all that is praiseworthy, admirable, and desirable in human lives but which is actively working against all that is praiseworthy and admirable."[7] It is only against the background of evil that the importance of some of the most ordinary, but indispensable, decencies of public and private life is illuminated. For Hampshire, such evil cannot be prevented by substantial conceptions of justice over which there may be little agreement in society. He argues that what is required in such situations is basic procedural justice. This procedural justice is part of "a bare minimum which is entirely negative and without this bare minimum as a foundation no morality directed towards the greater goods can be applicable and can survive in practice."[8] Justice, in this context, involves fair procedures of negotiation, a sort of machinery of arbitration that forms the basis for the recognition of untidy and temporary compromises between incompatible visions of a better way of life.[9] It is a means of enabling different conceptions of the good life to coexist and as far as possible to survive without any substantial reconciliation between them and without a search for the common ground. This coexistence is possible by virtue of a restraint accepted by everyone on unmeasured ambition, on limitless self-assertion, and on the obsessive desire for an ever-larger slice of the cake; and because people involved in even the fiercest of disputes are prepared to recognize the need to balance argument against argument, concession against concession. Basic procedural justice makes possible a minimally decent life, which has a value independent of any wider conception of the good.

Further reflection on the notions of minimal decency and basic procedural justice and on the relationship between the two enables a better grasp of the context and function of truth commissions. For a start, the phrase "minimally decent" implies that the best available ethical standards in a society, even by its own lights, remain unrealized. A minimally decent society is not free of exploitation, injustice, or demeaning behavior. It may not even embody political equality. Yet, it is a social order in which almost every voice is heard, some visibility for everyone is ensured in the political domain, and even the most marginalized and exploited are part of negotiations, however unequal the conditions under which they take place. There remain asymmetries in such a society, but it is not asymmetrically (or symmetrically) *barbaric*. In short, a system of basic procedural justice keeps negotiations going and thereby prevents barbarism. On the other hand, in a barbaric society, where basic procedural justice is dismembered, the entire mechanism of negotiation and arbitration has vanished. Usually, the violation of norms of procedural justice begins with the politically motivated deployment of excessive force. In the early stages of regression into barbarism, gross violations of basic rights—that is, physical intimidation, torture, murder, and even massacres—occur on a fairly large scale. Active deliberation and opposition is brutally terminated. As indifference and submissiveness are routinely generated in a depoliticized environment, the initial use of excessive force makes physical coercion more or less redundant. The point worth making here is that in either case, the demise of basic procedural justice is a *political* evil, which creates political victims.

A person who is robbed on a highway or systematically exploited on agricultural land or in a factory is a victim, but not a political victim. Political victims are those who are threatened, coerced, or killed because of their attempt to define and shape the character of their own society, and to determine the course of what it might become in the future. When political victims suffer violence, they are not merely harmed physically, however. The act of violence transmits an unambiguous, unequivocal message, that their views on the common good—on matters of public significance—do not count, that their side of the argument has no worth and will not be heard, that they will not be recognized as participants in any debate, and, finally, that to negotiate, or even reach a compromise with them, is worthless. In effect, it signals their disappearance from the public domain. When excluded from the political domain, such persons may be described as politically dead, as was the case with the law-abiding but politically silenced subjects of former communist states.[10] If the collapse of basic procedural justice brings political death, then clearly its restoration marks the political rebirth of members of a society. This helps explain why, by making the restoration of basic procedural justice their primary objective, truth commissions focus primarily on the rehabilitation of political victims.

Political victims usually, though not always, are victims of structurally generated *social* injustice. Exclusion from political processes is frequently accompanied by severe social and economic disadvantages. Clearly, not all forms of grave injustice in the past are of a political nature.[11] But if truth commissions focus on the rehabilitation of political victims, then it is not part of their brief to aim at the social rehabilitation of victims—to deal with gross social injustices of the past. Since some measure of social justice for groups who have in the past suffered grave social harm is usually necessary for reconciliation, an important reason is suggested as to why truth commissions need not aim at reconciliation.

But why should they not aim higher? A better understanding of the precise context within which truth commissions operate explains why their objectives must be restricted to restoring a minimally decent order. It is crucial to remember that when transiting from a barbaric to a minimally decent condition, societies are beginning their ascent from hell and are taking the first faltering steps away from a situation of gross injustice. When it comes to such societies standing precariously on the threshold of moral restoration, it is important that we remain firmly anchored in low-level ground realities and begin our search for relevant moral principles from there. We must not first reach out for high, nearly perfect ethical standards only subsequently to judge ground realities from that perspective. And the reality on the ground is that the only thing of which people are certain is that enough evil has been wrought from which relief is urgently required.

It is important to understand fully the significance of this point. It does not mean that enmity or estrangement has ceased between victims and perpetrators or between conflicting groups. Nor does it mean that they have begun to view each other with equal respect. Such attitudes may not even be on the distant horizon of a society resurfacing from an evil past. However, it does mean that a space has opened up for a new order on terms not entirely unfavorable to all political actors—that a temporary reprieve from civil war or tyranny exists, together with the hope that hostilities can be prevented in future. It also means that force has begun to give way to negotiation; and although relative advantage still accrues to one group, no one has a sense of complete victory or defeat. To be sure, relations of force characteristic of barbaric societies are not totally dismantled, but the process has begun to loosen their tenacious grip.

Normally, such transitional moments emerge out of a settlement in which former oppressors refuse to share power unless guaranteed that they will escape the criminal justice system characteristic of a minimally decent society. Alternatively, they typically arise because former victims do not fully control the new order they have set up and lack the power to implement their own conception of justice. However, such transitional moments also can come about by other means. It is entirely possible that former oppressors are comprehensively vanquished but that current victors, victims of the previously existing barbaric society, refuse on moral grounds to avenge themselves, or fully to implement the conventional criminal justice system. In short, former victims refuse on moral grounds to don the mantle of victors, a position Mohandas K. Gandhi might well have taken.

At issue here are transitional situations of extreme complexity, replete with moral possibilities, including grave moral danger. The danger is obvious: victims may forever remain victims and their society may never cease to be barbaric. But what is often missed is that seeds of moral progress are also present herein because former victims are saved the awesome responsibility of wielding absolute power and therefore may escape the devastating consequences of being corrupted by its use. As a result, the possibility is foreclosed that past wrongs will be annulled only by fresh acts of equally excessive wrongdoing; for example, as in the former Soviet Union. Instead, we are presented with the possibility of confronting past wrongs by means other than the use of force or the willful manipulation of the criminal justice system. So what may begin as mere political constraint opens up (minimally) moral possibilities. It is these possibilities that lend moral weight to such mechanisms as a truth commission.

A proper moral response must be formulated with the greatest possible sensitivity to evil and its aftermath. Not all conceivable moral responses are contextually appropriate. In my view, at least three possible responses exist. A morally relevant distinction is not made by the first response between a stable society governed by rules of basic procedural justice (a minimally decent society) and a society moving gradually toward procedural justice or at the start of a process of consolidating it (the transition of a barbaric society to a minimally decent one). This first position argues that the same system of moral rules is applicable to both these situations. When people kill mercilessly, betray friends and family, and save their own skins at the expense of loved ones, they breach the same moral norms that a serial killer violates when he strikes. The moral response to this violation must be identical. The second position recognizes the difference between a minimally decent society and a barbaric one. It also recognizes that reliance on a substantial morality, or even on the complete set of rules of procedural justice, is impracticable during a period of transition from a barbaric to a minimally decent society. However, it does not adequately see, as the third position does, that the issue is not merely one of impracticability but is also one of sensitivity to standards of appropriateness in relevant situations. It cannot understand that the move to a minimally decent society also requires that a group or even an entire collectivity be reeducated into a system of morality. Basic procedural justice is a cultural artifact, not a natural instinct, and individuals can lose their moral moorings if the group with which they identify drops altogether out of the institution of morality. The third position carefully notes this significant fact and admits that it is a mistake to elide the distinction between stable and transitional societies and unwise, even morally dangerous, to ask for more in transitional situations.

A further point to note is the impact of the breakdown of basic procedural justice on the personal lives of victims. Hampshire rightly points out that when Adolf Hitler deliberately substituted force for negotiation, creating thereby a pliant and demoralized mass fit for domination, he destroyed morality itself in public life.[12] However, I wonder if Hampshire is correct in saying that "morality survived in families, among friends, in professions and perhaps in commerce." Evil has a way not merely of spilling over from the public into the private domain but of pervading our intimate realms as well. When morality is destroyed in public life, it does not leave the rest of the social world unaffected. Friends, lovers, and members of the family can all be complicitous.

The world is peopled with intimate enemies. No one may be presumed innocent. The very distinction between friend and enemy, between those who you
love and those you intensely hate, is blurred. Veena Das, the Indian sociolo-
gist, reporting on victims of the massacre of Sikhs in Delhi in 1984, writes of
how the traumatic violence of the crowd suddenly revealed to one of its victims
the fragility of her kinship universe.[13] Shanti, the victim, disclosed, "It was my
own mama [mother's brother] who had advised my husband to hide. He revealed the hiding places of the Siglikar Sikhs to the leaders of the mob. He
bartered their lives for his own protection. Go and see his house. Not even a
broken spoon has been looted."[14] Rosenberg provides a moving account of
Vera and Knud Wollenberger, husband and wife, dissident members of the
peace circle in communist East Germany who risked their jobs and their freedom and were constantly spied upon by the Stasi. After the fall of the Berlin
Wall, Vera joined the East German parliament and campaigned for Stasi victims to access their personal files. When she eventually succeeded in accessing
her own file, it was full of reports from a Stasi informer, code named "Donald,"
containing information that could have been known to only one person.
"Donald" was her own husband.[15]

The horror of this monstrous universe can hardly be overstated. The misfortune of complete friendlessness, a life without love, is one of the greatest
evils that can befall human beings. And precisely this state results from the
breakdown of basic procedural justice; not only are people deprived of a minimally decent public domain but also of love and affection in private life. Conversely, the restoration of basic procedural justice revives not only a healthy
public arena but also intimate living. If a function of truth commissions is to
reinstate basic procedural justice, then they have a crucial role to play in eventually restoring warmth among friends and family.

How Do Truth Commissions Work?

How does a truth commission facilitate the transition from a barbaric to a
minimally decent society? How does it stabilize basic procedural justice? For
this to happen—for the moral threshold to be crossed—the entire society, and
particularly the victims of barbarism, must begin to *believe* that conditions of
civil war, tyranny, or gross injustice have receded, and that henceforth decisions are likely to be made by negotiation rather than be imposed by brute
force. They must begin to trust one another and have faith in the process. This
is unlikely to happen if a widespread feeling among victims persists that
wrongs done to them in the past are not even acknowledged. It is crucial for
developing faith in the process of negotiation that grave injustices in the past
be publicly acknowledged *as* grave injustices, as evils, and that perpetrators of
this evil own up to full responsibility for their wrongful acts. Victims also need

to move from passive disengagement with the world to active engagement with it.

This reengagement is effected by the fulfillment of two characteristic obligations. First, an obligation to oneself, to learn again to live one's life and rebuild relations with fellow citizens as well as with friends and family. Second, an obligation to others, particularly to the loved ones who have been killed. Victims and survivors need to tell stories of their victimizations, relate their versions of events, and point out the aggressors and amplify their aggressions. In doing so, victims express retributive emotions of deep resentment, moral hatred, and the cry for justice. Because physical injury also leaves them mentally scarred and with little self-respect, they need to reclaim their self-esteem as well. A truth commission helps achieve such goals and is an instrument by which a belief in the end of an era of gross injustice is collectively generated and reinforced. In fact, by announcing that basic procedural justice is firmly installed, a truth commission helps brings to life a new (minimally) moral order, an important symbolic requirement. When a truth commission successfully performs these functions, it restores the public health of a traumatized society and helps mend the deeply fractured intimacy among victims of barbarism. For all these reasons, truth commissions are necessary (are morally required) in transitional societies.

Against the argument that truth commissions are necessary for societies in transition from barbarism to minimal decency, two opposing criticisms can be leveled. For some, truth commissions inherently do more than is required. Those who hold this view inundate the victim with advice to check emotions. Rather than tell publicly and remember past injustice, victims are exhorted to forget. They are asked to contain hatred and overcome resentment—in short, either to condone or immediately to forgive. Revenge, to which resentment may lead them, they are told, is unbecoming of civilized people, and full of terrible consequences for society. These critics draw a distinction between the felt needs of the victim and the real needs of the entire community and suggest that the two often run against one another. Instead of focusing on the past, the victim is told to think of the future. In brief, in this view, truth commissions are dangerous or, at best, unnecessary.

The opposite view holds that a truth commission does far too little and is inadequate or merely cosmetic, at best. Its fact-finding function can be performed by narrowly conceived commissions to investigate rights abuses. Its cathartic functions can as easily be performed by private organizations. What the victims need, so the argument goes, is real social justice, not symbolic reparations that follow forced forgiveness. Besides, how can murderers be allowed to walk free merely by disclosing what is public knowledge anyway? Therefore, truth commissions can neither provide an adequate strategy to deal with past injustices nor achieve reconciliation. The very idea of a truth commission, they say, is flawed.

Why Not Forget?

It is well known that remembrance of past harm reinforces asymmetries of power. The fear of physical suffering in the future feeds on the remembrance of past acts of repression. Such thinking encourages passivity and obedience in victims, and this in turn serves the interests of the powerful. But such remembrances cut both ways. If memory of suffering is kept alive, reprisal may occur at future, inopportune moments. Therefore, among perpetrators, a motivated forgetfulness of their own wrongdoing, accompanied by the hope that victims will quickly forget past sufferings, is not uncommon at a time when asymmetries of power are in the process of being dissolved. In this context, calls to let bygones be bygones—to wipe the slate clean or to start afresh—work unabashedly in favor of perpetrators of crime. In any case, forgetting cannot be brought about intentionally. The demand on the victim to forget past injustices is in reality an injunction to forgive or not publicly to recall past injustices.

Most calls to forget disguise the attempt to prevent victims from publicly remembering in the fear that "there is a dragon living on the patio and we had better not provoke it."[16] But it is doubtful if this is a good strategy for repairing wounds or achieving reconciliation. When persons are wronged, they are not only made to suffer physically but are mentally scarred. The most injurious suffering is the damage to their sense of self-respect. As Murphy points out, when a person is wronged, he or she receives a message of marginality and irrelevance.[17] The wrongdoer conveys that, in his scheme of things, the victim counts for nothing. Since self-esteem hinges upon a critical opinion of the other, the message sent by the wrongdoer significantly lowers the self-esteem of the wronged. In these circumstances, the insult and degradation inflicted constitute a deeper moral injury.

The demand that past injustices be forgotten does not address this loss of self-esteem. Indeed, it inflicts further damage. Asking victims to forget past evils is to treat them as if no great wrong has been done to them, as if they have nothing to feel resentful about. This can only diminish them further. Forgetting specific wrongs fails to achieve its putative objective, a point to which Waldron has drawn our attention: "When we are told to let bygones be bygones, we need to bear in mind also that the forgetfulness being urged on us is seldom the blank slate of historical oblivion. Thinking quickly fills up the vacuum with plausible tales of self-satisfaction, on the one side, and self-deprecation on the other."[18] Beneficiaries of injustice then come to believe that gains accrue to them due to the virtue of their race or culture, and victims too easily accept that their misfortune is caused by inherent inferiority.

Waldron is on to something important here. The call to forget reinforces the loss of self-esteem in the victim. Furthermore, moral injuries that are neglected putrefy demoralization in the victim. Under these conditions, perpetrators feel that they can get away with murder and grow in confidence that such injuries can be inflicted without resistance even in the future. Therefore, rather than prevent wrong acts, forgetting ends up facilitating them. Proper remembrance alone restores dignity and self-respect to the victim.

A proper remembrance is critical if the wounds of the victim are to be healed. It is also necessary to fulfill the collective need of a badly damaged society. This view sits uneasily with the uncomfortable fact, to which Wolin has drawn our attention, that while societies remember their heroic deeds they suppress memories of collective injustice.[19] Wolin wonders if collective memory is an accomplice of injustice and whether by its silence on collective wrongs, it does not signify the very limits of justice. But he also asks if a society can ever afford to remember events in which members feel tainted by a "kind of corporate complicity in an act of injustice done in their name." Can France remember the St. Bartholomew's Day Massacre, America its Civil War, or India its partition? Can these horrific events be remembered by being represented in civic rituals? One person who thought collective forgetting necessary was the English philosopher Thomas Hobbes. For Hobbes, suppression of memories of past wrongs was essential, because if society were treated as a building made of stones, then some stones that have an "irregularity of figure take more room from others" and so must be discarded.[20] Hobbes's covenant was a device to incorporate social amnesia into the foundation of society, a necessary condition of which is the dehistoricization of human beings.

But is dehistoricization possible? I think not. "Muslims" invaded India in the twelfth century, but for many Hindus, Muslims continue to be invaders who may kill, destroy, or convert them. The conquest of Quebec by the English happened more than two centuries ago, but the project of Quebec nationalists "involves a reconquest of the conquest." A large part of nationalist agenda all over the world, Ignatieff rightly reminds us, is about settling old scores. In so many countries people remarkably similar in most essential respects appear to lunge at each others' throats simply because once upon a time one ruled over the other. A simple strategy of forgetting has simply not worked. Besides, it is to live in a fool's paradise to imagine that as grievances recede into the past and are half-forgotten, they will somehow cease to be real. As Ignatieff puts it, "Collective Myth has no need of personal memory or experience to retain its force."[21] Only an appropriate engagement with the past makes for a liveable common future. It is true that one must guard against cosmetic remembrance; an engagement with the past must take place simultaneously at the level of gut, reason, and emotion. If not properly addressed, grievances and resentments resurface. Oddly, animosity between groups is sustained even when it goes against their current interests. This happens because emotional reactions ingrained in the human mind remain insensitive to altered circumstances and are bequeathed from generation to generation. Like property, animosities are inherited too![22]

Nonetheless, former victims and fragmented societies eventually need to get on with their lives rather than be consumed by their suffering. Perhaps victims need to forget just about as much as they need to remember.[23] People who carry deep resentments and grievances against others are hardly likely to build a society together. Therefore, to ask people to forget is not entirely unreasonable. Timing is the essence of the issue. Forgetting too quickly or without redress, by failing to heal adequately, inevitably brings with it a society haunted by its past. One cannot forget entirely, too soon, and without a modicum of justice. Clearly, while some forgetting at an appropriate time is necessary, a complete erasure is neither sufficient nor desirable for healing or for the consolidation of a minimally decent society. Moreover, while specific acts of wrongdoing need to be forgotten eventually, a general sense of the wrong and of the horror of evil acts must never be allowed to recede from collective memory. Such remembering is crucial to the prevention of wrongdoing in the future. Without a proper engagement with the past and the institutionalization of remembrance, societies are condemned to repeat, reenact, and relive the horror. Forgetting is not a good strategy for societies transiting to a minimally decent condition.

Remembrance as Acknowledgment

Two kinds of rememberings are needed to deal with crimes committed in the past. The first is a kind of commemoration, usually embodied in constitutional guarantees and collective rituals or social memorials that ensure that the moral dimension of certain events never eludes the collective memory of society.[24] The point behind such generalized remembering of wrongdoing is to prevent its recurrence.[25] Truth commissions may indirectly facilitate this form of remembrance, but they must be concerned primarily with the public recall of specific wrongdoing. This second kind of remembrance enabled by them is contrasted with deliberate concealment. Public recall of a crime brings it out into the open, challenges its denial by its perpetrators, and contests versions that by sanitizing events, distort their true character. The purpose behind it is to get perpetrators or complicitous beneficiaries to admit to the knowledge of and to own up to responsibility for the crime. People need to replace a generalized, diffused sense of what has happened with a more accurate account. They simply need to know the facts: Is the missing person alive? If dead, how did he die and on whose orders? Where is the burial site? Or, did he get a proper funeral? They need, wherever possible, to identify government officials who have direct responsibility for the crime as well as the wider array of people collectively responsible for harm. More important, there exists a need to know not only the nuts and bolts of the repressive machinery, but where relevant, to acknowledge a pattern of political injustice and of harm, injury, and suffering inflicted on generations of victims by structured legal and political institutions and to highlight the less visible pain and damage caused by them. This is important because behind the drama of political repression, detention, torture, and murder there also lies a painful story of lives mutilated by unjust political institutions—the half-visible story of broken families and personal betrayals.[26]

Getting this second kind of acknowledgment is not easy. It is not always easy for victims to publicize their injuries. Without conditions that bolster confidence and reduce fear and, in extreme cases, treat traumatic emotional disorders, victims are usually reticent about entering the public domain. It is well known that only a minuscule proportion of rape victims acknowledge, let alone file, cases. Du Toit tells us that in South Africa the disproportionate number of women who came forward to tell their stories to the South African Truth and Reconciliation Commission (TRC) hardly ever talked about themselves but focused on husbands, sons, or other men in their lives.[27] Das, in a study of survivors of the riots that followed Indira Gandhi's assassination in Delhi in 1984, notes how male survivors felt both guilty for having survived and ashamed at having failed in their obligations to the dead, traumatic emotions that induce loss of face and extreme reluctance to talk.[28] Das explains the public withdrawal of these men by reference to their sense of having betrayed close kinspersons, to their shame at having escaped in the garb of women, and their humiliation and loss of self-esteem at having cut their hair and shaved their beards—important signs of Sikh identity. Compounding all of this trauma was a sense of impotence generated by the failure to take revenge. Innumerable cases exist of victims and survivors for whom the overwhelming need to tell is matched only by a serious inability to do so. In many instances, this is due to the psychological process of numbing that protects the inner self from unbearable external assaults.[29] It is also caused by a certain framing of time by which victims typically fail to distance themselves from the past. Shanti, who lost her husband and three sons in the massacre, and later committed suicide, could not bring herself even to think of the immediate future.[30] Such persons have to relearn how to live again, or be taught how to reengage with their world, before they can make their stories public. Besides, victims are frequently unable to risk reengagement for fear that in the process they may forget what happened to their dead.[31]

A further problem has to do with how such persons frame their stories. Das tells us how it is not untypical of victims to depict a massacre as a natural disaster. "She carries on as if she were the only one to suffer a loss. Look at the world around us. Everyone was affected. A storm came upon us and it destroyed everything in its way. Can we save anyone from such a storm?"[32] If the source of grief is purely natural, why not suffer it with dignity in silence? Why make a narrative of grief that must be endured? Why bring into the public domain grief that is not even caused by another human agent? A final issue concerns the nature of the public arena where stories are told. People need to be convinced that public spaces specifically chosen for this purpose are significant and that their listeners are serious, sympathetic, and unbiased. Both the arena and the persons therein must possess a stamp of authority. Initially, I found it puzzling that victims required official recognition and validation of their stories. Subsequently, I realized that this must have to do with the authority of the modern state, and the accompanying premium attached to citizenship. Among people living in relative poverty, especially in societies such as India's, it must also have to do with a certain normative attitude toward the state: viewing it as an intimate benefactor. When presented with massive evidence of the state being continuously distant and uncaring, victims, if they are publicly to recall, need to regain confidence in the state as an intimate benefactor. In other cultural contexts, people must regain trust in the impartiality of the state before they can begin to tell their stories to state officials.

To get perpetrators to acknowledge responsibility for a crime is as difficult as it is to get beneficiaries to admit complicity or even their knowledge of it. An entirely different psychological process is in motion that demands almost as much attention as the one that concerns victims. Fearing excessive punishment, perpetrators may not confess. Acknowledgment is awkward, deeply embarrassing, and unlikely to be achieved voluntarily or smoothly. There is a deeper problem in that the authority of ideological rhetoric compels most people actively to censor the testimony of their own experience. Besides, why surrender if you can cope with your guilt? I have often wondered how people can live with the fact of the grave harm they have caused others. One unsavory answer is that even purely negative self-assertion generates a great sense of accomplishment in people. The gain in pride and in the sense of power can be achieved as much by hurting others as by helping them. Sadly, some get an enormous pleasure out of kicking others. Humans, in pursuit of self-affirmation, have a vast capacity to shrug off wrongs done to others. Nationalist passion thrives on a rhetoric of self-affirmation propelled by people uniting around imaginary grievances against others.[33] Sometimes lies and denials of crimes also feed into negative self-assertion. Thus, not only the fear of punishment but also false pride and negative self-affirmation prevent people from acknowledging the wrongs that they know about or have committed, when it suits them to do so. The TRC faced this difficulty. Even President Frederik W. de Klerk, who ritualistically offered an apology to those who suffered the indignities and humiliation of racial discrimination, continued to deny any personal knowledge of some of the worst abuses of human rights.[34] This is why truth commissions must be commended if they succeed in persuading perpetrators to acknowledge their crimes.[35]

Acknowledgment as an Operative Act

Acknowledgment is an achievement for another reason. Public remembrance of past injustice and its acknowledgment of it by the wrongdoer are part of a series of acts that Skorupski calls "operative."[36] A social fact is not a fact because it is out there in the world, independent of people's beliefs about it, but, as is well known, is partly constituted by beliefs. For it to remain a fact, the beliefs constituting it must remain stable. This stability is achieved not by an inner steadfastness on the part of individuals but largely by collective acts that function to mark them out *as* facts. Similarly, the significance of events or states of affairs is also constituted by collective practices. Their particular human significance has no publicly perceptible form other than that given by collective practices within a particular culture. There is no way in which this significance can be publicly known unless it is made known through these practices. In short, social facts and their significance depend for their perpetuity on stable beliefs and focused remembrance, neither of which is possible without collective practices. This role of pointing out the public significance of things is traditionally performed by rituals and ceremonies, more generally by what is called symbolic action.[37] The fence that marks out a property boundary is not an optional extra but is crucial to people in retaining a sense of private property. The act of coronation confirming a new king in office is not a superfluous luxury but is central to a recognition of the new status of the person, and this in turn is a precondition for the efficacy of any future act of the royalty. Among such symbolic acts are those performed solely to set up new patterns of rules, that is, operative acts. The example of coronation given above not only establishes a social fact and underlines its significance, but in an important sense also creates it. Now, my claim is that the kind of public acknowledgment that truth commissions make possible constitutes such an operative act. A body of citizens through a complex set of institutions, including a truth commission, launches a new order bound by a new set of rules and, possibly, a system of rights. One function of a truth commission is to contribute to the performance of such operative acts that mark the inauguration of a new moral order. The recognition that grave wrongs have been committed in the past, that people have been severely victimized, and that individuals, groups, and even whole communities have been identified for their crimes announces and underlines this new moral regime and gives future victims the confidence required for their reentry into political processes of negotiation. True, this is a symbolic function, but its symbolic aspect must not be treated as something one can do without; rather, it is constitutive of a system of basic procedural justice. It is no doubt also true that truth commissions cannot perform this function entirely on their own. It is a mistake to believe that truth commissions can carry this burden exclusively on their shoulders, but it is equally mistaken to fail to see their contribution in the announcement and inauguration of a new order.

Against the view that we should simply forget and bury the past and look to the future, forgetting either benefits past oppressors or leaves complex problems relating to the past unresolved. Against the contrary view that public acknowledgment of evil does too little for the victim, I have argued that, if properly understood and appropriately secured, such acknowledgment must be seen as an achievement. Both arguments together constitute a defense of the idea of a truth commission as a complex strategy by which to deal with the past and help societies stabilize a system of basic procedural justice. They establish that a struggle for minimalist morality (the third response) is not a shameful compromise but an appropriate response in the aftermath of evil. The question that still remains to be answered is whether truth commissions can achieve more. Can they fix collective responsibility and also become appropriate mechanisms of forgiveness?

Symmetrical and Asymmetrical Barbarism

Norms of basic procedural justice can come apart if either all relevant parties withdraw their consent or when only one of them does so. When no party abides by norms of basic procedural justice, we descend into a symmetrically barbaric society. When only one violates these norms and others are keen to enforce them, an asymmetrically barbaric society results. The condition of Jews in Nazi Germany and of blacks under the apartheid regime in South Africa illustrates asymmetrical barbarism. So does the massive repression by the state of its own citizens in Argentina and Chile. On the other hand, the violence that plagued Hindu-Muslim relations in the years before and after the partition of India exemplifies symmetrical barbarism. Deliberately to withdraw allegiance to norms of basic procedural justice—to abandon the moral viewpoint—is to aim at evil and be guided by it. In an asymmetrically barbaric society, a particular group (an ethnic/religious/race–based community or the class of political elites), by its violation of minimally moral rules, bears a primary responsibility for evil. Other groups in this situation, normally the victims, bear no such responsibility and, indeed, continue to hold on to a distinctively moral viewpoint. The case of symmetrically barbaric societies is different. Everyone in societies altogether beyond the pale of morality shares the responsibility for social and political evil. All hell has broken loose, and, slightly to alter a phrase borrowed from Hampshire, there is "madness in *every* soul."[38] Therefore, the very distinction between perpetrators and victims appears here to have collapsed. Given this distinction, some mechanism such as a truth commission is necessary and sufficient for restoring minimal decency in symmetrically barbaric societies. However, in asymmetrically barbaric societies, a truth commission is necessary but not sufficient.

Two clarifications are in order. The first dispels the possible impression, stemming from talk of "necessary and sufficient conditions" that truth commissions can single-handedly restore minimal decency. To arrive at a minimally decent order, a society transiting from barbarism necessarily requires both forward-looking and backward-looking institutions. Forward-looking institutions are so called because they are justified primarily in terms of principles that deal with current or future issues and problems, say an electoral commission to ensure fair and free elections or a market-regulating institution to rectify current economic injustice. Institutions are backward-looking when they are justified primarily in terms of principles that compensate, say, for past harm, or deal specifically with grave injustice in the past. I take a truth commission to be a backward-looking institution designed primarily to rehabilitate political victims.

Such a backward-looking institution is necessary (morally required) in the transition to a minimally decent society. When societies move away from symmetrical barbarism, a truth commission suffices for this purpose. However, in the case of asymmetrical barbarism, a truth commission is not sufficient to deal even with grave injustice in the past.[39] Remembrance, acknowledgement, and admission of collective responsibility are just not enough. Other strategies and institutions, say public trials of the most notorious of perpetrators or policies designed to restore political self-confidence among former victims, will be necessary to bring about a stable, minimally decent order.

All barbaric societies need not be neatly categorized as symmetrical or asymmetrical. Indeed, most societies without basic procedural justice tend rapidly to slide from one kind of barbarism to another. For instance, victims resisting their oppressors may be disproportionately violent, turning into perpetrators of greater evil, and completely annuling the moral advantage they had previously possessed. Rwanda is a case in point, where Tutsi were exterminated by Hutu.[40] But not long ago, Rwanda exemplified symmetrical barbarism; and as we go farther back, we find Tutsi systematically victimizing Hutu. The distinction between symmetrical and asymmetrical barbarism is not easy to sustain.

It is not enough to have minimal decency as an objective. Necessary also is a sensitivity to the kind of barbarism left behind. If, in transiting from situations of asymmetric barbarism, we behave as though we are getting away from symmetric barbarism, then, we may regress farther into already existing circles of hell. Consider the period of the partition of India. The fear and radical uncertainty generated by new borders drawn on the basis of religion forced people from their homes in the hope of living securely with people of their own ilk. More than 10 million people crossed borders. It is an understatement to say that this "transfer of populations" was violent. Nearly 1 million were slaughtered, and almost 100,000 women were abducted and raped by marauders belonging to a religion other than their own. Responsibility for this savagery cannot be laid at the door of any single religious group.[41] It makes little sense in such situations to revive the distinction between victim and perpetrator or to make the "victim's status as victim the constitutive pillar of a new political order."[42] The restoration of the moral order, and, in particular the consolidation of basic procedural justice, is the primary need in such situations. A truth commission or some equivalent mechanism is necessary and sufficient for this purpose.

Truth Commission for Future Reconciliation?

My third claim is that a truth commission must not aim to bring about reconciliation, but try only to create a minimally decent society—no mean feat, anyhow. By reconciliation, I mean a cancellation of enmity or estrangement via a morally grounded forgiveness, achievable only when perpetrators and beneficiaries of past injustice acknowledge collective responsibility for wrongdoing and shed their prejudices, and when victims, through the same process, regain their self-respect. The view that truth commissions should aim at reconciliation is usually criticized for two reasons, with which I disagree. The first challenges the coherence of the notion of collective responsibility and therefore finds the very question of collective forgiveness redundant. The second argument criticizes the idea of forgiveness as morally inappropriate. I do not find the notion of collective responsibility incoherent nor the idea of forgiveness morally unworthy. For me, a victimized group can forgive former perpetrators if it owns up collectively to responsibility for wrongdoing and repents. I use "responsibility" not as a legal liability for an act.[43] It is linked rather to what men and women decide to do. I believe that most of our acts and decisions are irreducibly social, and, therefore, responsibility for them is social, too.[44]

Three things follow. First, the domain of moral responsibility spills over beyond what is directly caused by an individual. Second, an entire collectivity can be held responsible for harm to others.[45] Third, guilt and blame must be seen to lie on a continuum, which also contains shame, remorse, regret, and the feeling of being tainted.[46] In short, groups may be held morally responsible for wrongs and individuals can partake of that responsibility, be guilty, or feel tainted.

Why should the victim forgive? Forgiveness implies forswearing resentment toward the person who inflicted moral injury.[47] It is hard to take the view that the forswearing of resentment is always morally appropriate. After all, there is nothing intrinsically wrong in resenting perpetrators of evil. Indeed, since such emotions are woven into one's sense of self-respect, persons who do not resent wrongs done them invariably lack self-respect. Under what conditions is it morally justified to forgive? Clearly, only when the self-respect of victims is enhanced by forgiveness, or at least is not undermined by it. This in turn happens when former perpetrators admit their wrongdoing, distance themselves from the wrongful act, and join the victims in condemning the act as well as their own past. Only under these conditions can the self-respect of victims be restored and enhanced.

Is it possible to achieve such a goal within the functional parameters of a truth commission? Truth commissions cannot aim to bring about reconciliation through this process of collective acknowledgment of grave wrongs-*cum*-forgiveness because reconciliation requires a profound change in the identities of people—a deep, rather long drawn out process. The experiential process of shedding prejudice and owning up to responsibility for wrongs done to others begins with the wrongdoers admitting the absence of a good reason for their acts. This must turn into an acknowledgment that the bad reason for the actions spring from the deepest recesses of their beings. Since a genuine confrontation takes place not just in the mind but at the level of gut and feeling, the acknowledgment that "I have hitherto been the wrong kind of person" is bound to be extremely painful. We might say of such persons that in such moments their souls are punished. This punishment of the soul must necessarily involve a profound change of identity, which must be witnessed by the victims if they are to be convinced that forgiveness is appropriate. Truth commissions that must operate within a compressed time frame, in the immediate aftermath of evil, are simply not equipped to bear the burden of effecting or encompassing this fundamental transformation.[48] Truth commissions can create conditions for reconciliation in the future. But such reconciliation, if and when it comes about, can be only a fortunate by-product of the truth commission.

It might be argued that it is improper to have forgiveness even as a long-term goal. One well-known argument against forgiveness is that it is deeply tied to Christian morality—at any rate that it takes us beyond ordinary morality into the domain of high religion. Victims in South Africa have complained bitterly that the justification of forgiveness derives from a particular moral vision with which they do not identify and that therefore it is not incumbent upon them to heed the plea to forgive. Others object that forgiveness must come from within, and only victims have the proper standing to do so. One cannot forgive under compulsion, nor can others forgive on behalf of a victim. A third criticism of forgiveness is that it has the effect of erasing wrongdoing—that it is an invitation to reconcile with rather than conquer evil. Finally, it is also argued that the plea for general amnesty with which it is linked can only lead to enraged victims opting for personal acts of vengeance. The demand for forgiveness in this view can only exacerbate settling of scores outside the rule of law.

It is true that Christianity provides an important source for the justification of forgiveness.[49] Within Christianity, it is widely recognized that since the propensity to wrongdoing is pervasive, forgiveness should be generally available, too. As original sinners, we seek forgiveness from God. As sinners in our day-to-day existence, we must seek forgiveness from each other. From the availability of a virtue in one religious tradition, it hardly follows that it is unavailable in others.[50] More important, atheistic humanism, with no connection whatsoever to religion, must have place for forgiveness, too. Even unbelievers can and should admit that in the course of living our lives we wrong others, particularly those about whom we care deeply. If we care about the people that we have wronged, we would certainly want them to forgive us. Indeed, a humanist must accept that at the heart of the human condition lies a radical fallibility that it is futile to try to overcome totally. We need forgiveness from each other, alas, because without God-like features we often commit wrong, and because there may be no God to forgive us. As Murphy notes, "We do all need and desire forgiveness and would not want to live in a world where forgiveness was not regarded as a healing and restoring virtue."[51] Furthermore, the domain where this virtue is exercised need not only be private. We need and expect forgiveness even within the wider public domain. I am not entirely convinced by the view that forgiveness is exclusively tied to one religious tradition or that unbelievers have no need for it.

The criticism that forgiveness bypasses the act of wrongdoing is not justified either. To forgive is not to convert a wrong into a right. It is not to justify the wrong done. Nor is it identical with excusing the wrong done, as when one excuses a child for causing some harm on the ground that he cannot really be held responsible for it. The process of forgiveness begins only after proper recognition of wrongdoing and is conditional upon it. Since the wrong is not simply whitewashed, to forgive is not to compromise with evil. Nor does forgiveness entail amnesty.

Forgiveness is not to be confused with mercy.[52] This confusion may well have lain at the heart of the South African TRC in its early stages.[53] Reasons for forgiveness are not automatically reasons for mercy. A victim may forgive a wrongdoer but not be entitled to free one of legal accountability. Conversely, out of mercy we may reduce punishment for the wrongdoers but not forgive them. To act out of compassion is not to forgive, though the two may be related. Finally, forgiveness is not a virtue in all contexts and is appropriate only when it is consistent with the dignity and self-respect of the victim. One cannot forgive for the future good of the society, if personal costs are excessive. The good of the community cannot provide reasons for unconditional forgiveness. Perpetrators cannot be forgiven if they neither acknowledge nor repent a crime. Nor are the victims ready for forgiveness if they retain the feeling that their suffering has not been properly acknowledged. Without proper repentance, persons who have killed or tortured may repeat the crime. If there is no forgiveness from within, "then the door is open to private acts of vengeance and retribution."[54]

Notes

1. I am grateful to Robert Meister, Veena Das, Mahmood Mamdani, Neeladri Bhattacharya, Kumar Shahani, Shalini Advani, Sudipta Kaviraj, and especially Tani Sandhu and Alok Rai for helpful discussions on this paper. Thanks are also due to the editors of this volume for their valuable suggestions.

2. The term "reconciliation" can be interpreted in two ways. On the first, stronger interpretation, reconciliation means a cancellation of estrangement via, say, forgiveness in order to establish substantive agreement on moral issues. On the second, weaker interpretation, it means cancellation of enmity with the help of a culture of reciprocity and mutual respect in order to have minimal disagreement on moral issues. (As I understand it, in their contribution to this volume, this is roughly what Gutmann and Thompson have in mind.) In my view, truth commissions may be unduly burdened if they aim at reconciliation in either of these two senses. Reconciliation presupposes a firm consensus on thick values. The objective of a minimally decent society presupposes much less; there need be only a diffused sense all around that we have had enough of evil, that we must get away from it, and that the means by which we do so must not themselves be evil. The necessity of getting over estrangement or dealing with one another with mutual respect is not felt, at least not in the immediate aftermath of evil.

3. Throughout this chapter, I have used the term society instead of the bulkier term "social formation"; and by social formation, I have something specific in mind—the manner in which a certain type of human collectivity comes into being as well as that human collectivity. Such a collectivity may be a small configuration within a community, a large community within a society, or interacting communities within a large political order such as the nation-state or indeed the entire world order or a part thereof. It is possible for a minimally decent social formation to exist within a larger barbaric society and, likewise, for a barbaric social formation to be found within a larger minimally decent society. One of the cases I mention, the massacre of Sikhs in Delhi in 1984, is a barbaric social formation on a relatively small scale. Its existence did not imply that the whole of India had turned barbaric. Of course, the entire sociopolitical order, such as a nation-state, may be barbaric or minimally decent. My use of these terms is flexible enough to include both small communities and large societies. Two further points: First, all societies remain at the edge of barbarism. None is able permanently to cross the threshold of minimal decency. Indeed, many societies sustain their own decency by directly perpetrating evil upon other societies. Second, the terms "minimally decent" and "barbaric" cut across the usual typology of socialist and capitalist social formations. Both capitalist and socialist societies have been known to be equally

barbaric or minimally decent. In my view, we need a complex, two-tiered morality to judge social formations: First, to test if they have crossed the threshold of minimal decency and then to begin making other cross-societal, moral judgments.

4. Thomas Nagel, *Other Minds* (New York, 1995), 213–214.

5. Stuart Hampshire, *Innocence and Experience* (Cambridge, 1989), 75. The association of the concept of evil with the idea of original sin, and more generally with theology, is certainly one reason why secular philosophers are reluctant to give it the attention it deserves. But its neglect is due also to postwar euphoria—a general sense of well-being throughout the industrialized world—and to a motivated lack of interest in theorizing about the great injustices of colonialism and its destructive consequences in the non-Western world. By giving us the idea of basic procedural justice, and with his renewed emphasis on evil, Hampshire has filled major lacuna in political philosophy. My use of the term "evil" follows L. M. Thomas's account of an evil act. An evil act must be a wrongful act, done in an appropriate way, that has the right moral gravity. The right moral gravity of an act is characterized either by its inherent or its quantitative hideousness or by both. For example, the rape and massacre of a large number of women. See Thomas, *Vessels of Evil: American Slavery and the Holocaust* (Philadelphia,1992). See also James P. Sterba's review of the book in *Ethics* CVI (1996): 424–448.

6. Hampshire, *Innocence*, 8, 69.

7. Ibid., 67.

8. Ibid., 72.

9. Ibid., 72–78, 109.

10. The idea of "political death" is similar to the notion of "social death" deployed by Orlando Patterson in *Slavery and Social Death* (Cambridge, 1982).

11. Mahmood Mamdani draws a distinction between injustice within the legal framework of apartheid and the injustice of apartheid itself. Once this distinction is drawn we can focus alternately on victims of apartheid narrowly defined, that is, militants victimized as they struggled against apartheid and those victims who suffered under the "day-to-day web of regulations that was apartheid." Mamdani, "Reconciliation without Justice," *South African Review of Books* CIV (1996).

12. Hampshire, *Innocence*, 75

13. Veena Das, "Our Work to Cry: Your Work to Listen," in *Mirrors of Violence* (Delhi, 1990), 347–348.

14. Ibid.

15. Tina Rosenberg, *The Haunted Land* (New York, 1996), xi–xii.

16. Quoted from Tina Rosenberg, in Alex Boraine, Janet Levy, and Ronel Scheffer (eds.), *Dealing with the Past* (Cape Town, 1997), 66.

17. Jeffrie G. Murphy, "Forgiveness and Resentment," in Jeffrie Murphy and Jean Hampton, *Forgiveness and Mercy* (Cambridge, 1990), 25.

18. Jeremy Waldron, "Superseding Historic Injustice," *Ethics* CIII (1992): 6.

19. Sheldon Wolin, "Injustice and Collective Memory," in *The Presence of the Past* (Baltimore, 1989), 32–46.

20. Ibid., 37.

21. Michael Ignatieff, *Blood and Belonging* (New York, 1993), 153.

22. See David Hume, "Of Parties in General," in *Political Writings* (Indianapolis, 1994), 160.

23. Michael Lapsley, a member of the African National Congress, was a victim of a letter bomb in which he lost both his hands and an eye and suffered shattered eardrums. He writes, "For a very small amount of time I thought it would have been better to have died. I had never met anyone without hands so I did not know that life could be meaningful. I was faced with some important questions and one of them was: Do I allow my life to be consumed with hatred, bitterness, self-pity and desire for revenge? Later I realised that if I was to spend the rest of my life looking for revenge or hunting for those who had sent me that letter bomb, it would consume me. The result was that I was able to say: 'I am going to live my life as fully, as joyfully, as completely as possible and that is my victory.'" Das notes that the behavior of women victims of the Sikh massacre in 1984 in Delhi—their tendency to grab everything from various relief agencies—did not match middle-class expectations of dignified behavior and was initially very puzzling. Later, she saw it as a healthy sign of women recovering and reengaging in life. "The need to corner as many relief goods as they could get gave some structure to women's activities and helped them to think of the future, to symbolize it in the new commodities that relief was bringing in their lives." See Das, *Mirrors*, 366.

24. For an illuminating discussion of these issues in the context of the United States and for the view that the national memory of the figure of Lincoln performs a function in U.S political culture similar to the one performed by truth commissions in other nations, see Robert Meister, "Living in the Aftermath of Evil: Notes on the Political Culture of National Recovery," unpublished (1997).

25. Indeed, this determination is also entailed by acknowledgment of the second kind. An acknowledgment that an act was immoral is a moral judgment and, like all moral judgments, has implications for action. Therefore, to acknowledge past injustice is to commit ourselves to avoiding it in the future.

26. Albie Sachs must have had this distinction in mind when he said, "It is enormously frustrating to me to know there are millions of people who want to share this country, to share their humanity and open up their hearts—not just Mandela who is noted for this. But they cannot do it because the other side will not acknowledge that apartheid was more than a mistake. It not only caused pain—it was fundamentally humiliating, inhuman, and cruel. It is one thing to recognise the facts of apartheid, it is another to acknowledge the pain, humiliation and indignities it caused." Albie Sachs in Boraine, Levy, and Scheffer, *Dealing*, 23–24.

27. Henry J. Steiner (ed.), *Truth Commissions: A Comparative Assessment* (Cambridge, 1997), 25–26.

28. Das, *Mirrors*, 384–388.

29. Ibid., 358.

30. Ibid., 359.

31. Ibid.

32. Ibid., 349.

33. See the excellent discussion in Ignatieff, *Blood*, 162.

34. See Timothy Garton Ash, "True Confessions," *New York Review of Books* XLIV (1997): 33–38.

35. In this respect, the South African TRC may well have failed, for far fewer of the violators have come forward to acknowledge their wrongdoing than was expected.

36. On operative acts and more generally on symbolic acts, see John Skorupski, *Symbol and Theory* (Cambridge,1976), 93–103.

37. See Skorupski, *Symbol.*

38. Hampshire, *Innocence*, 189.

39. A truth commission is one of the many backward-looking institutions available to deal with past injustice. In symmetrically barbaric societies, it is sufficient. In asymmetrically barbaric societies, we need a commission and other backward-looking institutions to deal with past injustice. Strictly speaking, a commission is an unnecessary but sufficient part of an insufficient but necessary background condition for the realization of a minimally decent society.

40. For an illuminating discussion of Rwanda, see Mamdani, "From Conquest to Consent as the Basis of State-Formation: Reflections on Rwanda," *New Left Review* CCXVI (1996): 3–36.

41. For a discussion of partition-related violence in India, see Ritu Menon and Kamla Bhasin, *Borders and Boundaries* (Delhi, 1998); Urvashi Butalia, *The Other Side of Silence* (Delhi, 1998); and Mushirul Hasan (ed.), *India Partition: Process, Strategy and Mobilization* (Delhi, 1993).

42. I here react to the discussion among Kanan Makiya, Charles Maier, and Yael Tamir at the meeting on truth commissions organized by the World Peace Foundation. Clearly, there exists a situation where the new moral order must not immediately erase the status of the victim, just as it would be wrong to retain it in another. The answer to Kanan Makiya's question, "Should we establish commonality on the basis of rights or on the recognition of pain," must be determined contextually. See Steiner, *Truth Commissions*, 31.

43. For a discussion of collective responsibility I rely entirely on Larry May, *Sharing Responsibility* (Chicago, 1992), 38, 106. For my purpose, unlike May, I do not distinguish between collective and shared responsibility.

44. My own views on the irreducibly social nature of human action is to be found in Rajeev Bhargava, *Individualism in Social Science* (Oxford, 1992), 199–220.

45. Of course, this is entirely consistent with the view that members of such a collectivity are responsible in varying degrees, depending largely on the quantum of power exercised by them.

46. May, *Sharing*, 34.

47. See the excellent discussion of this issue in Murphy and Hampton, *Forgiveness*, 43; J. L. Mackie, *Persons and Values* (Oxford, 1985), 206–219; and Murphy and Hampton, *Forgiveness*, 24, 47.

48. In my view, anxiety over the capacity of truth commissions to promote reconciliation is groundless, and at best, premature. See the report by Kate Dunn, "Will S. Africa's Report bring action?" in *Christian Science Monitor* 30 October 1998, where the veteran antiapartheid campaigner, Helen Suzman, wonders whether the TRC succeeded in promoting reconciliation. Truth commissions are meant to encourage the controlled expression of "difficult and troubling emotions," not suppress them. And the expression of such emotions is bound to temporarily exacerbate tension between groups, not bring about immediate reconciliation. That, incidentally, is why truth commissions must aim to consolidate a minimally decent society, not aim for "higher" goals such as reconciliation.

49. Ibid.

50. For example, Gandhi believed that in Hindu scriptures forgiveness is the highest virtue. See *The Collected Works of Mahatma Gandhi* (New Delhi, 1982), CXXXVI, 70.

51. See Murphy and Hampton, *Forgiveness*, 30–31.

52. Ibid., 34.

53. The TRC, it may be recalled, had to decide who got amnesty in return for a complete description of political crimes committed by the perpetrators. Many feared that this amounted to something like a general amnesty. Critics of the TRC, such as President Mbeki, have repeatedly asserted that a general amnesty will never be accepted by the people of South Africa.

54. See Rosenberg, in Boraine, Levy, and Scheffer, *Dealing*, 67.

IV

Moral Ambition Within and Beyond Political Constraints

REFLECTIONS ON RESTORATIVE JUSTICE

ELIZABETH KISS[1]

"WE'VE heard the truth. There is even talk about reconciliation. But where's the justice?"[2] This, according to the *Final Report* issued in November 1998 by South Africa's Truth and Reconciliation Commission (TRC), was a "common refrain" among observers of the commission's work. It is easy to understand why many would view justice as a casualty of the truth commission process. Under the terms of South Africa's negotiated transition from apartheid to democracy, those who had committed gross human rights violations for political reasons, whether in defense of the apartheid regime or in efforts to overthrow it, received amnesty if they made full public disclosure of their crimes. Perpetrators thus got off "scot-free," escaping criminal prosecution and in some cases even being freed from prison years after they had been tried and convicted.[3] Amnesty extinguished civil as well as criminal liability, a point upheld by the South African Constitutional Court when it rejected a lawsuit filed by the families of murdered antiapartheid activists Steve Biko, Griffith Mxenge, and others who alleged that their rights to seek judicial redress had been unconstitutionally violated.[4]

If justice requires the prosecution and punishment of those who commit gross human rights violations—which the South African Parliament defined as "killing, abduction, torture, or severe ill-treatment"—then the amnesty offered by the TRC violates justice.[5] Can the TRC be defended against, or in spite of, this criticism? Its supporters tend to appeal to two very different kinds of considerations in justifying the commission's work. First, they argue that the amnesty provisions were simply the best deal the African National Congress (ANC) was able to extract from the South African government during the negotiated transition to democracy. Although it would have been morally preferable to prosecute human rights violators, this proved "impossible" given the "military stalemate" between the state and the liberation movements.[6] With no prospect of a decisive victory over the minority white regime, the ANC was compelled to acquiesce in the amnesty guarantees demanded by

National Party leaders, both to secure a settlement and to stave off a direct threat by the security forces to disrupt the 1994 democratic elections.[7] On this view, the amnesty granted by the TRC did indeed sacrifice justice. Or, at best, it salvaged "certain essential elements" of justice by virtue of the uniquely South African innovation of making amnesty individual and conditional on public disclosure of specific misdeeds.[8] The decision to sacrifice or compromise justice was morally justified, however, because it was, or was reasonably regarded as being, necessary to achieve a successful transition from a profoundly unjust regime to a democratic one.

The second type of justification offered is quite different. It asserts that the work of the TRC, including its controversial amnesty provisions, achieves or promotes important moral values, values that are far less likely to be attained through prosecutions. Thus the TRC's *Final Report* argues that "even if the South African transition had occurred without any amnesty agreement, even if criminal prosecution had been politically feasible," prosecutions would have yielded much less truth about what happened and why, and far fewer opportunities for closure, healing, and reconciliation.[9] Nor is it only values other than justice that are better served by the TRC. While acknowledging that the TRC failed to provide retributive justice, the commission argues that it has promoted another kind of justice, restorative justice, "which is concerned not so much with punishment as with correcting imbalances, restoring broken relationships—with healing, harmony and reconciliation."[10] Justice should not be seen "merely as retribution," and "the tendency to equate justice with retribution must be challenged and the concept of restorative justice considered as an alternative."[11] Indeed, the report suggests, "strengthening the restorative dimensions of justice" was critical to the TRC's efforts to fulfill its constitutional mandate to help build a bridge between "the past of a deeply divided society characterised by strife, conflict, untold suffering and injustice, and a future founded on the recognition of human rights, democracy and peaceful coexistence and development opportunities for all South Africans, irrespective of colour, race, class, belief or sex."[12]

Curiously, these two kinds of justifications have been offered by the same people almost in the same breath, and both are prominently featured in the commission's report.[13] At first glance this seems odd, for surely it is very different to claim that the TRC was compelled by political necessity to do something unjust and to assert that its actions promoted a more ambitious and expansive vision of justice. Nevertheless, I argue that this dual perspective—of reluctant realpolitik and of visionary moral ambition—captures a core element of the truth commission experience as it has emerged over the past two decades in over a dozen countries.

Truth commissions are a recent invention, designed to provide societies in transition with a way to deal with their legacies of mass violence, abuse, and injustice.[14] They are authoritative bodies given a mandate to develop an official account of past brutalities, in the hopes that doing so will help prevent a recurrence of such violations. In most cases, transitional regimes emerge under difficult and unstable conditions, constrained by limited resources and threatened by the continued presence of former elites who still possess considerable military, judicial, and economic power. This is certainly as true in South Africa as it was, for instance, in Chile, where former dictator Augusto Pinochet remained head of the armed forces, and in Argentina, where civilian president Raul Alfonsin needed to placate the same military establishment that had waged the dirty war. These conditions place severe constraints on what truth commissions can do. As a result, almost all commissions have exhibited some features—grants of amnesty to perpetrators, selective investigation of crimes, or a failure to "name names"—that revealed them to be, in Weschler's vivid phrase, "mired in the muck of forced compromise."[15]

But there is another side to the story. In their efforts to fulfill their mandates under these difficult circumstances, truth commissions have struggled with basic questions about what justice requires in relation to survivors, perpetrators, and entire nations scarred by a brutal past. Out of these struggles are emerging new vocabularies of truth and justice as well as a new institutional repertoire for pursuing them. Developed through a remarkable learning process involving participants from around the world, especially from Latin America, Eastern Europe, and Africa, this repertoire encompasses multiple tasks and aims.[16] Truth commissions generate authoritative historical accounts, issue recommendations for institutional change, and direct a national morality play that places victims of injustice on center stage. They combine investigative, judicial, political, educational, therapeutic, and even spiritual functions. This proliferation of functions and aims reflects what I call the *moral ambition* of truth commissions, their determination to honor multiple moral considerations and to pursue profound and nuanced moral ends. In the process, truth commissioners have affirmed the value of "narrative" as well as of "forensic" forms of truth, and have come to speak of justice as reconciliation, national healing, and moral reconstruction. More to the point, they have developed concrete practices aimed at furthering these goals, practices that stretch the conventional limits of judicial and political action. All of these features of truth commissions are clearly discernible in the South African TRC, the most morally ambitious commission to date. And they are dramatically encapsulated in the commission's efforts to promote what it calls "restorative justice."

Is such moral ambition legitimate or wise? In particular, is restorative justice truly a distinctive type or dimension of justice, one that is different from, and in some cases more important than, retributive justice? If so, can restorative justice be promoted through a truth commission? Or, as some critics charge, is restorative justice both conceptually muddled and politically illegitimate? I defend restorative justice as a coherent and legitimate, though risky, framework for seeking to rectify profound injustice. Although it cannot refute the legitimacy of retributive justice, restorative justice presents an ambitious and inspiring alternative. It is important, however, that its proponents be mindful of the risks involved in pursuing restorative justice, and of the limitations of truth commissions as instruments for accomplishing such a project.

The Role of Truth: Acknowledgment, Therapy, and Justice

The "essence" of a commitment to restorative justice, according to the TRC's report, is an effort to restore and affirm the human and civil dignity of victims.[17] When truth commissions were first established two decades ago, this was not envisaged as an important, or even necessarily relevant, aspect of their purpose. Instead, it has emerged out of reflection on the actual experiences of truth commissions.

As their name implies, truth commissions are created, first and foremost, to establish the truth about past injustices. Sometimes this requires unearthing information that has been hidden from the public. The TRC, for example, succeeded in exhuming the bodies of almost fifty activists who had been abducted, killed, and buried in unmarked graves.[18] But even when most of the facts about a crime or atrocity are well known, it is vital to a society's prospects for justice that they be publicly and officially acknowledged.[19]

Establishing the truth is instrumental to justice in at least two ways. Truth serves justice in a basic sense stressed by the Argentinian truth commission in its report *Nunca Mas*: without truth one cannot distinguish the innocent from the guilty.[20] Less directly, truth serves justice by overcoming fear and distrust and by breaking the cycles of violence and oppression that characterize profoundly unjust societies. As the TRC report put it,

> The Commission was founded in the belief that, in order to build the "historic bridge" of which the interim Constitution speaks [between "a deeply divided past of untold suffering and injustice" and "a future founded on the recognition of human rights"], one must establish "as complete a picture as possible" of the injustices committed in the past. This must be coupled with a public, official acknowledgement of the "untold suffering" which resulted from those injustices.[21]

Some have cast doubt on the value of revealing such truths, worrying that there is already too much fixation on past wounds and that, as Elon put it, "A little forgetfulness might be in order."[22] The past, they warn, can become an indulgence and an obsession, playing into our capacity for what Breytenbach has called "scab-picking curiosity."[23] There may well be some wisdom in these warnings. But a policy of enforced amnesia is simply not a viable alternative for fledgling democracies emerging from a period of gross human rights violations. Moreover, many people have concluded that, just as wounds fester when they are not exposed to the open air, so unacknowledged injustice can poison societies and produce the cycles of distrust, hatred, and violence we have witnessed in many parts of the world, including the Balkans, Rwanda, and the Middle East.

Even more dangerous, perhaps, than ignored injustices are distortions and disinformation. The TRC made a special point of emphasizing how its work has decisively discredited some widely circulated accusations and counteraccusations.[24] In addition, "partisan" or "selective" accounts of past conflicts can "easily provide the basis for mobilisation towards further conflicts."[25] For instance, selective narratives of suffering can lead previously victimized groups to victimize others in turn. Krog has speculated that the atrocities suffered by Afrikaners at the hands of the British in the Anglo-Boer War (1899–1902) helped to shape the brutalities of apartheid.[26] A similar argument might be made about Israeli behavior toward Palestinians. What is needed to counteract these tendencies is "an inclusive remembering of painful truths about the past."[27] Thus, while Archbishop Desmond Tutu's assertion that there is "no healing without truth" is more of a working hypothesis than a demonstrated fact, it is reasonable, on the available evidence, to believe that truth-gathering can help to prevent a recurrence of the injustices of the past.[28]

Truth commissions originally gathered victim testimony in order to construct an official account of past abuses. However, a growing number of commission participants have begun to find value in the process of listening to such testimony. Some highlight the therapeutic value of giving testimony; for others, it represents a form of doing justice to victims. Both views signal important shifts in the theory and practice of truth commissions.

Many survivors of human rights violations—whether in Chile, Sri Lanka, or South Africa—attest to the healing power of telling their story to an official commission after a lifetime of being ignored, disrespected, and abused by state officials.[29] For instance, when asked by a commissioner how he felt after testifying before the TRC, one South African man, blinded as the result of an assault by a police officer, replied, "I feel what has been making me sick all the time is the fact that I couldn't tell my story. But now . . . it feels like I got my sight back by coming here."[30] Telling the truth about their wounds can heal the wounded—and perhaps listening to such stories can help heal societies.[31]

Of course, the therapeutic aspects of the work of truth commissions can be viewed as incidental to their core mission of establishing the truth. Indeed, some critics have referred dismissively to the TRC's Human Rights Violations Committee as a "kleenex commission."[32] Others, more thoughtfully, warn that an overemphasis on the therapeutic does a disservice to survivors who regard themselves not as patients in need of healing but as citizens entitled to justice.[33] While such warnings are important, healing deserves attention as an important part of what truth commissions can accomplish.

But the taking of survivor testimony has another dimension beyond, and independent of, its potential as a source of healing: it is an important means of doing justice to victims. In an article entitled "Truth as Justice," Popkin and Roht-Arriaza contend that providing a platform for victims is one of the core tasks of truth commissions, not merely as a way of obtaining information but also from the standpoint of justice.[34] Truth and justice are intrinsically, and not just instrumentally, connected. Those whose lives were shattered are entitled to have their suffering acknowledged and their dignity affirmed, to know that their "pain is real and worthy of attention."[35] We have an obligation to tell them, in the words of TRC commissioner Pumla Gobodo-Madikizela, "You are right, you were damaged, and *it was wrong.*"[36] More important, we have an obligation to listen, to "give them an opportunity to relate their own accounts of the violations of which they are the victim."[37] Justice requires that we treat people as ends in themselves. We affirm the dignity and agency of those who have been brutalized by attending to their voices and making their stories a part of the historical record.

Placing healing and victim-centered justice at the heart of a truth commission's work has required commissions to invent new practices and norms. These include norms of respectful listening, which allow people to tell their stories without interruption; rituals of acknowledgement and respect (such as the practice, in stark contrast to that prevalent in courtrooms, of commissioners rising when witnesses enter to give evidence); and the provision of support services by psychologists and social workers.[38] Members of the TRC honored victims in other ways as well, by singing and praying with them, visiting the sites of atrocities, and participating in reburials and public rituals of remembrance.[39]

The practices of a victim-centered justice seek to recognize the dignity and voice of those who have suffered. They are reminiscent of Fraser's arguments that "recognition" is a distinct form of justice beyond both retributive and distributive justice. Justice as recognition entails acknowledging the distinctive identity of the other, striving to repair damage done to him or her through violence, stigmatization, and disrespect, and including his or her stories in our collective histories.[40] The practices developed by the TRC offer important insights into what justice as recognition requires. Thus the theory and practice of truth commissions has led to a nuanced idea of victim-centered justice, and to a new repertoire of practices by which to honor the dignity of former victims of oppression.

This victim-centered vision of justice affirms that, in societies emerging from a period of repression, justice requires "an inclusive remembering of painful truths about the past" and a commitment to allow victims to tell their stories.[41] Neither of these tasks is likely to be accomplished through prosecutions. First, because of their focus on particular perpetrators and charges and their constraints by rules of evidence, trials lack the narrative scope of truth commissions and do not yield comprehensive accounts of regimes.[42] Thus the TRC was able to reconstruct a much more complete picture of human rights violations than would have come out through efforts to prosecute individual perpetrators.[43] Second, because of the rules of due process and the norms of an adversarial legal system, trials cannot do justice to victims in the sense that this result is promoted through victim testimony. Prosecution witnesses at trials undergo constant interruption and aggressive cross-examination; they are not treated with the deference and respect that truth commissions can accord to victims giving testimony.[44] In the TRC hearings, the testimony of witnesses was not treated as "arguments or claims in a court of law," but rather as "personal or narrative truth" providing "unique insights into the pain of South Africa's past."[45]

Moreover, in its effort to develop as complete a picture as possible of past injustices, the TRC was not only concerned with victims' perspectives; its mandate also extended to an effort to understand "the motives and perspectives of the persons responsible" for gross human rights violations.[46] This meant that the commission gave amnesty applicants opportunities to explain themselves, and regarded the testimony of perpetrators as an important feature of what it called "social, or dialogue truth."[47] In his foreword to the commission's report, Tutu provided a striking illustration of this spirit of understanding when he noted that, although he firmly believed that "apartheid was an intrinsically evil system," he tried to understand the "insights and perspectives" of its supporters and believed that some of them "were not driven by malicious motives," but "genuinely believed" that apartheid offered "the best solution to the complexities of a multiracial land with citizens at very different levels of economic, social, and educational development."[48]

While perpetrators deserved a fair hearing, the commission sought, not to excuse them, but to assign "political accountability and moral responsibility" to those who had committed some of apartheid's most egregious crimes.[49] Whether truth commissions that lack the power of prosecution can achieve such accountability is one of the most difficult questions confronting defenders of restorative justice.

Justice and Accountability: The Problem of Amnesty

If truth commissions have a moral Achilles' heel, it is the issue of amnesty. Doing justice to the past and to its victims entails holding those who committed abuses accountable. Accountability, in turn, evokes the idea of retributive justice, of legal prosecution and punishment. In principle, truth commissions are compatible with, and indeed can be precursors to, judicial prosecutions. This was in fact the assumption underlying the work of the Argentinian Truth

Commission in the early 1980s: that its findings would subsequently be used by the Argentinian judiciary to prosecute members of the military junta who had committed gross human rights violations. Five hundred officers were indeed tried on the basis of the truth commission's report. In the end, however, the effort to punish perpetrators of the dirty war foundered on legal and political obstacles. Faced with judicial chaos and the threat of a coup, the government halted the prosecutions and issued a blanket amnesty for soldiers and police. Since then, truth commissions have come to be viewed more as alternatives to trials than as precursors to them.

The reasons for this development are numerous. Legal obstacles to prosecutions include problems of due process raised by the prospect of prosecuting people for crimes committed under different legal regimes, statutes of limitations, evidentiary problems inherent in crimes of secrecy like torture, abduction, and extrajudicial murder, and the defense available to many perpetrators that they were acting under orders. In some cases outgoing regimes have tried to indemnify themselves by passing self-amnesty laws; or, as in South Africa, they have made a guarantee of amnesty the sine qua non of their acquiescence to a negotiated transition.

Political obstacles to prosecution are no less formidable. Transitional regimes often face an unsympathetic judiciary dominated by supporters of the old regime, uncooperative police and security forces, inadequate resources and expertise, and the threat of military coup or civil unrest. Truth commissions are thus hobbled from the start in their efforts to hold perpetrators accountable.

Even as they have continued to be shaped by these constraints and compromises, however, truth commissions have sought to reach beyond them in order to achieve some degree of accountability. For instance, commissions have sought to identify those responsible for human rights violations even in circumstances in which they could not publish this information, much less use it as the basis for legal prosecutions. Thus, for instance, the Chilean Truth Commission submitted a list of alleged perpetrators to the country's president. In addition, most truth commissions prepare a report offering specific recommendations for legislative, political, institutional, educational, or other changes that are needed to ensure that abuses do not recur. While attenuated, this, too, provides a measure of accountability, for it establishes as a matter of public record the institutional mechanisms responsible for past abuses. By identifying structural causes of human rights violations, commission reports reveal systematic patterns of accountability that may be a valuable resource for future political mobilization.

The South African TRC presents the most striking example of an innovative attempt to establish mechanisms of accountability in the face of severe political constraints. With a commitment to amnesty guaranteed by the interim constitution, the new government needed to determine the exact form amnesty would take. After extensive parliamentary and public debate, a policy was drafted that made amnesty individual rather than collective, and conditional on full, public, disclosure by perpetrators. This novel approach to amnesty was morally innovative in three ways. First, it upheld the principle usually repudiated by amnesties, the principle of individual moral accountability. As the TRC's final report rightly stresses, the amnesty provisions did not give perpetrators impunity but provided "a considerable degree of accountability."[50] Perpetrators had to disclose publicly what they had done. The TRC firmly upheld this principle over the objections of some in the ANC who argued that antiapartheid activists were involved in a just war and therefore should not be held accountable for gross human rights violations.[51]

The second moral innovation accomplished by South Africa's amnesty provisions was that applicants for amnesty were tried in the court of public opinion. Previous truth commissions had met in private. In South Africa, public hearings and extensive coverage by the media ensured that perpetrators could not hide behind the wall of silence and anonymity that has protected the torturers and murderers of so many regimes. Victims had a right to confront their abusers during amnesty hearings, holding them accountable in an especially powerful way. These confrontations sometimes achieved what the TRC characterizes as one of the key elements of restorative justice, the idea that crimes and offenses are injuries done to another person, violations against individual human beings rather than against "faceless" institutions.[52] So, for instance, Ashley Forbes was able to confront his torturer, policeman Jeffrey Benzien, and compel him to "demonstrate" his torture techniques at the amnesty hearing. Forbes then asked Benzien, "What kind of a man does this to another human being?"[53]

South Africa's third moral innovation was that its amnesty law created incentives for truth-telling, so that applications for amnesty became vehicles for uncovering truths about past abuses. Those who failed to apply for amnesty remained vulnerable to criminal or civil charges. Persons named as perpetrators in testimony given to the Committee on Human Rights were contacted and invited to apply for amnesty. Perpetrators could be denied amnesty if they failed to make full disclosure of their participation in gross human rights violations, or if they failed to persuade the commission that they had acted out of political motives.[54] Given the requirements of "full disclosure," the incentive to close ranks was eroded and a substantial number of perpetrators sought to explain or excuse themselves by naming those who had ordered them to act. For instance, five officers who had killed unarmed demonstrators implicated General Johan van der Merwe as the one who had given them orders to fire. The general applied for amnesty in turn, and implicated two of his superiors. In this way accountability could be established along a chain of command, a feat that has proved almost impossible to accomplish through trials.[55] This model of individual amnesty represents an important innovation and a positive precedent for future truth commissions.

These accomplishments of the South African amnesty provisions do not alter the fact that some people who had committed brutal crimes were granted amnesty and allowed to continue with their lives. In this sense, as the TRC report rightly acknowledges, retributive justice was not done. For some human rights advocates this amounts to the failure to uphold an absolute moral and legal imperative to prosecute those who have committed gross human rights violations.[56] Many critics also noted that, while the commission's Amnesty Committee was empowered to grant or deny amnesty, victims who testified before the commission would wait for years to receive reparations. The TRC came in for particular criticism for its failure to obtain more substantial interim reparations for victims.[57] Moreover, since amnesty was not contingent on expressions of remorse or contrition, on the grounds that these could be feigned so easily, some applicants pointedly refused to apologize and adopted a self-righteous and supercilious tone. Others, seemingly untouched by the process, mechanically confessed only the bare minimum to satisfy the requirements of disclosure and sought to excuse their own conduct by portraying themselves as obedient functionaries or victims of "ideological brainwashing." Small wonder that some victims and their families were frustrated or enraged by the TRC process.[58]

On the other hand, the case of General Magnus Malan, former army chief and defense minister, is instructive. While the TRC was doing its work, Malan was prosecuted for authorizing hit squads and assassinations. After eighteen months and twelve million rand in taxpayer-supported court costs, he was acquitted. Later, however, Malan appeared before the commission and told his own story, denying some allegations but admitting to much more than his trial had disclosed.[59]

While the TRC's encounters with the highest-ranking leaders of apartheid, former prime ministers/presidents Pieter W. Botha and Frederik W. de Klerk, were frustratingly inconclusive, it is clear that the truth commission process led to the identification of many more perpetrators than would have been revealed through prosecutions. Two large, high-profile postapartheid trials yielded only one conviction. By contrast, the TRC received amnesty applications from more than 7,000 people, an astonishing number given initial estimates that about 200 would apply.[60]

The extent to which the TRC succeeded in holding perpetrators accountable remains a matter of argument. Some express repugnance that a person like Benzien could receive amnesty and be allowed to return to work as a police officer. Others point out that the public and private opprobrium experienced by many perpetrators amounted to a powerful form of accountability and even punishment. Benzien, for instance, suffered a nervous breakdown, and other amnestied perpetrators were shunned by friends, spouses, and families.[61] In addition, many applicants, including those responsible for the death of Steve Biko, have been denied amnesty. Since amnesty hearings are scheduled to continue well into the year 2000, with a supplemental report from the

Amnesty Committee due after their conclusion, final judgments about the TRC's record on amnesty cannot be offered.

Although it was constrained from imposing full legal accountability on perpetrators, the TRC sought other ways to hold them accountable. The *Final Report* even criticized the TRC's own mandated procedures, arguing that "the fact that people are given their freedom without taking responsibility for some form of restitution remains a major problem with the amnesty process."[62] The commission's moral ambition in pursuing accountability for human rights violations is also evident in its hearings into the role of the professions and major institutions under apartheid and in its efforts to confront broader questions of accountability for apartheid's "ordinary violence" and injustice.[63]

As part of its effort to "establish as complete a picture as possible of the causes, nature and extent of the gross violations of human rights" and of the "antecedents, circumstances, factors and context of such violations," the TRC organized hearings on the roles of the media, the medical profession, business, political parties, the churches, and the legal system under apartheid.[64] These hearings attempted to establish the extent to which these institutions collaborated with both the extralegal and legal violence of apartheid. While the hearings were decidedly a mixed success—with the legal hearings, in particular, thwarted by the refusal of judges to appear before the commission—they nevertheless prompted a national debate about broader questions of what the TRC called "direct and indirect, individual and shared responsibility" for human rights violations.[65]

The TRC also encouraged ordinary South Africans to consider their accountability in upholding apartheid. For instance, it created a Register of Reconciliation, inviting people who were neither victims of gross human rights violations nor applicants for amnesty to send personal reflections.[66] People were encouraged to recognize "the little perpetrator in each one of us" and to acknowledge their "direct or indirect responsibility" for the "mundane but nonetheless traumatizing dimensions of apartheid life that had affected every single black South African."[67]

In the end, the TRC's ability to overcome the culture of impunity that has plagued so many countries in transition depends on the overall pattern of its own grants and denials of amnesty as well as on how the debate over whether to prosecute alleged perpetrators who were denied amnesty or who declined to apply for it is ultimately resolved. The TRC took a clear stand in this debate in 1999, when it presented to the National Director of Public Proseclutions a list of over one hundred names of persons it recommended for prosecution.[68] However, questions over the wisdom of post-TRC prosecutions continue to divide human rights advocates both inside and outside South Africa.[69]

Justice, whether retributive or restorative, demands full and fair accountability. In practice, such accountability is difficult to achieve in transitional situations like postapartheid South Africa. Nevertheless, despite the severe constraints of a politically imposed amnesty process, the TRC achieved a robust degree of accountability and reinforced the links between justice, accountability, and truth.

Reconciliation, Reparation, and Restorative Justice

Restorative justice includes a three-fold commitment (1) to affirm and restore the dignity of those whose human rights have been violated; (2) to hold perpetrators accountable, emphasizing the harm that they have done to individual human beings; and (3) to create social conditions in which human rights will be respected. As yet, all of these features are perfectly compatible with retributive justice. To be sure, trials rarely do justice to victims' voices in the way truth commissions have the capacity to do, and traditional conceptions of retributive justice place relatively little emphasis on restoring victims' dignity. Nevertheless, legal punishment of rights violators remains a powerful way of affirming the dignity of victims. Thus far, the difference between retributive and restorative justice appears to be one in emphasis and degree rather than in kind. It becomes much sharper when we consider a fourth aspect of restorative justice, its commitment to reconciliation. For while retributive justice demands that the guilty be punished, restorative justice, in Tutu's words, "is concerned not so much with punishment as with correcting imbalances, restoring broken relationships—with healing, harmony and reconciliation."[70] Thus, a key defining element of restorative justice is its privileging of reconciliation over retribution.

The roots of the TRC's commitment to reconciliation can be traced both to South African architects of the commission and to the history of truth commissions internationally. Themes of reconciliation and of a transcendent vision of justice were already evident in the Argentinian truth commission's report, which disavowed "vindictiveness and vengeance" and argued:

> All we are asking for is truth and justice, in the same way that the churches of different denominations have done, in the understanding that there can be no true reconciliation until the guilty repent and we have justice based on truth. If this does not happen, then the transcendent mission which the judicial power fulfills in all civilized countries will prove completely valueless.[71]

Significantly, this passage asks that the guilty "repent" rather than be punished. Punishment serves justice by imposing harm on those who have harmed others and by seeking to prevent or deter future harm. But repentance requires a moral transformation on the part of the perpetrator, and makes possible a transformed relationship between the perpetrator and others in the community.

The transformative aspirations of truth commissions have been articulated more fully by Zalaquett, a lawyer and Chilean truth commissioner. Zalaquett argues that the ultimate goal of truth commissions, and indeed of any attempt to deal systematically with past human rights abuses, is "to put back in place a moral order that has broken down or has been severely undermined, or to build up a just political order if none existed in historical memory."[72] The task of creating a just society is one of moral reconstruction. It entails efforts to repair the broken quality of human relationships throughout a society, including those between the former oppressor and the oppressed, and sets as its overriding goal the creation of conditions in which all citizens are accorded dignity and respect.

Moral reconstruction cannot be accomplished through judicial means alone; it is at once political, legal, cultural, moral, psychological, and spiritual. Many of those who participated in deliberations about a possible South African truth commission shared this expansive vision of the work a truth commission needed to do to contribute to such moral reconstruction. For instance, Justice Goldstone commented that he hoped the commission would merge two "streams," the "vital legal underpinning . . . without which such a commission could not succeed" and the "philosophical, religious and moral aspects without which the commission would be an empty legal vessel which would do a great deal of harm and achieve nothing."[73] And Justice Sachs noted with approval that the commission was being envisioned as an enterprise "that is primarily moral, cultural, psychological and human rather than one which is solely legal or instrumental."[74] He argued that the commission represented "what we have spent our whole lives fighting for. . . . It is the creation of a nation."[75]

Restorative justice does not *preclude* punishing the guilty. Indeed, punishment can be justified as a way of restoring moral order. Arendt characterized punishment and forgiveness as alternatives but not opposites, because both were "ways of attempting to put an end" to a cycle of vengeance, of action and reaction that "without interference could go on endlessly."[76] Nevertheless, proponents of restorative justice tend to privilege forgiveness or reconciliation over punishment, to emphasize the humanity of both victim and offender, and to seek personal and institutional transformation ahead of retribution.[77] As Zalaquett put it,

> There is a long-standing tradition, both religious and humanistic, that establishes a moral superiority of forgiveness and reconciliation over punishment. This is not a pious renunciation of justice. Rather, it means that if the reestablishment of a moral order may be similarly achieved through either path, the road of forgiveness and reconciliation should be preferred.[78]

The reason for this preference is that forgiveness is "more conducive to re-establishing the broken moral order because it presupposes the perpetrator's voluntary submission to the values that were violated. Such a solution is a better solution than to have to subdue the ... perpetrator by punishing him."[79] Zalaquett makes clear that forgiveness and reconciliation require that past injustices be uncovered and acknowledged, that perpetrators be held accountable, and that reparations be provided to those who were harmed. Thus justice as truth and accountability are essential elements of his vision of restorative justice. But he prefers the path of forgiveness and reconciliation because he believes it opens up moral possibilities for reconstructing a just society that are harder to achieve via the path of punishment.

During the South African transition, the priority of reconciliation over retribution was powerfully expressed through the exemplary magnanimity of President Nelson Mandela and through the ANC's willingness, unprecedented on the part of a victorious liberation movement, to acknowledge officially that there were victims and perpetrators on all sides. Indeed, the ANC appointed three commissions prior to the establishment of the TRC specifically to investigate allegations of human rights violations in ANC camps and detention centers. To be sure, subsequent relations between the ANC and the TRC were frequently stormy, and the ANC even mounted a court challenge to the *Final Report*. But it was a credit to both parties that these tensions never derailed the TRC process.

The postamble to the interim constitution set the tone for the TRC's work when it proclaimed "a need for understanding but not for vengeance, a need for reparation but not for retaliation, a need for *ubuntu* but not for victimization," invoking the African concept of *ubuntu*, or humaneness. As the commission's name indicated, its "overarching task" was not only to seek the truth but also to promote "national unity and reconciliation."[80] In his foreword to the TRC report, Tutu pointed to the necessity of reconciliation by invoking an image of South Africa "soaked in the blood of her children of all races and of all political persuasions."[81] The pervasive violence of apartheid and of the brutal struggles that it spawned had left South Africans bitterly divided by hatred and fear. The country's prospects for a more just and peaceful future depended on a willingness to reconcile and move forward. Reconciliation was not, however, a policy of "forgive and forget." As the TRC motto ("Truth ... the Road to Reconciliation") emphasized, its vision of reconciliation was premised on reconstructing as complete a picture as possible of the injustices of the past. Nor did reconciliation involve impunity or moral amnesty, for the commission sought to establish accountability for the crimes of the apartheid period. What was required was a renunciation of vengeance and violence in favor of a willingness to work together as South Africans.

As the commission's work proceeded, reconciliation and restorative justice became more and more explicitly its animating moral vision.[82] Its rhetoric and practice persistently championed reconciliation at the personal, interpersonal, community, and national levels in ways that were breathtakingly ambitious in a society emerging from years of brutal repression and communal violence.

While the amnesty process did not require perpetrators to apologize for their actions, commission hearings created an opportunity for repentance and forgiveness. The most extraordinary, and publicly celebrated, moments of those hearings occurred when individual victims and perpetrators reached out to one another and achieved some measure of reconciliation. Commissioners applauded those who repented and forgave, exhorted white South Africans to acknowledge their complicity in apartheid, and called on all South Africans to "forego bitterness, renounce resentment," "move past old hurt," and approach one another in a spirit of "generosity" and "magnanimity."[83] The TRC thus became an advocate and facilitator of reconciliation, challenging conventional models of judicial proceedings and commissions of inquiry.

Some people, both within and outside of the commission, were uneasy about this ambitious vision of reconciliation and argued that a more limited notion of peaceful coexistence was all that could and should be promoted. The commission's report acknowledged this concern and noted that it was also shared by some of those who gave testimony at the victims hearings.[84] Yet even those who most vigorously advocate criminal prosecutions in the aftermath of the TRC acknowledge that the participation of perpetrators within the TRC process had transformative significance for South Africa. In calling for the prosecution of rights violators who "snubbed" the TRC, human rights groups emphasized that perpetrators who came before the TRC and accepted "public shaming or accountability" thereby contributed to the creation of "a culture of human rights and respect for . . . institutions of justice."[85]

By privileging reconciliation over punishment, restorative justice seeks to transcend the traditional dichotomy between justice and mercy, incorporating dimensions of mercy into justice.[86] Yet the reconciliation sought through restorative justice does not come cheaply, either for perpetrators or for victims. Because neither remorse nor forgiveness can be demanded, or even expected, in South Africa's deeply divided and grossly unequal society, restorative justice requires a difficult balancing act between an insistence on accountability and a readiness to reconcile.[87] It also demands a recognition that reconciliation will be a lengthy and difficult project.

Three points emphasized in the *Final Report* serve as a useful corrective to any temptation to overstate the commission's success in achieving reconciliation. First, the report repeatedly stresses that reconciliation is a long-term goal and vision, and that the TRC can be no more than one part of a much larger process.[88] Second, the commission acknowledged that its task of promoting truth and reconciliation proved to be "riddled with tension." Disclosure of painful truths sometimes evoked anger and alienation rather than reconciliation, and the commission's efforts exacerbated some community conflicts even as they moderated others.[89] Finally, the report emphasizes that genuine reconciliation cannot occur without material reparations and redistribution of resources. The reparations proposed by the TRC, which include monetary payments to individuals as well as collective and symbolic reparations such as clinics to provide medical and counseling services, monuments, and the re-naming of parks and schools to honor the victims of repression, are inadequate in themselves.[90] Only a commitment to mitigate the pervasive inequities of apartheid and to provide social justice for black South Africans can sustain progress on the "road to reconciliation." A spirit of reconciliation, while neces-sary, is insufficient; "wide-ranging structural and institutional transformation" has to occur.[91] Ultimately, therefore, the TRC sought to honor its ambitious vision of reconciliation by emphasizing its own limitations and pointing be-yond itself to the many tasks still left to be done in the name of restorative justice.

Assessing the Ethics and Politics of Restorative Justice

Was the TRC justified in emphasizing restorative over retributive justice? The key questions are, first, is the idea of restorative justice truly an alternative conception or dimension of justice? Second, is it an appropriate goal for a public body like the TRC to pursue? And third, was the TRC's effort to promote restorative justice a good idea? Did it succeed in achieving its aims?

To pursue restorative justice in the face of a legacy of oppression and vio-lence means seeking to restore dignity and voice to victims of injustice, hold-ing perpetrators of injustice accountable for the harms they have inflicted on people, and adopting as an overriding goal the creation of conditions in which all are treated with respect.

In privileging reconciliation and reparation over punishment, restorative justice requires a leap of faith, a belief in the possibility of moral transforma-tion of both persons and institutions. As Arendt reminds us, punishment and forgiveness are both ways of seeking stable alternatives to vengeance and of constructing a legitimate moral order. Retributive justice and restorative jus-tice are therefore morally coherent and to some extent overlapping approaches.

While restorative justice is generally more morally ambitious, it cannot re-fute the moral logic of retributive justice. That is, it cannot deny the legitimacy of a demand for punishment and thus has no easy answers to provide to victims of injustice, who assert that their dignity will be restored only if they see their victimizers punished. All the proponents of restorative justice can do is offer these persons an alternative: an opportunity to tell their story, to confront their tormenters and hold them accountable, to receive reparations for the harms they have suffered, and to join in pursuing a project of transforming institu-tions and relationships so that they uphold human dignity. As tenuous as this last goal may seem compared with the satisfaction of seeing a criminal behind bars, it expresses the powerful and important idea that what is owed to victims of grave injustice is nothing less than a commitment to build a just society for them and their children. And while this goal also is affirmed within a conception of retributive justice, it has less priority than it does from within a restorative justice perspective.

Is restorative justice a legitimate goal for a public institution like the TRC? Ash argues that the goal of "reconciliation of all with all" is illiberal, because it deprives people of the essential liberal freedom of moral dissent. He champions more modest goals of "peaceful coexistence, cooperation, and tolerance" instead.[92] In its strongest form, Ash's charge that the TRC is illiberal has little force. South Africans could, and did, dissent from the work of the TRC and its vision of restorative justice, in the press and at the commission hearings themselves. Some sued the government (albeit unsuccessfully) for violating their constitutional right to seek judicial redress against perpetrators. The TRC's report makes no attempt to hide this dissension, and neither the commission nor the government interfered with anyone's freedom to dissent. There are, however, three related objections to restorative justice, implicit in Ash's concerns, which do need to be taken seriously.

The first is that the TRC unjustly put psychological pressure on people who refused to forgive. This is wrong, not because it interferes with their right to dissent or their freedom of speech (it does not), but rather because it fails to acknowledge the moral legitimacy of their anger. It is wrong to pressure victims of abuse to reconcile with their oppressors, and doubly wrong when this pressure comes from those of us who have not been victimized. An ethic of forgiveness, Hampton has argued, must acknowledge the legitimacy of what she calls "moral hatred," which is the righteous condemnation of wrongdoers and the refusal to reconcile with them, especially while they remain committed to a morally wicked cause.[93]

Hampton is right to remind us that we must treat survivors who express "moral hatred" with respect. At issue, though, is whether the very existence of the TRC, as an official institution that seeks to facilitate reconciliation, constitutes a denial of the legitimacy of such moral hatred. Clearly, the TRC was not neutral on the question of restorative versus retributive justice. In fact, its mandate explicitly required it to promote reconciliation. It did strive for impartiality and objectivity in other aspects of its work; for instance, in its efforts to uncover facts about human rights violations, or to question applicants for amnesty. But on the issue of reconciliation the TRC was entrusted with a role of publicly advocating and promoting reconciliation and the creation of a multiracial democratic society.

The TRC's mandate derived from an act of Parliament and was developed out of extensive public discussion. Thus the decision to privilege reconciliation over punishment had a great deal of democratic legitimacy, more than if the commission had been created through a presidential order, as was the case in other countries. The TRC also derived moral authority from the support of President Mandela, whose own commitment to reconciliation could not be reproached for a failure to understand the plight of victims of injustice. Thus the TRC was legitimately authorized to pursue reconciliation. At the same time, it was morally obligated to acknowledge the legitimacy of a demand for retributive justice. An analogy might be to a government's efforts to mobilize its citizens to fight a just war, while acknowledging the legitimacy of conscientious objection. Thus the existence of a public body that promotes reconciliation is not offensive, unless it fails to treat victims who dissent from that perspective with respect.

Hampton's insistence on the legitimacy of "moral hatred" reminds us of the moral complexity of issues of punishment and reconciliation. This complexity was beautifully captured by the South African Constitutional Court in its ruling rejecting the lawsuit brought by murdered activists' families against the TRC's amnesty policy. In explaining the court's decision Justice Ismail Mahomed described the TRC as

> a difficult, sensitive, perhaps even agonising, balancing act between the need for justice to victims of past abuse and the need for reconciliation and rapid transition to a new future; between encouragement to wrongdoers to help in the discovery of truth and the need for reparations for the victims of that truth; between a correction in the old and the creation of a new. It is an exercise of immense difficulty interacting in a vast network of political, emotional, ethical, and logistical considerations. . . . The results may well often be imperfect and . . . support the message of Kant that "out of the crooked timber of humanity no straight thing was ever made."[94]

Did this spirit of humility inform the attitudes of commissioners in their dealings with victims? Or did the commission pressure witnesses who came before it, and convey disapproval of those who refused to offer words of forgiveness? These are questions only eyewitnesses and participants can answer.[95] Perhaps, though, it is a recognition of the legitimacy of demands for retributive justice that prompts the TRC's defenders to offer dual justifications for their work, invoking political necessity in the face of victims' moral anger and affirming restorative justice before other audiences.

In its *Final Report*, the commission does acknowledge the legitimacy of anger on the part of victims. However, its language shows a troubling tendency to obscure the difference between a desire for revenge and a demand for retributive justice. Thus it states that "the desire for revenge is an understandable human response" and notes that commissioners were "exhilarated by the magnanimity of those who should by rights be consumed by bitterness and a lust for revenge."[96] A statement acknowledging that anger was not only understandable but morally justified would have been more appropriate.

A second objection to the TRC's pursuit of restorative justice is that its underlying ethic of forgiveness and reconciliation is distinctively Christian and therefore inappropriate to inject into the public sphere of a diverse and democratic society. This charge was made by a number of the TRC's critics and was explicitly acknowledged in the commission's report.[97] Concern about the religious basis of restorative justice can mean a number of different things. It may be a fear that a minority religious view is being imposed on a diverse society through the illegitimate use of coercive state power. Or it may be a concern that religious claims are being endorsed by a state-sponsored body like the TRC that are not shared by or even comprehensible to other citizens. Finally, the concern may be that as a religious ethic the idea of reconciliation is relevant to personal relationships but not to civic or political ones.

Without a doubt, the TRC did employ religious rhetoric, thanks above all to Tutu, its chairman. For instance, Tutu concluded the foreword to the commission's report by invoking an image of South Africans as "the rainbow people of God."[98] Theological arguments also featured prominently during public discussions prior to the establishment of the TRC. For instance, de Gruchy argued that it was important to maintain a theological dimension to public discourse about the South African transition because otherwise an understanding of the significance of the transition would be impoverished. "The theological goes beyond the moral," he argued. "The moral says there must be justice; the theological concurs, but adds that justice must lead to reconciliation and that reconciliation must acknowledge the need for justice. There is more at stake than morality."[99] In a similar vein, Chikane argued for the need to preserve the "deeper and more critical" meanings of the word "reconciliation," which emerge from theological and religious discourse.[100]

It is worth noting, however, that restorative justice has been championed by people from many different traditions, religions, and cultures, from the Japanese to the Maori of New Zealand, and that the TRC traced the notion of restorative justice both to "Judaeo-Christian tradition" and to "African traditional values" like *ubuntu*.[101] In its genesis, restorative justice is not narrowly and exclusively Christian. Moreover, it is not concerned with exclusively theological concepts like the salvation of the soul, but with themes like human dignity, respect, and mercy that qualify for what Rawls has termed "public reason," in the sense that they are comprehensible to free and equal citizens in a pluralistic democracy.[102]

Given the parliamentary mandate of the TRC, and the wide-ranging public debate that accompanied the commission's work, the first concern about the religious basis of restorative justice, that it is a coercive imposition of religion on a diverse society, seems misplaced. And as the themes of restorative justice are comprehensible outside of a context of Christian belief, and are indeed shared by many non-Christians, the second concern is also allayed.

Indeed, there is good reason to take restorative justice seriously even if it is derived from, and takes its full meaning within, a context of religious belief. In this case, theological arguments may offer deeper and more critical understandings of universal human experiences and of the requirements of a just society than are easily available within secular ethical discourse. In his analysis of the politics of forgiveness, Jones argues that a "theologically informed political imagination" that can envision such practices as "loving your enemies in the midst of brokenness" can provide a politically powerful antidote to hopelessness and despair.[103] Arguments from theology can inspire more imaginative thinking about ethics and politics, even among those who do not belong to a particular theological or religious tradition.

We have good reasons to take theological claims about forgiveness seriously as sources of moral arguments within diverse societies. There is, however, a third concern about the appropriateness of a theologically informed commitment to reconciliation, which Jones summarizes as follows: forgiveness is "personally helpful but socially and politically irrelevant," since "individual persons . . . forgive, but states seek justice." The relevance of forgiveness is limited, in this view, to the personal and private sphere and is irrelevant to the political and public.[104] This concern was explicitly mentioned in the commission's report as a "potentially dangerous confusion" between a personal, religious view of reconciliation and a political one.[105]

Jones counters by arguing that there is no reason to limit the scope of forgiveness to private life. He calls the effort to do so "a phony realism about what is possible and impossible" in public life.[106] In this he echoes a point Arendt made in *The Human Condition*. Arendt argued that while Jesus made what she called "the discovery of the role of forgiveness in the realm of human affairs" in a religious context and articulated it in religious language, "this is no reason to take it any less seriously in a strictly secular sense." The tendency not to theorize forgiveness in political terms, she added, reflected an unfortunate tendency for contemporary political thought to "exclude . . . a great variety of authentic political experiences."[107]

The belief that civic institutions are incapable of pursuing reconciliation reflects a failure of political imagination. A politics of vengeance is all too familiar from Rwanda, Serbia, and elsewhere. Why, then is reconciliation considered beyond the reach of political action? We have witnessed how President Mandela's moral magnanimity shaped the politics of the South African transition, and how the TRC created a public space in which some victims and perpetrators who came together in a spirit of *ubuntu* and forgiveness became empowered—and no doubt empowered others—to live and work together in a democratic South Africa.

What of Ash's admonition that it is better to pursue modest goals of peaceful coexistence than morally ambitious visions of reconciliation? This third and final challenge to the TRC is also the most important. Restorative justice is strongly oriented toward the future, toward institutional and moral transformation. The question is whether, in overreaching by attempting to pursue more morally ambitious goals, a truth commission might undermine its capacity to achieve the more modest goal of peaceful coexistence. If the TRC became "more a source of division than of unity," as some have charged, then perhaps proponents of restorative justice have good reason to trim their sails.[108]

Has the moral ambition of the TRC borne fruit? This question is difficult to assess, for two reasons. First, it is impossible to make a comparative judgment, since we cannot know what a more modest commission might have accomplished. And second, as the commission's report makes clear, the processes that it was trying to promote will take a long time. Nevertheless, it is possible to offer some tentative evaluations of the commission's work.

It is helpful to ask what it would have meant for the TRC to fail. Goldstone argues that the clearest sign of failure would have been for the commission to be ignored. Instead, it was astoundingly successful in engaging the South African public. Not only were TRC proceedings widely followed on television, radio, and in the newspapers, but the commission received over 22,000 submissions from victims and over 7,000 applications for amnesty.[109] As the fair and peaceful elections of 1999 amply demonstrate, the TRC did not cause South Africa's fragile democratic consensus to break down in the way some had predicted it would.

By the measure of public opinion polls, the commission had mixed success. So, for instance, a 1998 poll indicated that only half of all South Africans considered the commission fair and only 17 percent believed that it had promoted reconciliation.[110] This is hardly surprising, and the commission's report rightly suggests it would have been astonishing had the commission not generated criticism and opposition. Similarly, the commission's report noted that there was evidence that the information revealed by its work had increased people's anger about the past.[111] Is this evidence that the commission failed? I argue that it is foolish to expect overwhelming support for a commission like the TRC, and that it would have been utterly impossible to make dramatic strides toward racial reconciliation and harmony so quickly in the South African context.

A better measure of the commission's achievements might be whether it was able to avoid some moral pitfalls. For instance, had it lost credibility for being partisan, its effort to build national unity by acknowledging the victims and perpetrators on all sides of South Africa's social divisions would have had no chance of success. But while criticisms of bias were leveled against it in the lively public debate that surrounded the commission's work, overall it was remarkably even-handed, as its international prestige attests. If its work cheapened or trivialized the idea of reconciliation, the TRC would have been harmed. Instead, the commission's report placed very strong emphasis on the incompleteness of its efforts and on the long road to reconciliation. Still another moral pitfall, and one that occasioned considerable public debate surrounding the commission, was the fear that the commission's work, with its focus on gross human rights violations, would end up obscuring and in some sense excusing the ordinary violence and harms of apartheid as well as the pervasive economic injustice that continues to shape the lives of black South Africans today.

The TRC may have been a victim of its own success. In order to make its task of truth-gathering manageable, its mandate was limited to gross violations of human rights. This, however, had the danger of suggesting that these gross violations represented the sum total of apartheid's crimes against humanity. This dilemma is similar to that which has at times faced Amnesty International, which achieved great credibility and influence in the international human rights field, in part by virtue of its clear and limited mandate. However, over time the concerns raised by Amnesty International came to be viewed by some in the world community as the entire extent of human rights violations, and other human rights organizations criticized Amnesty for unintentionally obscuring the validity of their own areas of concern. In similar fashion, the TRC had to strive to ensure that it was viewed as part of the struggle for restorative justice rather than as the exclusive arena. It had to call attention to the plight of the ordinary victims of apartheid even as it justifiably limited its own investigations and reparations to those who had suffered gross violations of their rights, violations that were illegal even under the wicked legal system of apartheid. This was a point eloquently made by Sachs:

> The real reparation we want ties in with the constitution, the vote, with dignity, land, jobs, and education. If we get all those things and there is a sense of forward movement and the creation of a nation and a real, shared dignity in this country, then I think the pressure simply to punish, to penalise and have commissions of truth becomes much less. Although I strongly support a commission of truth, . . . the danger is that it should never be a substitute for . . . real dignity and the real overcoming of apartheid.[112]

In its report, the commission was very careful to emphasize the injustices of apartheid and to place its own work within a much broader context. However, advocates of restorative justice have to be vigilant in countering those who would say that, now that the commission has completed its work, the injustices of apartheid have been revealed and whites who were not among the perpetrators bear no special responsibility for rebuilding the lives of their black fellow citizens.

Is it possible to say that the commission succeeded in its ambitious goal of helping to build a bridge to a new, just, and unified South Africa? Its clearest achievement, surely, is that it has forever altered the official history of South Africa. This means not only that atrocities and lies have been revealed, but also

that scenes from commission hearings—the voices of victims and perpetrators—now form part of a new national narrative. These scenes reveal terrible
brutality but also extraordinary courage and magnanimity among South Africans of all races. In the words of Krog, an Afrikaner journalist and poet, the
commission "chiselled a way beyond racism and made space for all of our
voices."[113] Had the commission restricted itself to more modest goals—had its
concern been to report "just the facts" about apartheid-era atrocities—it could
not have created a context in which painful facts were embedded within a
national narrative that offered hope and a vision of a just future.

Finally, one of the most important ways in which the commission succeeded
in pursuing ambitious and nuanced moral goals was in the moral values it
exemplified in its own work. Its hearings dramatically portrayed a newly enfranchised black majority addressing its former oppressors with civility and
with a willingness to acknowledge the others' legitimate pain. In a moving
passage of the commission's report, Tutu noted,

> It was not the upholders of apartheid who introduced gross violations of human
> rights in this land. We would argue that what happened when 20,000 women and
> children died in the concentration camps during the Anglo-Boer War is a huge blot
> on our copy book. Indeed, if the key concepts of confession, forgiveness and reconcil-
> iation are central to the message of this report, it would be wonderful if one day some
> representative of the British/English community said to the Afrikaners, "We
> wronged you grievously. Forgive us." And it would be wonderful too if someone
> representing the Afrikaner community responded, "Yes, we forgive you—if you will
> perhaps let us tell our story, the story of our forebearers and the pain that has sat for
> so long in the pit of our stomachs, unacknowledged by you."[114]

In carrying on its work publicly, and in acknowledging dissenting arguments and moral complexity in its final report, the commission exemplified the
norms of a new democratic society. It also sought, in the report, to take seriously the criticisms and worries that had been raised against it, and to do
justice to the moral and political complexities of its own task. Tutu acknowledged that the commission itself had been a microcosm of South African society, "reflecting its alienation, suspicions, and lack of trust." He confessed that
the early meetings of the commission were "very difficult and filled with tension." But, he added, the commissioners had grown closer together despite
their hostile backgrounds, and had embraced their identity as "wounded
healers."[115]

The image of "wounded healers" aptly captures the power and ambiguity of
restorative justice. In the end, the TRC, by its willingness to pursue an ambitious and generous vision of restorative justice, "kept alive the idea of a common humanity" and set a tone for the South African transition that can be an
invaluable moral and political resource for future generations.[116]

Lessons for the Future

What lessons does the TRC and its commitment to restorative justice offer to the rest of the world? It is important to recognize that there are many aspects of the South African situation that would be hard to replicate in other societies. South Africa is fortunate in having leaders with the moral caliber and authority of Mandela and Tutu, as well as the presence of an established legal tradition that could provide a foundation for the work of the TRC even as it transcended the limits of conventional judicial institutions. With its black majority, South Africa is also an example of a society in which a group is "poised to reclaim or restart a nation under terms conducive to democracy, even as it continues to need the presence and resources of the white minority."[117] Of course, it still took courage and an enormous leap of faith for the architects of the TRC to commit to a vision of restorative justice. But in societies where hopes for a functioning democracy are far dimmer, where moral leadership is hard to find, or where warring communities are resistant to the thought of a shared future, the moral ambition of the TRC would quickly ring hollow.[118]

Although South Africa may be unique in some respects, the TRC offers many examples of creativity and innovation that can serve as models for future transitional regimes and truth commissions, especially its individual amnesty policy. The TRC experience should also encourage other societies to continue to modify the institutional repertoire of truth commissions. For instance, Goldstone urged the creation of a truth commission without amnesty provisions to complement the work of the War Crimes Tribunal in the former Yugoslavia, and this may well be a valuable model for other countries as well.[119] With the public nature of its hearings and the remarkable candor of its report, the TRC provides numerous lessons for future truth commissioners about the pitfalls and moral costs to avoid. It has also convincingly demonstrated that truth commissions are not just "second-best" responses to past injustice, but can provide a far fuller account of the crimes of the past and establish greater accountability among former elites than prosecutions are realistically able to do.[120] Truth commissions also offer a way of acknowledging and doing justice to situations in which there have been victims and perpetrators on multiple sides. This makes them an especially promising tool in the many situations—from Eastern and Central Europe to Ireland to the Middle East—where peaceful progress is continually hampered by competing narratives of oppression and the presence of harm and bitterness on all sides.

In the context of transitional justice, no mechanism to confront past abuses is beyond moral reproach. Not only are there difficult trade-offs between punishment and reconciliation, and between individual reparations and collective social development, but there are also new challenges and forms of injustice that easily are overlooked by transitional regimes. So, for instance, South Africa's disenfranchised township youth no longer are fighting against apartheid, but in many cases are succumbing to lives of crime; the challenge that they pose to South African democracy, as well as their ill-treatment by the police, raises an entirely new set of questions and challenges for proponents of restorative justice.[121]

There are lessons of a different order as well. The TRC was a stunning reminder of how much of the dynamism and creativity in the quest for justice is coming from people of color in general, and Africans in particular. Former U.S. ambassador to South Africa James Joseph has referred to the TRC as an African gift to the world at the start of what "may well be the African century," the century of "the potential of people of color."[122] South Africa's emergence as a model of ambitious and creative democratic politics challenges entrenched dismissive attitudes toward Africa across the world, and upsets the dire predictions made by many members of the American political establishment concerning the quality of black majority government in South Africa. A few years ago, for instance, Kristol criticized the widespread admiration for Tutu, writing "I am reasonably certain that if and when the ANC comes to power, he will be a vocal apologist for its tyranny and brutality."[123] Even as great a humanist as Havel, in his magnificent essay "The Power of the Powerless," referred dismissively in passing to Africa, arguing that the oppression of the posttotalitarian system in Eastern Europe was all the more shocking because its oppression was occurring not "in some ephemeral dictatorship run by a Ugandan bandit" but "in a system that embraces such a huge portion of civilized humankind and represents an integral, stable and respected part of the modern world."[124] Today, people around the world are looking to the South African TRC as a model.

The institutional repertoire of truth commissions may be helpful in developing innovative approaches to a variety of moral and political challenges within stable liberal democratic regimes such as the United States. As Levinson has argued, "every society is in transition," and all have their share of unacknowledged injustices with corrosive effects.[125] Coretta Scott King called for something like a truth commission—a body with the capacity to grant amnesty from prosecution in exchange for testimony—to reopen the case of her husband's assassination. Official acknowledgment has been absent or inadequate about many shameful aspects of American history that continue to haunt survivors and their descendents, from the Cherokee Trail of Tears to the staggering legacy of slavery and Jim Crow, and the continuing injuries of racism. Elements taken from truth commissions may be useful to efforts in these and other cases to establish official acknowledgment of wrongdoing and to do justice to the stories of survivors. The greatest value of the moral and political innovations of truth commissions may, however, be realizable on a far more local scale. For instance, the legacy of police brutality against African-Americans corrodes American democracy and contributes to cycles of violence, bitterness, and distrust. Many American communities have been trying to address this issue with civilian police oversight boards. In some cases, however, short-term public hearings incorporating some of the institutional aspects of a truth commission could accomplish more to air grievances, educate the public, offer reparations, and create opportunities to move forward in a spirit of reconciliation.

A commitment to restorative justice is, in Burton's words, "a thread looping around the world, putting in stitches here and there, building the fabric of this quest for justice."[126] The moral ambition of this effort in places like South Africa can inspire us to try to think more ambitiously about the possibilities for justice within our own circumstances.

Notes

1. I would like to thank the organizers and participants of two meetings on truth commissions, one at Harvard Law School in May 1996 organized by the World Peace Foundation, the Harvard Human Rights Program, and the Harvard Program in Ethics and the Professions, and one in Somerset West, South Africa, in May 1998 organized by the World Peace Foundation and attended by commissioners and staff of the Truth and Reconciliation Commission. It was a privilege to be present at both of these gatherings. I especially wish to thank Amy Gutmann, Martha Minow, Robert Rotberg, Graeme Simpson, Dennis Thompson, and Wilhelm Verwoerd for their responses to my paper. I also presented the paper to the University of Toronto Department of Political Science in December 1999, and I am grateful to all present for their stimulating questions and comments, most especially to David Dyzenhaus, Ran Hirschl, Cheryl Misak, Edward Morgan, Jennifer Nedelsky, Ayelet Shachar, and Melissa Williams. My thanks also to Lincoln Hancock for exceptional research assistance; to students in my class, Human Rights in Theory and Practice, for lively discussions about truth commissions; to my colleague Sheridan Johns for an excellent presentation to my class on the subject—and, as always, to Jeff Holzgrefe for his invaluable editorial and moral support.

2. TRC, *Final Report* (Cape Town, 1998), I, chap. 5, par. 3.

3. This point was stressed by Constitutional Court Justice Albie Sachs at an international meeting organized by the World Peace Foundation: Truth versus Justice: Can Truth Commissions Be Justified? (Somerset West, South Africa, 28–30 May 1998). (Hereafter called the *Truth v. Justice meeting*.)

4. *Azanian Peoples Organisation (AZAPO) and Others v. President of RSA and Others*, 1996 (8) BCLR 1015(CC), discussed in Martha Minow, *Between Vengeance and Forgiveness* (Boston, 1998), 56; David Dyzenhaus, *Judging the Judges, Judging Ourselves* (Oxford, 1998), 10.

5. Promotion of the National Unity and Reconciliation Act of 1995, section 1(1)(xix). This act established the TRC.

6. Chairperson Desmond M. Tutu, "Foreword," in *Final Report*, I, chap. 1, par. 21; ibid., chap. 5, par. 57.

7. These points were stressed by André du Toit and Albie Sachs at the *Truth v. Justice meeting*. See also *Final Report*, I, chap. 1, par. 22, 49.

8. Ibid., chap. 5, par. 61.

9. Ibid., par. 71, 73. See also I, chap. 1, par. 7, 24.

10. Ibid., I, chap. 5, par. 70, and chap. 1, par. 36.

11. Ibid., par. 54a.

12. Ibid., par. 82 and par. 82–85, 1. The quoted text comes from the postamble of the Interim Constitution of 1993. Constitution of the Republic of South Africa Act 1993, s. 232 (4).

13. For example, when Churchill Mxenge, brother of murdered antiapartheid lawyer Griffiths Mxenge and a strong critic of the TRC, confronted Tutu and accused him of failing to uphold justice, Tutu first appealed to political necessity, and later affirmed the importance of restorative justice. Minow, *Vengeance and Forgiveness*, 81, citing Tina Rosenberg, "A Reporter at Large: Recovering from Apartheid," *New Yorker*, 18 November 1996, 90.

14. For a useful comparative study, see Priscilla B. Hayner, "Fifteen Truth Commission—1974 to 1994: A Comparative Study," in Neil J. Kritz (ed.), *Transitional Justice* (Washington, D.C., 1995), I, 225–261.

15. Lawrence Weschler, "Afterword," *A Miracle, A Universe: Settling Accounts with Torturers* (New York, 1990).

16. For a vivid description of this process see the forewords and introductions to Alex Boraine, Janet Levy, and Ronel Scheffer (eds.), *Dealing with the Past: Truth and Reconciliation in South Africa* (Cape Town, 1994); and Alex Boraine and Janet Levy (eds.), *The Healing of a Nation?* (Cape Town, 1995).

17. *Final Report*, I, chap. 5, par. 89.

18. Ibid., chap. 1, par. 29.

19. This crucial difference between knowledge and acknowledgment, which is stressed in most of the literature on truth commissions, has been attributed to Thomas Nagel. See Weschler, *A Miracle, A Universe*, 4.

20. Ernesto Sabato, "Prologue," to *Nunca Mas* (New York, 1986), 5.

21. *Final Report*, I, chap. 5, par. 2.

22. Amos Elon, "The Politics of Memory," *New York Review of Books*, 7 October 1995, 5.

23. Breyten Breytenbach, "Appendix," in Boraine, Levy, and Scheffer, *Dealing with the Past*, 162.

24. *Final Report*, I, ch. 5, par. 34.

25. Ibid., 51.

26. Antjie Krog, "The South African Road," in Boraine and Levy, *Healing of a Nation?* 112–119.

27. *Final Report*, I, chap. 5, par. 51.

28. Ibid., chap. 1, par. 16.

29. See Henry J. Steiner (ed.), *Truth Commissions: A Comparative Assessment* (Cambridge, Mass., 1997), especially comments by José Zalaquett and Manouri Muttetuwegama.

30. Testimony of Lucas Baba Sikwepere, quoted in Minow, *Between Vengeance and Forgiveness*, 67.

31. For an insightful discussion of the capacity of truth commissions to heal individuals and collectivities, see ibid., 61–79.

32. This criticism is cited by TRC member Pumla Gobodo-Madikizela, in "On Reconciliation: Reflecting on the Truth Commission," December 1996, on the official website of the Truth and Reconciliation Commission at http://www.truth.org.za.

33. For arguments for and against the therapeutic value of truth commissions, see Steiner, *Truth Commissions*.

34. Margaret Popkin and Naomi Roht-Arriaza, "Truth as Justice: Investigatory Commissions in Latin America," in Kritz, *Transitional Justice*, I , 262.

35. *Final Report*, I, chap. 5, par. 22, 45.

36. Comments of Gobodo-Madikizela, quoted in Minow, *Between Vengeance and Forgiveness*, 60; emphasis added.

37. *Final Report*, I, chap. 5, par. 89.

38. Lindy Wilson, "Can Truth Bring Reconciliation?" a public lecture at the Center for Documentary Studies, Duke University, 21 April 1998.

39. "TRC and Families to Visit Murder Site of 12 Youths," Truth and Reconciliation Commssion press release, 2 April 1998; http://www.truth.org.za.

40. Nancy Fraser, "From Redistribution to Recognition? Dilemmas of Justice in a 'Post-Socialist' Age," *Justice Interruptus* (New York, 1997), 11–39.

41. *Final Report*, I, chap. 5, par. 51.

42. Minow, *Between Vengeance and Forgiveness*, 60.

43. *Final Report*, I, chap. 5, par. 66, 71–73; I, chap. 1, par. 7.

44. Minow, *Between Vengeance and Forgiveness*, 60; Comments of Albie Sachs at *Truth v. Justice* meeting, Somerset West, South Africa, 28–30 May 1998.

45. *Final Report*, I, chap. 5, par. 36.

46. Ibid., par. 97.

47. Ibid., par. 39–42.

48. Ibid., chap. 1, par. 56.

49. Ibid., chap. 5, par. 96.

50. Ibid., par. 57–61.

51. Ibid., chap. 1, par. 41, and chap. 4, par. 64–81.

52. Ibid., chap. 5, par. 89, 82.

53. Wilson, "Can Truth Bring Reconciliation?"

54. For an example of a finding denying amnesty on grounds of failure to make full disclosure, see "Amnesty Decision: Gerhardus Johannes Nieuwoudt (AM 3920/96)"; http://www.truth.org.za/amnesty/45.html.

55. Minow, *Between Vengeance and Forgiveness*, 59.

56. Aryeh Neier is among the most vocal advocates of an imperative to prosecute violators of human rights. For a good summary of his arguments and his ongoing debate with José Zalaquett, see Boraine, Levy, and Scheffer, *Dealing with the Past*, 2–15. See also Diane Orentlicher, "The Duty to Prosecute Human Rights Violations of a Prior Regime," *Yale Law Journal* C (1991): 2537–2615.

57. Antjie Krog, *Country of My Skull* (Johannesburg, 1998), 278.

58. Dyzenhaus, *Judging the Judges*, 10.

59. *Final Report*, I, chap. 5, par. 73; Minow, *Between Vengeance and Forgiveness*, 89–90.

60. Krog, *Country of My Skull*, 121.

61. Dumisa Ntsebeza, panel presentation, "Lessons for the World: The Uses of

Truth Commissions," Truth v. Justice meeting, Somerset West, South Africa, 28–30 May 1998. See also Dyzenhaus, *Judging the Judges*, 10; Krog, *Country of My Skull*, 76.

62. *Final Report*, I, chap. 5, par. 100.

63. The distinction between "ordinary" and "extraordinary" violence in apartheid is discussed in Dyzenhaus, *Judging the Judges*, 6–7.

64. Ibid., 25–26.

65. Dyzenhaus, *Judging the Judges*, is an excellent analysis of the hearing on the legal profession. See also *Final Report*, I, chap. 5, par. 110.

66. Minow, *Between Vengeance and Forgiveness*, 75.

67. *Final Report*, I, chap. 5, par. 107–108.

68. "TRC Urges that Scores Be Charged," *The Star*, 25 May 1999 (available at http://archive.iol.co.za/Archives/1999/9905/25/freedom3day4.htm).

69. See, for instance, the *Call for Prosecutions* issued by a coalition on nongovernmental organizations in November 1998, as well as the heated public debate between Barney Pityana, chair of the South African Human Rights Commission, and human rights organizations and other commentators in July 1999. The text of the *Call for Prosecutions* and further information about these debates may be found at the website of the Centre for the Study of Violence and Reconciliation, http://www.wits.ac.za/csvr/press.htm. See also Piers Pigon, "No Reconciliation Possible without Investigation," *Daily Mail and Guardian*, 4 August 1999 (available at http://www.mg.co.za/mg/news/99aug1/4augboipatong.html.), and "South Africa: No Impunity for Perpetrators of Human Rights Abuses," Amnesty International Press Release, 30 July 1999 (http://www.amnesty.org.uk/news/press/releases/30_july_1999-2.shtml).

70. *Final Report*, chap. 1, par. 36.

71. "Prologue," to *Nunca Mas*, 5.

72. José Zalaquett in Boraine and Levy, *The Healing of a Nation?* 45.

73. Comments by Richard Goldstone, in ibid., 120.

74. Comments by Albie Sachs, in ibid., 103.

75. Comments by Albie Sachs, in Boraine, Levy, and Scheffer, *Dealing with the Past*, 146.

76. Hannah Arendt, *The Human Condition* (Chicago, 1958), 241.

77. Minow, *Between Vengeance and Forgiveness*, 92; Dyzenhaus, *Judging the Judges*, 6.

78. Zalaquett, in Boraine and Levy, *The Healing of Nation?* 46.

79. Ibid., 46–47.

80. *Final Report*, I, chap. 5, par. 10.

81. Ibid., chap. 1, par. 1.

82. See, for instance, the press club speech by Archbishop Tutu on 21 October 1997 and Howard Zehr, "South Africa's Truth and Reconciliation Commission Is an Unprecedented Experiment of Breathtaking Stakes," *Mennonite Central Committee News Service*, 7 March 1997; both on http://www. truth.org.za.

83. *Final Report*, I, chap. 5, par. 50–52, and chap. 1, par. 67, 71.

84. Ibid., chap. 5, par. 20.

85. "NGO Response to Dr. Barney Pityana's Call to Stop Apartheid Prosecutions," 30 July 1999 (http://www.wits.ac.za/csvr/press.htm).

86. My thanks to Robert Keohane for a discussion that helped me formulate this point. The dichotomy between justice and mercy is one of the archetypal "right versus

right" dilemmas discussed in Rushworth Kidder, *How Good People Make Tough Choices* (New York, 1995), 109–126. See also 13–29.

87. Jonathan Allen offers an acute analysis of this balancing act as a principled compromise between justice and reconciliation in "Balancing Justice and Social Unity: Political Theory and the Idea of a Truth and Reconciliation Commission," *University of Toronto Law Journal* XLIX (1999): 320, 325, 338.

88. Ibid., par. 1, 6, 27, and chap. 4, par. 42–59.

89. Ibid., par. 3, 14, 18.

90. Minow, *Between Vengeance and Forgiveness*, 92–93. Reparations continue to be an unfinished item on the South African government's agenda. See "One Year Since the TRC Report: Where Are the Reparations? (http://www.wits.ac.za/csvr/press.htm).

91. *Final Report*, I, chap. 5, par. 26, 52.

92. Timothy Garton Ash, "True Confessions," *New York Review of Books*, 17 July 1997.

93. Jeffrie Murphy and Jean Hampton, *Forgiveness and Mercy* (New York, 1988), 80, 149.

94. *AZAPO and Others v. President of RSA and Others*, cited in Dyzenhaus, *Judging the Judges*, 24–25, note 49.

95. One commissioner did suggest that she thought that the TRC unintentionally pressured victims to express a willingness to reconcile. *Truth v. Justice meeting* (Somerset West, South Africa), 28–30 May 1998.

96. *Final Report*, I, chap. 1, par. 68, 71; I, chap. 5, par. 54a.

97. South African political commentator Steven Friedman is one such critic. See Dyzenhaus, *Judging the Judges*, 11, note 19; *Final Report*, I, chap. 5, par. 19–20.

98. Ibid., chap. 1, par. 93.

99. Comments of John de Gruchy, in Boraine, Levy, and Scheffer, *Dealing with the Past*, 141–143.

100. Comments of Frank Chikane, in Boraine and Levy, *Healing of a Nation?* 100–101.

101. Minow, *Between Vengeance and Forgiveness*, 91–92, and *Final Report*, I, chap. 5, par. 84–85.

102. John Rawls, *Political Liberalism* (New York, 1993), 213–254.

103. L. Gregory Jones, *Embodying Forgiveness: A Theological Analysis* (Grand Rapids, Mich., 1995), 267.

104. Ibid., 239, 267.

105. *Final Report*, I, chap. 5, par. 19.

106. Jones, *Embodying Forgiveness*, 267.

107. Arendt, *Human Condition*, 238–239.

108. Steven Friedman, cited in Dyzenhaus, *Judging the Judges*, 11.

109. Richard Goldstone, "Foreword," in Minow, *Between Vengeance and Forgiveness*, xii.

110. "Only Half of People Feel TRC is Fair and Unbiased: Survey," *Reports from the South African Press Association*, 5 March 1998; http://www.truth.org.za/sapa389.

111. *Final Report*, I, chap. 1, par. 68.

112. Albie Sachs, in Boraine, Levy, and Scheffer, *Dealing with the Past*, 24.

113. Krog, *Country of My Skull*, 278.

114. *Final Report*, I, chap. 1, par. 65.

115. Ibid., par. 89.

116. Krog, *Country of My Skull*, 278.

117. Minow, *Between Vengeance and Forgiveness*, 63.

118. My thanks to Peter Russell for helping me to sharpen this point.

119. Goldstone, "Foreword," in Minow, *Between Vengeance and Forgiveness*, x.

120. This point is also argued by Minow, *Between Vengeance and Forgiveness*, 88.

121. This point was stressed by Graeme Simpson at the *Truth v. Justice meeting*.

122. James A. Joseph, "Reconstruction and Reconciliation in South Africa: The Role of Race," Mitchell Hart Memorial Lecture, Duke University, 23 April 1998.

123. Irving Kristol, "Human Rights: The Hidden Agenda," in Walter Laquer and Barry Rubin (eds), *The Human Rights Reader* (New York, 1989), 393.

124. Vaclav Havel, "The Power of the Powerless," in *Open Letters: Selected Writings 1965–1990* (New York, 1991), 189.

125. Comment by Sanford Levinson, *Truth v. Justice meeting*.

126. Comments of Mary Burton, in Boraine, Levy, and Scheffer, *Dealing with the Past*, 120.

V

Truth Commissions, Transitional Justice, and Civil Society

DAVID A. CROCKER[1]

MANY societies seeking a just transition from authoritarian regimes or civil wars to democracy have employed official truth commissions to investigate systematic violations of internationally recognized human rights.[2] These abuses—which include extrajudicial killing, genocide, disappearance, rape, torture, and severe ill-treatment—may have been committed by a previous government against its own citizens (or those of other countries), by its opponents, or by combatants in a civil or international armed conflict. Recently utilized in South Africa and Guatemala, such investigative bodies have been employed in twenty countries and are being considered for such nations as Bosnia, Cambodia, Indonesia, and Kenya. Truth commissions can contribute to achieving many important goals in societies during the transition to democracy. But they must be supplemented by other measures and institutions, such as trials and judicial punishment.

This chapter suggests eight goals for reckoning with past wrongs and, in the light of that framework, assesses the strengths and weaknesses of official investigatory bodies. This chapter further shows that a nation's civil society—especially when it practices public deliberation or deliberative democracy—is indispensable to the success of truth commissions and, more generally, to reckoning with past wrongs. This chapter contends that *international* civil society may play a useful role in advancing the goals of national truth commissions and transitional justice.

The Challenge of Transitional Justice

The question of "transitional justice," is, How should a fledgling democracy reckon with severe human rights abuses that earlier authoritarian regimes, their opponents, or combatants in an internal armed conflict have committed? Sometimes the term "transitional justice" is used to refer exclusively to penal justice and even to retributive interpretations of trials and punishment. Here it is employed more broadly to cover such concerns as compensatory, distributive, and restorative justice. The challenge for new democracy is to respond appropriately to past evils without undermining the new democracy or jeopardizing prospects for future development.[3]

Societies in transition to democracy have employed many means in reckoning with human rights abuses that a prior regime or its opponents have committed. In addition to domestic trials, amnesties, and investigatory bodies, these measures embrace but are not limited to international war crime tribunals; social shaming and banning of perpetrators from public office ("lustration"); public access to police records; public apology or memorials to victims; reburial or reparation of victims; literary and historical writing; and general or individual impunity (the ignoring or accepting of past violations).

To decide among these tools, as well as to fashion, combine, prioritize, and sequence them, a society ideally should consider what it is trying to accomplish as well as its institutional and political capabilities and limitations.

Strengths and Limitations of Truth Commissions

To evaluate truth commissions as one kind of measure, as well as any particular truth commission, requires standards of assessment. What standards should be used and where should they come from? Earlier, I clarified and defended a plurality of goals that have emerged from worldwide moral deliberation on transitional justice.[4] In this chapter I employ those goals as criteria to evaluate truth commissions and to indicate where such bodies need to be supplemented or corrected by other tools.

Truth

To meet the challenges of transitional justice, a society should investigate, establish, and publicly disseminate the truth about past atrocities. What Boraine calls "forensic truth" or "hard facts" is information about whose moral and legal rights were violated, by whom, how, when, where, and why.[5] Given the moral significance of individual accountability, the identity of individual perpetrators should be brought to light. There is also what has been called "emotional truth"—knowledge concerning the psychological and physical impact on victims and their loved ones of rights abuses and the threat of such abuses. Just as important is less individualized and more general truth, such as reasonable interpretations of state actions and those of the state's opponents, as well as causal explanations of the chain of command, institutional structures, and economic problems that resulted in rights violations.

Knowledge about the past is important in itself. One way to make this point is to say that victims and their descendants have a moral right to know the truth about human rights abuses. Moreover, without having reasonably complete truth, none of the other goals in transitional justice, to be discussed presently, are likely to be realized. Appropriate sanctions are impossible without having a reasonable certainty about the identity of perpetrators and the nature of their involvement. Public acknowledgment must refer to specific occurrences, while reparations presuppose the accurate identification of victims and the kinds of harms they suffered. If reconciliation in any of its several senses is to take place, there must be some agreement about what happened and why. Former enemies are unlikely to be reconciled if what count as lies for one side are verities for the other.

It is not enough to discern the truth; the truth also should be accessible to the public, especially if it is to contribute to other urgent goals such as public deliberation. Some commissions—in order to safeguard witnesses if not the commissioners themselves—have conducted their hearings and deliberations in private. South Africa's Truth and Reconciliation Commission (TRC), however, was particularly successful in making its activities public and transparent: it gathered testimony in various locations throughout the nation; its proceedings were accessible to many South Africans. The media in many of the country's languages extensively covered these activities, especially the hearings on individual human rights violations and amnesty applications.

Although some truth commissions have "named names," their chief virtue is discerning overall patterns, institutional context, and, to a lesser extent, the general causes and consequences of atrocities. In taking testimony directly from the principals, sometimes not long after the violations being investigated, truth commissions play an indispensable role in getting a reasonably full picture of what happened and the ongoing consequences in people's lives. Unlike judicial efforts to determine legal guilt or innocence, official investigatory bodies also can profile examples of moral heroism in the face of barbarism. Proponents of a truth commission for Bosnia, for example, emphasize the role of such a body in profiling Serbs that aided their Muslim neighbors (and vice versa): "Against the backdrop of all the evil that has taken place, the tale of the good is a part of the history to be revealed."[6]

Truth commissions, however, also have limitations with respect to revealing truth. In order to get their work done in one, two, or three years, truth commissions must select only a few hundred or thousand among a multitude of cases to investigate in depth. Furthermore, truth commissions usually lack the power of subpoena and cross-examination, cannot search and seize evidence, and cannot independently corroborate witness testimony. Finally, official investigatory bodies, even when they avail themselves of historical studies, are often disadvantaged in comparison to historians. Professional historians are likely to have more time and skill in gaining access to documents, sifting through facts, unmasking distortions and lies, assessing explanatory hypotheses, and ascribing responsibility.[7]

One of the most difficult issues for a truth commission with respect to the goal of truth concerns the issue of whether there is "one truth or many." Although most "forensic truths" will be relatively noncontroversial, citizens and even members of the truth commission itself may differ over comprehensive patterns of interpretation—especially over who or what is most responsible for atrocities. How should these differences be handled in a truth commission's final report? One way, which Chile's National Commission on Truth and Reconciliation practiced, is to employ general (and sometimes vague or ambiguous) terms in order to achieve unanimity at the expense of precision. A second method is to strive for agreement but also to identify issues that remain matters of contention. In a third approach, which would resemble the practice of the U.S. Supreme Court, unresolved disagreements would be formulated as majority and minority judgments in the same or even in separate reports. Although these last two approaches to disagreement would be respectful of societal pluralism and stimulate further public deliberation, they would have the serious disadvantage of undermining the authoritative or collective character of an official truth commission's final report.

Public Platform for Victims

In any society meeting the challenge of transitional justice, victims or their families should be provided with a platform to tell their stories and have their testimony publicly acknowledged. When victims are able to give their accounts and when they receive sympathy for their suffering, they are respected as persons and are treated with dignity rather than—as before—treated with contempt. The public character of the platform is essential, for secrecy about human rights abuses, enforced through violence and intimidation, was one of the conditions that made possible extensive campaigns of terror.

Depending on the number of testimonies taken and the context in which this is done, truth commissions often do well in attaining the present goal. South Africa's TRC took more than 22,000 testimonies from victims or their families, made its sessions public, encouraged extensive media coverage, including extensive radio coverage and nightly and weekly TV recaps of highlights, and maintained a web site.

Accountability and Punishment

Full transitional justice requires that there be fair ascriptions to individuals and groups on all sides of responsibility for past abuses and the meting out of appropriate sanctions to perpetrators. Sanctions may range from legal imprisonment, fines, compensatory payments, and prohibitions on holding public office to public shaming.

Many questions about responsibility and punishment remain to be answered. How, for example, should accountability be assigned? How should we understand the degrees and kinds of responsibility with respect to the planning, execution, provision of material support for, and concealment of, atrocities? How should "sins of commission" be compared morally to "sins of omission"? To what extent are groups—particular police or military units, political parties, or professional groups such as medical associations—responsible for rights violations? Without a suitably nuanced view of accountability or responsibility, a society falls into the morally objectionable options of, on the one hand, whitewash and amnesia, or, on the other hand, the demonization of all members of an opposing group.[8]

Similar questions may be asked with respect to sanctions, whether criminal, civil, or nonlegal. What types of sanctions are appropriate for what violations, and on what bases? Should a theory of criminal punishment include a retributive element, and, if so, how should it be understood? Can it be distinguished from revenge, and how should it be institutionalized in relation to the other functions of punishment, such as protection, deterrence, rehabilitation, restoration, and moral education?[9]

At first glance it might appear that truth commissions make no contribution to accountability and sanctions.[10] Indeed, it might be argued that truth commissions are designed precisely as a morally second-best alternative when attributions of guilt and punishment are ruled out because of fears that legal prosecution would further divide a society in need of healing or imperil a new and incomplete democracy by provoking an authoritarian or military takeover. Societies have often chosen truth commissions when amnesty or other laws enacted by the prior authoritarian government to protect itself and its functionaries have (largely) blocked the legal route. Alternatively, some have defended the claim that truth commissions—and especially the TRC—are not morally second best but have advanced beyond penal and retributive justice to something called "restorative justice," defined as rehabilitating perpetrators and victims and (re)establishing relationships based on equal concern and respect.[11]

This judgment—that truth commissions are incompatible with accountability and sanctions—is mistaken, however, for three reasons. First, when a truth commission names the names of (likely) individual and group perpetrators, that commission is contributing to the ending of a culture of impunity in which rights violators get away scot-free. In Argentina those named by that country's truth commission report, *Nunca Mas* (Never Again), have been subject to social stigmatization. Fellow citizens shun former military leaders and publicly express opprobrium by cursing and spitting. In South Africa, perpetrators from many walks of life—including physicians and scientists as well as police and military personnel—have to face their own families who, prior to truth commission hearings, may have had no idea that their spouses or parents were complicitous in horrendous acts. Sanctions need not be legal in order to impose a burden and control rights abuses. Moreover, with respect to holding perpetrators accountable, truth commissions often have an advantage over trials and legal punishment because—in comparison with the latter—the former usually can be launched and concluded more rapidly, cost less, and address the (alleged) crimes of more people.[12]

Second, as the cases of Argentina, Chile, Guatemala, and South Africa make clear, the work of truth commissions can be compatible with trials and punishments. In South Africa, the trial, verdict, sentencing, and imprisonment of police death squad commander and assassin Eugene de Kock took place just as the TRC began its proceedings.[13] In Argentina and Chile, criminal proceedings followed the publication of each country's truth commission report. Hence, those countries that choose to make a just transition by means of official investigatory bodies need not forgo the additional tool of trial and punishment. Even more, in South Africa trials and truth commissions worked together, for the threat of trial and punishment was a powerful incentive for those suspected of atrocities to apply for amnesty and tell the truth. As an editorial in a South African newspaper observed in 1996, "The perhaps unintended combination of judicial stick and truth commission carrot has emerged as a potent force in flushing out former operatives who have adopted a wait-and-see attitude."[14]

Third, truth commissions often contribute directly to judicial processes by which perpetrators are held legally accountable and sanctioned by fines, imprisonment, compensation to victims, community service, or prohibitions on public careers. The Argentine and Chilean truth commissions recommended to their respective judicial authorities that certain individuals be prosecuted, and the commissions provided evidence for judicial processes. Furthermore, the Amnesty Committee of the South African TRC has rejected amnesty requests from and urged prosecution of persons whom the committee judged to have lied, violated rights with *non*political intent, or caused harm disproportionate to the agent's political aim. And those who never applied for amnesty are subject to legal prosecutions and civil suits.

Guatemala's Commission on Historical Clarification (CEH), initially criticized because its mandate prohibited it from having any judicial intent or effect, surprised most observers when it took advantage of provisions in Guatemala's National Reconciliation Law (NRL) that held that amnesty could not be granted for genocide, torture, and forced disappearance. Finding that state agents committed acts of genocide against the Mayan people in four locations from 1981 to 1983, the CEH was not content merely to recommend further investigation (by government and civil society) of those who had disappeared, the exhumation of bodies, and reparations; it also urged trials and punishment for those who had committed acts in violation of the international Genocide Convention and not exempted by the NRL amnesty agreement.[15]

Finally, insofar as a truth commission makes recommendations to remedy the earlier causes of rights violations, it is in a good position to help transform the judicial system and, thereby, increase the possibility of fair judicial processes and punishment in the future.[16] Hence, a truth commission's success in getting at the truth is compatible with and often contributes to the assignment of responsibility and imposition of legal and other sanctions.

While truth commissions have particular merit in promptly addressing the causes and consequences of systematic abuses and the related contours of collective responsibility, trials are more suitable for holding accountable individual political leaders and the architects of atrocities. The either/or of "truth v. justice" must be avoided; both truth commissions and trials have distinctive and mutually supplementary roles in achieving the multiple goals of transitional justice.

Rule of Law

Transitional societies should comply with the rule of law, which, as Luban argues, is one of the abiding legacies of Nuremberg.[17] The rule of law includes respect for due process, in the sense of procedural fairness, publicity, and impartiality. Like cases must be treated alike, *ex post facto* laws eschewed, and private revenge prohibited. Rule of law is especially important in a new and fragile democracy bent on distinguishing itself from prior authoritarianism, institutionalized bias, or the "rule of the gun."

The most obvious application of the ideal of the rule of law is in and through a nation's courts and its other judicial bodies. Yet truth commissions also may presuppose, illustrate, and strengthen the rule of law. Truth commissions depend on the rule of law to the extent that enabling legislation or constitutional provisions—such as the postamble to South Africa's Interim Constitution—authorize them. Even a duly constituted investigatory body, however, might be biased against one side in an earlier conflict or dictatorship. And in encouraging victims to give testimony, truth commissions usually fail to give those accused or their attorneys the right to confront and cross-examine their accusers.

On the other hand, truth commissions can implement the rule of law to the extent that they are public, investigate all sides in a conflict, recognize ways in which perpetrators can also be victims, and adopt measures to reduce bias.[18] One such measure is to appoint commission members who represent various and opposing political factions and who have reputations for fairness. Those who write the final report must be vigilant against (but not overcompensate for) unintentional racial, class, or ideological bias.[19] Further, a truth commission respects due process when persons who come before it are treated even-handedly and impartially.

Compensation to Victims

Compensation, restitution, or reparation, in the form of income, medical services, or educational and other opportunities, should be paid to individuals and groups whose rights have been violated. Depending on the scope of its mandate and the duration of its existence, a truth commission may contribute to compensation. In Chile, a body institutionally separate from the nation's Truth and Reconciliation Commission compensated the survivors of human rights abuses and the families of victims. This division of labor came about because while the truth commission had to complete its work in a relatively short time, a longer period was needed for deciding on criteria for compensation and for identifying and treating harms, some of which emerged years after being inflicted. The TRC's Reparation and Rehabilitation Committee (R & R) is following the Chilean model. Although it implemented some "Urgent Interim Relief" toward the end of the TRC's life, the R & R's power was almost exclusively that of making recommendations to Parliament, which—if accepted—would be implemented by a permanent body, the President's Fund.

Though truth commissions should not be artificially limited to achieving only one aim, such as truth, they should not be expected to do too many things, either. Following Chile's example, South Africa is implementing a nuanced "reparation and rehabilitation policy" that defends reparation on both moral ("restoration of dignity") and legal grounds and provides several types of both individual and communal reparation. Individuals are compensated both through monetary packages, which take into account severity of harm, number of dependents, and access to services, and through services such as reburials and the providing of headstones.

One criticism of the TRC, however, is that it has failed to provide needed support for those who testified before it. After having testified before the TRC, some victims reported that afterwards they suffered flashbacks, sleeplessness, and depression. Not having received the material or other compensation that they believed they had been promised or due, these victims insist they have become expendable means to the end of the TRC's work.[20] It would seem, however, that these criticisms should be directed less at the TRC and more at the South African government or international donors for failing, up to this point at least, to aid and compensate victims in a timely and adequate manner.

Institutional Reform and Long-term Development

To reckon fully with past wrongs, an emerging democracy must identify the causes of past abuses and take steps to reform the law and basic institutions to reduce the possibility that such violations will be repeated. Basic institutions include the judiciary, the police, the military, the land tenure system, the tax system, and the structure of economic opportunities. One temptation in post-conflict or postauthoritarian societies is to permit euphoria (which comes with the cessation of hostilities and the launching of a new democracy) to preempt the hard work needed to remove the fundamental causes of injustice and guard against their repetition.

In both Guatemala and South Africa, for example, the fundamental causes of repression and human rights abuses were racism and economic inequality. A transitional democratic society must try to remove such deep causes of human rights abuses, and it must do so in a way that will deepen its democracy and promote just economic development in the future. The long-term development goal should be that all persons, regardless of race, ethnicity, or inherited wealth, should have opportunities to participate politically and live minimally decent lives.

What, if anything, can a truth commission contribute to such an ambitious goal for transitional justice? First, insofar as its search for truth involves a grasp of the complex causes of past human rights abuses, a truth commission is well positioned to make recommendations for institutional reform. Because of its public prominence, an official investigative body is likely to provoke public debate and encourage national and international efforts to ensure *nunca mas* (never again). Second, a truth commission's actions can be directly linked to reduction of poverty and racism. For example, confessed perpetrators may make reparations to their victims by contributing time or money to society-wide poverty alleviation. Third, the TRC's sectoral approach to institutional reform and long-term development was an important breakthrough in transitional justice; the TRC held hearings in such sectors or institutions as health, business, the judiciary, the media, prisons, and faith communities, and it encouraged each to engage in a process of institutional self-examination and reform. Fourth, as Gutmann and Thompson argue, a truth commission can contribute to long-term democratization and equal respect for all citizens by practicing in its "process" what it preaches in its "product."[21]

Reconciliation

A newly democratic society in transition from a conflictual or repressive past should aim to reconcile former enemies and reintegrate them into society.

There are at least three meanings of reconciliation, ranging from "thinner" to "thicker" conceptions. On the most minimal account, reconciliation is nothing more than "simple coexistence," which means no more than that former enemies comply with the law instead of killing each other.[22] Although this modus vivendi is better than violent conflict, transitional societies should aim for more: while they may continue to disagree and even be adversaries, former enemies must not only live together nonviolently but respect each other as fellow citizens as well. Osiel calls this kind of reconciliation "liberal social solidarity," while Gutmann and Thompson term it "democratic reciprocity."[23] Among other things, this means that people hear each other out, enter into a give-and-take with each other about matters of public policy, build on areas of common concern, and forge compromises with which all can live.

A third and more robust conception of reconciliation has sometimes been attributed to the truth commissions of Chile and South Africa—reconciliation as a shared comprehensive vision, mutual healing and restoration, or mutual forgiveness.[24] (Both of these commissions include the word "reconciliation" in their names.) These "thicker" conceptions of reconciliation are much more difficult to defend than the "thinner" notions. There are both practical and moral reasons to favor the first and second over the third notion of reconciliation.

First, the reduction of enmity between former adversaries—let alone the seeking and granting of forgiveness—is less likely to happen through the short-term efforts of a truth commission than when former enemies work together on common projects over a period of years, for example, in the same political, economic, and civil organizations. Transitional justice takes time (often many generations) and goes through several phases; there are limits to what a truth commission can do in one or two years. The best hope often lies in a new generation that has not experienced past conflicts. Second, truth commissions can permit and even encourage both confessions of guilt and mutual forgiveness, especially in a society in which a religious imperative to forgiveness is widely accepted. Yet to prescribe these acts legally would be to compromise the moral autonomy of both victims and perpetrators as well as promote feigned professions of guilt and contrition. More generally, it is morally objectionable as well as impractical for a truth commission or any other governmental body to force people to agree about the past, forgive the sins committed against them, or love one another.

Public Deliberation

Given the second sense of reconciliation just discussed, a newly democratic and transitional society should aim to include public debate and deliberation in its goals and strategies for transitional justice. It is unlikely that in any given society there will be full agreement about the aims and means for dealing with past abuses. Moreover, all good things do not always go together, for sometimes achieving one end will be at the expense of (fully) achieving another. Legal sanctions against human rights violators can imperil a fragile democracy in which the military body responsible for the earlier abuses still wields social and political power. In order to protect witnesses or secure testimony from alleged perpetrators, a truth commission's interrogation of witnesses or alleged perpetrators sometimes may have to take place behind closed doors. Testimony by victims and confessions by perpetrators, at least in the short run, may worsen relations among former enemies.[25] Truth commissions, let alone trials, use resources that could be employed in poverty alleviation.

What can be aspired to is that disagreements about ends, trade-offs, and means will be reduced as much as possible through public deliberation that permits a fair hearing for all and promotes morally acceptable compromises.[26] The goal of public deliberation is relevant for an investigative body's composition. One reason the Argentine, Chilean, and South African truth commissions gained legitimacy was that their respective members represented a wide spectrum of political positions.

The public deliberation norm should also guide a commission's mode of operation. Whenever possible, a truth commission's activities should go on in public rather than behind closed doors and be accessible—linguistically and in other ways—to every citizen. Various truth commissions have realized this goal of public deliberation and decision making in different ways and to different degrees. The TRC, for example, sought to practice deliberative give-and-take internally; publicly vetted its procedures, problems, and preliminary conclusions; stimulated enormous public debate and comment; and was willing to respond to public criticism. Its eventual report stimulated at least as much public discussion as did reports in Argentina and Chile.

Domestic Civil Society and Transitional Justice

A nation's civil society is often well suited to decide on and give priority to the ends of transitional justice as well as to design, implement, monitor, and improve various means to achieve them. In particular, without a vigorous domestic civil society, backed up on occasion by certain types of international civil society, new democracies are unlikely to establish effective truth commissions.

Three models emphasize different aspects of civil society relevant to transitional justice. An antigovernmental model, in which civil society includes all and only nonstate bodies, emphasizes that civil society can be a bulwark of freedom against an oppressive state.[27] An associational model conceives of civil society as a third sector between the (coercive) state and the market.[28] It recognizes that private associations can generate civically valuable by-products (social trust, civic capacities) as well as civically noxious attitudes (clannishness, private revenge, and resistance to democratic change).[29] A third—the public sphere model—focuses on how civil society groups, especially those that are internally democratic and egalitarian, nourish the kind of informed public opinion that makes viable democratic government possible.[30]

These three models alert us to the positive and negative roles civil society organizations can play in transitional justice and to the challenge that social pluralism poses to a just and democratic transition. Although usually appointed by a government's executive or legislature, official truth commissions can be viewed either as parts of civil society or as hybrid entities that mediate between the state and civil society. Truth commissions are normally composed of prestigious and respected citizens not holding public office, and often these citizens represent important nongovernmental organizations (NGOs) a spectrum of political outlooks, commercial groups, and religious institutions.

Formation of Truth Commissions

Civil society groups have played crucial roles in establishing truth commissions. Conversely, in countries with a weak civil society, such as the Democratic Republic of the Congo, neither official nor unofficial truth commissions have been established.

Groups in South Africa's civil society—through conferences and public hearings—helped forge the idea of a truth commission. A presidentially appointed committee, many of whose members represented civil society, received nominations for TRC commissioners and recommended twenty-five to President Mandela, who appointed seventeen.[31]

In the difficult and drawn-out peace negotiations between the Guatemalan government and the Guatemalan National Revolutionary Union (URNG), its guerrilla movement, civil society played a strong role. The UN-brokered Framework Agreement signed in January 1994 "recognized the role played [in earlier negotiations] . . . by the various sectors of organized civil society and gave them a legitimate place within the negotiating process in an Assembly of Civil Society (ACS)."[32] Chaired by the highly respected cleric Monsignor Rodolfo Quezada Toruño, the ASC formulated and transmitted, to the negotiating parties and the UN mediator, the ASC's consensus positions on the various topics being negotiated, including the formation of a truth commission, an agreement on indigenous rights, and an agreement on socioeconomic goals.[33] Moreover, the Guatemalan Alliance against Impunity was crucial in influencing a National Reconciliation Law that, in advance of similar Latin American laws, excluded crimes such as genocide from its amnesty provisions.[34]

Investigation

Civil society groups can be enormously helpful and even indispensable in obtaining the truth about the past. During the seventeen-year Pinochet dictatorship, two religious organizations—the ecumenical Comité de Cooperación Para la Paz en Chile (1974–1975) and the Roman Catholic Church's Vicaría de la Solidaridad (1976–1992)—collected thousands of judicial transcripts concerning disappearances. Such records were invaluable for the investigations of the presidentially appointed National Commission for Truth and Reconciliation, which had to complete its work in only eighteen months. In Uruguay, a nongovernmental report on governmental abuses committed between 1972 and 1985 was more comprehensive, accurate, and widely distributed than the little-known and anemic government report.[35]

In Guatemala, prior to the peace accords and the founding of the CEH, the Guatemala City archdiocese's human rights office launched the unofficial Project for the Recovery of Historical Memory (REMHI).[36] Increasingly dissatisfied with CEH's limited mandate, meager resources, and initially slow progress, REMHI engaged in what Popkin has called "the most comprehensive civil society effort to investigate a country's past atrocities."[37] Local citizens, whom REMHI trained as "ambassadors of reconciliation," recorded more than 6,000 testimonies, which communal leaders, elected by their villages, gave in their native (Indian) language. On 24 April 1998, REMHI presented and summarized its report, "Guatemala: Nunca Mas." A press release and public lecture charged that the army and so-called civilian self-defense patrols were responsible for by far the greatest percentage of the 150,000 deaths and 50,000 disappearances in the war. Because Guatemalan illiteracy is so high, diffusion of the report employed theater, radio, videos, public workshops, and ceremonies. REMHI, like other Guatemalan human rights groups and the CEH itself, has directly contributed to truth about the past and manifested respect for victims by providing them with a platform in their own language.

The challenges and dangers involved in uncovering truth about past evil were tragically underscored two days after the presentation of REMHI report: Auxiliary Bishop Gerardi Conedera, the director of the archdiocese's human rights office and coordinator of the report, was brutally bludgeoned to death in his home in Guatemala City.

Adversarial Public Action

Some organizations in a nation's civil society devote themselves to monitoring and evaluating the government's (and wider society's) actual steps toward achieving peace, democratization, and transitional justice. One role of civil society is to constitute an independent agency to assess whether promises are kept and rhetoric becomes reality. Such monitoring and assessment is part of what Sen calls "public action" designed to advance the public good.[38] Possible actions include public petitions, protests and marches (sometimes with pictures of the "disappeared"), strikes, press conferences, public forums, public burials of the remains of those recently exhumed, and complaints addressed to public officials.

Each of these activities helps undermine what Leo Valladares, the Honduran human rights ombudsman, calls the "culture of impunity."[39] In such a culture, government officials, the police and military, and ordinary citizens routinely break the law without fear of punishment, for there is a shared understanding that each person will be silent about the other's abuses as long as the favor is returned. Many NGOs in transitional societies are seeking to replace such a culture of impunity with a "culture of responsibility" or a "culture of rights" in which citizens are responsible for respecting human and legal rights and publicly protesting their violation. As the 1996 report of Honduras's National Commission of Human Rights puts it:

> Civil Society ought to join forces so that judicial reform is a reality, and this requires the strengthening of a democratic and human rights culture in order to halt the epidemic of corruption and be able to save our democratic institutions. As the Commissioner has expressed it: "Democracy is shown not only at the ballot box but also by accusations, by opposition to official abuse and corruption, and by the system of justice. Hence, democracy ought to fight so that injustice is the exception and justice the rule."[40]

In Guatemala, NGOs have not always agreed in their assessment of governmental efforts to implement transitional justice. Some civic groups pressured the official Guatemalan truth commission to violate their legal mandate and name perpetrators. Others urged that "naming names" risks a blanket amnesty (as occurred in El Salvador) or a return of military repression (as was threatened in Argentina), subjects those incorrectly named to undeserved abuse, and distracts attention from the general pattern (and remedy) of human rights abuses.

Even an investigative body as internationally applauded as the South African TRC is not immune to criticism from South African civil society. The Centre for the Study of Violence and Reconciliation and the Khulumani Victim Support Group, for example, criticized the TRC for overemphasizing the ideal of reconciliation-as-forgiveness and failing to give sufficient attention to other goals of transitional justice such as accountability, punitive justice, and compensatory support for victims. They argued that the TRC should collaborate more fully with NGOs—for example, by contributing to NGO efforts to organize survivor support groups.[41]

The Public Sphere and Public Deliberation

The civil public sphere clearly functions in countries undergoing transitional justice insofar as the mass media and civic groups promote a society-wide debate that evaluates and seeks to improve the ends and means of transitional justice. For instance, South African newspapers and television reported daily on the TRC's work. They also provided opportunities for a spectrum of critics and defenders of the commission. Likewise, since the mid-1980s, many Guatemalan newspapers have enlarged and invigorated the public sphere by reporting and commenting on the peace process, and by opening their pages to a variety of public opinion.

The foregoing examples illustrate what a country's civil society, however conceived, and its civil public sphere, in particular, may do to advance the aims of transitional justice. Civil society, however, is not without some limitations, and there are some dangers in putting undue (and the wrong kind of) emphasis on it.

Groups in civil society, especially following prolonged authoritarianism, may be very weak and disunited, and thereby limited in their potential impact on transitional justice. Just as civil society groups can differ considerably within a given national society, so too the civil societies of particular nations or regions exhibit much variety. Civic groups and national civil societies as a whole differ with respect to longevity, vitality, formality, resources and sustainability, orientation (inward or outward), internal structure (democratic vs. hierarchical), and external relations (grassroots, regionally/nationally federated, or internationally linked). Depending on their type and social context, many groups and networks are limited in what they can contribute to transitional justice, for often they have scant resources, outreach, and staying power. They may rise and fall before they are able to make much of a difference in the lives of their members or the larger society. Their knowledge of similar groups or networks also may be limited so that they are unable to learn from each other. Their scope may be entirely at the "grass roots," preventing them from influencing national institutions. Even worse, some civil society groups may be bent on vengeance or amnesia, two morally defective goals for societies in transition.[42]

Given these limitations, societies undergoing transitional justice should beware of certain dangers in thinking about the potential roles of civil society in meeting the challenges of transitional justice and democratic development. First, civil society must not be idealized as the new source of salvation, permanently assuming roles that other actors, including national and local governments, should play. As innovator, facilitator, critic, educator, and (temporary) substitute, there is much that civil society can contribute to transitional justice. Yet, here as in other areas, the state must be "brought back in," for government has an indispensable role with respect to some forms of prosecution, punishment, investigation, compensation, and commemoration.[43] And just as civil society can supplement and correct the state, a democratizing state may fortify and help unify a weak, timid, and fragmented civil society. This outcome is especially likely when a truth commission conducts activities that are public and decentralized; seeks civil society's continual evaluation of its work; cooperates with parallel or supplemental civil society initiatives (such as medical attention to victims); and, upon the conclusion of its work, recommends ways in which civil society might continue the struggle to right past wrongs.

A second peril is the opposite of the first, namely, that civil society will narrow its scope, functioning as an assortment of exclusively inward-oriented voluntary associations, and thereby fail to assess, debate with, and influence other institutions that affect transitional justice. A self-help group of human rights victims or perpetrators, while important in a free and pluralistic society, is not all that civil society can be in relation to the challenge of transitional justice. Especially when trials and truth commissions finish their work, citizens and civil society groups have important outward-oriented responsibilities and opportunities. In a radio interview at the end of the TRC's work, Tutu observed that the commission by itself could not bring about reconciliation and that "each south African is going to have to say, 'What is the contribution I am going to be making to what will be a national project?'"[44]

A third peril is that civil society will lose its independence and become a mere rubber stamp—rather than a monitor and critic—of the government. Cases in point are Uruguay's truth commission and Yugoslavia's television since 1989, which is either controlled by government or practices self-censorship.[45]

International Civil Society and Transitional Justice

It is in relation to the strengths, limitations, and dangers of domestic civil societies that we can best understand the ways in which international civil society (ICS) may contribute to a nation's transitional justice. The paradigm cases of international civil society are voluntary associations such as the Roman Catholic Church, Doctors Without Borders, the International Campaign to Ban Land Mines, the International Red Cross, and the International Soccer Federation. These nonstate organizations and movements are composed of members whose concerns extend to other nations and to international structures and issues.[46] My emphasis here is on globally oriented networks of individuals and voluntary *institutions* and not merely on world moral *opinion*, let alone the public opinion of powerful Western nations.

There are two types of ICSs and a closely related type of international institution: civil society groups from one country that aid the efforts of civil society groups in another country, undergoing transitional justice; international not-for-profit organizations and movements; and transnational institutions such as the Organization of American States and institutions within the United Nations system. The first type, an internationally oriented domestic civil society, is illustrated by the Washington Office on Latin America (WOLA), a group that emphasizes police, judicial, and economic reform. Composed largely of U.S. citizens, this U.S. advocacy group supplies moral and financial support and U.S. speaking opportunities to representatives of NGOs from countries such as Guatemala. Moreover, WOLA transmits lessons that domestic societies learn about transitional justice in one country to similar societies confronting the challenge of transitional justice in other countries.

The second type of ICS is illustrated by a profusion of heterogeneous international NGOs; movements usually composed of members from many nations. The term "globalization" is often used to denote global capital flows and transnational economic institutions. There is, however, another kind of globalization—movements and NGOs that investigate, debate, and help implement policies of many kinds in particular nations and regions. This network is constantly changing and often lacks formal institutional definition; sometimes an ICS is little more than a "virtual community" committed to a common cause and linked by e-mail, fax, and list servers. Still the contributions to transitional justice by groups of this second type should not be underestimated.

Consider the global scholarly community concerned with issues of righting past wrongs in the context of democratic transitions.[47] It generates conferences, often subsidized by private philanthropic organizations such as the Aspen Institute, the Soros Open Society Foundation, the Friedrich Ebert Foundation (Germany), the Instituto de Defensa Legal (Peru), and the World Peace Foundation (U.S.A.). These organizations bring together scholars, policymakers, and policy analysts to understand, compare, and improve approaches to transitional justice. A notable achievement in this area is the United States Institute of Peace's important three-volume study, *Transitional Justice: How Emerging Democracies Reckon with Former Regimes*.[48] Emphasizing both national and international assessments of the ends and means of transitional justice, these three volumes include general essays, twenty-one country studies, and a collection of laws, rulings, and reports that have emerged in the last fifty years. Thanks to these and similar studies, when a country embarks on a path to transitional justice, its government and domestic societies will have intellectual resources and practical models on which to draw. They will not, as ex-President Raúl Alfonsín said about Argentina's efforts in the 1980s, have to invent "their approach from nothing."[49] With international philanthropic support, those designing and implementing South

Africa's TRC learned valuable lessons from the Chilean and other truth commissions.

Also noteworthy are the international investigatory/advocacy groups that conduct inquiries into and denounce human rights violations, monitor human rights compliance, and make recommendations as to how past abuses should be treated and future violations prevented. By providing international attention and support, these international groups can also lend legitimacy to and strengthen the hand of domestic civil groups and democratically elected governments in pursuing the goals of transitional justice.[50] Funded by a variety of private and national sources, these ICSs include Amnesty International and Human Rights Watch, the NGO Coalition for an International Criminal Court, and the Joint Evaluation of Emergency Assistance to Rwanda, the last being an international team that investigated the international response to the Rwandan massacre. Through their published documents and press conferences, these sorts of groups can inform domestic and world opinion and contribute to public deliberation about what should be done.

Closely related to international civil society, but a product of intergovernmental cooperation, are those organizations of the United Nations system that play a variety of roles in national transitional justice. Although the UN has been beset with financial problems (partially due to the failure of the United States to pay its dues), waste, and inefficiencies, it has contributed to transitional justice in several significant ways. In 1991, responding to a request by the Salvadoran government and the political opposition, the UN established, funded, and provided personnel to the Salvadoran truth commission. Later in Guatemala, the United Nations Human Rights Observer Mission in Guatemala (MINUGUA) facilitated the peace negotiations, including agreements between the contending parties with respect to truth commissions and other measures of transitional justice.[51] The UN also established and funds two ad hoc international criminal courts, the International Criminal Tribunal for the Former Yugoslavia and the International Criminal Tribunal for Rwanda.

In sum, the UN has tried to influence and assist states in transition, encouraging them to forgo morally untenable approaches, such as private revenge, victor's justice, and impunity, and to adopt mechanisms likely to realize the multiple legitimate aims of transitional justice. In these efforts the UN has a mixed record, ranging from an important—if not unqualified—success in El Salvador, to slow progress in Guatemala, Bosnia, and Rwanda, and to a controversial and still unimplemented agreement for an International Criminal Court.[52]

There are distinctive merits, effects, and limitations of ICS with respect to transitional justice when assessed in relation to the roles of national governments and domestic civil societies. ICS (and international regimes) can promote transitional justice by providing to domestic civic groups and democratically elected governments with material resources, lessons learned by other new democracies, international legitimacy, and moral support. Such assistance may be indispensable as domestic civil groups and fledgling democracies face the forces of revenge or appeals to social amnesia. ICS can also adopt an adversarial role and criticize or temporarily substitute for domestic civic groups and national governments when there is good reason to believe that they have succumbed to unjust or antidemocratic forces.

Whether in a collaborative or adversarial relation to domestic civil societies and national governments, ICS plays an important role in hammering out, justifying, and diffusing universally applicable norms relevant to transitional justice.[53] Conversely, these norms, which include universally accepted human rights, are one impetus for what Mandela calls "the creation of an international community predicated on human dignity and justice."[54] International civil society is deepened and widened by appeal to a fundamental normative perspective that includes, in addition to universal human rights, the fundamental goals to which a new democracy should aspire in designing and evaluating its attempts to deal with a terrible past.[55]

Yet, ICS can also weaken or prevent a society from effectively meeting the challenges of transitional justice. As Nino rightly insists, too much or the wrong kind of international response to a country's past rights violations can do more harm than good.[56]

International involvement and intemperate appeals to universal human rights can give some factions—for instance, the military—the pretext to reject, as an "outside job," international recommendations or pressure. In El Salvador, the fact that three non-Salvadorans composed the Salvadoran Truth commission was used as public justification for the government to declare—the week after the commission's report was released—a general amnesty for all those individuals charged with violating rights during the civil war. Furthermore, international aid for domestic transitional justice can backfire. Instead of nurturing robust domestic civil societies, public deliberation, and responsive governments, international support for a nation's democratic transition in fact may insulate governmental efforts from domestic criticism. In turn this insulation may cause reduction of public deliberation, the narrowing of the national consensus, and, thereby, the loss of popular support for the government's efforts. For example, instead of trying to address the objections of some of its most trenchant critics, South Africa's TRC sometimes took refuge in the consolation offered by its many international supporters.

Finally, due to ignorance of a transitional society's particular challenges, ICS's timing may be wrong.[57] It may act too soon, before conditions are ripe and to the detriment of future domestic efforts. Both within and without Bosnia, there has been a vigorous debate about whether that divided country is ready for the truth and reconciliation commission being promoted by such groups as the United States Institute of Peace.[58] Or ICS may stay involved too long, and hence prevent a nation's government and civil society from developing its own capabilities. Finally ICS may act too late, after a window of opportunity has been closed.

To mitigate such risks, groups in ICS must interact with both governmental and civil groups in the transitional society. Moreover, ICS must become knowledgeable about the particular society in transition as well as recognize that each new democracy has the *primary* and *ongoing* responsibility for achieving the multiple goals of transitional justice. Not only does this responsibility imply the government's duty—often by means of an official truth commission—to investigate, sanction, and compensate rights violations, but it also supports rights of citizens to public deliberation, adversarial public action, and democratic rule. Like domestic civil society, however, a well-informed international civil society is often helpful, sometimes indispensable, but never sufficient if a new democracy is to utilize truth commissions and other means to meet the complex challenges of transitional justice.[59]

Notes

1. I am grateful to Patrick Ball, David P. Crocker, Edna D. Crocker, Cristián Parker, Margaret Popkin, Robert I. Rotberg, Michael Slote, Dennis Thompson, Wilhelm Verwoerd, and my colleagues at the Institute for Philosophy and Public Policy and the School of Public Affairs—especially Sue Dwyer, Peter Engelke, Arthur Evenchik, Robert K. Fullinwider, and William A. Galston—for helpful comments on earlier versions of this essay. I also owe thanks to the World Peace Foundation South African Truth and Reconciliation Commission Conference, Somerset West, South Africa, 28–30 May 1998.

2. The best multidisciplinary collections on transitional justice are Neil J. Kritz (ed.), *Transitional Justice: How Emerging Democracies Reckon with Former Regimes*: I, *General Considerations*; II, *Country Studies*; III, *Laws, Rulings, and Reports* (Washington, D.C., 1995); Naomi Roht-Arriaza, (ed.), *Impunity and Human Rights in International Law and Practice* (New York, 1995); and A. James McAdams (ed.), *Transitional Justice and the Rule of Law in New Democracies* (London, 1997). See also Martha Minow, *Between Vengeance and Forgiveness: Facing History after Genocide and Mass Violence* (Boston, 1998).

3. Nations other than new democracies also have occasion to decide what they "should do about a difficult past." Timothy Garton Ash, "The Truth About Dictatorship," *New York Review of Books* XLV (19 February 1998), 35. For these broader issues, see Ash's essay and David A. Crocker, "Reckoning with Past Wrongs: A Normative Framework," *Ethics & International Affairs* XIII (1999): 43–64.

4. David A. Crocker, "Transitional Justice and International Civil Society: Toward a Normative Framework," *Constellations* V (1998): 492–517; "Civil Society and Transitional Justice," in Robert Fullinwider (ed.), *Civil Society, Democracy, and Civic Renewal* (Lanham, Md., 1999), 375–401; and Crocker, "Reckoning with Past Wrongs."

5. Alex Boraine, "The Societal and Conflictual Conditions That Are Necessary or Conducive to Truth Commissions," World Peace Foundation and South African Truth and Reconciliation Commission Conference, Somerset West, South Africa, 28–30 May 1998.

6. Neil J. Kritz, "Is a Truth Commission Appropriate in the Former Yugoslavia?" International Conference on War Crimes Trials, Belgrade, Yugoslavia, 7–8 November 1998, 3. See also Neil J. Kritz and William A. Stuebner, "A Truth and Reconciliation Commission for Bosnia and Herzegovina: Why, How, and When?" Victimology Symposium, Sarajevo, Bosnia, 9–11 May 1998.

7. In Santos Juliá et al., *Las Victimas de la Guerra Civil* (Madrid, 1999), Spanish historians and social scientists give an insightful accounting of the horrendous wrongs committed by all sides in the Spanish Civil War of 1936–1939 and by the Franco dictatorship that lasted until 1976. The volume, shattering the conventional image of Spain as a successful example of "forgive and forget," also details the way in which Franco as well as his democratic successors dealt—in very different ways—with forty years of atrocities and repression.

8. See Carlos Nino, *Radical Evil on Trial* (New Haven, 1996), ix–x.

9. See, for example, Jean Hampton, "The Retributive Idea," in Jeffrie G. Murphy and Jean Hampton, *Forgiveness and Mercy* (New York, 1988), 111–161; Naomi Roht-Arriaza, "Punishment, Redress, and Pardon: Theoretical and Psychological Approaches," in Roht-Arriaza (ed.), *Impunity and Human Rights*, 13–23; Michael Moore, *Placing Blame: A General Theory of the Criminal Law* (Oxford, 1997); and Aryeh Neier, *War Crimes: Brutality, Genocide, Terror and the Struggle for Justice* (New York, 1998), 80–85.

10. See Jennifer Llewellyn, "Justice for South Africa: Restorative Justice and the South African Truth and Reconciliation Commission," in Christine Koggel (ed.), *Moral Issues in Global Perspective* (Peterborough, Ont., 1999), 96–107.

11. Ibid., 103–105.

12. See Kritz and Stuebner, "A Truth and Reconciliation Commission."

13. See Eugene de Kock (as told to Jeremy Gordin), *A Long Night's Damage: Working for the Apartheid State* (Saxonwold, South Africa, 1998).

14. "Between the Carrot and Stick," *Sunday Independent*, 14 July 1996, 10.

15. Margaret Popkin and Nehal Bhuta, "Latin American Amnesties in Comparative Perspective," *Ethics & International Affairs* XIII (1999): 117–118. See also "Guatemala Memory of Silence, Report of the Commission on Historical Clarification, Conclusion and Recommendation" (25 February 1999), 58.

16. Priscilla Hayner, "Official Truth-Seeking: A Tool for Peacemaking?" Preliminary Discussion Paper, Committee on International Conflict Resolution, National Research Council, 16 June 1998, 15–16; Hayner, "In Pursuit of Justice and Reconciliation: Contributions of Truth Telling," in Cynthia J. Arnson (ed.), *Comparative Peace Processes in Latin America* (Washington, D.C., 1999), 366–368.

17. David Luban, "The Legacies of Nuremberg," in *Legal Modernism* (Ann Arbor, 1994), 344–346. Cf. Lon L. Fuller, *The Morality of Law* (New Haven, 1977; rev. ed.), 33–39.

18. See Sanford Levinson, "Trials, Commissions, and Investigating Committees: The Elusive Search for Norms of Due Process" (in this volume).

19. Wilhelm Verwoerd, "The Commission Report: History? Advocacy? A Verdict,"

World Peace Foundation and South African Truth and Reconciliation Commission Conference, Somerset West, South Africa, 28–30 May 1998.

20. Susanne Daley, "In Apartheid Injury, Agony Is Relived but Not Put to Rest," *New York Times*, 17 July 1997, A1, A10.

21. Amy Gutmann and Dennis Thompson, "The Moral Foundations of Truth Commissions" (in this volume).

22. Charles Villa-Vicencio, "A Different Kind of Justice: The South African Truth and Reconciliation Commission," *Contemporary Justice Review* I (1999): 407–428.

23. Mark Osiel argues that what he calls "liberal" or "discursive social solidarity" can be promoted "through public deliberation over continuing *dis*agreement, a process by which rules constrain conflict within nonlethal bounds and often inspire increasing mutual respect among adversaries." Osiel, *Mass Atrocity, Collective Memory, and the Law* (New Brunswick, N.J., 1997), 17n. 22; see also 47–51, 204n. 136, 263–165). See also Gutmann and Thompson, "Moral Foundations."

24. See Donald Shriver, *An Ethic for Enemies: Forgiveness in Politics* (New York, 1995).

25. See Gilbert A. Lewthwaite, "In South Africa, Much Truth Yields Little Reconciliation," *Baltimore Sun*, 30 July 1998, 12.

26. See James Bohman, *Public Deliberation: Pluralism, Complexity, and Democracy* (Cambridge, Mass., 1996). See also Amy Gutmann and Dennis Thompson, *Democracy and Disagreement* (Cambridge, Mass., 1996).

27. See Michael Ignatieff, "On Civil Society: Why Eastern Europe's Revolutions Could Succeed," *Foreign Affairs* LXXIV (1995): 128–136. Ignatieff captures the spirit of the antigovernment model when he observes that for the East European intellectuals in the 1970s and 1980s, civil society was "the kind of place where you do not change the street signs every time you change the regime" (128).

28. See Benjamin R. Barber, "Clansmen, Consumers and Citizens: Three Takes on Civil Society," in Fullinwider (ed.), *Civil Society*, 9–29.

29. See Robert D. Putnam, "Bowling Alone: America's Declining Social Capital," *Journal of Democracy* VI (1995): 65–78.

30. See Jean L. Cohen, "American Civil Society Talk," in Fullinwider (ed.), *Civil Society*, 55–85.

31. Alex Boraine, "Truth and Reconciliation in South Africa: The Third Way" (in this volume).

32. Teresa Whitfield, "The Role of the United Nations in El Salvador and Guatemala: A Preliminary Comparison," in Arnson (ed.), *Comparative Peace Processes*, 270–271.

33. Ibid., 271.

34. Popkin and Bhuta, "Latin American Amnesties," 116.

35. Priscilla Hayner, "Fifteen Truth Commissions—1974–1993: A Comparative Study," *Human Rights Quarterly* XVI (1994): 232–233.

36. REMHI, *Guatemala: Never Again! The Official Report of the Human Rights Office, Archdiocese of Guatemala* (Maryknoll, N.Y. 1999). (An abridged English translation of *Guatemala: Nunca M'as, Informe projecto interdiócesano de recuperación* de la memoria *histórica* [Guatemala City, 1998]).

37. Margaret Popkin, personal communication, 22 April 1998.

38. Amartya Sen and Jean Drèze, *Hunger and Public Action* (Oxford, 1989), 275–279.

39. Leo Valladares, interview, 8 August 1997.

40. *El Difícil tránsito hacia la democracia: 1nforme sobre derechos humanos, 1996* (Honduras, 1996), 20–21. The translation is my own.

41. Graeme Simpson, "Lessons for the World: The Uses of Truth Commissions," presentation to the World Peace Foundation and South African Truth and Reconciliation Commission Meeting, Somerset West, South Africa, 28–30 May 1998.

42. See Crocker, "Transitional Justice and International Civil Society," 495–496.

43. See Michael Schudson, "The 'Public Sphere' and Its Problems: Bringing the State (Back) In," *Notre Dame Journal of Law, Ethics and Public Policy* VIII (1994): 529–546. For a compelling argument that (un)civil society also contains groups that imperil democratization and justice, see Xiaorong Li, "Democracy and Uncivil Society: A Critique of Civil Society Determinism," in Fullinwider (ed.), *Civil Society*, 403–418.

44. Cited in Lewthwaite, "In South Africa," 12A.

45. Hayner, "Fifteen Truth Commissions," 616–617. Warren Zimmerman, "The Last Ambassador: A Memoir of the Collapse of Yugoslavia," *Foreign Affairs* LXX (1995): 12.

46. Cf. Gordon A. Christenson, "World Civil Society and the International Rule of Law," *Human Rights Quarterly* XIX (1997): 731.

47. See Naomi Roht-Arriaza, "Conclusion: Combating Impunity," in Roht-Arriaza (ed.), *Impunity and Human Rights*, 295.

48. See note 2.

49. Kritz, "The Dilemmas of Transitional Justice," in Kritz (ed.), *Transitional Justice*, I, xxi.

50. Roht-Arriaza, "Conclusion: Combating Impunity," 302.

51. Whitfield, "The Role of the United Nations."

52. See Steven R. Ratner and Jason S. Abrams, *Accountability for Human Rights Atrocities in International Law: Beyond the Nuremberg Legacy* (Oxford, 1997); Belinda Cooper (ed.), *War Crimes: The Legacy of Nuremberg* (New York, 1999).

53. Roht-Arriaza, "Conclusion: Combating Impunity," 294. For the role of ICS in forging and promoting international human rights, see Michael Ignatieff, "Human Rights: The Midlife Crisis," *New York Review of Books* XLVI (20 May1999): 58–62.

54. Nelson Mandela, "Foreword," in Kritz (ed.), *Transitional Justice*, I, xi.

55. Kathryn A. Sikkink points out, "Chilean organizations formed to confront government repression, especially the Vicaria de Solidaridad, became models for human rights groups throughout Latin America and a source of information and inspiration for human rights activists in the United States and Europe." See "Nongovernmental Organizations, Democracy, and Human Rights in Latin America," in Tom Farer (ed.), *Beyond Sovereignty: Collectively Defending Democracy in the Americas* (Baltimore, 1996), 155.

56. Carlos Nino, "Response: The Duty to Punish Past Abuses of Human Rights Put into Context: The Case of Argentina," in Kritz (ed.), *Transitional Justice*, I, 417–436.

57. See Anita Isaacs, "International Support for Democratization: A Map and Some Policy Guidelines Derived from the Four Case Studies," in Farer (ed.), *Beyond Sovereignty*, 281–282.

58. Kritz and Stuebner, "A Truth and Reconciliation Commission."

59. See Sikkink, "Nongovernmental Organizations," 160–168.

VI

The Moral Foundations of the South African TRC

TRUTH AS ACKNOWLEDGMENT AND
JUSTICE AS RECOGNITION

ANDRÉ DU TOIT

CONCEPTUALLY, truth commissions are extraordinarily complex enterprises: their primary concerns are as much political as moral in ways that both invoke and recast history and law.[1] If truth commissions address fundamental moral questions—of justice and truth, violence and violation, accountability and reparation—they do so not at the level of theoretical reflection or by means of established institutions but as eminently political projects. Conversely, the politics of truth commissions is informed by distinctively moral notions and objectives to a degree that is unusual in modern and secular societies.

The moral foundations of truth commissions need to be distinguished from a number of related but distinct considerations, including those of the relevant *historical circumstances*, the enabling *political conditions*, the specific *legal mandates*, and the available *conceptual frameworks*. These are all in different ways relevant to, but do not determine, the question of the *moral foundations* of truth commissions:

- First, truth commissions typically operate in certain *historical contexts*, that of transitions from authoritarian or totalitarian regimes to a more democratic dispensation. More generally, truth commissions function in what may be termed the circumstances of transitional justice; that is, when a democratic political culture of rights and accountability needs to be established in the aftermath of massive violations of human rights.[2] This applies to the South African case, but its particular circumstances are also those of the transition from apartheid to a nonracial democracy. As we will see, this historical circumstance raises special difficulties for the South African Truth and Reconciliation Commission (TRC).

- Second, there is the question of the enabling *political conditions*. For the TRC these are very much that of a negotiated political settlement between the National Party (NP) government and the African National Congress (ANC) in circumstances where many had anticipated the quite different outcomes of either a liberation struggle resulting in the seizure of power or the endgame of open civil war and/or partition. Given such political conditions, there could be no question of victors' justice on the model of the Nuremberg trials. However, what is politically possible and desirable is not what is morally required; conversely, it also does not follow that if a certain kind of "justice" is not politically possible then any other alternative must amount to a moral compromise. The political compromise may or may not be a moral compromise.

- Third, there is the matter of the specific *legislative mandates*. In the case of the TRC, an act of Parliament stipulated that it was to include the provision of amnesty, albeit conditional on individual application and full disclosure. Moreover, this act was directly based on the "postamble" to the Interim Constitution. It bound Parliament itself to provide for amnesty, irrespective of moral or political arguments to the contrary. From a constitutional and legal perspective, the option of choosing "justice" rather than amnesty was effectively foreclosed. As far as the moral foundations of the TRC are concerned, though, this cannot be the last word.
- Finally, there is the question of available *conceptual frameworks*. In authoritarian societies these include the traditions and mentalities that had in the past sanctioned or legitimated abuses and atrocities.[3] The availability or emergence of new and alternative models of political and moral thought may contribute to the possibility of a collective learning experience.

These historical circumstances, enabling political conditions, specific legal mandates, and available conceptual frameworks are not to be confused with the *moral foundations* of the TRC. These will have to be found with reference to appropriate moral principles and criteria. The TRC's constitutive moral conceptions of "truth and reconciliation" may be explicated more specifically in terms of *truth as acknowledgment* and *justice as recognition*, and these principles can provide a coherent alternative, at least in the circumstances of transitional justice, to retributive notions of justice requiring criminal prosecution and punishment. In other words, core notions of the TRC—associated especially with the victims' hearings—provide the outlines for a justifiable and coherent conception of transitional justice. Saying so does not mean that the TRC was able to sustain this moral conception consistently, or that other and even alternative notions of justice and truth did not also function in the TRC process.

The TRC's approach to transitional justice need not be construed as a moral compromise, sacrificing justice for the sake of truth and reconciliation. The moral foundations of truth commissions require a closer consideration of the distinctive features and requirements of the circumstances of *transitional justice*, in addition to the general moral considerations underlying notions of justice familiar to established liberal democracies. Thus, Gutmann and Thompson in this book argue that the moral justification of truth commissions should be not just moral *in perspective* and moral *in practice*, but "should be moral *in principle*: it should explicitly appeal to rights or goods that are morally comparable to the justice that is being sacrificed."[4] This conclusion appears to assume that in principle the demands of justice are the same even in radically different kinds of historical circumstances, and that the key question concerns the other goods and values with which justice may need to be balanced. This chapter advances a different perspective on the moral foundations of truth commissions in general and the TRC in particular. It argues that, consistent with justice itself, understanding the moral foundations of truth commissions may require different principles applied in fundamentally different kinds of historical circumstances, such as those of transitional justice.

This difference flows from Rawls's basic distinction between the *general conception* of justice and the *special conception* of justice. Although Rawls's principles of justice apply to issues of social or distributive justice and not to the criminal or retributive justice, the distinction itself need not be confined to distributive justice. A concern for "transitional justice" responds to a similar need to apply moral considerations of justice more generally and not only in the familiar but nevertheless "special" circumstances of established liberal democracies.[5]

It is in the context of transitional justice that truth commissions function. If they do not conform to the demands of the "special" conception of (retributive) justice familiar to us *within* established liberal democracies, it does not mean that they may not—especially in these transitional circumstances—be required by a more "general" conception of justice. The moral conceptions informing the victims' hearings of the TRC—that is, the principles of truth as acknowledgment and justice as recognition—may be construed as appropriate applications of a more "general" conception of justice in such transitional contexts. So, far from amounting to a moral compromise—sacrificing (retributive) justice for the sake of truth and reconciliation—they are in accordance with the requirements of *justice* more generally in these transitional circumstances and serve to prepare the way for the conditions under which the "special" conception of justice, familiar to established liberal democracies, may be introduced.

The Moral Conceptions of Truth Commissions as Founding Projects

Truth commissions are not part and parcel of the regular institutional arrangements of "normal" democracies. They are *historical founding projects* in the transitional context of introducing and consolidating a new democratic dispensation and/or a culture of rights and accountability following massive violations of human rights under the prior regime. They are best understood as responses to the special *moral and political needs* of this kind of historical context; that is, those arising from attempts to found a new democratic order in the aftermath of the political atrocities and/or social injustices of a prior regime. Contextually, truth commissions are thus best understood as expressions of a new democratic resolve and political will coupled with the public acknowledgment of great wrongs done to individuals and communities. Their moral and political objectives can be encapsulated in an allusive phrase such as the Argentinian "Nunca Mas" ("Never Again"). It need not be spelled out *what* it is that should not be allowed to happen again, and even less *why* this must not happen. *In this historical context* it is overwhelmingly and transparently clear to all concerned what the open-ended reference involves (e.g., the "disappearances," the political killings and tortures). Similarly, the phrase adopted by the TRC as its banner—Truth the Road to Reconciliation—simply assumes that it will be evident *who* needs to be reconciled and *what* truth is required.

As historical founding projects, truth commissions may be compared to constitution-making. Similar to a constitutional assembly, charged with the task of drawing up a new constitution, the TRC was not a permanent institution, but was meant to facilitate the launching of a new era. Unlike the *forward-looking* founding function of establishing a constitution, the founding function of truth commissions is also *backward-looking*; typically, truth commissions are in the business of "dealing with the past." For this reason, truth commissions have been unfavorably compared with constitution-making. Ackerman has argued that, given the limited amount of moral capital available to any historical founding action in transitional contexts and in view of the divisive conflicts likely to be unleashed by backward-looking projects in these circumstances, constitution-making should be the preferred option.[6] However, as the conjunction of the TRC and the Constitutional Assembly demonstrates in the South African case, these were not mutually exclusive alternatives. Moreover, it would be misleading to conceive of truth commissions as backward-looking only; compared to historians' concerns with the past, they are primarily aimed at establishing a new moral and political order. If truth commissions are backward-looking, they are so precisely as historical founding projects; they deal with the past not for its own sake but in order to clear the way for a new beginning.

Compared to constitution-making, truth commissions also operate at a different level. Truth commissions are not so much concerned with the specifics of establishing the legal and institutional framework for a new political order as they are in serving to generate and consolidate new and distinctive conceptions of political morality that can henceforth inform the political culture. Though dependent on the available conceptual frameworks, the distinctive contributions of truth commissions are bound up with, and indeed require, novel moral and political conceptions as their own constitutive principles. In the case of the TRC, its constitutive moral conception may, as a first approximation, be found in the novel and contested notion of *truth and reconciliation*. This term has often been understood to depart from more familiar conceptions of retributive and social *justice*, while it is sometimes suggested that it may involve alternative notions of "restorative justice."[7]

Diagnosing the Needs for Transitional Justice

Circumstances of transitional justice cover a range of different historical situations, while the massive violations of human rights by prior regimes vary across a number of relevant political and moral dimensions. Truth commissions may be an appropriate and justifiable response in certain contexts, and less so or not at all in other contexts. A political and moral diagnosis is required, and this may be correct in its assessment of the primary moral needs in this particular historical context, or it may be mistaken. Diagnoses of the nature of the prior regime and its violations of human rights may differ significantly with regard to such factors as the following:

- The prior regime may have been *sectorally based* or *systemic* in character. In this regard, Rosenberg has made a suggestive distinction between a "regime of criminals," allowing clear distinctions between identifiable sets of perpetrators, victims, and beneficiaries, and a "criminal regime," where the distinctions between perpetrators, victims, and beneficiaries are unclear and problematic and collaborators have a larger role. Broadly speaking, the former has been more characteristic of various Latin American cases of transitions from authoritarian rule, while the latter applies more to the Eastern European experience of transitional justice in the aftermath of totalitarian regimes.[8] In this perspective, it is no accident that truth commissions have been salient mechanisms for transitional justice in Chile and Argentina but not in Czechoslovakia or Poland. In the Latin American cases, the core issue of the "disappearances" and the torture of political opponents by the military and death squads posed urgent questions of truth. The situation is different where all were, to some degree, made complicit by the prior regime's systemic injustices. If, in the words of Havel, "All of us are responsible, each to a different degree . . . none of us is merely a victim," then it is not so clear what truth concerning whom—victims, perpetrators, collaborators, and bystanders?—needs to be established, or indeed whether a truth commission would be the appropriate response.[9] (Thus, in the Czech case, lustration proved highly problematic in establishing the truth regarding the different categories of informers who had collaborated with the security police.)
- "Dealing with the past" inevitably involves basic choices and trade-offs, including the relative priorities to be given to the interests of perpetrators, victims, beneficiaries, collaborators, bystanders, or others. Depending on the nature of the prior regime and of its political atrocities, the urgent moral need may be to give priority

to dealing either with *perpetrators* (by bringing them to justice), or *victims* (through restoring their human and civic dignity), or more generally, *beneficiaries* (through social and economic redistribution).

Different approaches to transitional justice can be defined with regard to their respective priorities. Thus, the Nuremberg trials paradigmatically established the priority of prosecuting and punishing perpetrators, while the Czech lustration laws are striking in giving priority, not in the first instance to dealing with the perpetrators (or, for that matter, the victims), but rather in focusing on the *informers and collaborators*.

In general, truth commissions as a distinctive approach to transitional justice reflect a double choice for "truth" rather than (retributive and social) justice. First, truth commissions typically give priority to gross human rights violations rather than to systemic injustices, and thus diagnose the primary moral need as that of having to deal with victims and perpetrators rather than with beneficiaries and bystanders or collaborators. This implies a choice for the imperatives of individual justice and truth over those of social or distributive justice. Second, and within this narrower focus on gross human rights violations, truth commissions differ from tribunals in giving priority to hearings in which the victims can tell their own stories, rather than seeking the prosecution and punishment of perpetrators. This implies a choice for "truth" (of victims) over (retributive) justice. Whether this amounts to a correct moral and political response to the needs of transitional justice will be a matter for applied diagnosis in the particular historical circumstances concerned, as well as for a more specific explication of the moral conception involved in this commitment to "truth"; that is, those of truth as acknowledgment and justice as recognition.

In the case of the South African transition, the mandate of the TRC, significantly, was formulated in terms of the need to address gross human rights violations—"the killing, attempted killing, abduction, [and] severe ill-treatment or torture" of past political conflicts. This reflected a specific moral and political diagnosis of the transition from apartheid, one putting the need to deal with individual victims and perpetrators of political atrocities in priority order as against the imperatives of social and systemic justice. Implicitly, this choice could not but relegate the systemic, institutionalized and structural aspects of apartheid—including the pass laws, forced removals, and Bantu education—to a contextual status. Central to such a project were the perpetrators and victims of particular political atrocities, rather than the collaborators with and beneficiaries from the social injustice and systemic inequalities of apartheid. Moreover, this focus on gross human rights violations was distinctly victim-oriented.

At its outset the TRC process was especially concerned with providing opportunity for hearings at which victims could tell their own stories in a nonadversarial context. This expressed a recognition of the urgent need to restore the human and civic dignity of victims of gross human rights violations. As far as perpetrators were concerned, what was required was full disclosure as a condition for amnesty, not prosecution and punishment; it amounted to an exchange of truth for indemnity. Taken together, this combination reflected a basic choice for "truth" as against retributive (and by implication social) justice. It constituted a distinctive moral conception with its own moral priorities, that of a commitment to *truth as acknowledgment*.

The moral foundations of the TRC depend on the appropriateness of this diagnosis in a context of the transitional justice facing postapartheid South Africa. The complication is that the South African case involves both elements of a "criminal regime" and those of a "regime of criminals." Dealing with the past in the South African case involves questions about *both* death squads, torture, killings, and disappearances *and* the systemic injustices of apartheid such as the pass laws, forced removals, and Bantu education. The main challenges to the moral priorities of the TRC are characteristically derived from one or another of these elements. Thus, one kind of challenge, forcefully articulated by Mamdani, invokes the claims of *social justice* versus *truth and reconciliation*.[10] This amounts to asserting the primary moral needs for measures of transitional justice to address the structural and systemic features of apartheid. In an important sense this challenge does not accept the TRC's special focus on political atrocities; it insists on the primacy of apartheid as a criminal regime even more than as a regime of criminals (Mamdani is concerned to shift the attention from the perpetrators and victims to the beneficiaries of apartheid as a system of exploitation). The second challenge accepts the TRC's special focus on gross violations of human rights, but demands that the perpetrators be prosecuted and punished. This challenge poses the imperatives of (criminal and retributive) *justice* against the objectives of *truth and reconciliation*.[11] In the South African context this effectively amounts to an insistence on the diagnosis of apartheid as a regime of criminals.

Insofar as these challenges draw on undoubted elements of the apartheid regime, they do have considerable force. They were also reflected in the TRC process itself, which by no means provided a single and unambiguous answer to these tensions between justice and truth or reconciliation. In practice, the TRC was a complex and sometimes unstable combination of different ways of relating the demands of justice and truth in responding to the different and conflicting moral needs in these particular circumstances of transitional justice. The moral conceptions of truth as acknowledgment and justice as recognition on which this chapter is focused need to be situated within this overall context; they evolved in conjunction with certain key aspects of the TRC, especially in connection with the victims' hearings, but they do not apply to all aspects of the TRC's activities.

The Changing Meanings of Truth and Reconciliation in the TRC as a Democratic Enterprise

Unlike its Latin American counterparts, and probably uniquely in the comparative international history of truth commissions, the South African TRC was itself a notably *public* and *democratic* enterprise. This feature accounts for some of its strengths and also for many of its greatest problems:

- First, it should be noted that the TRC was not, like many of its counterparts elsewhere, a presidential commission or even an international tribunal, but a parliamentary commission. Not only was the establishment of the TRC uniquely preceded by an extended public debate concerning its general objectives, but its specific mandate and procedures were fashioned through a process of parliamentary hearings and debates with the participation of all major political parties.
- This public and democratic character was sustained in the actual proceedings of the TRC. To an unusual extent the TRC conducted its business in full public view. If the Chilean commission likewise arranged a series of hearings at which victims could come forward to tell their stories and have these officially acknowledged, it was with the crucial difference that this did not happen in public or with ongoing coverage by the media. The Latin American models only went public once they were ready and had been authorized to do so. In this respect the ongoing TRC hearings were comparable more to political trials as public events and deliberate exercises in political education.[12] The TRC's public hearings, though, differed from political trials in that they lacked the specific focus possible in the prosecution of particular cases. The TRC could not rely on the courts' established authority. While framing its proceedings in terms of an encompassing narrative of truth and reconciliation, the hearings still allowed victims and others to "tell their own stories"; not infrequently, doing so produced local or sectional narratives in tension with or even contesting the generalized framework proposed by the TRC. In these respects, too, the process was notably democratic.[13]
- More generally, the TRC had in large part to fashion its own task and agenda through an ongoing process of highly public and publicized pressures and negotiations. As far as the issue of amnesty was concerned, for example, the TRC was not charged with investigating the cases of a predefined set of alleged perpetrators. Since individuals had to apply for amnesty, the TRC actually had to persuade or pressure reluctant perpetrators to avail themselves of this opportunity—and a considerable part of this persuasion was played out in full public view.
- Finally, the TRC also moved into a number of different areas that did not necessarily follow from its formal structure, including the hearings devoted to the submissions of the various political parties, as well as a series of "sectoral hearings" focusing, in turn, on the health sector, the press, the judiciary, the business community, and the churches. In the comparative history of truth commissions

these sectoral hearings were a South African innovation. They were not primarily focused on particular individuals, whether perpetrators or victims, but were more contextual in orientation. To some extent this can be taken as an attempt by the TRC to address the underlying challenge of transitional justice in the postapartheid context: how to balance the concern with *individual* cases of political atrocities and gross violations of human rights with the *structural* features of apartheid as a system of exploitation and oppression. This is also reflected in the focus on institutional matters, rather than on the personal accountability of individuals that characterized the "perpetrator findings" in the eventual TRC *Final Report*.[14]

The TRC's public and democratic character increased both its risks and its opportunities as an ongoing *process* relative to the eventual *product* (in the sense of its *Final Report*). It follows that there was no strong separation of process and product as with other truth commissions. The South African TRC's *Final Report* could not have the same dramatic impact as the Chilean TRC's report, or that of the Argentinean *Nunca Mas*, as the public presentation of previously undisclosed "truths" in an authoritative and well-defined finished product.[15]

The relevant point is that, due both to its democratic character and to the close fusion of process and product, the constitutive moral conception of the TRC cannot readily be fixed in a single or unambiguous sense. Instead, we find that in practice the *meaning and interpretation* of truth and reconciliation, as stated objectives of the TRC, shifted over time as different sets of agents became involved at several stages of the overall process and located their ideas within different *framing narratives*. The TRC's constitutive moral conception of truth as acknowledgment was thus extended, complemented, and contested in various ways by related and alternative conceptions.[16] There were four different stages in this development:

- During the preparatory and planning stages of the TRC the *political* sense of reconciliation—that of elite pacts rooted in the experience of negotiated settlements and implicitly understood in terms of a master narrative of future *nation-building*—was most pronounced.
- During the early stages of the TRC's actual work a pronounced *religious and therapeutic* sense of reconciliation through the disclosure of truth—of some transforming process of personal, social, and spritual renewal—became more salient. The appointment of Archbishop Tutu as chairperson, along with a number of other religious leaders as well as individuals from the counseling professions on the TRC, led to the increasing prominence of a religious and therapeutic discourse and the symbolism of "healing" and "reconciliation."
- More generally the victims' hearings provided a public space and recognized opportunity for a range of individuals to "*tell their own stories*," rooted in diverse local and communal settings, and to have them officially acknowledged. The TRC effectively created a sympathetic and caring framework for the bereaved and traumatized, far removed from the adversarial procedures of a court of law, with assistants

on hand to comfort those in distress as well as to provide for multiple simultaneous translations from the witnesses' languages of choice. Substantial numbers availed themselves of the opportunity to participate in these public procedures for restoring and affirming the human and civic dignity of the victims. But the TRC's own conception of these events and its particular framing of the hearings did not exhaust their significance. Precisely by enabling people to tell their stories, they enabled them to some extent do so in their own more ambiguous or alternative terms, often implicitly and even explicitly in tension with the TRC's framing narratives of violation, disclosure, reconciliation, and perhaps even forgiveness. (Thus, some insisted that they were activists in a liberation struggle, not victims but survivors.) At the same time the sustained revelation, through the TRC process itself, of so many atrocities tended to reinforce a countervailing popular narrative demanding (retributive) "justice" and punishment.

- The Commission's efforts to draw representatives of the main political parties and of different sectors of civil society into the TRC process through various special and sectoral hearings also met with somewhat mixed success. The party political representatives tended to use the opportunity to assert their own partisan narratives for framing the political atrocities of the past, and had considerable difficulty in accepting accountability on the terms proposed by the TRC. Instead, they opted for their own versions of political or collective responsibility. Some political parties and leaders refused to cooperate with the Commission and increasingly challenged its bona fides, with the National Party (NP) even taking the TRC to court. The judiciary refused to participate in the legal sector hearing, claiming that participation would compromise its independence.[17] In other cases the sectoral hearings merely provided a further terrain where the different protagonists, rather than transcending past divisions and conflicts, continued to pursue their own agendas.

- Subsequently, as the *quasi-judicial and adversarial procedures* of the amnesty hearings began to take center stage, the TRC's practice shifted from acknowledging truth as a means of reconciliation to the imperatives of observing the *procedural rights* of those implicated by the disclosures and allegations in the course of this process. At other hearings, too, lawyers and legal procedures played an increasingly prominent role.

- Finally, with the publication of the TRC's *Final Report*, it emerged that in the Commission's own view the victims' hearings had been only one phase of the process and had increasingly been subordinated to the methodology of systematic data processing and the corroboration of statements as a basis for the objective of making *victim and perpetrator findings*. Instead of achieving closure to the TRC process, this finding served to bring the Commission into confrontation with the ANC.[18]

If the complications and tensions in the interpretation of the TRC's moral and political objectives are intimately linked to the public and democratic character of the process, they also precluded any authoritative imposition of a clear and definitive version. Alternative moral conceptions and political narratives emerged in the course of the TRC process; they were likewise grounded in particular diagnoses of the moral and political needs of postapartheid South Africa. The question of their moral foundation concerns whether or not they can be validated in relation to the circumstances of transitional justice. This chapter does not pursue this question with regard to these alternative moral conceptions, but is specifically concerned with investigating the moral foundations of the TRC by explicating its constituent conceptions of *truth as acknowledgement* and *justice as recognition*. If these notions were most closely associated with the victims' hearings during the earlier part of the TRC process, they may also be best suited to provide a coherent and distinctive justification for the role of truth commissions in the circumstances of transitional justice.

Truth as Acknowledgment

As the term itself suggests, the constitutive principle of truth commissions must be tied up with some notion of "truth." However, here we need to tread with care. Truth is a dangerous word, often used loosely if not metaphorically. "The word 'Truth' makes me uncomfortable," wrote Krog, the poet, on having to report on the TRC. "The word 'truth' still trips the tongue. . . . I prefer the word 'lie.' The moment the lie raises its head, I smell blood. Because it is there where the truth is closest."[19] In political contexts truth, more often than not, is subject to ideological manipulation, and to charge an official commission with establishing the "truth" raises Orwellian alarms about doublespeak and political show trials as "degradation rituals."[20] It is vital to distinguish and unpack the relevant senses of truth in order to explicate the distinctive moral conception informing the project of the TRC.

In contexts of transitional justice, *truth* will evidently be focused on disclosing the political atrocities of the prior regime and in past conflicts. But this is a complex matter: it is not only a question of gaining knowledge of the relevant facts regarding the killings or tortures, but even more a matter of finding appropriate ways to acknowledge them. In this connection, Nagel focused on the crucial distinction between *knowledge* and *acknowledgment*.[21] This distinction involves two different senses of truth: the *factual truths*, relevant to the forensic processes of gaining and confirming knowledge of particular events and circumstances, and *truth as acknowledgment*, the crucial issue for transitional justice. Both senses of truth are relevant to the objectives of truth commissions, with the former serving the latter:

- The need to know the "truth" about the political atrocities of prior regimes reflects (in part) a definite lack of relevant *factual knowledge*. Often this will prove a massive, difficult, and complex forensic task: witnesses are hard to find or unreliable and under all sorts of pressures, records are destroyed or have been falsified, and even basic particulars are contested on all sides. In many cases it may not be possible to gain reliable knowledge or to demonstrate conclusions beyond a reasonable doubt. Yet this must clearly must be a major part of the work of any truth commission: to establish and extend a reliable database, to test the many allegations in circulation, and to corroborate the statements made by various parties. Unless this task is properly done the foundation for any further historical or political function of truth commissions will be missing. Victims and their relatives need to *know* what happened to their loved ones before they can forgive or engage in any process of reconciliation. More generally, truth commissions may significantly add to the sum of knowledge of past political atrocities; and if they do not manage to establish the whole truth in all its particulars, they can at least set definite limits to those who for political reasons would wish to *deny* the very occurrence of these atrocities.[22] But their functions should not only, or even primarily, be considered in these terms. Though it will always be relevant to inquire what, if any, new knowledge a truth commission has added to what had previously been known about political atrocities, or to what extent it succeeded in resolving particular contested cases, this may not be its most important contribution to the truth concerning such atrocities.

- Even under the prior regime the truth of ongoing political atrocities or human rights violations such as torture are in a sense already *known* (certainly to the perpetrators and victims themselves; to some degree to their immediate relations, colleagues, and friends; and to a lesser extent in the wider community). Officially, though, the occurrence of these violations is often denied categorically. Thus, the South African government long insisted that it held no political prisoners, much less admitted that they were victims of torture or abuse. Where deaths in detention became publicly known, these were consistently ascribed to natural or other causes. Unofficially, though, some individuals and sections in the security forces were widely known as notorious torturers and killers. In such cases the issue is not so much that of a lack of *knowledge* as of the refusal to *acknowledge* the existence of these political atrocities. This is, in the first instance, a political issue. Precisely because, at one level, the reality of the atrocities and violations will be known only too well to those concerned, the effective refusal to acknowledge them in public amounts to a basic demonstration of political power. For the victims, this actually is a redoubling of the basic violation: the literal violation consists of the actual pain, suffering, and trauma visited on them; the political violation consists in the refusal (publicly) to acknowledge it. The latter amounts to a denial of the human and civic dignity of the victims. For the perpetrators, it likewise serves to define their power: not only are they in a position to do terrible things to others, but they can do so with impunity. It is one thing if political atrocities are the work of unknown perpetrators, who thereby manage to escape punishment under the law. Politically, it is a different situation if the perpetrators are known as such, but are in a position to deny the very existence of their victims or atrocities, thereby asserting their own impunity.

• For the successor regime, an insistence on processes of public *acknowledgment* of political atrocities and human rights violations may thus constitute a special political priority, and in this regard truth commissions can play a vital role. For victims they can provide appropriate forums and procedures for the particularized *restoration of their human and civic dignity.* Strictly speaking, the actual pain and suffering involved in past political atrocities and gross human rights violations can never be undone. The victims of political killings cannot be brought back to life, nor can the harm and trauma of torture and abuse somehow be negated. What can be done, though, is publicly to restore the civic and human dignity of these victims precisely by acknowledging the truth of what was done to them. This was the function and purpose of the victims' hearings where people were enabled to tell their own stories, and to have them publicly acknowledged in nonadversarial procedures.

In the particular circumstances of transitional justice in postapartheid South Africa, the conception of truth as acknowledgment embodied in the victims' hearings of the TRC thus represented a political choice for the priority of restoring the civic and human dignity of the victims of gross human rights violations. In considering the significance of this particular choice, it may be compared to the alternative option of a "democratic" transition. That would merely consist of the formal restoration of citizenship and civic rights to those who had been denied those rights under apartheid. That was the significance of the "founding election" of 1994 for South Africans generally: it represented the effective as much as the symbolic restoration of basic citizenship. As such a founding action, the founding election was forward-looking, rather than backward-looking. Now consider the effect of such a founding election without anything like a backward-looking truth commission. It could have been deemed sufficient that all South Africans would *henceforth* be able to exercise equal political rights. Without a TRC, where would that have left the victims of gross human rights violations and the perpetrators of political atrocities? Former victims and killers or torturers alike would have counted among the henceforth-equal citizens of this new South African democracy—but without any special acknowledgment of prior violations. The TRC reflects a moral and political diagnosis that—at least in the case of victims and perpetrators of gross human rights violations—a general and formal restoration of citizenship alone would not be sufficient. Something more needed to be done: justice required a particularized procedure of public acknowledgment to restore human and civic dignity, and to exact some measure of accountability from the perpetrators.

It needs to be stressed that the significance of this choice for truth as acknowledgment operates primarily at a public and a political level. It is a mistake to assume that participation in the victims' hearings of the TRC could somehow guarantee the *personal* healing of traumas due to the gross human rights violations concerned. The procedures involved in the public restoration of the victims' civic dignity may or may not also contribute to personal healing, but that cannot be its primary purpose. Personal healing and social reconciliation at this level need to be distinguished from the political significance of truth as acknowledgment.[23] Consider a further possible alternative option, one that would give priority to the *therapeutic* objectives of personal healing. It is possible to conceive of a process through which substantial numbers of victims and perpetrators would be identified for professional psychological and pastoral counseling aimed at individual healing and interpersonal reconciliation. This process would differ from the TRC in that it would not involve public acknowledgment but would operate in private and professional contexts. What difference would it make to victims and perpetrators if the therapeutic objectives of personal healing and interpersonal reconciliation could actually be achieved in this way? Clearly, the difference would primarily be a political one; at the personal level victims and perpetrators would, by definition, be "healed" and "reconciled"—but without any public acknowledgment of the truth of the gross human rights violations or some measure of accountability for the political atrocities concerned. If personal healing and interpersonal reconciliation were the primary objectives, then it need not matter that the double denial of the victims' human dignity had not been publicly addressed or the perpetrators called to some form of accountability—so long as victims and perpetrators alike were individually healed and reconciled. As against this result, the conception of truth as acknowledgment informing the victims' hearings of the TRC reflects a different set of priorities. On this view, the point is precisely that representatives of the state and civil society should take public responsibility for the restoration of the human and civic dignity of victims whose suffering at the hands of the state or political agents had so long been denied—that is the political significance of truth as acknowledgment.

Justice as Recognition

This chapter has discussed the *political* functions and significance of the constitutive conception of truth as acknowledgment that informed the objectives and practice of the TRC, and of the victims' hearings in particular. What about the *moral* foundations of the TRC: how is this notion of truth as acknowledgment related to the concerns of transitional justice? We distinguish the specific sense of justice relevant in this context, that of *justice as recognition* involved in the restoration of the human and civic dignity of victims, from both that of *criminal and retributive justice* and that of *social and distributive justice*. In practice, the respective senses of truth and justice are related in different ways through the particular processes and procedures involved in such matters as criminal prosecutions and public hearings. These processes involve distinctive assumptions and implications regarding the relative priority of, or a particular focus on, perpetrators and/or victims. In the case of prosecutions seeking criminal and retributive justice, the structure of the adversarial system amounts to a special focus on the perpetrator as the accused who is subject to punishment, but must be presumed innocent until proved guilty. "Truth" in this context, as Minow among others has shown, is confined to what may be relevant to the *criminal guilt or innocence* of the perpetrator.[24] What about the *victim's truth*, or the many other complex and multifaceted aspects of the truth relevant to a particular case? So far as the practice of criminal justice is concerned, victims may indeed be presumed to have a basic interest in seeing retributive justice done to perpetrators, but otherwise they cannot expect any special consideration. The testimony of victims, too, are only admissible in accordance with strict rules of evidence and may be subject to potentially hostile cross-questioning. In practice, as the experience of victims in criminal trials for rape has shown, the process of obtaining *criminal justice* for perpetrators may well revisit on victims a further traumatic experience compounding the original violation.

Compared to the adversarial structure of the criminal justice system and its focus on the accused, truth commissions represent an alternative way of linking truth and justice that puts victims first. The relevant sense of justice, which is intimately connected with that of truth as acknowledgment, is that of *justice as recognition*: the justice involved in the respect for other persons as equal sources of truth and bearers of rights.[25] In practice, this requires a fundamentally different orientation to that of the criminal justice system in the form of victim-centered public hearings—nonadversarial and supportive forums structured in ways to enable the acknowledgment of victims "telling their own stories." These often will not accord with the rules of evidence required in criminal proceedings; nor do they necessarily measure up to the requirements of natural justice and the *audi alterem partem* (hear the other side) rule, especially when these testimonies implicate others. What is at stake when victims are enabled to "tell their own stories" is not just the specific factual statements, but the right of framing them from their own perspectives and being recognized as legitimate sources of truth with claims to rights and justice. The relevant sense of truth is of a more holistic *narrative truth*—that involved in the overall framing of the events and experiences that together make up the victim's own "story." In a sense all individuals will have their own "story," perpetrators as much as victims, but perpetrators are not invited to tell *their* "own stories." They disclose and acknowledge in a forum of public accountability their parts in the political atrocities of the past. It is only insofar as the narrative truth of these stories fits the overall objectives of both justice as recognition and truth as acknowledgment, and thus serves to restore the victims' human and civic dignity and secure some measure of accountability from perpetrators, that it will accord with the moral conception informing truth commissions as a mechanism for transitional justice.

In what way does the notion of justice as recognition, linked to that of truth as acknowledgment, provide an appropriate *moral foundation* for the TRC? We distinguish carefully between the principles of justice familiar within consolidated liberal democracies (or what Rawls terms the *special conception* of justice) and the specific needs of transitional justice (compatible with the *general conception* of justice). Abstracted from the circumstances of transitional justice, the idea of a need for the restoration of the civic and human dignity of victims of gross human rights violations may well seem incoherent, if not tautologous. At this level of abstraction, the Kantian terms of equal respect for persons as moral agents, the moral imperatives—treating each person as an end, and never as a means to an end—are assumed to apply across the board to victims and perpetrators alike. Given these assumptions, within the moral and political framework of established liberal democracies, perpetrators of gross human rights violations stand morally condemned for their violations of the rights of others; for their part, perpetrators have failed in the most basic duty of showing respect for other persons. But what about the moral status of the victims of such gross violations of human rights? In terms of the *special conception* of justice, given the moral and political assumptions of established liberal democracies, it can hardly be conceived that victims, even of gross human rights violations, have thereby lost their moral status as persons to be respected as ends in themselves.

It is the moral measure of the political atrocities involved in torture, killing, or other gross abuses that these are perpetrated on persons whose rights and dignity should have been respected. But, if given the set of assumptions underlying the functioning of established liberal democracies, the human and civic dignity of victims can never be "lost," how can there be any special moral need for the *restoration* of such human and civic dignity? In terms of the *special conception* of justice, there is no need for the notion of justice as recognition except in terms of the respect owed to all persons as bearers of rights, victims and perpetrators alike. This is the sense involved in that respect for equal rights and justice that is fundamental to the very notion of the rule of law on which stable legal institutions in liberal democracies are founded. But it is precisely the concern of *transitional justice* that these regular institutions cannot yet be taken for granted; under the prior regime, the very foundations of law and of public institutions were perverted.

A new culture of rights and equal citizenship must still be ensured. There is a very real (historical) sense in which the human and civic dignity of some—in particular, the victims of political atrocities and gross violations of human rights—have been denied and now need to be publicly affirmed if the democratic transition is to be consolidated. In this perspective, justice as recognition must then involve more than just the abstract (Kantian) sense of moral respect, and is this further sense of justice as recognition that requires the special remedies provided by truth commissions as a means to transitional justice.[26]

We have argued that *truth as acknowledgment* and *justice as recognition*, as moral conceptions informing the practice of the TRC, are distinctive and coherent ideas relevant to transitional justice and need not involve a moral compromise in which (retributive) justice is sacrificed for the sake of some other value or good. Rather, at the level of Rawls's *general conception*, both truth as acknowledgment and justice as recognition can be derived from the requirements of justice itself in the circumstances of transitional justice. The notion of truth as acknowledgment has been related especially to the basic political objective of restoring the civic and human dignity of victims of gross violations of human rights. With regard to the complex notion of justice as recognition, it is the loss of basic self-confidence and of socially recognized self-esteem, over and above the general sense of moral self-respect, that is specifically relevant to projects of transitional justice. This differs from what, by analogy to Rawls, we would call the *special conception* of (retributive) justice, so familiar in the context of consolidated liberal democracies, insofar as the pertinent senses of justice as recognition do not assume established liberal democracies or stable institutions of law and order, and could therefore apply more widely, for example, also to historical transitions from authoritarian regimes.

It is in these circumstances of transitional justice that there are special moral and political needs for restoring the civic and human dignity of victims, their basic self-confidence and their socially recognized self-esteem. However, even if the distinctive notions of truth as acknowledgment and justice as recognition are coherent and relevant to transitional justice, the actual practices informed by them are not self-validating thereby. The moral and political justification of such practices depend on whether or not they are based on a correct assessment of the primary moral needs in that particular transitional context. In this connection, the "mixed" nature of the South African transition from apartheid, involving both elements of a "criminal regime" as well as those of a "regime of criminals," pose special complications.

The notions of truth as acknowledgment and justice of recognition, as explored in this chapter, relate especially to the victims' hearings that featured notably during the initial phase of the TRC. However, the victims' hearings constituted only one part of the complex and many-layered activities of the TRC process. Other activities of the TRC, such as the amnesty process, or the making of perpetrator findings in the TRC *Final Report*, were informed by different moral notions. These, too, derive from specific assessments of the special moral and political needs in the transition from apartheid, as do the various justice-based challenges to the TRC. In various ways they constitute different historical diagnoses translated into moral and political priorities. None is self-validating; and their moral justification will depend both on the demands of transitional justice and on the actual features of the particular transition involved. Even so, the notions of truth as acknowledgment and justice as recognition, which informed the victims' hearings as one crucial part of the TRC process, provide a coherent alternative to notions of justice based on criminal prosecution and punishment and, as such, provide a morally justifiable model of transitional justice.

Notes

1. Neil J. Kritz (ed.), *Transitional Justice: How Emerging Democracies Reckon with Former Regimes* (Washington, D.C., 1995), 3 volumes.

2. Jon Elster, "Coming to Terms with the Past: A Framework for the Study of Justice in the Transition to Democracy," *Archives European Sociology* XXXIX (1998): 7–48; Luc Huyse, "Justice after Transition: On the Choices Successor Elites Make in Dealing with the Past,"*Law and Social Inquiry* XX (1995): 51–78. The point of departure for the comparative study of transitions from authoritarian rule in this context is Guillermo O'Donnell, Philippe Schmitter, and Laurence Whitehead (eds.), *Transitions from Authoritarian Rule* (Baltimore, 1986), 4 volumes.

3. Cf. Carlos Nino on the background trends in Argentinian history—ideological dualism, corporatism, anomie, and concentration of power—which help explain the massive violations of human rights that occurred under prior regimes: *Radical Evil on Trial* (New Haven, 1996), 44–49. In the South African case, the moral and intellectual legacies of apartheid and racism are similarly relevant.

4. Amy Gutmann and Dennis Thompson, "The Moral Foundations of Truth Commissions," Chapter II in this volume (emphasis added).

5. John Rawls's terminology may well be misleading here insofar as the "special" conception of justice may suggest a connection with exceptional (e.g. transitional) circumstances. It is important to stress that the connections line up the other way around: it is the "general" conception of justice that applies also to unfamiliar, developmental, and transitional circumstances and not only to the norm of established liberal democracies, as tends to be the case with the "special" conception of justice.

6. Bruce Ackerman, *The Future of the Liberal Revolution* (New Haven, 1992).

7. For some instances of discussions and position papers relevant to the TRC's own evolving understanding of truth and justice, see Alex Boraine, "Can 'Truth Telling' Promote Reconciliation?" unpublished paper (1998); Charles Villa-Vicencio, "A Different Kind of Justice: The South African Truth and Reconciliation Commission," unpublished paper (1997); Wilhelm Verwoerd, "Justice after Apartheid?: Reflections on the South African Truth and Reconciliation Commission," unpublished paper (1997).

8. Tina Rosenberg, *The Haunted Land: Facing Europe's Ghosts after Communism* (New York, 1995), 400–401.

9. Vaclav Havel, "The Great Moral Stake of the Moment," *Newsweek*, 15 January 1990, cited in Aviezer Tucker, "Paranoids May Be Persecuted: Post-totalitarian Justice," paper presented to the Columbia University Mellon Seminar on Transitional Justice, 1998.

10. Mahmood Mamdani, "When Does Reconciliation Turn into a Denial of Jus-

tice?" Human Sciences Research Council Lecture, Pretoria, 18 February 1998; cf. also Mamdani, "Reconciliation without Justice," *South African Review of Books* (November/December 1996).

11. Cf. Aryeh Neier, "What Should Be Done about the Guilty?" *New York Review of Books*, 1 February 1990; Diane F. Orentlicher, "Settling Accounts: The Duty to Prosecute Human Rights Violations of a Prior Regime," and Carlos S. Nino, "Response: The Duty to Punish Past Abuses of Human Rights Put into Context: The Case of Argentina," *Yale Law Journal* C (1991), 2539–2615, 2619–2640; Nino, *Radical Evil*, 107–148.

12. Cf. Mark J. Osiel, "Ever Again: Legal Remembrance of Administrative Massacre," *University of Pennsylvania Law Review* CXLIV (1995), 505–690.

13. But see Chapter I, note 1.

14. For a fuller account and critical analysis, see André du Toit, "Perpetrator Findings as Artificial Even-handedness? The TRC's Contested Judgements of Moral and Political Accountability for Gross Human Rights Violations," paper presented at "Commissioning the Past," University of the Witwatersrand History Conference, 1999.

15. Juan E. Mendez, *Truth and Partial Justice in Argentina: An Update* (New York, 1991), cited in Kritz, *Transitional Justice*, II, 330.

16. See also Graeme Simpson, "A Brief Evaluation of South Africa's Truth and Reconciliation Commission: Some Lessons for Societies in Transition," incidental publication (in brochure form), Centre for the Study of Violence and Reconciliation (Johannesburg, 1998).

17. Cf. David Dyzenhaus, *Judging the Judges, Judging Ourselves: Truth, Reconciliation and the Apartheid Legal Order* (Oxford, 1998).

18. Du Toit, "Perpetrator Findings."

19. Antjie Krog, *Country of My Skull* (Johannesburg, 1998), 36.

20. Osiel, "Ever Again," 510, with reference to Harold Garfinkel, "Conditions of Successful Degradation Ceremonies," *American Journal of Sociology* LXI (1956): 420.

21. Thomas Nagel, cited in Lawrence Weschler, "Afterword," in *State Crimes: Punishment or Pardon* (Washington, D.C., 1989), 93. Cf. Lawrence Weschler, *A Miracle, a Universe: Settling Accounts with Torturers* (New York, 1990), 4.

22. Michael Ignatieff, "Articles of Faith," *Index on Censorship* XXV (1996): 111–113.

23. Brendon Hamber, "Dealing with the Past and the Psychology of Reconciliation: The TRC, a Psychological Perspective," paper presented at the Fourth International Symposium on "The Contributions of Psychology to Peace," Cape Town, 1995; Hamber, "Do Sleeping Dogs Lie? The Psychological Implications of the TRC in South Africa," Occasional Paper of the Centre for the Study of Violence and Reconciliation (Johannesburg, 1997).

24. Martha Minow, *Between Vengeance and Forgiveness* (New York, 1998); cf. also Simpson, "A Brief Evaluation," 12–13.

25. Jonathan Allen, "Balancing Justice and Social Unity: Political Theory and the Idea of a Truth and Reconciliation Commission," *University of Toronto Law Journal* XLIX (1999), 315–353.

26. See Elizabeth Kiss, "Moral Ambition Within and Beyond Political Constraints: Reflections on Restorative Justice," Chapter IV in this book.

VII

Truth and Reconciliation in South Africa

THE THIRD WAY

ALEX BORAINE

South Africa has experienced racism and oppression of one form or another ever since the earliest days of colonialism. There are those who argued that the period under review for the commission in South Africa should have started as far back as the first arrival of white settlers in 1652. Others were of the view that at the very least one should look at the period that began with South Africa's first constitution in 1910. Many maintain that the starting point should be 1948 when the National Party came into power. After careful consideration, the Standing Committee on Justice in South Africa's Parliament decided to recommend that the period to be covered should be March 1960 to December 1993. The first date coincides with the banning of political organizations, severe oppression of any resistance to apartheid, and the Sharpeville massacre. The end date was arbitrarily chosen as the date when the negotiation teams decided on an amnesty provision in the Interim Constitution (this date was later changed to 10 May 1994, largely to include a number of right-wing Afrikaners who engaged in violent acts immediately prior to the election in April 1994).

In 1910, when the first South African constitution was promulgated, it characterized white hegemony and was fundamentally undemocratic, excluding as it did the vast majority of the population. It was also structurally racist, because the exclusion of the majority was in terms of skin color. However, this undemocratic and racist constitution was further entrenched when the National Party (NP) came into power in 1948. Under the NP, through its policy of apartheid, a structure of domination was enforced that was not only a denial of basic political rights but a systematic piece of social engineering that embraced every area of life from birth to death. Thus, the system of apartheid determined state policies relating to the franchise as well as to land, housing, residence, schools and universities, transport, health services, sports, hotels, restaurants, and even cemeteries.

Apartheid was a system of minority domination of statutorily defined color groups on a territorial, residential, political, social, and economic basis. It was a system that was entrenched for almost fifty years.

Although the cards seemed to be stacked against South Africa achieving a relatively peaceful and relatively democratic election, the transition from oppression, exclusivity, and resistance to a new negotiated, democratic order in 1994 was realized. The chains that bound the majority of her people in what appeared to be perpetual servitude were shattered. Many people, both within South Africa and beyond its borders, have described this transition as nothing short of a miracle.

Because of the social and economic legacy of apartheid there remained unfinished business. Without effectively dealing with that unfinished business, it was impossible to sustain the miracle, consolidate democracy, and ensure a peaceful future for all South Africans. With the transformation, there was also a compelling need to restore the moral order. Hence the creation of the Truth and Reconciliation Commission (TRC).

The commission believed that the healing process in South Africa began with an honest assessment and diagnosis of the sickness within that society. The TRC provided South Africans, both perpetrators and victims, with an opportunity to face the past and its consequences and to start afresh. The TRC was an opportunity to make a serious contribution in order to deal finally with the past without dwelling in it and to help create the conditions for a truly new South Africa.

While it is true that South Africa's Commission has been shaped very much by its own history and the circumstances and the nature of its particular and peculiar transition, there are many similarities to the experiences in Eastern Europe and South America that impinged on the TRC:

- a shift from totalitarianism to a form of democracy;
- a negotiated settlement—not a revolutionary process;
- a legacy of oppression and serious violations of human rights;
- a fragile democracy and a precarious unity;
- a commitment to the attainment of a culture of human rights and a respect for the rule of law; and
- a determination to make it impossible for the gross violations of human rights of the past to happen again.

South Africa, in company with many other countries, had to face up to three critical questions:

- First, how do emerging democracies deal with past violations of human rights?
- Second, how do new democratic governments deal with leaders and individuals who were responsible for disappearances, death squads, psychological and physical torture, and other violations of human rights?
- Third, how does a new democracy deal with the fact that some of the perpetrators remain part of the new government and/or security forces or hold important positions in public life?

Hayner reminds us that there have been nineteen truth commissions in sixteen countries over the last twenty years, including those in formation.[1] In the work leading up to the appointment of the TRC, we were greatly influenced and assisted in studying many of these commissions, particularly those in Chile and Argentina.

There were several choices open to South Africa as it sought to come to terms with its past. First, a blanket or general amnesty was proposed. This was strongly preferred by the former government, led by President Frederik W. de Klerk, as well as the security forces, including the military and the police. This option, however, was untenable for the African National Congress (ANC), representing the majority of people who had suffered gross human rights violations in the past.

The second option was that of calling to account those who were directly responsible for the gross human rights violations that took place and of putting them on trial and prosecuting them so that justice could be seen to be done. This approach, akin to the Nuremberg Trials, was for a very long period strongly supported by the members of the liberation movements while they were still in exile.

As Thabo Mbeki, then Deputy President of South Africa, put it, "Within the ANC the cry was to 'catch the bastards and hang them' but we realised that you could not simultaneously prepare for a peaceful transition. If we had not taken this route I don't know where the country would be today. Had there been a threat of Nuremberg-style trials over members of the apartheid security establishment we would never have undergone the peaceful change."[2]

A third option was the one that gained majority support—to appoint a special commission that was at first referred to as a "truth commission" and was later introduced formally as a "truth and reconciliation commission." This commission would offer the possibility of truth relating to victims and perpetrators, the restoration of dignity for victims and survivors, a limited amnesty, and a search for healing and reconciliation.

Richard Goldstone, a judge on the Constitutional Court of South Africa, put it this way, "The decision to opt for a Truth and Reconciliation Commission was an important compromise. If the ANC had insisted on Nuremberg-style trials for the leaders of the former apartheid government, there would have been no peaceful transition to democracy, and if the former government had insisted on blanket amnesty then, similarly, the negotiations would have broken down. A bloody revolution sooner rather than later would have been inevitable. The Truth and Reconciliation Commission is therefore a bridge from the old to the new."[3]

While there can be little doubt that Mbeki's commitment to "a peaceful transition" was a valid reason for not following the Nuremberg option, there can be no doubt that the strength of the right-wing and state military and security forces was a major factor that informed choices at the negotiating table. Mbeki made it absolutely clear, in a private interview with President Nelson Mandela, that senior generals of the security forces had personally warned him of dire consequences if members of the security forces had to face compulsory trials and prosecutions following the election. According to

Mandela, they threatened to make a peaceful election totally impossible. Some compromise had to be made and, in the postamble of the Interim Constitution, provision was made for the granting of amnesty to advance reconciliation and reconstruction and for its legislative implementation.

The point has already been made that South Africa learned a great deal from other countries who had undergone transitions toward democracy, but there are some unique features to the South African model.

Unique Features of the South African Model

The process by which South Africa arrived at its commission is quite different from any other that I know. It was essentially democratic and gave as many people as possible an opportunity to participate in the formation of the TRC.

The idea of a truth commission came first from the ANC prior to the election in 1994. Ironically, that is, seen against the background of widespread human rights violations committed by the South African state over many decades, the ANC was accused of perpetrating human rights violations in some of its camps while in exile. The response of the ANC was to appoint an internal commission of inquiry. A report was published, but there was considerable criticism in that it lacked impartiality. A second independent commission was appointed.

Its findings were made known to the national executive of the ANC, and its decision was that there were grounds for criticism, but that the critique should be seen against the overall human rights violations that had gripped South Africa over a very long period. The way to resolve this question was to appoint a truth commission.

A very important contribution was made by Kader Asmal when he held the Chair of Human Rights at the University of the Western Cape and delivered an inaugural lecture entitled "Victims, Survivors and Citizens—Human Rights, Reparations and Reconciliation."[4] Many who either heard or read the lecture lent their voices in support of South Africa having its own commission.

Two major conferences were held under the auspices of Justice in Transition, a nongovernmental organization. The first, entitled "Dealing with the Past," was held in 1994 in Cape Town. A number of leading scholars and human rights practitioners from Eastern Europe, Central Europe, and South America were invited to share their experiences with South Africans. A book was published under the title of the conference, *Dealing with the Past: Truth & Reconciliation in South Africa*, and was distributed widely throughout South Africa.[5]

A second conference, held in July of the same year, also in Cape Town, was entitled "Truth and Reconciliation." The majority of participants were from

South Africa, but there were key participants from Chile and Argentina as well. Dullah Omar, the Minister of Justice, who had been appointed soon after the election, was the keynote speaker. He outlined the idea of a commission, notice of which he had already announced in Parliament. A second book was published by Justice in Transition under the title *The Healing of a Nation?*[6] A number of workshops and conferences were held throughout South Africa to look at the concept of a truth and reconciliation commission, and these deliberations contributed significantly to the final model.

Input from civil society was placed before the Parliamentary Standing Committee on Justice, which was charged with the finalization of the necessary legislation. Public hearings were held, and these were followed by the debate in Parliament itself, where the Promotion of National Unity and Reconciliation Bill was finally passed by an overwhelming majority.

One further contribution to the democratic process was Mandela's decision to appoint a small, representative committee consisting of individuals from major political parties and civil society who together accepted responsibility for the selection process leading to the appointment of members of the TRC. People from all walks of life were encouraged to nominate potential appointees and about three hundred names were received by the selection committee. After a lengthy process, which involved public hearings, the committee sent twenty-five names to Mandela, and he, in consultation with his cabinet, appointed seventeen commissioners.

From the very outset, the process leading to the actual promulgation of the Act as well as the appointment of the commissioners was as open, as transparent, and as democratic as possible.

Parliamentary Legislation

The act of Parliament that brought the TRC into being was very different from that of other commissions. In most instances, commissions have been appointed by the president or prime minister of the country concerned. They have had to work out their own procedures, objectives, methodologies, and other concerns. The benefit of a commission being based in an act of parliament is that a democratically elected group of people participated in the debate and finalized the content of the commission. Objectives were clearly set out, restraints were laid down, and the commissioners had to abide by the act.

In the South African Act, provision was made for seventeen commissioners, serving full-time. The Act also provided for three separate committees:

- The Human Rights Committee, which conducted public hearings for victims and survivors. A prescribed form was made available for all applicants to complete.

While many victims and survivors appeared in public before the TRC, thousands more completed the application form itself. Nearly 23,000 applications were received before the TRC ended. The first public hearings for victims and survivors took place in East London in 1996.

- The Reparation and Rehabilitation Committee, which was charged with developing a policy for long-term reparations as well as urgent interim relief. It was decided very early not to finalize any such policy until the Human Rights Committee hearings were complete so that the policy could be informed by the victims/survivors themselves.
- The Amnesty Committee, which heard applications for amnesty through 2000.

A critical decision, made during the Standing Committee hearings, opened the TRC to the media and to the general public. Doing so placed a heavy burden on the commissioners, who traveled throughout South Africa conducting hearings. They were constantly under the scrutiny of the media and the public. The entire nation thus participated in the hearings and the work of the commission from the very beginning through radio, television, and print media. Anyone could attend any of the hearings. Transparency was assured. Also, this method ensured a strong educative opportunity so that truth-telling, healing, and reconciliation were not confined to a small group but were available to the entire nation.

Powers Granted to the Commission

A further difference from most commissions is the powers that were vested in the TRC. The commission had powers of subpoena and of search and seizure. This enabled the TRC to invite alleged perpetrators, or those who might have critical information, to come before the TRC.

It also meant that the TRC could secure files and documents that had been secreted away by the previous government and its agents. Thus, agreements were made by political parties and by military and security institutions to make public submissions to the commission.

The South African model also widened the mandate to include public hearings of major institutions such as political parties, the legal system, business, labor and health sectors, the faith communities, and the armed forces.

Amnesty Provisions

The provision of amnesty to perpetrators of gross human rights violations had been and is a source of heated debate and controversy. South Africa did not escape this debate. Many prominent jurists and human rights activists were totally opposed to any form of amnesty. "Blanket amnesty" is inherently contradictory.

> "How can I ever have peace when every day I risk meeting my unpunished torturer in the neighbourhood?"
>   (Tortured ex–political prisoner, Argentina, in a personal discussion with the author when he visited Argentina in 1996.)

> "How is reconciliation possible when lies and denials are institutionalised by the responsible authorities?"
>   (Human rights activist, Santiago, Chile, 1996; in the author's discussion with a mother whose son had "disappeared.")

and

> "No government can forgive. No commission can forgive. They don't know my pain—only I can forgive and I must know before I can forgive."
>   (Widow testifying to a TRC amnesty hearing in South Africa in 1997.)[7]

A serious question that faced all involved in the process leading up to the TRC was, How does it limit crass impunity? There is, of course, considerable merit in securing justice that is achieved through prosecution and that does strike a blow at impunity. Further, it is such a process that helps to give back to victims in some measure their personal and social dignity and to an extent can expose the truth. But this process has limitations. Full justice is not always possible in a society in transition.

My own view was that when considering historic human rights violations committed during a period of oppression and conflict, the historical, political, and social circumstances as well as the nature of the particular transition must be borne in mind. In the case of South Africa, the resolution of conflict was through negotiation, not through victory on the field of battle, nor through the collapse of a former regime. Inevitably, negotiation politics involved a search for consensus, and this includes compromise.

Even when a war crimes tribunal has been appointed, it is not always possible to fulfill in its entirety the mandate to bring to book all of those who were directly involved in gross human rights violations. In the former Yugoslavia and in Rwanda it will not be possible to bring all those implicated in gross human rights violations before tribunals. In addition, criminal prosecutions are time-consuming, and securing evidence leading to a conviction is often problematic. Most countries are unable to afford costly trials, so relatively few will be prosecuted. The majority of offenders will go free.

A very important point to make is that in war crimes tribunals the final word is punishment. But in a deeply divided society this cannot be the final word if healing and reconciliation are to be achieved. Stern measures have to be taken against genocide, but consideration must always be given to reconciliation so that the risk of the process being repeated is to some extent diminished. There is a strong case for a mechanism similar to a truth and reconciliation commission to be introduced into countries that have experienced widespread conflict and remain deeply divided.

In the South African case, attempts were made to limit impunity. The first decision was to reject a general amnesty. In many other ways the amnesty provisions have tried to ensure that amnesty is not something cheap and easily accessible:

- First, amnesty had to be applied for on an individual basis—there was no blanket amnesty.
- Second, applicants for amnesty had to complete a prescribed form that called for very detailed information relating to specific human rights violations.
- Third, applicants had to make a "full disclosure" of their human rights violations in order to qualify for amnesty.
- Fourth, in most instances applicants had to appear before the Amnesty Committee in open hearings.
- Fifth, there was a time limit set in terms of the Act. Only those gross human rights violations committed in the period 1960 to 1994 were considered for amnesty. Then, there was a specified period during which amnesty applications had to be made, from the time of the promulgation of the Act, which was in December 1995, to 10 May 1997.
- Finally, a list of criteria laid down in the Act determined whether the applicant for amnesty would be successful.

Whether a particular act, omission, or offence is an act associated with a political objective was decided with reference to the following criteria:

- the motive of the person who committed the act, omission, or offence;
- the context in which the act, omission, or offence took place, and, in particular, whether the act, omission or offence was committed in the course of or as part of a political uprising, disturbance, or event, or in reaction thereto;
- the legal and factual nature of the act, omission, or offence, including the gravity of the act, omission, or offence;
- the object or objective of the act, omission, or offence and in particular whether the act, omission, or offence was primarily directed at a political opponent or state property, at personnel, or against private property or individuals;
- whether the act, omission, or offence was committed in the execution of an order of, or on behalf of, or with the approval of, the organization, institution, liberation movement, or body of which the person who committed the act was a member, an agent, or a supporter; and
- the relationship between the act, omission, or offence and the political objective

pursued, and in particular the directness and proximity of the relationship and the proportionality of the act, omission, or offence to the objective pursued.

However, it did not include the following criteria:

* for personal gain: provided that an act, omission, or offence by any person who acted and received money or anything of value as an informer of the State or a former state, political organization, or liberation movement shall not be excluded only on the grounds of that person having received money or anything of value for his or her information; or
* out of personal malice, ill-will, or spite, directed against the victim of the acts committed.

Finally, it is important to bear in mind that the truth and reconciliation process was not a substitute for criminal justice. A number of trials and prosecutions took place simultaneously with the work of the TRC. The combination of judicial stick and TRC carrot emerged as a potent force in flushing out former operatives who adopted a "wait-and-see" approach in relation to the commission.

Notwithstanding the above, there were problems relating to the amnesty provisions. There were those in South Africa—some organizations and individual families—who had suffered very grievously from human rights violations and believed that there ought to have been no amnesty provisions whatsoever. They wanted nothing more and nothing less than trials, prosecutions, and punishment. More especially, they were concerned that in terms of the act those who applied for amnesty and were successful would never again be liable, either criminally or civilly. Some were even prepared to accept that if one had to pursue the way of amnesty as a price for peace and stability in South Africa, there still ought to have been an opportunity to bring civil actions against either the organization, the state, or the individual.

There were those who felt so strongly about the question of amnesty that they brought a case against the TRC before the Constitutional Court of South Africa. The court ruled in favor of the TRC. It did so on the grounds that the Constitution (Section 33) sanctioned the right of limitation to access to the court based on the postamble of the Constitution granting amnesty. It also held that the amnesty provisions were not inconsistent with international norms and did not breach South Africa's obligations in terms of public international law instruments. It relied on the distinctions between conflicts between parties within the same state versus, for example, conflicts between a colonial power and a struggle for self-determination against colonial and alien domination. Despite this ruling, there still remained deep-seated opposition to the amnesty provisions.

On the other hand, there was also a strong view that if reconciliation was to become a reality in South Africa, both victim and perpetrator had to be encouraged to participate in the life and work of the TRC. The dilemma was that if people were encouraged to apply for amnesty but were still liable in a criminal court or in a civil court, what would be the incentive for their coming forward? There needed to be a window, or a period of grace, to give public expression to private grief and suffering and to grant a second chance to those who participated in gross human rights violations under particular circumstances and during a particular period in a country in conflict.

South Africa's experience is very similar to that of many other countries in that witness after witness at the Human Rights Committee hearings emphasized their deep fundamental need to know the truth surrounding the loss of a loved one. Over and over again people pleaded to know what happened to a father, a mother, a sister, a brother, a son, or a daughter. They wanted to know where he or she was buried. They wanted to know why they were killed and under what circumstances. This was a common refrain at every public hearing. Almost exactly the same set of words has been used by witnesses whether they lived in South America, Northern Ireland, or South Africa. Their plea in different languages has been, "I want to forgive but I must know who to forgive and for what." In other words, knowing the details and circumstances of the human rights violation in itself is part of the healing process.

But how will they know the truth if perpetrators do not come forward? The fact of the matter is that repression and concealment have been with South Africa for generations. There is very little likelihood of new evidence coming to light or even witnesses being prepared to testify. The only way victims were going to know some of the truth was for perpetrators to tell their stories. This may have been small comfort, but in terms of the pleas of victims it was of some consolation to them as they tried to reconstruct their lives.

Truth revealed offered not only comfort and peace of mind but also a limited form of justice. Amnesty was a price that South Africa had to pay for a relatively peaceful transition. It was also a price many victims had to pay in order to know some of the truth of their horrendous past.

Amnesty was the price South Africa paid for a free and fair election and a relatively peaceful transition. The haunting question, which has yet to be answered, is, Are the needs and objectives of the state synonymous with those of the violated individual?

Essentially, the TRC was committed to the development of a human rights culture and a respect for the rule of law in South Africa. In this sense, the commission was not so much about the past as it was about coming to terms with contemporary challenges and future goals. It is, however, impossible to cope with the present, invaded as it is by the dark shadows of the past, and it is impossible to plan with any certainty for the future without jettisoning some of the baggage from the past that threatens to overwhelm and paralyze every effort. In attempting to build for the future there is an irreducible minimum, and that is a commitment to truth. As President Patricio Aylwin of Chile said when he assumed office in 1990:

> This leaves the excruciating problem of human rights violations and other violent crimes which have caused so many victims and so much suffering in the past. They are an open wound in our national soul that cannot be ignored. Nor can it heal merely through mere forgetfulness.
>
> To close our eyes and pretend none of this ever happened would be to maintain at the core of our society a source of pain, division, hatred and violence. Only the disclosure of the truth and the search for justice can create the moral climate in which reconciliation and peace will flourish.[8]

However costly the search for truth and knowing the truth might be, it is of fundamental importance if South Africa is to achieve a degree of peace and unity.

South Africa has come out of a period in which its society was based on lies and deceit. Radio and television were little more than giant propaganda factories producing a packaged product to reinforce oppression and exclusivity. The search for truth and the recording of that truth exorcised the fantasy of denial that makes transformation impossible.

A critical question is What kind of truth-telling lay at the heart of the TRC's work? The TRC distinguished four kinds of truth. First, there is *factual or forensic truth*. The act that governed the work of the TRC required it to "prepare a comprehensive report which sets out its activities and findings based on factual and objective information and evidence collected or received by it or placed at its disposal" [Section 4(e)].

This mandate operated at two levels. First, for findings at an individual level. The TRC was required to make findings on particular incidents with regard to specific people—concerning what happened to whom; where, when, and how; and who was involved. In order to fulfill this mandate, the TRC adopted an inclusive policy of verification and corroboration to ensure that findings were based on accurate and factual information.

At the second level, the TRC was responsible for findings on contexts, causes, and patterns of violations. It was this search for patterns underlying gross human rights violations that engaged the commission at a very broad and deep level.

While the TRC, through its Investigative Unit, database, and research, attempted to perform with the highest degree of efficiency, there are always limits in the search for truth and even in truth telling.

Ignatieff's words are pertinent:

> All that a truth commission can achieve is to reduce the number of lies that can be circulated unchallenged in public discourse. In Argentina, its work has made it

impossible to claim, for example, that the military did not throw half-dead victims in the sea from helicopters. In Chile, it is no longer permissible to assert in public that the Pinochet regime did not dispatch thousands of entirely innocent people.[9]

In South Africa, it is no longer possible for so many people to claim that "they did not know." It has become impossible to claim that the practice of torture by state security forces was not systematic and widespread, to claim that only a few "rotten eggs" or "bad apples" committed gross violations of human rights. It has become impossible to claim that accounts of gross human rights violations in ANC camps were merely the consequence of state disinformation.

The second kind of truth is *personal and/or narrative truth*. Through the telling of their own stories, both victims and perpetrators gave meaning to their multilayered experiences of the South African story. Through the media these personal truths have been communicated to the broader public. Oral tradition was a central feature of the commission's process. Explicit in the Act was an affirmation of the healing potential of truth telling.

One of the objectives of the TRC was to "restore the human and civil dignity of victims by granting them an opportunity to relate their own accounts of the violations of which they [were] the victims."[10] The stories listened to did not come to us as "arguments" or claims as in a court of law. They were often heart-wrenching, conveying unique insights into the pain of our past. To listen to one man relate how his wife and baby were cruelly murdered is much more powerful than all the statistics in the world, and it gives insight into the conflicts of the past.

By facilitating the telling of "stories," the TRC not only helped to uncover the existing facts about past abuses but also assisted in the creation of "narrative truth." The TRC contributed to the process of reconciliation by giving voice to individual subjective experiences. The TRC was about the task of "restored" memory and humanity.[11]

The third truth is *social or "dialogical" truth*. Judge Albie Sachs, even before the TRC began its work, talked about "microscope truth" and "dialogue truth." "The first—microscopic truth—is factual and verifiable and can be documented and proved. Dialogue truth, on the other hand, is social truth, truth of experience that is established through interaction, discussion and debate."[12]

Finally, there is *healing and restorative truth*. The Act required the TRC to look back to the past and forward to the future. The truth the TRC was required to establish contributed to the reparation of the damage inflicted and to the prevention of it ever happening again. But, for healing to be a possibility, knowledge in itself is not enough. Knowledge must be accompanied by *acknowledgment* of accountability. Public acknowledgment that thousands of South Africans had paid a very high price for democracy affirmed the human dignity of the victims and survivors. It was an integral part of the healing of the South African society.

South Africans desperately needed to create a *common memory* that could be acknowledged by those who created and implemented the apartheid system, by those who fought against it, and by the many more who were in the middle and claimed not to know what was happening in their country.

Reconciliation

The TRC was criticized from its very inception. Yet, these were its goals:

- To establish the truth in relation to past events as well as the motives for and circumstances in which gross violations of human rights have occurred, and to make the findings known in order to prevent a repetition of such acts in the future.
- To pursue national unity. The well-being of all South African citizens and peace require reconciliation between the peoples of South Africa and the reconstruction of society.
- To obtain understanding but not vengeance. There was a need for reparation but not for retaliation—a need for *ubuntu* but not for victimization.
- To advance reconciliation and reconstruction. Amnesty was to be granted in respect of acts, omissions, and offenses associated with political objectives committed in the course of the conflicts of the past.

There is a Zulu saying that "all truth is bitter," and there is no doubt that many in South Africa found the disclosures made by the TRC unpalatable. Many victims and survivors had to revisit their own experiences of grief and mourning, while those who claimed not to know that gross human rights violations were taking place have had to come to terms with the fact that either their eyes were tightly shut or they actually did know what was happening but preferred not to acknowledge it. This is never easy individually or collectively.

It is for this last reason, possibly, that there was so much direct opposition to the TRC. A number of individuals, through their lawyers, took the TRC to court, in the main protesting against the lack of due process. The National Party, always lukewarm if not hostile to the TRC, finally decided to take the chairperson and the deputy chairperson of the commission to court, demanding a public apology from the former and the resignation of the latter. The Inkatha Freedom Party referred a long list of complaints against the TRC to the nation's Public Protector.

Many white Afrikaners accused the TRC of being biased and one-sided. They made their feelings known in newspapers and on radio and television programs, but also in anonymous letters, many of which were extremely threatening. Some of the commissioners received a barrage of anonymous

phone calls, including death threats. The TRC was not only born in controversy, with very powerful constituencies opposed to it at its very inception, but
that opposition continued. What price then reconciliation?

It must be conceded that although the opportunities presented by the appointment of the TRC were far-reaching, nevertheless there were clear limitations as well. In the same way, the healing of a nation and the bringing about
of a genuine reconciliation could not be achieved merely by holding conferences or writing books. There is no guarantee that through the life and work
of the TRC healing and reconciliation was automatically guaranteed.

Discussion, debate, analysis, listening, and the recording of the truth can
constitute a significant part of the healing process, but only that. Much, much
more will need to take place over many years. The wounds incurred in the long
and bitter period of repression and resistance are too deep to be trivialized by
imagining that a single initiative can on its own bring about a peaceful, stable,
and restored society. In particular, it must be restated that without measurable
steps taken to address the ever-widening gap between wealth and poverty,
conflict rather than reconciliation will be the order of the day.

At best the TRC could, through its work and through its recommendations,
lay down what could be termed building blocks that could point to the possibility of coexistence, and of mutual respect, leading to the long, difficult, and
painful process of reconciliation. That in itself was a significant contribution.

The TRC achieved the following:

First, it broke the deathly silence surrounding the grotesque consequences
of apartheid. The TRC was enjoined to "establish as complete a picture as
possible of gross human rights violations perpetrated between 1960 and 1994
by conducting investigations and hearings."[13] These investigations and hearings were not merely scientific and legal but also essentially human. Thousands of victims and survivors from all parts of South Africa appeared before
the TRC and told their simple and yet powerful stories of human suffering
and indignity. As a consequence, the stories of victimization and human rights
violations have been told not merely in statistics and incidents but with a
poignant human voice. Furthermore, the victims/survivors themselves have
experienced a degree of catharsis because, for the very first time, they have
been received by a compassionate and a sympathetic state-appointed commission. Their experience prior to this was of a hostile state. When loved ones
were missing, those left went first to the local police station and were treated
in many instances as nuisances, and in many more as people who were of no
consequence. When they went to state hospitals looking for sons and daugh-
ters and fathers and mothers, they received similar treatment. It was no better
when they went to the mortuary in a final attempt to find a missing person. In
going before the TRC, they were being received publicly, with dignity.

Second, against the background of a country where for decades a cover-up was the order of the day and propaganda masqueraded as truth, the TRC's ability to bring forth truths thus far not known was perhaps one of its greatest contributions to an open society. Many victims who never had known who had taken their loved ones into custody, where they had been taken, under what circumstances, the nature of the torture, and the manner of the killing, now know. Perpetrators came forward, not in their scores, not in their hundreds, but in their thousands, to confess their involvement in gross human rights violations. The truth, in no small measure, was uncovered. There has an emerging pattern that helped to create an understanding and appreciation of what had taken place in a climate created by politicians and in a system implemented by generals and by foot soldiers.

There was also not only an accumulation of knowledge but, in many instances, of acknowledgment. Through the hearings of major institutions, including political parties, the business and labor sectors, the health community, the media, the judiciary, the faith community, and others, many people publicly acknowledged their own collusion with apartheid. This acknowledgment should never be underestimated in a generous response from those who have been victimized and indeed dehumanized in the past. The generosity of spirit by the majority of victims/survivors was one of the most remarkable experiences of those of us who sat on the commission, and this feeling spilled over into the wider community.

Acknowledgment went one step further. The TRC made it impossible particularly for white South Africans, to continue to declare "I did not know." If they did not know then, they certainly know now. It takes a conscious effort to avoid the story of South Africa's TRC.

A remarkable feature of the commission was the media coverage of its progress. There was hardly a day since the beginning of 1996 to late 1998 when newspapers did not feature the TRC, either on their front pages or in editorials and feature articles. As far as television was concerned, hardly a day went by without the life and work of the TRC being featured on its major news bulletins, over and above a highly professional and effective one-hour weekly program on a major television station. But radio probably had a greater impact. Not only were hearings broadcast live throughout South Africa for four hours per day, but broadcasts, commentaries, discussions, and debates featured prominently in all the eleven languages used in South Africa so that even those unable to read or write participated in the developing story emerging from the work of the TRC.

Finally, within the restraints of a negotiated settlement, major compromises were made. It can be argued that the TRC, despite those restraints, has achieved the best possible outcome. South Africa decided to say no to amnesia and yes to remembrance; to say no to full-scale prosecutions and trials and yes to forgiveness. South Africa chose the third way. Those who committed violations of human rights, if they applied for amnesty, in many instances went free. In South Africa's circumstances, where there was no victor and vanquished, it had no real alternative.

For South Africa, as in many other countries, the central tension is between the politics of compromise and a radical notion of justice. This tension has been expressed in different ways by different analyses of the process from authoritarian rule in South America and Eastern Europe to a democratic form of government, and it is a genuinely universal issue.

Political scientists state the dilemma somewhat more pragmatically. For them, it is the need for democratic or stable democratization as against the notion of justice, equality, and restitution.

Another way of stating the tension is to distinguish between retributive justice on the one hand and a prudential focus on the common good and future injustice on the other. The former is the Nuremberg model, based on the positive duty of successive governments to dispense justice for past crimes. That approach, as an analysis of the Nuremberg trials will reveal, has very real limitations and, indeed, challenges the very notion of justice itself. Furthermore, many countries emerge from a totalitarian system not via a military victory but through a state of collapse and/or through negotiation and therefore have to deal with the messy business of compromise. Restorative rather than retributive justice can be a potent force for transformation and healing.

In South Africa the transition was essentially determined by a political compromise, and a recurring question was, Was there a moral basis to that compromise?

In a real sense there was. It is morally defensible to argue that amnesty was the price South Africa had to pay for peace and stability. Whether in fact a military coup was a reality or not, these things are certain: if negotiation politics had not succeeded the bitter conflict would have continued, many more human rights violations would have occurred, and hundreds, possibly thousands, would have been killed. Hard choices had to be made, and it does not follow that the choices that were made lie easily on the consciences of the politicians who made them. The alternative was far less desirable, and potentially much more destructive.

One of the overarching problems that the TRC faced was the unwillingness of some political leaders to accept accountability for the past. As in so many other parts of the world it was the foot soldiers, the middle management of the security forces, and even the generals who were blamed for implementing the policies and laws devised by political parties and political leaders.

The political leaders of the previous regime found it excruciatingly difficult to assume accountability for the consequences of the racial laws that they placed on the statute book. They found it even more difficult to accept that the climate created by those laws made it possible for gross human rights violations to occur.

The moral order can only be restored when the process begins where people make the laws; that is, in parliament. It can only flourish when judges and magistrates interpret those laws for the benefit of the disadvantaged, the oppressed, and the poor. Reconciliation begins when new laws and their interpretation are implemented. Without political will and courage they remain words and phrases with no life.

This has begun to emerge in South Africa. In the TRC, in government, in civil society, and in the professions, there is a determination that what was experienced in the past must never happen again. It is this new spirit, this commitment, that was primarily the TRC's greatest contribution to a country emerging from a very dark night of the soul into a new day.

Notes

1. Priscilla B. Hayner, "Fifteen Truth Commissions—1974 to 1994: A Comparative Study," *Human Rights Quarterly* XVI (1994): 597–655.

2. Interview *Cape Times*, 24 February 1997.

3. Hauser Lecture, New York University, 22 January 1997.

4. Inaugural Lecture, University of Western Cape, 25 May 1992.

5. Alex Boraine, Janet Levy, and Ronel Scheffer (eds.), *Dealing with the Past: Truth & Reconciliation in South Africa* (Cape Town, 1994; 2d ed., 1996).

6. Alex Boraine and Janet Levy (eds.), *The Healing of a Nation?* (Cape Town, 1995).

7. The citations for these quotes are in the text.

8. Speech given in Chile's parliament, 1990.

9. Michael Ignatieff, "Articles of Faith," *Index of Censorship* V (1996): 113.

10. The Promotion of National Unity and Reconciliation Act, 1995.

11. Antjie Krog, "The South African Road," in Boraine, *Dealing*, 118.

12. Ibid., 105.

13. The Promotion of National Unity and Reconciliation Act, 1995.

VIII

The Uses of Truth Commissions

LESSONS FOR THE WORLD

DUMISA B. NTSEBEZA

THERE are some ways in which the South African Truth and Reconciliation Commission (TRC) is a unique experience; by all accounts it captured the imagination of the world, having attracted as it has done not only the local media attention but also the world media. We can justifiably make a case for what could possibly, or rather even, *should* inform other truth commissions in the future.[1]

The Promotion of National Unity and Reconciliation Act 34 of 1995, as amended, was established essentially to investigate and establish as complete a picture as possible of the nature, causes, and extent of gross violations of human rights that were committed during the thirty-four years, 1960 to 1994. These gross violations of human rights were to be investigated insofar as they emanated from the conflicts of the past. The Act also enjoined the TRC to establish the fate or whereabouts of the victims of such violations.

The Act provided for the granting of amnesty to persons who made a full disclosure of all the relevant facts relating to acts associated with a political motive, committed in the course of the conflicts of the past during the thirty-four-year period. The Act also prescribed that victims should be afforded an opportunity to relate the violations they suffered. The TRC had to take measures aimed at the granting of reparations and at the rehabilitation and the restoration of the human and civil dignity of all victims of gross violations of human rights.

The Act evolved from the postamble to the Interim Constitution Act 200 of 1993, which came at the end of a four-year-long negotiation process that itself was a consequence of a political compromise between the contending parties. It recognized that:

1. South Africa's past was that of a deeply divided society characterized by strife, conflict, untold suffering, and injustice.

2. The future had the potential of being founded on the recognition of human rights, democracy, and peaceful coexistence and development opportunities for all South Africans, irrespective of color, race, class, belief, or sex.

3. There was a need for reconciliation between the people of South Africa in order for peace and national unity to endure and for reconstruction of society to take place.

4. Whereas in the past, humanitarian principles were transgressed, leaving South Africa with a legacy of hatred, fear, guilt, and revenge, the new Constitution, guaranteeing as it did rights and freedoms to individuals, laid a secure foundation on the basis of which there could be understanding instead of revenge, reparation instead of retaliation, *ubuntu* instead of victimization.

5. Central to the whole reconciliation process and the reconstruction of society, the postamble stated, was the requirement to grant amnesty in respect of acts, omissions, and offenses associated with political objectives and committed in the course of the conflicts of the past.

The postamble was a recognition that the political transition that spelled the death of apartheid was neither a reform of apartheid nor a revolutionary overthrow of the apartheid order. It was a negotiated settlement, a political compromise—one that produced a constitution that provided for the establishment of "mechanisms, criteria and procedures, including tribunals, if any, through which amnesty shall be dealt with at any time after the law has been passed."

That South Africa could only go the route of the TRC and not the way, for example, of the war crimes tribunal in The Hague seems to have been captured in the judgment of the South African Constitutional Court, *Azanian Peoples Organization (AZAPO) and Others v. President of the Republic of South Africa and Others*, 1996(4) SA 671(CC).

In that judgment, Justice Ismail Mahomed quoted with approval:

The call to punish human rights criminals can present complex and agonising problems that have no single or simple solution. While the debate over the Nuremberg trials still goes on, that episode—trials of war criminals of a defeated nation—was simplicity itself as compared to the subtle and dangerous issues that can divide a country when it undertakes to punish its own violators. A nation divided during a repressive regime does not emerge suddenly united when the time of repression has passed. The human rights criminals are fellow citizens, living alongside everyone else, and they may be very powerful and dangerous. If the army and the police have been the agencies of terror, the soldiers and the cops aren't going to turn overnight into paragons of respect for human rights. Their numbers and their expert management of deadly weapons remain significant facts of life. . . . The soldiers and the police may be biding their time, waiting and conspiring to return to power. They may be seeking to keep or win sympathisers in the population at large. If they are treated too harshly—or if the net of punishment is cast too widely—there may be a backlash that plays into their hands. But their victims cannot simply forgive and forget.

These problems are not abstract generalities. They describe tough realities in more than a dozen countries. If, as we hope, more nations are freed from regimes of terror, similar problems will continue to arise.

Since the situations vary, the nature of the problems varies from place to place.[2]

Despite its critics, and despite the view of others that Nuremberg-type trials should have been the option, the TRC process was the only one possible in the conditions of transition in 1994.[3]

What lessons can be drawn from the South African and other truth commissions?

Civil and Human Dignity to Victims

One of the enduring aims and objectives of the TRC was to restore to victims of gross violations of human rights their civil and human dignity by providing them with an opportunity to tell their own stories of victimhood.

This aspect was movingly confirmed by Nohle Mohapi, the wife of Mapetla Mohapi. Mapetla had been a leader in the Black Consciousness Movement. In 1977 he was arrested and detained in terms of the then very notorious Section 6 of the Terrorism Act of 1967, which provided, *inter alia*, for solitary confinement in conditions where only the security police had access to a detained person; no lawyer, friend, or relative could have access to a detainee for an indefinite period.

Mohapi had been found hanged in his cell, with a suicide note. This immediately became an area of contestation; Mrs. Mohapi claimed that her husband had been murdered by the state. All her efforts, through the legal processes of an inquest and civil action, came to naught. Instead, she was mulcted with huge costs, and at every appearance she was made to feel that she was the guilty party—*she* was the troublemaker. Her only sin was seeking to know the truth about what had happened to her husband.

Nineteen years later, after the very first TRC hearings with her, she told the media that she finally felt relieved. The TRC environment had been friendly. For the first time, she felt dignified and honored because she was testifying before people who seemed to understand the pain she had carried for almost two decades. The TRC seemed to believe her, which was a new experience.

The TRC realized that it had never known what the process was doing to victims. It struck us members of the TRC that the mere opportunity for victims to tell their stories was so important for them that the TRC would have been remiss—in its endeavor to heal those wounded by the evils of the past—had it not allowed them to do so. Besides, it was clear that Mrs. Mohapi had been relieved when she realized that her matter was now going genuinely to be investigated—that every genuine effort would be made to discover the truth.

That made her feel dignified. That gave her a sense that her civil dignity as an equal citizen before the law was being taken seriously and respected.

Mrs. Mohapi exemplified a number of victims and survivors whose civil and human dignity were restored by being able to tell their stories to the TRC. Her experience was reminiscent of a second story. On being asked by the TRC chairman to sit down before and during a testimony, a woman remarked that in all the years that she had dealt with officialdom around issues of her victimization, she had never been asked to sit down. It made a lot of difference to her and to her sense of dignity.

Criminal Justice and the Exposure of Truth

The amnesty process has rightly been condemned as one that provides perpetrators of the most heinous crimes with an opportunity to walk the streets as free persons. Subject to certain conditions, the process also involves the suspension of civil and criminal proceedings pending the consideration and disposal of the application for amnesty.[4]

The amnesty provision engendered much debate and, in one instance involved a litigation process right up to the Constitutional Court.[5] There are those who have argued that the amnesty process is an unconscionable betrayal of the feelings of the victims. It allows them to escape retributory justice. The argument has been strongly made that only criminal justice, in the sense of making sure that those who have committed terrible deeds are tried, convicted, and sent to jail, is the answer for criminal acts committed in the past. Punishment is the only form of justice that perpetrators of violence, torture, and severe ill-treatment can ever hope to get. Indeed, Griffiths Mxenge's brother, an outspoken critic of the amnesty process, and one of the applicants in the AZAPO case, strongly argued that the least that should have happened, to the murderers of his brother was that they should have been sentenced after conviction (after which the president, in the exercise of his prerogative, could grant them amnesty after they had served a significant period of imprisonment).[6]

The first critique of this argument is that it assumes that there has always been evidence available for a successful prosecution. The reality, of course, is that no such evidence has been available. Nor was there a willingness on the part of the apartheid establishment to do anything with the available evidence. Either evidence was destroyed, or the state machinery covered up all traces.

A case in point is that of the so-called Cradock Four, United Democratic Front (UDF) activists, among them Matthew Goniwe, who were murdered in 1985 between Cradock and Port Elizabeth, in South Africa. There had always been a popular belief that the police had killed them, but no evidence could be found. The criminal justice system provided for an inquest before a magistrate.

At the inquest, the legal representatives of the police argued the likelihood that the UDF activists had fallen victim to an internecine war of attrition between the UDF and AZAPO—another incidence of the so-called black-on-black violence. They pushed this thesis so strongly that it is known that one of the family lawyers began to believe it. The eventual finding was that no one was to blame. The truth was thoroughly suppressed or, at best, confused through the criminal justice system. The families still suffered from non-confirmation of their suspicions. The law had not availed them.

About four years later, a second inquest was held, now before the Judge President of the Eastern Cape Provincial Division. This second inquest had been sparked off by a note from Colonel Lourens du Plessis, then an operative of Military Intelligence, to Brigadier Joffel van der Westhuizen of the South African Defence Force (Special Forces). The note was to the effect that Matthew Goniwe, Sparrow Mkonto, Mbulelo Goniwe, and others were to be "permanently removed from society." As it turned out, Goniwe and Mkonto (with Fort Calata and Sicelo Mhlawuli) had indeed been murdered. Despite the note, and despite the matter being heard by a judge president, truth suffered. This time, the judge found that he could not find, as fact, whether it was the army or the police who had murdered the four activists, although he was satisfied that one or the other had been responsible.

Truth suffered after this second attempt by the families to learn what had happened to their loved ones. The law courts could not provide the answer. Once again, the perpetrators got off and the families were deprived of an opportunity to reconcile with the manner of the deaths on the basis of knowing what had happened. Had the process been different—were the perpetrators ever to come forward to the TRC by way of amnesty applications—not only would the truth come out in a "full disclosure" by the amnesty applicants, but the families also would learn for the first time the details of what had happened to their loved ones.

When the victims' families did appear before the TRC's Amnesty Committee, they began to get a very good dose of the truth. It might not have been the entire truth, but for the first time the families could put faces to deeds. Whether doing so leads to healing, and to reconciliation, time will tell. For now, some truth has come to light only through the amnesty process. The TRC succeeded in exposing the truth. Two attempts by the criminal justice system had failed to do so.

A second assumption that the criminal justice argument makes is that every prosecution, even assuming there is evidence (not just mere information), will either expose the truth or result in a conviction. The trial of General Magnus Malan, in which all the accused were acquitted at various stages, was a clear demonstration of the failure of the criminal justice either to expose the truth or to achieve its stated objective, namely, retributive justice.[7] Even though the court found that the massacre was carried out by Inkatha Freedom Party supporters paid by the South African Defence Force, (a) it could not be proved that the six Inkatha supporters before the Court were in fact the perpetrators; (b) state witnesses were unreliable; (c) many of the statements had been tampered with; and (d) "Project Marion" documents could be given innocent interpretation.

The case fell on its face because it depended on a causal link being established between the training of Inkatha supporters in Namibia's Caprivi strip and the killing of UDF supporters in Kwa Makhutha. That causal link could have been established only if the trainees had been called; but the state prosecution did not call this evidence.

This trial and the verdict, far from reconciling the split community in KwaZulu Natal particularly, and the rest of South African society generally, further divided society. Progressive legal organizations such as the National Association of Democratic Lawyers (NADEL) hinted at the lack of confidence that human rights lawyers had in a nontransformed judiciary and prosecutorial services. NADEL called for a moratorium on all prosecutions of human-rights-violations-related crimes until the entire judicio-legal system had been totally transformed, had become representative, and had gained legitimacy in the eyes of the majority of the people.[8]

The TRC's chairman observed that the trial's outcome demonstrated that the TRC offered a better prospect of establishing the truth about the past than a criminal trial.[9] The TRC held a special hearing to which the trainees were called. They told us, *inter alia*, that they had been recruited on the basis that they were Inkatha supporters. During training they had been instructed to return and kill ANC supporters, the UDF members. It took the TRC process to bring out the truth.

Punishment—Is Retribution the Only Form of Effective Punishment?

The traditional argument is that wrongdoers must suffer the consequences of their choices. On conviction, they go to jail. In some jurisdictions, for the more serious crimes—which would be characterized as gross violations of human rights by our Act—the death sentence is competent.

Except for my opposition to the death sentence for a variety of reasons, I have, ordinarily, no strong argument against this view. However, I have since interrogated my own premises for concluding that the only effective punishment is retribution—even for heinous crimes.

The process of getting amnesty was structured in such a way that it achieved a variety of objectives. It placed a high price on the acquisition of amnesty. Second, it did not have the uncertainties sometimes associated with the criminal justice system, especially when convicted persons protest their innocence until execution, in some cases, only for it to be discovered that they were wrongly convicted.

Further, retributive justice destroys a culture of impunity on the part of the perpetrators. It is clear that there is a need to restore humanity to perpetrators and to reintegrate them into society. The process of seeking amnesty results in public shaming. It creates new victims in the form of spouses, children, parents, and relatives of perpetrators—people who had been unaware of what these perpetrators did. This is so because, in terms of the Act, amnesty applicants testified in public. They made full disclosures, in the glare of nationwide (and even worldwide) publicity. Maybe for the very first time these disclosures were known to wives, friends, and children. These people, who regularly went to church and behaved like law-abiding citizens, had the darker side of their lives exposed in public. To South African society, especially the white community, exposing what took place shattered many illusions.

For amnesty applicants to be prepared to run the gauntlet of public dismay, censure, and even ostracism was a heavy price to pay. Amnesty was not cheap. It was a process that traumatized not only the applicants and the victims but those communities that operated under illusions. For perpetrators, such exposures are their own punishment, and thus an element of justice itself. In that way, the TRC was a unique court of truth.

Villa-Vicencio, in an unpublished paper entitled "A Different Kind of Justice" (1997), observed that the concern of opponents of the amnesty process was that it lacked justice. The TRC was seen to err in the direction of cheap forgiveness.[10] He argued, however, that there was a case to be made for an alternative type of justice—political restorative justice, which addressed the legitimate concerns of victims and survivors while seeking to reintegrate perpetrators into the community.[11]

Villa-Vicencio said that full disclosure, in public, ensured the emergence of a collective understanding of the truth about the past. Further, the public censure of those responsible for gross violations happened only through this amnesty process. The censure of one's fellow citizens, he argued, and of generations to come, is a form of justice that, in a certain way, is as severe as languishing in prison.[12]

The aim of restorative justice is salutary because it does not seek to ignore the past, something that a blanket amnesty would have accomplished. It compels the perpetrators to take responsibility for redressing past wrongs. Respite (for perpetrators), in time, inevitably gives way to the return of suppressed memories that haunt and torment the present.

Boraine makes that point very powerfully when he states, "It was in order to avoid an amnesty which amounted to little more than impunity that we attempted to introduce an amnesty programme which included accountability and disclosure."[13] Boraine rejected blanket amnesty because:

1. Impunity threatens belief in a democratic society. The fact that those responsible for former violations are not put on trial and a demand for justice (criminal justice) is denied creates doubts and fears about democratic ideas and ideals.

2. Impunity confuses and creates ambiguous social, moral, and psychological limits. A society that does not investigate or punish serious crimes blurs the norms of right and wrong. It creates ambiguity and a disrespect for laws and prohibition.

3. The lies and denials are institutionalized and are defended by the laws of the country. One law prohibits violence and force, while another protects wrongdoers against fair trial and punishment.

4. Impunity tempts people to take the law into their own hands.

5. Impunity invalidates and denies what has happened and thereby limits the possibility of effective communication between fellow citizens. The lack of official verification of former events leaves room for doubts and skepticism about the stories told. This reduces the scope for collective mourning and a collective working through the suffering.

6. Impunity strengthens powerlessness, guilt, and shame.

7. Impunity affects belief in the future and may leave a historical "no man's land" in which there is both an official and an unofficial version of events—something that may give rise to historical stagnation, limiting the possibility of moving ahead and creating a common just society.

It is thus true that the South African model, regard being given to the criteria and the tests to be satisfied by an applicant (the so-called Norgaard principles), endeavors to strike a *via media* (a middle way) between blanket amnesty and the sledgehammer of retributive justice of the criminal courts.[14]

Indeed, retribution, in terms of the Act, has only been suspended to the extent of reciprocation by perpetrators who will not escape prosecution if they either fail to apply for amnesty or fail to make a full disclosure resulting in the failure of the application. A case in point is that of Ferdi Barnard, who was widely suspected to have been responsible for the murder of an academic from the University of the Witwatersrand. He did not apply for amnesty and was successfully prosecuted for the murder, inter alia, of Richard Webster.

The TRC's amnesty process constituted a delicate balance between the "carrot" of absolving perpetrators from criminal and civil liability and the "stick" of the prosecution of perpetrators in the criminal courts, where they can be convicted and sentenced.

Agency for Fundamental Social Change

Even if all the truth can be exposed, if the conditions of the ordinary people have not changed since the advent of the democratic order, all the truth telling, and the knowledge by victims that comes with it, will have been in vain. In some way, society might be in danger of its own success in exposing the truth.

The TRC was only one element in a project to transform South Africa from a repressive, virtually oligarchical society to a democracy. It could only act as one of the agents of transformation. It had the function of making recommendations to the nation via its final report.

Terreblanche called for the establishment of a second truth commission, the task of which would be to investigate the nature and extent of what he called the "[structural] exploitation inherent in the power structures of the political system of *white political supremacy* and of the economic system of *racial capitalism*." He called for the investigation of what he termed *systemic exploitation* of the majority by a minority over a period of at least one hundred years.[15] He argued that without a clear understanding of the systemic nature of the exploitation that had occurred, it would not be possible for beneficiaries (mainly whites) to make the necessary confession, to show the necessary repentance, and to experience the necessary conversions. Without systemic justice, he argued, true reconciliation might prove to be unattainable. Terreblanche called on the TRC to do whatever it could to investigate the *systemic* relationship between (mainly white) *beneficiaries* and (mainly black) victims.[16] One of the practical steps that Terreblanche recommended was that white businesses should volunteer to pay a wealth tax, a suggestion that stirred a hornet's nest of opposition.

Conclusion

Barney Pityana, chair of the South African Human Rights Commission, has heavily criticized the TRC:

1. Was any dignity restored when many told their stories in the full glare of television cameras? Pityana says that he knows many who would not subject themselves to what they considered an indignity. He says that they also felt helpless in the face of lies that the amnesty applicants told. He ends by suggesting that "such a [public] spectacle was not necessarily ennobling but demeaning of their human dignity."

2. The TRC was wrong to hold the view that "whatever the circumstances, moral reprobation was the same for deeds like murder even if it was in the course of fighting a legitimate war"; that the moral opprobrium of the ANC's treatment of its prisoners of war could not be "equated with that of the enemy state" because "surely some moral distinction had to be made," something that he says the TRC report failed to make.

3. Restorative justice does not square with our "strong call for the prosecution of those who were not granted amnesty or who failed to apply for amnesty." He argues that the prosecutions as recommended by us "would drag for a long time without any guarantee of convictions. His simple (if not simplistic!) solution is that "those who have escaped the net of the TRC must receive forgiveness by the nation . . . [because] we cannot afford the futility of the Magnus Malan trials."[17]

4. The TRC failed to help South Africa with the challenge of reconciliation. He claimed that "some of us often felt that the Commission was too anxious to give signs and symbols of forgiveness and reconciliation." The TRC, he claims, has left "all of us with an unfinished business which now becomes the task of all of us."[18]

Since the publication of the TRC's *Final Report* in 1998, many commissioners have been invited to countries in transition. In all of these countries, the TRC process has been hailed as a miracle. On tour, I have made the following points, all positive lessons for the world.

1. As far as South Africa is concerned, anyone who doubts that South Africa is a better place after the TRC process must ask oneself the question: "How would South Africa be had there been no TRC?" I am clear in my own mind that the answer is obvious. We would still be saddled with guilt in the way that Namibia now is, hence the calls there by human rights groups for some form of TRC.

Did the process uncover all the truth? I cannot pretend that it did, especially if one is looking for truth with a capital *T*, a very elusive concept at the best of times. If, however, the question is whether we have put on the table more facts that, but for the TRC process, would never have seen the light of day, then the answer is that we gave South Africa a fairly good dose of the truth.

I would go so far as to suggest that the virtually violence-free elections in South Africa in 1999 owe a lot to the TRC process. People of South Africa, in turning out in the huge numbers that they did (almost 80 percent of registered voters) and returning the prodemocracy ANC in ever-increasing numbers, were giving an indication that only parties that promise a future of peace, freedom, and equality should be returned to Parliament. I argue that the three years or so during which the people of South Africa were being reminded by testimony after testimony of the horrors of the apartheid were a time during which these accounts of South Africa's past were constantly present in our minds in a way that reminded us, even as we went to vote, that there shall never be a return to that evil past.

2. As for the world, the most abiding lesson is that in a conflict situation like the one in Guinea-Bissau, at the end of which there are no clear winners and no clear losers, the only alternative to a war of attrition can be a process like the TRC. If one looks at the Angolan conflict, which has left Angola destroyed after a quarter of a century of internecine warfare, one realizes that where outright military victory is not viable, other alternatives must be found.

In order to ensure relatively lasting peace, however, amnesty must not be cheapened, for example, by it being granted upon request with no conditions. Blanket amnesty, as the saga around General Augusto Pinochet's arrest in the United Kingdom demonstrated, leads to resentment because the recipients usually conduct themselves with galling impunity.

For that reason, even though the guns in Sierra Leone were silenced in 1999, lasting peace will remain elusive if those who were involved in horrible atrocities are not dealt with. In that country there may well be a need for an amnesty process like the one adopted in South Africa.

Finally, in South Africa, a Nuremberg-type process would have been less than successful. As the TRC *Final Report* showed (and as the amnesty process demonstrated), the major perpetrators of gross violations of human rights were apartheid security officers. They came forward, in most cases, because the process promised indemnification from prosecution and civil liability. To have sought to prosecute them would have meant that the democratic government was hopeful that they would go out and investigate themselves in a manner that would have produced evidence that could secure convictions. This result would have been improbable (if not impossible) to achieve.

Besides, it could possibly have produced a terrible right-wing backlash at a time when the loyalty of most of the white people had not been won over. Six years of democracy in South Africa has eroded any probability of a backlash happening, and that has been demonstrated by the failure of the Freedom Front to make an impact in the 1999 elections even though its support was traditionally from those who were militaristic and supportive of a separatist white independent Volkstaat.

Notes

1. The Winnie Mandela and the United Football Club hearing being a case in point. During that hearing we learned that the only occasion before that date that had attracted such media attention was Mandela's release on 2 February 1990.

2. Marvin Frankel and Ellen Saideman, *Out of the Shadows of the Night: The Struggle for International Human Rights* (New York, 1989), 103–104.

3. Indeed, it is said that the postamble, in fact, came about as a consequence of an intervention by the armed forces in November 1993. They advised constitutional negotiators that they were aware that right-wing formations were aiming to bomb the elections out of existence; that they were able and willing to prevent that, but that they were not willing to go to jail thereafter. They wanted a guarantee that amnesty would be granted to them, hence the references in the postamble.

4. See the Azanian People's Organization (AZAPO) case.

5. Ibid.

6. Ibid.

7. This was a trial in which former defence minister General Magnus Malan, former defence force Generals Jan Geldenhuys and Kat Liebenberg, and nine military intelligence officers and six SADF-trained Inkatha supporters faced charges of murder, attempted murder, and conspiracy to murder, all arising out of a night attack on the home at KwaMakhutha of UDF activist Victor Ntuli on 21 January 1987.

8. As per Krish Govender, publicity secretary, NADEL, *Sunday Times*, 13 October 1996, 5.

9. *City Press*, 13 October 1996, 4.

10. See also Charles Villa-Viscencio's other unpublished paper, "The Burden of Moral Guilt: Its Theological and Political Implications," 22–23.

11. Villa-Vicencio, "A Different Kind of Justice," 5.

12. Ibid., 6.

13. Alex Boraine, "Alternatives and Adjuncts to Criminal Prosecutions" (written text of paper presented at "Justice in Cataclysm: Criminal Tribunals in the Wake of Mass Violence," Brussels, Belgium, 20–21 July 1996), 3–4.

14. In its submissions to the TRC, the National Party called for general amnesty, arguing that the Norgaard principles militated against successful amnesty applications. The TRC's Amnesty Committee was not persuaded by this submission.

15. Sampie Terreblanche, "Law and Injustice as Outcome of Economic Policies" (written text of a paper presented at the University of Stellenbosch, March 1997), 19–21.

16. Ibid., 20–21.

17. Pityana was once a lieutenant of Steve Biko, and a colleague of Mapetla Mohapi and Nohle Mohapi, of the Black Consciousness Movement. Pityana's remarks do not square up with Nohle Mohapi's views on the question of the cathartic effect on her of her public testimony, and the sense of dignity that she felt for the first time when she testified before the TRC. Further, I am not confident that Mrs. Biko shares Pityana's view that the killers of her husband who have failed to get amnesty must not be prosecuted. I am certain she has been outraged by Pityana's call that "those who have escaped the TRC net . . . must receive forgiveness by the nation."

18. Barney Pityana, speech given at the Twenty-ninth Provincial Synod of the Church of the Province of Southern Africa, 16 July 1999.

IX

Amnesty, Truth, and Reconciliation

REFLECTIONS ON THE

SOUTH AFRICAN AMNESTY PROCESS

RONALD C. SLYE[1]

THE granting of amnesty to individuals for acts constituting gross violations of human rights is one of the most controversial mechanisms contemporary societies have used to address violent pasts.[2] While South Africa has adopted a qualitatively different approach to amnesty than its peers, it is not immune from such controversy. Many have debated whether granting amnesty for the worst violations of human rights is morally prohibited or illegal under international law, whether criminal prosecutions are better vehicles than self-styled truth commissions for addressing past violations of human rights, and whether, in the case of South Africa, the parties that negotiated the transition should have agreed to an amnesty. There has been little discussion, however, of the relationship between the granting of amnesty—including, in the case of South Africa, the process by which amnesty is granted—and the stated goals of truth and reconciliation.

How much does amnesty contribute to the quantity and quality of truth? Do we know more about past violations because of an amnesty, and is that additional information useful in understanding why such violations occurred and knowing how to prevent their future occurrence? Addressing these questions near the end of the amnesty process, I conclude that the South African amnesty increases both the quantity and quality of information we possess about past violations.

How much does amnesty contribute to reconciliation? There are two necessary conditions for reconciliation: accountability, and the creation of a human rights culture (a political culture that values human dignity and the rule of law). Accountability is an important component of any process of reconciliation that follows a period of systematic human rights abuses. Without some accountability for past violations, reconciliation is at best false and at worst impossible. Although accountability is a necessary condition for reconciliation, the creation of a human rights culture concerns the quality of such reconciliation. One can imagine a society that meets a minimum definition of reconciliation—that is, a society that is stable and, maybe temporarily, peaceful—that does not recognize the dignity of each of its members.[3] This is not a desirable state of reconciliation. By reconciliation I mean something more than the absence of violent conflict. A society is not reconciled with its violent past unless it works toward the creation of a culture of respect for fundamental human rights. The question is whether the granting of amnesty in South Africa contributes to the creation of such a culture, or not.

What is meant by "amnesty"? Generally, amnesties are official acts that provide an individual with protection from liability—civil, criminal, or both—for past acts. A survey of amnesties granted throughout history reveals an enormous variety of acts that fall under this generic label.[4] Many of these amnesties have as their purpose the concealment of facts about past violations, and the denial of accountability for such violations. The question raised so provocatively by South Africa is whether the granting of amnesty *must* detract from the goals of truth, reconciliation, accountability, and the creation of a human rights culture. The amnesty procedure administered by South Africa's Truth and Reconciliation Commission (TRC) was the most sophisticated amnesty undertaken in modern times, if not in any time, for acts that constitute violations of fundamental international human rights. To the extent that the South African amnesty contributes to, rather than detracts from, these important goals, it provides a useful model for creating and judging future amnesties; to the extent that the South African amnesty is consistent in its failure with many of its predecessors, it provides powerful evidence for those who decry amnesties in any and all forms.

Truth and Judicial Alternatives

Does the granting of amnesty for gross violations of human rights contribute to a society's understanding of its past? In other words, does it contribute to the "truth"? Without delving into the important issue of what we mean by "truth" in this context, all that I ask is whether the granting of amnesty contributes to a society's shared understanding of its past. That is, given the information that amnesty adds to the public record, can we say that such information provides additional and important insights into what happened and why?

Prior to the case of South Africa, contemporary amnesties added little if anything to public knowledge or acknowledgment about a society's past. This is not to say, however, that they added nothing. It is somewhat ironic that an effort to use a mechanism to prohibit inquiry and accountability in fact provides a minimal, if very unsatisfactory, level of both. Implicit in any granting of amnesty is an underlying crime for which an individual or a group desires protection from prosecution and liability. A desire for amnesty thus implies a belief by those requesting it—or in many cases demanding it—that there is some exposure of liability for which they require protection. Of course, part of such a desire may be justified—or rationalized—as based on a fear of illegitimate prosecutions driven not by any requirement of justice but by politics: the fear of the group recently removed from power of being persecuted by the new group in power. Yet this fear of politically motivated prosecutions cannot completely explain a desire for amnesty. The mere granting of amnesty would be insufficient protection from such politically driven actions. Amnesties may always be ignored, or overturned, for political or other reasons if the new group in power is determined to punish members of the old regime.[5]

Except for the minimal significance that we can attribute to the desire of an individual or class of individuals to be granted amnesty, amnesties have traditionally had the effect of preventing inquiry and denying accountability. Contemporary amnesties granted for human rights abuses rarely, if ever, identify individual recipients.[6] They apply to a class of people, or to a class of acts, or to all acts during a particular time period. We may conclude from such amnesties that some individuals recognize that violations occurred for which protection from prosecution is needed, but we learn nothing new from the granting of the amnesty concerning who perpetrated such acts and why.

One of the major innovations of the TRC was an amnesty procedure that had as its major purpose revelation. There was the acknowledgment by interested parties of the need for amnesty—the acknowledgment that violations occurred for which legal protection was required—that we find in all amnesties. We know that this was a need recognized by all the major parties to the transitional negotiations—the National Party (NP), the African National Congress (ANC), and the Inkatha Freedom Party (IFP). Although the NP was the major force in the negotiations pushing for a blanket amnesty to cover acts covered by the apartheid regime, the ANC was also interested in some form of amnesty for acts its members had committed during the liberation struggle. The IFP continued to call for a general blanket amnesty for its members, and with rare exceptions its members refused to participate in the amnesty process. Unlike other amnesties, however, the South African one required that individuals identify themselves through applying and making full disclosure of the activities for which they wanted amnesty. This requirement of self-initiation and disclosure had a number of important consequences that make such a process better suited than a traditional trial to the needs of a society in transition.

Proponents of criminal trials over truth commissions argue that the former actively includes the accused perpetrator in the search for truth and accountability.[7] The argument is that a trial forces a defendant to confront his or her accusers and to engage them in a search for the truth. Conversely, trials provide a safe space in which victims may confront their perpetrators. The trial creates a rule-governed space within which a formal dialogue takes place among victims, the accused, and society (represented by the government).

Truth produced from trials, according to Nino, the late Argentinean philosopher-lawyer, is "much more precise and much more dramatic" than truth produced from commissions, because in the former the accused contributes to his story.[8]

There are two important claims about the utility of trials over commissions. The first claim is based on the participation of the accused in their trial. Such participation has two important effects: it contributes to the rehabilitation and societal reintegration of the accused by including them in the national deliberative process; and it allows the accused to explain, and even justify, their actions, and thus provides an important perspective on the truth and context of past events. The claim is that by ensuring the participation of the accused in this national dialogue, trials enhance the dignity of the accused and thus increase prospects for rehabilitation and reintegration. Participation by the accused also provides important raw information—facts, perspectives, and motivations—necessary for a proper discussion about the past. It provides information that can only come from the accused, which enhances the quality of public discussion and the shared understanding that such discussion produces.

The second claim for trials concerns the quality of the information produced. The claim is that trials produce better quality information because they not only provide direct testimony from the accused, but also produce information that has been subjected to the rigors of legal process and the rules of evidence. The argument is that trials produce information that is more reliable.

One of the important lessons of the South African amnesty process is the demonstration that formal trials are not the only forums within which these goals can be met—and that in fact trials may not be the best forums.[9] Comparing the participation of the accused in a trial as opposed to an amnesty hearing, there is no question that the quality of the participation is at least as good in the latter as in the former. In fact, it seems clear that in South Africa the amnesty hearings have resulted in substantially more participation by the accused than one finds in a typical trial. In a trial setting, the accused may, and often does, participate passively. It is the state, or the victim, that initiates the process that demands the presence of the accused. The information that forms the basis for the trial—or to use Nino's characterization, the "story" or "narration"[10]—is provided by the state and the victims. The accused are placed in a defensive position. Their goal is to escape liability, and thus to raise as much doubt as possible about the claims of the state or the accuseds' alleged victims. There is no requirement that a defendant in a criminal or civil trial testify; and while the accused may challenge the testimony of others and offer their own evidence and testimony, this is often done vicariously through their lawyer.

The dynamic of the amnesty hearing is quite different. The accused persons initiate the proceeding, for they are affirmatively seeking a benefit. The applicants provide—or at least want to appear to provide—a full disclosure of the details of the acts for which they want amnesty. Information thus comes from the accused, which is then evaluated and challenged by the victims and the state (through the amnesty committee). The amnesty applicants participate voluntarily in the process.[11] This does not necessarily mean that the *quality* of the information produced by the amnesty hearing is better than that produced at a criminal trial. In terms of the *participation* of the accused, however, there is a strong argument that the amnesty hearing process created in South Africa provided just as much, if not more, participation by the accused than a trial.

The fact that amnesty hearings may be more successful than trials in increasing the quality of the *participation* of the accused does not mean that the quality of the *information* produced from the hearings is better. The claim of those who defend trials is that the technical rules of a court produce a better quality of truth than proceedings not governed by such rules. In other words, the highly developed rules of evidence, procedure, and proof that govern a trial ensure that a fact established in such a setting is more likely to be true than if it had been established or asserted in another forum where such rules do not apply. This claim is based on the *procedure* by which information is developed and tested in a formal trial. While the type of procedural rules used is certainly important, an examination of the *purposes* for which these procedures are designed provides some useful additional insights into how we might compare the quality of the information produced in trials as opposed to the South African amnesty hearings.

The purpose of a criminal trial is to determine whether the evidence presented against the accused is sufficiently compelling to permit the court to feel justified in imposing punishment. Stated somewhat differently, the question is whether we are satisfied that we have sufficiently minimized the probability that we may be about to punish an innocent person. Certainly for achieving such a purpose, the rules of evidence and procedure are critically important. The purpose of such a highly structured process is to minimize the danger of producing a false positive; that is, to minimize the danger that we will conclude that persons are guilty when in fact they are not. A cost of this process is the increased possibility of a false negative—concluding that something did not happen in the eyes of the law when in fact it did; that some persons are not responsible for a violation when in fact they are. This is not to say that even the best crafted and implemented rules of procedure and evidence may not produce a false positive. These rules are designed to diminish the possibility of such a false positive to an acceptable level, given the consequences (i.e., punishment), but do not claim to eliminate entirely such a risk.

The purpose of an amnesty hearing is not to minimize the probability that we may be about to punish an innocent defendant. An amnesty process has already made the decision not to punish the guilty—or at least not to punish in the traditional sense that we think of punishment. The issue in the amnesty hearing is whether the applicant is revealing sufficient information—whether he or she is making "full disclosure" of the acts for which amnesty is wanted. The important questions to be answered are why? who else was involved? and how? The amnesty process—as distinct from the entire truth and reconciliation process—is more concerned with the amount and quality of the information revealed by the accused than with the amount and quality of the total information produced.

As far as the quality of the information produced, if an amnesty applicant testifies that he or she committed a particular violation, there is little reason to doubt the veracity of the claim.[12] This does not mean, of course, that the information produced by the amnesty hearing is not flawed. Both trials and amnesty hearings suffer from a similar phenomenon—defendants and applicants will tailor their testimony based on the legal requirements for, in the first case, acquittal, and in the second, amnesty. The fact that an individual's testimony is distorted by his or her interest is not particularly insightful. The interesting question is not whether the testimony is in fact distorted, but in what ways is it distorted? Thus in the case of a trial, defendants may argue that they did not do the act in question, or that they did not do the act intentionally, or that they committed the act but it did not have the legal significance that the state claims.[13] Under the South African amnesty, there were three major requirements: (1) that the applicant make "full disclosure"; (2) that the act for which the applicant is applying for amnesty be "associated with a political objective"; and (3) that the act for which the applicant is seeking amnesty was not committed for personal gain or out of personal malice, ill-will, or spite.[14]

The first requirement, that an applicant make full disclosure, was obviously intended to encourage the disclosure of as much information as possible. As far as I know there was no clear guidance on what would have constituted a failure to make full disclosure, although as of this writing there has been at least one decision not to grant amnesty based on the applicant's failure to make full disclosure.[15] This lack of guidance may in fact be intentional—the idea being to create an incentive based on uncertainty that the applicant flood the committee with information irrespective of its seeming significance or importance, and leaving it to the committee and the commission to separate the significant from the mundane. The effect of this requirement was that individual applicants had an incentive to disclose as much damaging material about themselves and their colleagues as they believed the commission's investigative team had been able to uncover. Uncertainty concerning both the applicable standard and the information possessed by the TRC created a favorable incentive for the disclosure of information.[16]

The remaining two requirements for amnesty resulted in applicants for amnesty characterizing the acts for which they were applying as being associated with a political organization or movement, and those opposing a particular amnesty application arguing that the acts were not in fact political. Since one of the ways to meet the political objective requirement was to establish that the act was ordered by a political party or organization, such entities may influence whether an individual receives amnesty or not.[17] Thus, if a political organization stated that it had in fact approved a particular act, it was more likely that an individual applicant might have received amnesty. If a political organization denied authorizing a particular act, an individual applicant may have had a difficult time convincing the amnesty committee that the act fit within the legislation's definition of an act with a political objective.[18] This leaves open the possibility that political parties might have confirmed or denied the official nature of an applicant's activities based on their then current political interests.

The requirement that an act be associated with a political objective in order to qualify for amnesty meant that acts for which there was no political meaning at the time of their commission were spoken of as political acts.[19] Conversely, some acts that seemed to be clearly associated with a political objective were characterized by those opposing an amnesty application as motivated not by politics but by malice or ill-will.[20]

Such testimonial distortions affect the information produced by the amnesty process on at least three levels. First, they affect our interpretation of the political importance of the act in question. Acts for which amnesty is granted are thus presumed to have been in furtherance of some political objective. Second, they focus our attention on the question of whether the act was in furtherance of a political objective or not, and detract from other important questions surrounding a violation. In some cases this has resulted in fascinating discussions about what a political objective is. Is deliberately killing an individual because he or she is white a political act in the context of a racist system of government?[21] The attention paid to political objective means, however, that other aspects of a particular act may be ignored or given less emphasis than they deserve. Thus, the utility of using violent rather than peaceful means to pursue a particular objective; the impact of an act on its victims and other members of a community; and the connection between one individual's or organization's decision to resort to violence on other similar decisions are all issues that, while not completely ignored in the amnesty process, are much less central than the issue of political objective. Third, they diminish our understanding of the real perspectives and motives that influenced an individual's actions. It is not inconceivable that a member of the security forces may have chosen to kill a particular antiapartheid activist at a particular time in order to further some personal objective; for example, to steal the victim's money or car, to further certain career objectives, or to embarrass rivals in a sister organization. It is similarly not inconceivable that some acts committed against the apartheid state may have been as much motivated by personal gain as political ideology.[22] An individual act can qualify as one associated with a political objective even if the individual who committed the act did not have strong political beliefs. Conversely, an individual act may not qualify as a political act even though the individual clearly believed that he or she was acting politically.[23] By either exaggerating or downplaying the political motivations of an individual, we were given a false picture of what in fact caused a particular violation.

Finally, trials are most effective as a forum in which the state or plaintiff presents a wealth of evidence to "prove" the liability of the accused. Such a trial presupposes that the state or plaintiff has ready access to such evidence. The problem facing South Africa, and indeed facing any country that has undergone a similar negotiated transition, was that the information implicating individuals was not readily at hand. Information necessary for a successful prosecution may be deliberately hidden, destroyed, or just hard to find for new government officials who are unfamiliar with the workings of the institutions in which they find themselves.[24]

Even with these qualifications, however, there is no doubt that the quantity, and probably also the quality, of the information elicited from the amnesty hearings was higher than what would have been elicited from criminal trials. In the *Final Report* of the TRC, the Amnesty Committee noted that many important participants in past violations had applied for amnesty.[25] The implication was that much information had been revealed that otherwise would not have been. In fact, a significant amount of information in the *Final Report* concerning past atrocities and individual responsibilities came from the amnesty hearings.[26]

History and Reconciliation

Even if we accept that the granting of amnesty, at least through a procedure like the South African one, increases a society's knowledge about its past, does that knowledge, or something else connected to the amnesty process, contribute to reconciliation? Or, to put the question another way, does the amnesty process and the information it elicits diminish the possibility of reconciliation? If the ability of a society to achieve a true and stable reconciliation is inversely related to the *amount* of information kept secret, then the amnesty process clearly contributes to reconciliation. Proponents of this position argue that the question of how a particular disclosure will affect the prospects for reconciliation is misguided. This is so, the argument goes, because reconciliation based on the suppression of *any* information is a false reconciliation that will eventually self-destruct. The recurring controversies concerning the extent of complicity by Western nations with the Nazi government are proof of the folly of such attempts to achieve reconciliation at the cost of truth. Yet, this absolutist argument clearly is open to question. As an empirical matter one could look, for example, at the revived interest in French complicity during the German occupation and argue that the myth of clean hands and French resistance were necessary for the creation of a stable and democratic postwar French government.[27] A similar argument might be made concerning the disclosure of the complicity of other Western governments, financial institutions, and corporations. Evaluating these two paths of reconciliation—immediate disclosure of the truth versus myth creation—by their effects is difficult. We do not yet know what the long-term effect the present revelations will have on the popular legitimacy of those Western governments and institutions that have been identified as being complicitous with Nazi Germany. Nor do we know what effect such revelations will have on the trust and respect among generations, groups, or nations. Similarly, we do not know what sort of society France, for example, would have become if the truth of Vichy France had been thoroughly revealed and discussed immediately after World War II.

It may be that the de facto path taken by Europe—a combination of the two paths with a temporal dimension: short-term myth-making combined with periodic revelations in the future—is the best one for moving forward and adequately confronting the past. The question of time—*when* is it best to examine the past for the purpose of reconciliation?—is an important one. Attempts to answer the *when* question can quickly devolve to a discussion of the comparative advantages of history and law. The tensions between historical and legal judgments make the attempt to combine the two in something like a truth commission all the more intriguing. A historian's judgment is one that derives its legitimacy in part from its temporal distance—the belief that contemporaries cannot evaluate events of their own time, for they are too close to, and too interested in, the events under examination. It is only with the passage of time that a more objective truth and a more balanced judgment can be achieved. A more sophisticated version of this argument is that distance shifts the bias of the historian from one directly related to the period under examination to one primarily embedded in another time and maybe another place. At its most ideal, the historian's craft is a method of deliberation across time—a conversation among individuals with differing perspectives, interests, and beliefs, out of which conversation the outline of an accepted truth begins to emerge.

The law, in contrast to history, is interested in judging quickly—as close as possible to the time of the events being examined. This is because a purpose of the legal system is immediately to condemn or ratify past acts in order, in part, to affect future conduct. This is achieved through the mostly controlled exercise of power, coercion, and even violence. For legal accountability, swiftness is important. In fact, the law generally discourages judgments concerning acts that occurred distantly in the past. Thus, statutes of limitations and the equitable doctrine of laches extinguish causes of action after the passage of a certain period of time. Law's focus on the present is explained in part by its consequences—law's power to punish and impose costs. The passage of time has two important effects on the quality and utility of legal judgments: evidence changes and disappears, and expectations and priorities shift. Our comfort with judgments that have as their consequence some form of punishment diminishes with the death, disappearance, and forgetfulness of witnesses. In addition to its impact on our confidence in the content of our judgments, the passage of time also affects our sense of fairness. The utility of law and its judgments is dependent in part on its promise of finality.[28] Without such finality—with the threat of law intervening years or decades later to readjust relations based on past acts—individuals would be more reluctant to plan and invest productively, for such plans and investments could be thwarted at any time.[29] The argument is that at some point we have to put the past behind us to honor present expectations about the future.[30]

What is the relevance of this admittedly brief comparison of law and history to the discussion of amnesty and reconciliation? Reconciliation requires that the goals of both law and history be met: that some form of accountability (legal judgment) and understanding (historical judgment) be combined. An amnesty process like South Africa's is the closest thing we have yet seen to achieve the goals of both disciplines. The demands of legal accountability are met—at least in part—and the raw material for an accurate and informed temporal discussion of the past is increased. To assist historical judging, the amnesty hearings produce contemporaneous statements by individuals of what they did and why—information that otherwise would not be available.[31] While the presence of such information does not ensure that a society like South Africa will develop an accurate history that is acceptable to most of its members, it does produce a contemporaneous record that will provide the basis for a more accurate process of historical judgment.

Accountability and Reconciliation

But what of law and the importance of accountability? Reconciliation is not possible without accountability for two reasons: one cannot be reconciled if there is a feeling of injustice; and the lack of accountability for the past endangers the creation of a human rights culture. The first concerns the effect of accountability, or the lack thereof, on people's ability and willingness to reconcile. The importance of accountability to reconciliation is important not only because of its impact on victims but also for its impact on perpetrators. It is difficult for victims to reconcile themselves with an individual or class of perpetrators if there is a widespread feeling that the perpetrators of past crimes are "getting away with it." To the extent that the amnesty procedures create some level of accountability that is recognized by the victims, it encourages reconciliation. The issue can be restated as follows: Do the victims or society have a legitimate claim against perpetrators despite the amnesty procedure?—a claim that may be asserted legitimately at some point in the future. If they do not, then reconciliation is furthered. If they do, victims will be dissatisfied until they can satisfy such a claim, and perpetrators will be resentful when they do. More important, groups and communities that identify with victims or perpetrators will also feel dissatisfied or resentful.

Accountability is also important to the perpetrators and their ability and willingness to contribute to reconciliation. Accountability may increase the possibility that perpetrators will be reintegrated into society by bringing some form of closure to that chapter of their life. In other words, it creates the ability of the perpetrators to say, "Yes, I did commit a wrong, but I have paid my debt and am now entitled to be an equal participant in society." There are those who argue that the act of punishment provides a psychological benefit to the accused that permits such a claim.[32] For an example, we need only look to the confession in 1995 of Adolfo Scilingo, an Argentinean military official. Despite receiving legal protection for his crimes, Scilingo felt compelled to confess the details of his involvement in the Argentinean dirty war, including his participation in the dumping of sedated civilians into the ocean from military planes. Or look to the decision in 1998 of Katherine Ann Power, an American fugitive who, after more than twenty years of successfully evading the police, turned herself in to be tried for the murder of a police officer. Power was convicted and sentenced and, after serving some years in prison, refused a chance at parole in order to express the genuineness of her remorse to the victim's family. The issue with the perpetrators is whether they are justified in claiming that they have paid their dues to society and to the victims. In other words, do they have a recognizable defense to the claim asserted by a victim or society that "they got away with it"?

If accountability contributes to reconciliation, the question is how much accountability was there in the South African amnesty process? There is no question that the South African amnesty process provided more accountability than any other truth commission, not to mention any other amnesty. Applicants were required to identify themselves individually as persons in need of amnesty, and to describe at least minimally the acts for which they believe they needed, and were entitled to, such protection. Those applicants seeking amnesty for the worst violations—gross violations of human rights—were required to participate in a public hearing where they were questioned by both the committee members and, in most cases, their victims, victims' families, and their representatives.[33] Through such hearings the perpetrators were required to recount their misdeeds. They were required to state unequivocally, "Yes, I did commit an act that constitutes a gross violation of human rights." Many did use the hearing as an opportunity to explain and even justify their actions.

As a calling to account, the amnesty hearings were effective. Through their applications and participation in public hearings, amnesty applicants accepted (if at times defiantly) responsibility for their violations.[34] Although some argued that such public acceptance and exposure constituted a degree of punishment similar in kind, if not in degree, to what one gets in a criminal trial, one need not look for punishment to find accountability.[35] The existence or not of punishment may, however, affect our evaluation of the quality of accountability produced.

While the South African amnesty process clearly furthered accountability, the more important and difficult question is whether the amount of accountability achieved was enough to ensure effective and long-term reconciliation. This is an empirical question that we may not be able to answer with sufficient confidence for a long time. We can, however, point to positive contributions that the amnesty process made to the reconciliation process. The amnesty hearings, along with the other hearings of the TRC, provided a space within which individual acts of reconciliation—statements of forgiveness, empathy, and acceptance—could occur, and did occur. These examples of reconciliation are all the more powerful since they are neither mandated nor encouraged by the amnesty requirements.[36]

Such acts of reconciliation are important at two levels: at the individual level, between victims and perpetrators; and at the societal level. The impact at the individual level is obvious. There are at least two ways that such individual acts of reconciliation contribute to a broader society-wide process of reconciliation. First, such individual examples act as models for other individual reconciliations. Thus, a mother's forgiveness and acceptance of her son's killer acts as a spark for similar acts of reconciliation—the theory being that if she can find it in her heart to forgive her son's killer, I can find it in mine to forgive the person who tortured me. Second, examples of acts of reconciliation between victims and perpetrators of gross violations of human rights can act as proxies for a process of reconciliation among groups in society; for example, between blacks and whites; between coloureds and blacks; between supporters of the IFP and the ANC; and between black policemen and their immediate communities. It encourages individuals who may not have an identifiable victim or perpetrator on the other side of their violation, but who contributed to or suffered from such violations, to participate in the larger process of reconciliation.

It is not clear how much this idealized notion of the effect of such acts of reconciliation occurred in South Africa. The hearings were primarily attended by victims and their supporters; with some exceptions the white population was noticeably absent, raising the question of how much the message of such reconciliatory acts penetrated certain communities. At the same time, there was anecdotal evidence that individuals who used to claim that stories of state complicity in torture and murder were exaggerated no longer felt comfortable making such claims. There are few, if any, who can now argue that death squad operations like Vlakpaas did not exist; that people were not tortured;

that civilians were not targeted or terrorized.[37] This is so in no small part because some individuals came forward and took responsibility. Many always knew that such acts had been committed. The importance of the amnesty hearings was that they provided a space in which individuals *acknowledged* their participation, thus providing personal and official validation of what many already knew, and making it that much harder for individuals to deny the truth of the atrocities. To paraphrase Ignatieff, the hearings and other revelations succeeded in reducing the number of lies that circulated unchallenged.[38]

Creation of a Human Rights Culture

The question left for the future is how effective the amnesty process—its revelations of what happened and its attempt at accountability—will be in creating a reconciled society, a society that strives to respect the dignity of all its members. There are, unfortunately, no modern historical examples of the granting of amnesties for gross violations of human rights to which we can turn to predict the future impact of the South African amnesty process. Many amnesties have been granted throughout history in a wide variety of civilizations. Either they are so old that we do not have enough information to evaluate their relevance to amnesties today, or they are so new that we do not know what their long-term impact will be. In the case of recent amnesties, there is some suggestion that amnesties that incorporate little if any accountability do not enjoy legitimacy a few years after their promulgation. Thus, the effective amnesties granted by the Argentinean government to members of the military have been challenged both abroad and at home. Abroad one sees the challenge in the criminal prosecutions in Spain and Italy. In Argentina one saw the challenge in the repeal of the laws that gave effective amnesty to the military, and the prosecution of Jorge Rafael Videla, the former military leader, for child kidnapping during his dictatorial reign. The amnesty and immunity that the former Chilean military dictator Augusto Pinochet Ugarte granted to himself did not protect him from his Chilean and European victims' efforts to hold him accountable before a Spanish court.

Although our knowledge of the long-term effects of amnesties on human rights violations is small, we can look for some insight into the use of amnesties in other settings. Amnesties have been used not only in the criminal context, but also in a variety of other areas involving legal compliance; in the United States, for example, in tax and immigration situations. Without going into too much detail, a look at the effect of tax amnesties provides some insights into what effect the South African amnesty might have on the future of that country, and how we might construct an amnesty that will make more likely the substantive vision of reconciliation articulated above.

A study by the Joint Committee on Taxation of the U.S. Congress looked at the effect of tax amnesties on short-term revenue gains and future compliance.[39] While the analogy is not perfect, the short-term revenue gain in the case of tax amnesties corresponds to the immediate benefit of the amnesty process—that is, the increase in information provided through the amnesty applications and hearings—while future compliance with tax laws corresponds with future compliance with human rights laws, an important condition for creating long-term reconciliation. The obvious concern in both the tax and the human rights fields is that the use of an amnesty will create an expectation that such amnesties will be available in the future, and thus decrease deterrence against future violations. The congressional report concluded that in the tax area there were two necessary conditions for an amnesty to succeed in maximizing short-term revenue while at the same time having little negative impact on future compliance: amnesties should be (1) rare, if not unique; and (2) combined with either a real or a perceived increase in enforcement. This result suggests that in the human rights context amnesties should also be rare—possibly limited to times of fundamental societal change involving a large proportion of a society's population. This result also suggests that such amnesties should be accompanied by visible activity in the area of future human rights compliance, such as increased law enforcement and governmental accountability.

One of the arguments made for amnesties in any setting is the importance of making a clean break with the past; or of creating a common starting point for all members of society from which a better future may be created.[40] Recent history has shown us that pure amnesties, at least in the case of gross violations of human rights, do not in fact achieve such lofty goals.[41] Whether an amnesty tailored more carefully to the needs of truth, accountability, and reconciliation is possible is the question posed by the South African amnesty process. The South African amnesty process furthered both truth and reconciliation to an extent unprecedented by any previous amnesty agreements. It increased both the quantity and the quality of the information available concerning past violations; and by providing some form of accountability, it increased the possibility of creating a substantive form of reconciliation that would further the creation of a stable democracy protective of human rights. While we may not know for years to come how useful this amnesty experiment will prove to be in creating a democratic South Africa that respects and protects all of its citizens' human rights, and how useful such a model may be for other societies undergoing a similar transition, it is clear that in the short run South Africa's amnesty process contributed much more than anything previously attempted.[42] But, is it enough? It is a question that history and historians are best at answering. While we can point to things that suggest reconciliation has been significantly furthered by the amnesty process, the empirical question of how stable and cohesive a society is produced as a result is one we are ill-equipped to answer at the moment. One thing we can conclude, however, is that the amnesty process has produced a wealth of information—"truth"—that will provide important raw material for future discussions and evaluations of South Africa's past. That, in turn, may help guide the present as it creates the future.

Notes

1. I thank the United States Institute of Peace for providing the funding for my research on amnesties for human rights abuses, out of which this article derives, and the participants of the World Peace Foundation conference on the South African Truth and Reconciliation Commission, held in Somerset West, May 1998.

2. Gross violations of human rights is a term of art in South Africa, defined in the legislation creating the Truth and Reconciliation Commission as the violation of an individual's human rights through killing, abduction, torture, or severe ill-treatment (Promotion of National Unity and Reconciliation Bill ["TRC Act"] [1995], section 1[ix]). By gross violations of human rights, I mean these violations as well as other violations recognized by international treaty and custom as violations of fundamental rights of individuals and groups.

3. For a more detailed discussion of what such a minimal definition of reconciliation might look like, see the discussion of a minimally decent society in the chapter by Rajeev Bhargava in this volume.

4. I have been examining amnesties granted throughout history in connection with a forthcoming book on the moral and legal legitimacy of amnesties for human rights violations, which will provide a more detailed description of the types of amnesties that have been used.

5. In fact, amnesties granted under one regime have been annulled by successor regimes. This was the case in Argentina, where an amnesty law passed by the military regime shortly before giving up power was reversed by the new democratically elected legislature. See Amnesty International, "Argentina: The Military Juntas and Human Rights," in Neil Kritz (ed.), *Transitional Justice* (Washington, D.C., 1995), II, 332. For a nuanced discussion of the moral and legal issues raised by the Argentine "self-amnesty law," see Carlos Nino, *Radical Evil on Trial* (New Haven, 1996), 64–65.

6. For example, in Uruguay amnesty was granted for police and military acts committed for a political motive prior to 1 March 1985. Beneficiaries of the Uruguayan amnesty would only be identified, if ever, when a civil or criminal claim was brought against an individual police or military official and that official raised the amnesty as a defense. In Argentina, a de facto amnesty was granted to all members of the military for any acts committed during a specific time period. In these and other contemporary amnesties, protection from civil and criminal claims is provided to classes of individuals, or to all acts committed within a certain time period. The result is that the beneficiaries of the amnesty are allowed—with a handful of exceptions—to remain anonymous. For the text of these and other recent amnesty laws, see Kritz, *Transitional Justice*, III.

7. Although some of the arguments made for and against criminal trials also apply to civil trials, there are important differences. I limit myself here to a comparison with criminal trials.

8. Nino, *Radical Evil*, 146.

9. To be fair to Nino in particular, I should note that he was writing before the creation of the South African TRC. Nino compared criminal trials to commissions like those set up in Argentina and Chile, where the accused were not required to, and did not, participate.

10. Nino, *Radical Evil*, 146.

11. This does not mean, of course, that there may be no pressure on an individual to apply for amnesty. The pressure to apply is directly related to the risk of being subject to a criminal or civil action, which in turn depends in part on the quality of the evidence available to the state and victims, and to the resources available to the state and victims to bring such an action.

12. Such a statement against interest may not be truthful. Applicants may be trying to cover for someone else; they may have been wrongfully convicted and now want to be released from jail; or they may wrongly but sincerely believe that they committed the act in question. Such a statement may also be incomplete. Applicants might state that they assaulted someone once, when in fact they assaulted them a number of times. An applicant's statement in that case is certainly incomplete and misleading. My only point here is that based on the statement we can safely assume that the applicant assaulted an individual *at least* once.

13. An example of the last assertion is, "Yes, I killed that person, but I was acting in self-defense."

14. TRC Act, section 20. There are other requirements that an applicant must have met in order to be eligible for amnesty—for example, that the act be committed within a particular period of time—but they do not have the same effect on an applicant's testimony as the three mentioned in the text.

15. It was not clear, for example, how much detail an applicant must provide, or whether some types of information were considered more significant than others. It was also not clear what type of contradictory information the committee recognized. Ironically, some opinions denying amnesty have pointed to contradictory statements made by the applicant or others in an apartheid-era court. See, for example, the decision regarding Nzimeni Jack Menera (Application 0015/96) (Decision of 12 August 1997). For a denial of amnesty for lack of full disclosure, see the decision regarding Gerhardus Johannes Nieuwodt (Application 3920/96) (Decision of 20 December 1997), where a victim's version of events that contradicted the applicant's was accepted by the amnesty committee as true.

16. There is no mechanism in the legislation that allows the rescission of a grant of amnesty if it is discovered later that an individual had not made full disclosure. This means that ideally applicants would want to reveal only as much information as the commission already possessed, and no more. It is not clear if a successful challenge could be brought in a court to overturn an amnesty decision if there were compelling new evidence that the applicant had not made full disclosure. It is also not clear who would have standing to bring such a challenge given the commission's limited life span.

17. The definition of an "act associated with a political objective" is formalistic. The definition looks at the nature of the act and at the authority of the individual committing the act. The amnesty committee downplayed the requirements concerning the nature of the act—for example, the gravity of the act and its proportionality to the

objective pursued—and focused more on the authority of the individual; for example, was the person a member or supporter of a publicly known political organization, or was the person ordered to commit the act in question by an authorized member of such an organization? For these requirements, see TRC Act at sections 20(2) and 20(3).

18. See the decision regarding Nzimeni Jack Menera (0015/96) (Decision of 12 August 1997), in which a victim submitted a letter from the ANC noting that certain acts of murder and other violence perpetrated by the amnesty applicant in the name of the ANC did not reflect the policies of, and thus were not authorized by, the ANC. Based on that letter, it would appear that the act in question would not qualify as an act committed with a political objective. At the amnesty hearing for Menera, held almost six years after this letter was written, however, the ANC supported his application as one that was legitimately undertaken in the name of the party.

19. Government security force members who killed a diamond dealer who had cheated them later claimed that the killing and cover-up were political. Antjie Krog, *Country of My Skull* (Johannesburg, 1998), 63. The test that the amnesty committee used to determine whether an act was political is a test based on the "Norgaard Principles"—principles developed by Carl Aage Norgaard, a Danish lawyer and former president of the European Commission on Human Rights, for the United Nations in the context of the Namibian transition. See "The Norgaard Principles," in Alex Boraine and Janet Levy (eds.), *The Healing of a Nation?* (Cape Town, 1995), 156–160.

20. For example, see the opposition of the Ribeiro family to the amnesty application of their parent's killers, in which the Ribeiro's children argue that because their parents were not supporters of the ANC, their killing was not political, but rather an (apolitical) attempt by the state to terrorize a community. See Stephane Bothma, "Policemen Have Shown No Remorse—Ribeiro," *Business Day* (4 March 1997): 2.

21. This was discussed extensively during the public hearings on the amnesty application of the killers of Amy Biehl, a student from the United States. See the transcript of the Amy Biehl hearing held in Cape Town on 8–9 July 1997 (on file with the author and with the offices of the TRC).

22. Whether acts with such mixed motives *should* be eligible for amnesty, or indeed whether the political nature of an act should play such a central role in determining eligibility for amnesty, are important questions that are beyond the scope of this chapter.

23. The legislation required that an individual's belief that he was acting politically be reasonable in order to qualify for amnesty (TRC Act, section 20[2][f]). For an example in which there was evidence that the individuals involved believed that they were acting politically—in amassing weapons to preserve a white state—but were denied amnesty, see the decision of Cornelius Johannes van Wyk (Application 1050/96) (Decision of 6 December 1996).

24. Trials may also be effective when the punishment at the other end is severe. Approximately 2,000 individuals in custody in Rwanda confessed to the crime of genocide after the execution of some of those already convicted. Those confessing hoped to take advantage of a provision of the Rwandan law that provided for reduced sentences for confessions. See "2,000 Rwandans Confess to Avoid Death Penalty," *New York Times*, 16 May 1998, A4. Of course, it is by no means clear how accurate these confessions in fact were, and the use of such means to elicit information raises a number of other issues of human rights beyond the scope of this chapter.

25. See South African Truth and Reconciliation Commission, *Final Report* (Cape Town, 1998), V, chap. 3, 112–113.

26. Upon the completion of the amnesty process, the commissioners will reconvene to determine whether information revealed in the post-*Report* amnesty hearings warrants an addendum or other modification of the *Final Report*.

27. Charles Maier, who has examined these issues far more thoroughly than I, raises this empirical question in his chapter in this volume.

28. Law manifests its preference for finality in such legal doctrines as estoppel, res ipsa loquitur, and stare decisis.

29. The assertion that law is more likely to get it right than history, or that the passage of time lessens our confidence in our judgments given the consequences, is questionable. One need only compare the cases of *Plessy v. Ferguson*, 163 U.S. 537 (1896), and *Brown v. Board of Education*, 349 U.S. 483 (1954) concerning apartheid in the United States, and the two Korematsu decisions concerning the internment of Japanese-Americans during World War II (*Korematsu v. United States*, 323 U.S. 214 [1944], and *Korematsu v. United States*, 584 F. Supp. 1406 [N.D. Cal. 1984]) to see how the judgment of law can be radically distorted by the prejudices of its era.

30. The general preference of law for finality is not clearly shared by the law of international human rights, which suggests that certain crimes like genocide and other crimes against humanity are not subject to any statute of limitations. See, for example, the Convention on the Non-Applicability of Statutory Limitations to War Crimes and Crimes Against Humanity, 660 U.N.T.S. 195, reprinted in 8 I.L.M. 168 (1969).

31. Some of this information might otherwise have become available in contemporaneous trials, and then later in memoirs, deathbed confessions, and posthumous revelations. The latter three means in particular are obviously subject to distortion by the passage of time.

32. See, e.g., Joseph Goldstein, "Police Discretion Not to Invoke the Criminal Process: Low-Visibility Decisions in the Administration of Justice," *Yale Law Journal* LXIX (1960): 544, note 4.

33. See note 2, *supra*, for the South African definition of gross violations of human rights.

34. In those cases where they do not accept such responsibility, applicants may be denied amnesty. For example, in their application, the killers of Steve Biko continued to insist that Biko's death was an accident for which they could not be held responsible. They were denied amnesty, and thus were exposed to future legal action by the state and the Biko family.

35. Other things that look like punishment occurred in, or as a result of, the amnesty hearings. Thus the hearings were extremely traumatic to the perpetrators and their families, in some cases resulting in the onset or exacerbation of post-traumatic stress syndrome, or in the applicant being ostracized by family, friends, colleagues, and former superiors. Such hearings were usually infinitely more traumatic to survivors, their families, and friends. I have discussed briefly the issue of accountability and punishment in Slye, "Justice and Amnesty," in Charles Villa-Vicencio and Wilhelm Verwoerd (eds.), *Looking Back, Thinking Forward: Reflections on the South African Truth and Reconciliation Commission* (Cape Town, 1999), 171–180.

36. There is no statutory requirement that amnesty applicants express remorse or sorrow for the consequences of their actions. Of course, some applicants may make a

strategic decision to include some indication of remorse or forgiveness with the hope of affecting a committee member's decision. There are, however, also examples of acts of reconciliation between amnesty applicants and their victims that occur outside of the amnesty hearing room, and at least initially outside of the public eye.

37. Vlakplas is the name of a farm outside Pretoria that was the headquarters of the most publicly notorious state-sponsored death squad in South Africa. See Eugene de Kock, *A Long Night's Damage* (Saxonwood, South Africa, 1998), 105–113.

38. Michael Ignatieff, "Articles of Faith," *Index on Censorship* V (1996): 113.

39. The report noted that thirty-four states plus the District of Colombia had implemented at least one general tax amnesty since 1983; seven states had implemented two such amnesties; and one had implemented three. The committee also looked at the experience of tax amnesties in other countries, noting that Ireland has had five such amnesties in the last six years, and that Italy has had over a dozen tax amnesties. Report JCS-2-98, 105th Cong., 2d sess. (30 January 1998).

40. For example, in ancient and medieval China amnesties were promulgated upon the accession of a new emperor as a signal of rebirth and renewal. Amnesties were also granted each spring for similar reasons. The practice of promulgating amnesties upon the accession of a new leader is still practiced in many Asian countries, and was practiced for centuries by some of the European monarchies. See Robert McKnight, *The Quality of Mercy: Amnesties and Traditional Chinese Justice* (Honolulu, 1981).

41. Thus, we have the foreign criminal trials involving Argentinean and Chilean defendants in Italy and Spain (most notoriously against the former Chilean dictator Augusto Pinochet Ugarte), the attempts to prosecute the former Argentinean military leader Jorge Rafael Videla for child abduction committed during his reign from 1976 to 1983, and the largely symbolic repeal of the Argentinean laws that created a de facto amnesty for the military.

42. We do not yet know how the amnesty committee and the commission will assess the effectiveness of the amnesty process. The discussion of amnesty in the *Final Report* made public in October 1998 is deliberately minimal, noting the fact that it would be premature to make any conclusions while the process is ongoing. See *Final Report*, V, chap. 3.

X

Amnesty's Justice

KENT GREENAWALT

Introduction

Does amnesty appropriately accompany the work of truth commissions? This chapter focuses on the relation of amnesty to justice, on the reasons for amnesties and the amnesties these reasons support, and on the process that is due to persons accused of gross violations of human rights, when they may be granted amnesty.

After an oppressive government has concealed murder, torture, and kidnapping that its police and military have committed, a successor regime attempting to establish a fair legal order may consider whether to establish some form of truth commission.[1] Against worries that raking the coals of past abuse will induce conflict and impede development toward a more just and happy future, powerful reasons exist for exposing the truth.[2] Such exposure allows families and friends of victims to learn what has happened; it provides an official acknowledgment of wrongs; it offers at least a minimal degree of accountability; it may promote psychological healing and reconciliation;[3] it may help discourage similar crimes in the future; it may assist in reconstituting the moral order, respect for human rights, and the rule of law; and it may contribute to a "common memory" on which the whole society may build. If past abuses have been numerous, no criminal process will be equipped to bring most of the guilty to justice. A truth commission can more effectively reveal the details of former crimes than can ordinary legal procedures.

By far the most troubling issue about creating truth commissions is the place of amnesty, whether the amnesty is general or individualized. Is conditioning the operation of a truth commission on the granting of amnesty to murderers and torturers morally acceptable?

"Amnesties" typically refer to exemptions from criminal liability accorded to classes of individuals before trial.[4] In United States history, for example, amnesties were granted for certain crimes committed during the Civil War and Vietnam War. Confederate soldiers were given amnesty for fighting the Union; soldiers and civilians who evaded service in Vietnam were subsequently relieved of the threat of prosecution. When individuals who have been tried and convicted subsequently have their penalties lifted, they are pardoned. In the United States, executive grants of immunity are usually called pardons, even when they precede prosecution; thus, President Gerald Ford, upon taking office, pardoned his predecessor, President Richard Nixon. Analytically, it makes sense to treat any exemption granted in advance as a kind of amnesty, since, for purposes of moral and political justification, the division between preprosecution and postconviction relief is the crucial one.[5]

Truth commissions can achieve some of the purposes of criminal trials, and amnesties may assist the work of truth commissions; but amnesties for murderers and torturers involve a degree of injustice. Is that injustice warranted? That depends to a large extent on social context and on exactly how a program for amnesty is formulated. This chapter raises such issues. Its most important practical conclusion is that political leaders considering an amnesty conjoined with a truth commission need to explore carefully the range of possibilities for amnesty.

Amnesties and Justice

Connections between Amnesty and Truth Commissions

For leaders of a new regime, the prospect of a truth commission bears importantly on the decision whether to grant amnesty to those who have committed grave abuses of human rights during a prior government. Justifications for amnesty connect to truth commissions in at least three significant ways. The most obvious tie is that by revealing past events, a commission serves some of the purposes of ordinary criminal trials. This will be particularly true if naming of violators is an aspect of the commission's efforts.[6]

The "naming of names" may occur through open testimony of victims, survivors, and witnesses, through confessions, or through official attribution by the commission. When a commission's proceedings are in secret, the public will learn names only through its report.[7]

Like criminal trials, a truth commission that names people creates a record of what crimes were committed by whom. This record will give *some* satisfaction to those who have suffered, and constitutes a kind of official acknowledgment and minimal accountability. The record can form the basis for informal social sanctions of public disapproval or ostracism, and of related shame, embarrassment, and disadvantage for the criminal. These informal sanctions can amount to serious "punishment," though they are not formal penalties directly imposed by the state.[8] To the degree that truth commissions serve the purposes of criminal, and civil, trials, an amnesty that eliminates the opportunity for standard trials may seem acceptable.

A second way in which amnesty can relate to a truth commission is as a precondition for its effective functioning. Members of the old regime, and perhaps its organized political opponents, may provide the commission with necessary cooperation only if they are assured that they, and those they care about, will receive amnesty.[9] Extensive amnesty may assist a truth commission to perform its job much more thoroughly.

Finally, amnesty can be relevant to broader objectives of a commission. If the aspiration is that a commission will operate in a short compass of time, laying the groundwork for more harmonious relations between former adversaries, continuing criminal trials may exacerbate old wounds and impede efforts to move beyond past wrongs.[10]

We should not think of amnesty and a possible truth commission as two unrelated questions that a new regime must face: "Should we grant amnesty?" "Should we have a truth commission?" Rather, the questions are: "If we want to have an effective truth commission, will some grant of amnesty be appropriate?" "Does the prospect of a truth commission make a grant of amnesty more acceptable than it would otherwise be?"

Justice and Consequences

Those who decide whether to include amnesty as an adjunct to a truth commission must face two basic issues. Does granting amnesty to murderers and torturers involve doing injustice? What might justify the state's doing such an injustice?

In the general vocabulary of moral considerations, doing injustice is intrinsically wrong, what is called a deontological constraint. Creating civil harmony is of consequential concern; harmonious relations are desirable consequences of prudent actions. When people remark, "The ends do not justify the means," they usually mean that someone should not do what is intrinsically wrong even to achieve good consequences. This claim reflects a priority of deontological constraints over consequential calculations. The granting of an amnesty might be regarded in precisely this way—as the committing of an injustice in order to achieve desirable consequences.

Some general comments help place in context how amnesty *should* be viewed. The abstract question whether people may commit injustice to achieve desirable consequences requires two comparisons, not one. The first comparison is between doing injustice now and any predictable favorable results, including the prevention of future injustices. The second comparison is between preventing future injustices and other favorable future consequences.

According to some moral philosophies, one should not commit injustice, no matter what will follow. Traditional natural-law moralists say, for example, that one should never intentionally kill an innocent person, even if that will save many other persons from being unjustly killed.[11] One need not embrace absolutist views to be troubled by the idea of governments doing injustices to achieve later benefits. Authorities are easily carried away, perceiving dangers that do not exist and grossly exaggerating risks of future harms. Leaders sometimes believe what they say; often they cynically manipulate subordinates and the public. In virtually every instance, leaders of old regimes have justified their own abuses in terms of grave national threats; and many foot soldiers in campaigns of murder and terror have believed that these threats were real. A new regime that acknowledges its plan to sacrifice present justice to promote future benefits creates a disturbing continuity similar to the justifications of the old regime.[12] Would it not be better for the new regime to say: "We will not do injustice, even if that involves some risk to future social peace and justice"?

If injustice is done to achieve future benefits, does the nature of the benefits matter? For those who emphasize *not doing injustice in the present*, the nature of likely results is not critical. But perhaps avoiding future injustice is a more compelling reason than most other future consequences. An armed uprising by a discontented military will cause injustice. If an unjust amnesty is granted to prevent an armed uprising, some injustices are done to prevent others. If justice has a priority over desirable social consequences, an unjust amnesty may be more defensible if it prevents predictable injustice.

Without trying to work out the details, I assume the following: Any absolutist view that governments should never do injustice is mistaken; but governments should not be able easily to justify doing injustice on the basis of predicted social benefits.[13] Ordinarily, justifications based on other social benefits should be less compelling than justifications based on preventing future injustices.[14]

One particularly poignant problem about amnesties arises if the old regime refuses to give way at all without a promise of amnesty. In the Republic of South Africa, for example, high officials in the ruling National Party said that they would not surrender power without amnesty.[15] Nelson Mandela and other leaders of the African National Congress (ANC) reasonably feared that a refusal to grant amnesty would yield an intensification of violent struggle with an uncertain outcome.

Is such a threat by an old regime relevant to what the new regime should agree to do? Our ordinary moral intuition is that threats make a difference. If a criminal credibly threatens to kill someone unless we steal a $1,000 necklace from an innocent person, we are justified in taking the necklace, because it is the lesser of two evils.[16] Our doing of an injustice prevents a more serious injustice by the threatener. A response to a grave threat may be justified even though the same action would not be warranted in the absence of any threat.

The threat of a regime not to give way can undoubtedly be grave. Its military, acting unjustly, may prevent the new regime from acquiring power and will exact a high cost in human life, even if it fails. Further, a civil war is a much less promising start for a new regime than a peaceful transition. When granting amnesty in a particular form has been made a condition of a peaceful transition in authority, a new regime may be morally justified in agreeing, even if the amnesty is morally inappropriate in various respects.

One variant of the idea that amnesty should not be granted in response to a threat of the old regime is the claim that international law condemns gross violations of human rights, that states have an obligation to prosecute the violators, and that a new regime is bound not to pardon violations committed under its predecessor. There are strong arguments that torture and political murder and other extreme violations of human rights by governments violate customary international law as well as important treaties. The more difficult issue concerns a duty to prosecute.

That duty is explicit under the Convention Against Torture; and interpretations of other treaties have inferred a duty to prosecute from an obligation to make guaranteed rights effective.[17] Orentlicher, one of the strongest proponents of such a duty, acknowledges that a new regime need not prosecute most violators—exemplary prosecutions will suffice—but she resists any assertion that a new regime might avoid prosecution altogether because of the pressure of circumstances.[18]

We can easily see the dilemma. If domestic pressures excuse governments from fulfilling these international obligations, new regimes will have a ready excuse to beg off from doing what international law requires. If these regimes lack an excuse, international law paradoxically requires that they refuse to take actions that may be necessary for a peaceful transition to power.[19]

Whatever international law may require, what is its force for a new regime in these circumstances? As a legal matter, no government has authority to wipe out its own international obligations or international law consequences outside the country, but the new regime can control legal consequences within its own borders. The moral force of international law in this context is more debatable. Is a new regime morally to blame if it does not satisfy a duty to prosecute? Just as an individual is morally justified in stealing a necklace to prevent a murder, a new regime may be justified in not penalizing horrendous crimes, when that is required to terminate the rule of those under whom the horrors are committed.

Democratic countries have shown little propensity to criticize nascent democracies that have agreed to amnesties under exigent circumstances.[20] Devoid of fear of international pressure to prosecute, and placing paramount value on a peaceful transition, a prospective new regime under a realistic threat of civil war will reasonably treat the nuances of international law as of secondary importance.

If political authorities, like ordinary citizens, sometimes may respond to threats by agreeing to conditions that they would not be otherwise justified in accepting, one needs to ask about any particular amnesty whether it would be justified in the absence of some grave threat, and whether, if not, it may be justified because of such a threat.[21] What follows focuses on the extent to which amnesty is appropriate according to ordinary justification, not justification because of a grave threat.[22]

Amnesty as a Kind of Injustice

Is granting an amnesty the doing of an injustice? Even if it is, can a truth commission produce benefits that justify the injustice, or yield a substitute justice that may be superior to criminal and civil liability?

One might wonder whether granting an amnesty can ever be the doing of an injustice. In Anglo-American law, the government has extensive discretion to choose whom to prosecute. Declining to prosecute is an omission to go forward. In the United States, giving some guilty people immunity in order to gain convictions of others is widely accepted.[23] Does this show—if the practice is defensible—that nonprosecution concerns public policy only, not justice?

Prosecutorial discretion and practices of granting immunity do not show that amnesty is merely a matter of public policy, rather than justice. An aspect of justice is prosecuting those responsible for terrible crimes. If a government openly failed, for no cogent reason, to prosecute a murderer, torturer, or rapist against whom it had overwhelming evidence, few would doubt that an injustice was done. A government owes prosecution to victims and their relatives and perhaps to the law-abiding public at large.[24] The presence of injustice is yet starker if immunity extends to civil consequences. Victims are then unable to redress the injustices a criminal has committed against them.

What nonprosecution and immunity do show is broad acceptance of the idea that some injustices *of this sort* are warranted to prevent other injustices. Few take the view that the injustice of not prosecuting people who should be prosecuted is never warranted.[25]

Justified Amnesties

When is amnesty unjust? When amnesty is unjust, can a truth commission's greater or different kind of justice (or some other benefits) cancel or make up for that injustice?[26]

In thinking about amnesty, one must be careful not to oversimplify the issue as being whether a truth commission is likely to be more or less valuable than prosecutions. That comparison becomes relevant for amnesty only if prosecution and a commission are not practically compatible. If the kind of truth commission one wants is fully compatible with criminal prosecution, a belief that the commission will be more valuable than prosecutions is hardly a reason to forgo prosecutions.

This issue of compatibility raises sharply the kind of amnesty a new regime might grant. Although one kind of amnesty may be unjust, another may not be. A truth commission that needs one kind of amnesty to function effectively may find a more sweeping amnesty unnecessary.[27] Refined evaluations must assess particular forms of amnesty in relation to particular forms of truth commissions within the context of actual societies.

There are seven dimensions along which amnesties may vary: (1) An amnesty may be blanket or limited, extended to all crimes committed within a particular period, or restricted to less serious crimes or to less responsible actors, or both.[28] (2) An amnesty may be automatic, covering all individuals within the classes named, or require applications by individuals. (3) For amnesties that require individual application, an individual may or may not have to disclose exactly what crimes he or she has committed. In South Africa, for example, individuals had to make a "full disclosure" of their violations of human rights; the amnesty covers only crimes that have been fully disclosed. (4) An amnesty may affect only criminal liability or also civil liability. (5) An amnesty may be total or partial. A partial amnesty is one that exempts those covered from the full measure of criminal and civil liability, but would allow some lesser degree of punishment or liability for damages. (6) An amnesty may or may not protect persons from consequences other than legal liability. Notably, it might ensure that individuals will not be fired from jobs on the basis of criminal acts that are revealed. (7) An amnesty from civil liability may or may not be accompanied by some alternative scheme to compensate victims.

Sometimes granting amnesty is not unjust; sometimes it is. This chapter is not the place to develop an account of just amnesty, but the American Civil War and the Vietnam War provide instructive illustrations.[29] From the national government's standpoint, the seceding South engaged in an illegal insurrection. Southern officers and soldiers were guilty of crimes punishable by death. Yet, any dispassionate observer had to acknowledge that decent, honorable men who respected the rights of others fought for the South.[30] At the highest level, Robert E. Lee resigned from the Union Army to lead the Confederate Army of Virginia. Whatever Lee's legal status, most people believed he had made an honorable choice. What he and other southern officers and soldiers did was legal according to the law that they recognized, and they acted openly, without shame. Opponents of the Vietnam War who resisted conscription also acted according to their moral sense, a sense that most people in the country came to believe was honestly informed, if not necessarily correct.[31] These men were exempted from prosecution for victimless crimes, not for focused attacks on particular individuals.

The behavior of torturers and political murderers is of vastly different moral quality, and attitudes reflect such a fact.[32] No doubt, within the tight circles of those involved, murders and tortures were accepted, but these acts remained grave crimes according to regular law, and the acts were not committed and acknowledged openly. Dispassionate outsiders may understand how "normal" people may be drawn to torture and murder, but they do not consider these to be the decent acts of honorable people.

Have I left out something huge—the political nature of most amnesties? The two American amnesties served political objectives; both were efforts to heal the United States after painful political conflicts and divisions. In each instance, those who committed crimes against a national sovereign were let off the hook. If amnesty is political, the central issue, a critic might say, is what will achieve political peace? If peace requires granting amnesty to murderers and torturers, so be it.

The political nature of amnesties is highly relevant to their being granted and to their design, but political expedience is not justice. One can illustrate the difference by putting a question about people who might be covered by amnesty. Do they *deserve* exemption from prosecution? If the answer is yes, they should get amnesty as a matter of justice. If the answer is no, and, further, they *deserve* prosecution, the amnesty is unjust, even if it is politically wise.[33] Those who murder and torture for oppressive regimes do not deserve amnesty; they deserve prosecution.[34]

One argument made for amnesty for the actual torturers and murderers is that it is unfair to punish them while the higher-ups who encouraged them and covered their own tracks go unpunished. Punishing the foot soldiers of torture and not their leaders is comparatively unjust, but it is *more* unjust to let everyone go free.[35] When crimes are committed by ordinary criminal organizations, it is unfair that the troops be punished when the leaders have insulated themselves, but it would not be more just to let the actual murderers and maimers go free.

Can a truth commission provide more, or better, justice than the justice of criminal prosecution? This question provokes a "numbers" argument and a "quality" argument about the possibly superior nature of truth commission justice.

The numbers argument does not deny that amnesty for torturers and murderers involves injustice, and that, indeed, for any given offenders, it would have been better had they been tried and convicted than let go free. The argument claims, nonetheless, that this injustice is outweighed by the gain in justice from the identification of offenders by a truth commission. With the time, expense, and procedural safeguards of criminal trials, and a conspiracy of silence by former officials who know the most about gross violations of human rights, a new regime relying on criminal prosecutions alone will be able to try and convict only a very small percentage of offenders, and these will be mainly minor figures who followed instructions. A truth commission may be able to identify a much larger percentage of offenders, and allow many more victims

and survivors to tell their stories. Each testimony by a victim and each identification of an offender achieves some portion of the justice of a criminal trial
and conviction.[36]

I want to illustrate this argument by assigning some highly artificial numerical figures to it. Suppose one predicts that, without a truth commission, convictions will occur for 5 percent of offenders, but that with a form of amnesty,
the truth commission will be able authoritatively to identify 50 percent of
offenders. One further estimates on some scale that the average amount of
justice of a typical truth commission testimony and identification is 25 percent
of the average amount of justice of a conviction. If we assume 1,000 offenders
and assign a number of 1 to the conviction of every offender, we can see that
relying on criminal prosecutions alone will produce a value of 50 (1000 x 1[the
value of each conviction] x .05 [the percentage of convictions]), whereas relying on a truth commission will yield a value of 125 (1000 x .25 [the value of
identification] x .50 [the percentage of identifications]). The truth commission
will achieve more justice than relying on criminal prosecution. If many more
people will be identified than could be convicted, the numbers argument is
strong.

What might be said against it? Someone might propose that identification
and amnesty achieve *none* of the justice of criminal conviction; but we have
seen that the benefits of victim and survivor testimony, of survivors' understanding of what has happened to loved ones, and of informal social sanctions
directed at the violators of human rights, do achieve *some* justice. A second
possible objection to the numbers argument is that amnesty sacrifices present
justice, and that deontological constraints of justice should not be violated for
future benefits. I suggest that such a rigid view of criminal prosecutions and
amnesty is unwarranted.

Lurking in the second objection is a rather different third objection—one
that relates to the nature of amnesty. Failure to convict is one thing, formal
exoneration is another. We can see this objection from the points of view of a
victim's family and of an ordinary criminal. The family might say, "We can
understand if you are unable, despite your best efforts, to gather enough evidence to convict the murderers, but for you to identify the murderers and
declare them formally free of any prosecution and civil liability, for you to
remove any fear they have that they might be penalized, is something else. It
is unjust for the state to declare that the murderers, without any prosecution
or penalty, now stand on the same basis as law-abiding citizens." The ordinary
criminal asks, "Why should I, who stole a modest amount of money, go to jail,
when torturers and murderers are declared beyond the reach of the law?"

These complaints bring home forcefully the point that amnesty is not just
a failure to convict. The injustice in the state's declaring that people who
committed terrible crimes can never be convicted goes beyond failing to

prosecute and convict.[37] This injustice, at a minimum, should cause us to look at the numbers differently, not to treat amnesty just like a failure to convict.

A different objection to the numbers argument is that it can easily lead to an oversimplification of options. Any careful evaluation should attend to alternative strategies. If convictions are going to be difficult, why not punish the worst offenders and let others go free?[38] Why not employ a strategy of selective immunity in order to get some offenders to testify against others? Or why not have prosecutors skim off the cases in which prosecution looks most promising, before granting any amnesties connected with a truth commission? Or why not maintain the prospect of minor penalties and/or civil liability rather than granting total amnesty—on the view that a large reduction in possible punishment will itself be sufficient to elicit most of the information a truth commission can obtain? Even if a truth commission with broad amnesty can achieve more justice than ordinary criminal processes, it may be that a combination of approaches will better than the stark options of prosecutions or a truth commission.[39] This objection to the numbers argument should leave us wary that a blanket amnesty, including providing safety from civil liability and being available to all offenders (or to all offenders who confess), is the best way to proceed.

A Different Kind of Justice?

Some defenders of the South African Truth and Reconciliation Commission (TRC) have suggested that it may achieve a different, possibly better, kind of justice than do criminal conviction and punishment—"restorative" justice.[40] The implication seems to be that even if an equal number of offenders could be identified, and an equal number of circumstances made clear by criminal prosecutions, the route of identification by a truth commission may be equally just (or more just), though involving a different kind of justice.

Preliminary Clarifications

Whether "restorative justice" is as good as, or better than, "ordinary justice" is of critical practical importance only insofar as one needs to choose between the two. If a truth commission could achieve the benefits of restorative justice without granting amnesty, one could have both restorative justice and ordinary justice. An estimate of the value of restorative justice does affect appraisal of the numbers argument, if amnesty increases identifications by the truth commission. And the comparative worth of the two forms of justice also comes into play if criminal prosecution directly impairs the value of what the truth commission does.[41]

Second, as we saw in respect to the numbers argument, choice is not necessarily either/or. One might think a truth commission could accomplish most of the value of restorative justice without a sweeping and full amnesty against criminal and civil prosecution.

A different clarification concerns remorse and forgiveness. If amnesty is conditioned on confession, it should not, cannot, also be conditioned on remorse. Remorse is too difficult for outsiders to discern, and insincere expressions of remorse are worse than no expressions at all. Also, forgiveness cannot be demanded or expected from victims or survivors. Forgiveness by some may be the fruit of a process, but it should not be the direct objective of a government procedure that lets victims and survivors tell their stories, and that identifies offenders.[42] At the most, one might claim that a process of free testimony, identification, and confession is more likely to yield genuine remorse and forgiveness than is criminal prosecution, and that a truth commission might encourage remorse and forgiveness.

Someone might raise the conceptual question whether the restorative benefits of a truth commission with amnesty constitute aspects of justice. Proponents urge that the free testimony of victims is preferable to the constrained processes of trial, but is this a matter of justice? If a truth commission heals wounds better than would a criminal trial, is that a matter of justice? These are difficult terminological questions, but we can largely avoid them. Truth commissions do undoubtedly achieve a measure of justice, judged even by the standards of ordinary justice. Positive aspects of what they do can be counted as part of their justice (whether those aspects are, strictly speaking, matters of justice or something else). In any event, the crucial issue is whether those aspects could justify forgoing the ordinary justice of criminal trials. If the benefits are great enough, and cannot be adequately achieved if criminal processes are also involved, the answer is "yes." How far the benefits are thought of as ones of justice or something else is not so important.[43]

Finally, "restorative justice" has a distinctly religious, perhaps peculiarly Christian, ring.[44] What relevance has that? A religious person might believe that one instance of genuine remorse or forgiveness is worth many criminal convictions, because remorse and forgiveness exemplify God's path for us. Some societies may be so religious that an explicit religious justification of this sort could be sufficient to justify the treatment of political criminals; but the benefits to be gained from a transitional process need usually to be defensible in terms of a human morality that crosscuts particular religious outlooks and does not rely on explicit theological premises.[45] Claims about restorative justice need not rest on theological premises, but the claims may look different when they are grounded on a broader base.

Restorative Justice for Individuals and Societies

"Restorative justice" may concern individuals who are directly involved and the community at large.

The individuals directly involved are offenders, on the one hand, and victims and survivors, on the other. Offenders who receive amnesty for horrible abuses of human rights are treated better than ordinary justice requires, and it is hard to imagine any standard *of justice* according to which their getting off "scot-free" from legal liability is just.[46] Because offenders are treated better than they deserve from the standpoint of justice, they have no complaint. But their undeservedly generous treatment is unjust from the standpoint of victims and survivors, and the whole community. That the offenders are identified and may feel remorse hardly cancels this injustice.[47]

Criminal punishment and the possibility of civil liability are the usual ways in which a political system tries to "do justice" for victims and survivors. Can a truth commission's processes substitute for this justice? For victims and survivors who have an opportunity to testify and face offenders and, at the end of the day, are reconciled to the men who have wronged them, perhaps a kind of justice is done. But victims and survivors cannot be expected to forgive, and it is arguable whether torturers and murderers deserve forgiveness if they are not willing to compensate those they have wronged terribly.[48] The opportunity to testify, and the identification of offenders, valuable as they are, are not an equivalent of criminal punishment and civil liability for those who have been wronged.

It might be suggested that civil liability is not important. Most offenders will lack resources to pay significant damages, and a system of public reparations may be in place.[49] One answer to the resource worry is that many officials of the old regime, especially higher-ups, will have more money than garden-variety criminals. A more significant answer tracks a point made about amnesty in general, as it compares with nonprosecution. Predicting that victims will not recover because offenders have little money is one thing; the government's declaring that offenders are legally free from any threat of liability is another.

As for public reparations, they do not provide the satisfaction of recovery from those who have committed the wrongs; and no public reparations are likely to approximate what one might be owed according to the usual standards of tort law. The comparative inadequacy of the reparations will be particularly great when a country is poor and the gross abuses of human rights have been extensive.[50]

Looked at from the standpoint of victims and their relatives, a truth commission's processes and identification do not achieve the justice of a criminal process plus potential civil liability.

Suppose it is claimed that this conclusion reflects a limited view of justice—that the possibility of restoring desirable relations between offenders and victims counts more than ordinary legal remedies. Were "restorative justice" with amnesty in general an improvement on punitive and compensatory justice, it should be more widely employed.[51] The fact that virtually no one suggests converting ordinary criminal and civil processes into identification without liability is evidence that almost everyone continues to regard ordinary justice as desirable justice for the individuals involved.[52]

An evaluation of "restorative justice" is affected by one's view of the informal sanctions of ostracism, disapproval, and disadvantage. I suggest that the likelihood of these sanctions diminishes *to some extent* the injustice of not punishing offenders. The application of these sanctions depends on some part of the community not fully forgiving the offender.[53] Would proponents of a remorse-forgiveness model really wish the identified, perhaps confessing, offenders of terrible crimes to be fully accepted by everyone, to proceed with their careers as if they had never done anything wrong?[54] That disapproval and its consequences are regarded as desirable features of the South African system of amnesty shows an attitude toward forgiveness that is complex and somewhat ambivalent, an attitude that those who have committed terrible wrongs against their fellows should not proceed through life unaffected.

A process of identification that includes victim testimony and offender confession may be healthy in opening possibilities of remorse and forgiveness; but, from the perspective of human morality (as it is, and as it reasonably should be), these possibilities do not make the process superior to ordinary criminal justice and civil liability in its justice toward individuals involved.

When one turns to the entire community, or large subcommunities, resolution is less clear-cut. In the typical transitional situation, there will have been government offenders (mostly police and military persons and their political superiors) and government opponents, and a large slice of the population in between.[55] Some representatives of the government, and perhaps some opponents, will have tortured and murdered for political objectives.[56] By granting amnesty, the new government signals that it will not seek revenge against members of the prior regime. In transitional circumstances, citizens may wonder how fair prosecutions could be, and even if their fairness is not in doubt, prosecutions may prevent healing between opposing forces.[57] If an amnesty reaches offenders on both sides, everyone may perceive a kind of reciprocal acceptance: your representatives will be free of liability, but, in return, so also will ours. A process of criminal prosecution, extending for years, might exacerbate old wounds in a way that a truth commission would not.

One could argue whether these possible benefits of a truth commission with amnesty count as aspects of justice or of broader social welfare, but the critical issue is whether these benefits justify sacrificing the justice achieved by criminal process and civil liability. In principle, the answer is "yes," although whether the benefits will occur is uncertain and depends on context. Not all societies will experience more healing because criminal prosecutions are avoided. One doubts, for instance, whether European Jews would have felt a comfortable part of post–World War II Europe if those who engineered the murders of millions of Jews were openly flourishing; one doubts that Bosnian Muslims will feel reconciled to Bosnian Serbs if amnesty is granted to sponsors of genocidal acts against their Muslim neighbors.

When one combines the argument about social healing with the "numbers argument," one has a strong case for some form of amnesty; but it is highly doubtful that the amnesty should be blanket and full.[58] Incentives for offenders to come forward to admit what they have done, as South Africa has proved, are crucial. Ideally, room should be left to prosecute especially egregious offenders against whom powerful evidence already exists.[59] All civil liability should not be foreclosed. Why not say that those whose confessed identity as offenders earns amnesty from criminal prosecution will be vulnerable to civil liability up to a percentage of their assets or income? The prospect of moderate civil liability would hold open some opportunity for redress of victims. It would probably not discourage offenders from admitting their guilt, since they could earn immunity from criminal prosecution and a *partial* civil immunity that would prevent them from being impoverished by having to pay damages.

Due Process for Claimed Offenders in a Process with Amnesty

Any system combining public testimony, identification of offenders in a public report, and amnesty raises the question of what process is due to those who, it is claimed, have committed grave crimes. As with other questions, we need to distinguish terminological issues from issues of substance, and to resist simple either/or thinking. The main terminological issue is what constitutes due process. The either/or approach to be avoided is that a straightforward choice must be made between the benefits of free public testimony and report identification, on the one hand, and protection of claimed offenders, on the other.

People who stand to suffer in some way from negative government action are not always entitled to the full panoply of protections that goes with the criminal process. The process that is "due" varies.[60] People who are named as offenders by witnesses or in a government report do not thereby suffer a loss of liberty or property; they are not owed the full process of a criminal defendant. Some settings are not compatible with full protection. If two opponents have decided to conciliate their dispute, formal processes can be a barrier. In other circumstances, the barriers to achieving full protection are time and resources.

The either/or way of thinking goes something like this: "Offenders are much better off under a truth commission, with a possibility of amnesty, than under vigorous criminal prosecution; and their being named is not a deprivation of liberty or property. Therefore, they should accept the consequences of the commission's process without complaint."

The problems are manifold. Being named as a murderer or torturer is a very serious matter, whether or not one is subject to subsequent criminal prosecution.[61] Further, the advantages of amnesty for actual offenders do not apply to people mistakenly named as offenders (who presumably would not be prosecuted or would be acquitted).[62] If a decision has been made to allow free victim testimony, the desirable informality of that procedure precludes immediate cross-examination by lawyers representing claimed offenders, but truth commissions should be very careful about who they allow to give public testimony, and they should be very careful who they name as offenders.[63] Also, they should provide an opportunity for named offenders to come forward and try to clear their names.[64] If truth commissions are careful, and few claimed offenders are innocent, the presence of such a procedure will afford some assurance to a public that those named are guilty. Although a degree of compromise of full procedural protections is necessary, the compromise should be no greater than is needed.

Conclusion

Amnesties for those who have committed murder and torture for oppressive governments are unjust. Possibilities for "restorative justice" do not eliminate elements of injustice in letting murderers and torturers go free. Nevertheless, some amnesty can often be justified as an adjunct of a truth commission. Amnesty can be a means to reduce future injustices and to deflect other grave social harms. One kind of justification is that a new regime's hands are tied by threats of civil war; but amnesty can be justified even when a new regime has greater flexibility.

Individual offenders in these circumstances do not deserve amnesty. Some form of amnesty is defensible to elicit greater truth about abuses and to promote healing in the society. If a truth commission can draw testimony from those to be granted amnesty, much more will be revealed about past abuses than would be possible in a series of criminal trials. And the process will take much less time.

The classes of those to receive amnesty should be carefully drawn, and amnesty should be granted only to those who are willing to step forward and admit what they have done. Typically, an amnesty should be partial in its effects. It should not immunize offenders from all civil liability. Offenders should be responsible to pay some damages to victims or their surviving relatives.

The problems of transitional justice are difficult and complex. Assisting a society to move to a more just and decent legal order is not simple. People can reasonably disagree about the outline of a desirable truth commission and about criteria for amnesty, if any amnesty is to be provided.

Notes

1. The discussion here assumes that the successor government represents a sharp break with the old regime. As Levinson emphasizes, the need to uncover systematic abuses can also arise for societies with continuity in government (Sanford Levinson, "Trials, Commissions, and Investigating Committees: The Elusive Search for Norms of Due Process," in this book).

2. Slye suggests that in some circumstances immediate revelation of the facts may not be desirable, although later disclosure may be helpful (Ronald Slye, "Amnesty, Truth, and Reconciliation: Reflections on the South African Amnesty Process," in this book). The degree of exposure that makes sense may depend partly on the kinds of wrongs done in the past. Holmes has written that enthusiasm for exposing Communist abuses has diminished quickly in most Eastern European countries; he describes a socially diffuse sense of complicity for the standard abuses under Communist regimes (Stephen Holmes, "The End of Decommunization," in Neil Kritz [ed.], *Transitional Justice* [Washington, D.C., 1995], I, 116–120).

3. Lisa M. Kois cautions, "It is difficult to know where to look for a illustrative example of successful national reconciliation or even what successful national reconciliation means." See Kois, "Walking that Fine Line: The Quest for Truth, Justice, and Reconciliation in Sri Lanka," unpublished paper (1998). The caution is well taken, but judging whether previously opposed groups in a society have become more or less reconciled is not too difficult.

4. See also Slye, "Reflections."

5. I shall not discuss pardons, understood as postconviction relief, further. What one can say in general is that conviction alone satisfies some objectives of a criminal process, but obviously not all. Insofar as pardon allows more benefits of the criminal process than does amnesty, it may be somewhat easier to justify. However, postconviction pardons may yield fewer benefits for the effectiveness of a truth commission. In particular, they may not encourage violators who have yet to be tried to disclose what they have done, and they do not prevent criminal proceedings from dragging on past the period during which a truth commission operates.

6. Thomas Burgenthal, one of the commissioners for the Commission for Truth in El Salvador, has an interesting discussion of its decision to name names and the pressure against their doing so (Thomas Burgenthal, "The United Nations Truth Commission for El Salvador," in Kritz, *Transitional Justice*, I, 293, 306–307). The issue of whether a commission report will provide names takes on overwhelming importance if the proceedings are confidential, as in El Salvador, and the report is public. See Kois, "Walking that Fine Line," on arguments pro and con. Priscilla B. Hayner ("Fifteen

NOTES   **205**

Truth Commissions—1974 to 1994: A Comparative Study," in Kritz, *Transitional Justice*, I, 225, 254–257) reports that until 1992, no truth commission had named names publicly. In Argentina, however, names submitted to the president had been leaked to the press. At a discussion of truth commissions, Yael Tamir remarked, "In the Middle East, when people are named as collaborators, they are in a very unpleasant situation, to put it mildly." Quoted in Henry Steiner (ed.), *Truth Commissions: A Comparative Assessment* (Cambridge, Mass., 1997), 46.

7. However, names may be leaked despite an official policy of secrecy.

8. A person identified as having committed gross abuses might lose his job in the military or police, but I do not consider that a formal penalty.

9. Alex Boraine ("Truth and Reconciliation Commission in South Africa: The Third Way," in this book) says that in South Africa perpetrators came forward in the "thousands." The incentive to speak will, of course, depend on the kind of amnesty given. If some people receive an amnesty without disclosing facts, they have little selfish reason to disclose.

10. Martha Minow writes, "It is far from clear that a truth commission can achieve therapeutic and reconciliation goals at the same time that prosecutions proceed" (Martha Minow, "The Hope for Healing: What Can Truth Commissions Do?" in this book).

11. Kent Greenawalt ("Natural Law and Political Choice: The General Justification Defense, Criteria for Political Action, and the Duty to Obey the Law," *Catholic Law Review* XXXVI [1986]: 1, 4–23), shows that such a position can be defended only on a particular assumption about God's role in human affairs.

12. See Amy Gutmann and Dennis Thompson, "The Moral Foundations of Truth Commissions," in this book.

13. Two problems exist: First, an absolute priority of justice over all other social values is not warranted. Governments are responsible for the lives of their citizens. If a government can prevent the loss of 10,000 lives through a natural catastrophe that does not involve injustice, doing so is more important than preventing the unjust failures to promote 10,000 employees. Second, just what consequences involve injustice is very slippery. Is the government's failure to save 10,000 lives unjust if it could have saved them? If so, any urgent government concern involving people's fates can be converted into an issue of justice. More generally, the line between justice and ordinary conditions of social welfare can be thin. Suppose, in the South African context, granting an amnesty would promote economic development. The dire poverty of vast sections of the population is substantially the result of the injustices of apartheid, including forced removals, passes, homelands, inadequate schools, and job discrimination. Any economic benefits that reach the black members of society might fairly by characterized as helping to redress the injustices of apartheid. On this reasonable account, the country's economic health is substantially a concern about economic justice.

I assume that in political life, government justifications should be judged not only according to some detached assessment in individual instances, but also according to whether it is desirable for governments to be able to advance these sorts of justifications. Some kinds of justifications may be dangerous because they are easy to put forward and the relevant facts are highly disputable.

14. Gutmann and Thompson say that moral justifications for truth commissions that sacrifice ordinary justice "should explicitly appeal to rights or goods that are morally

comparable to the justice that is being sacrificed." "Social stability" does not qualify; promoting "justice in the future" does. See Gutmann and Thompson, "Moral Foundations," in this book.

15. See, e.g., Boraine, "The Third Way," in this book.

16. Dennis Thompson has reminded me that it may sometimes be wrong to yield (or appear to yield) to a threat even if performing the act might otherwise be all right. A gift of $2,000 by me to a relative might be fine, but perhaps I would do something morally wrong if I provided the relative with $2,000 because (or after) he had blackmailed me.

17. The most elaborate argument for an international law duty to prosecute is made in Diane F. Orentlicher, "Settling Accounts: The Duty to Prosecute Human Rights Violations of a Prior Regime," in Kritz, *Transitional Justice*, I, 375. See also Aryeh Neier, "What Should Be Done about the Guilty?" in Kritz, *Transitional Justice*, I, 173, 179–180. John Dugard points out that apartheid itself is regarded as a crime in international law, and that South Africa may be failing in an obligation to punish leaders in the era of apartheid, quite apart from any participation by them in murders, tortures, and other brutalities (Dugard, "Retrospective Justice: International Law and the South African Model," in A. James McAdams [ed.], *Transitional Justice and the Rule of Law in New Democracies* [South Bend, Ind., 1997], 269).

18. Orentlicher, "Settling Accounts," 402–409, 413–416.

19. See Carlos Nino, "Response: The Duty to Punish Past Abuses of Human Rights Put into Context: The Case of Argentina," in Kritz, *Transitional Justice*, I, 417.

20. Ibid., 430.

21. This conclusion affects how I take the thoughtful discussion in Amy Gutmann and Dennis Thompson, "Moral Foundations." Insofar as their essay sets out to establish conditions without which a truth commission plus amnesty cannot be justified, I say that otherwise unacceptable features could be justified reactions to grave threats. The issues that they raise are ones that concern (1) justification in ordinary circumstances and (2) what makes an arrangement of a truth commission with amnesty *more or less* morally sound (whatever the circumstances of its creation).

22. I put aside an intermediate case in which the old regime does not threaten civil war, but the new regime fears reasonably that civil war will result if it does not grant a particular kind of amnesty.

23. See Levinson, "Trials, Commissions, and Investigating Committees," in this book.

24. That nonprosecution involves government inaction rather than action might make some difference, but the government's failure is still an injustice. See the comment of Dennis Thompson, in Steiner, *Truth Commissions*, 51. In characterizing nonprosecution as an injustice, I do not analyze the extent to which considerations of justice are ultimately separable from consequential considerations. I suggest the complexity of this issue in "Punishment," *Journal of Criminal Law and Criminology* LXXIV (1983): 343.

25. However, perhaps within other legal systems people may have a different view.

26. The best terminology is a subject of disagreement. Some people say that what would otherwise be an injustice is rendered not an injustice if the reasons for doing it are strong enough (even though the feature that seems unjust is not itself eliminated). Others say that the injustice remains, but is somehow warranted. Those who prefer the first vocabulary could talk about whether amnesty is prima facie unjust, leaving open the

possibility that it is not really unjust if the reasons for granting it are strong enough. I prefer the second approach, and talk about the possible injustice of granting amnesty; but I do not preclude the option that granting an unjust amnesty may be justified.

27. More precisely, some modest sacrifice in the achievement of a commission's goals may be acceptable in order to gain some convictions.

28. Any imaginable amnesty is somewhat limited. Not every crime committed by every criminal is the subject of amnesty.

29. See Kent Greenawalt, "Vietnam Amnesty—Problems of Justice and Line-Drawing," *Georgia Law Review* XI (1977): 1.

30. It might be fairly said that anyone who fought for the Confederacy did not respect the human rights of slaves; and it might be argued that this disrespect bore on whether amnesty should have been granted. It is of some relevance that some border states that remained within the Union retained slavery throughout the war. (Slavery within "loyal" states was not covered by the Emancipation Proclamation.)

31. Some draft evaders and others who qualified for amnesty did not act for conscientious reasons, but a high percentage did so.

32. I do not mean to suggest that the moral status of the acts is determined by public attitudes. Without making the argument, I am assuming that these differences in attitude are responsive to moral differences in behavior. Public attitudes count directly in decisions about amnesty in some calculus of political feasibility.

33. I pass over the intermediate possibility that law violators neither deserve amnesty nor prosecution, that either disposition would be appropriate as far as a result is concerned. In that event, an amnesty is not unjust, though it is not required by justice.

34. There is a rather different "political" argument. It is that people, including authorities of the state, are swept up in political movements, and cannot be blamed for what they do as parts of these movements. At least as to choices that could have been made otherwise, this argument seems unappealing for most of those who torture and murder.

35. However, one might argue on behalf of some subordinates that they were reasonably ignorant that orders they were receiving were illegal or that they were subject to duress (for example, that they might themselves have been killed if they did not obey an order to kill). When such arguments are powerful, they make the case for amnesty stronger.

36. Slye says that, in terms of participation by those accused and quality of information, the proceedings of the TRC are probably superior to criminal trials (Slye, "Reflections," in this book). Boraine has suggested that truth is a limited form of justice (Boraine, "The Third Way," in this book). Aryeh Neier, a strong proponent of prosecutions, believes that the "truth phase" of the government, in acknowledging the responsibility of its agents and making public exactly what happened, is more important than the "justice phase" of prosecution and conviction (Neier, "What Should Be Done," 180). Lawrence Weschler puts the dilemma and the numbers argument succinctly. "[T]he families of extremely prominent murdered people, such as Steve Biko and Griffiths Mxenge . . . are among the few people who might reasonably expect to get justice. But their opportunity for justice might deprive millions of people of the possibility of truth. The trade-off is clear. Justice might be rendered in a few highly publicized cases. Or many people might have the opportunity to know of the loved one's fate. I prefer more truth for more people" (Weschler, in Steiner, *Truth Commissions*, 52).

37. *If* a failure to prosecute were based on corruption, favoritism, or indolence, that might be as unjust as amnesty, though in a somewhat different way.

38. In a report of an Aspen Institute conference, Alice Henkin wrote, "Several participants suggested that while there may be room for governmental discretion in dealing with the perpetrators of lesser crimes, gross abuses such as genocide, torture, disappearance and extrajudicial or summary executions must always be criminally prosecuted and punished" (Alice H. Henkin, "State Crimes: Punishment or Pardon" [Conference Report], in Kritz, *Transitional Justice*, IV, 184, 187). Writing about international law duties, Orentlicher acknowledges that new regimes could not be expected to punish all of those who committed even very serious crimes. She suggests that exemplary trials are all right, if the persons prosecuted are those most responsible or those involved in the most notorious crimes. See Orentlicher, "Settling Accounts," 404–409. In Argentina, members of the military accepted prosecutions of disgraced leaders, but threatened an uprising when prosecution of middle level officers was a prospect. See Kois, "Walking that Fine Line."

39. The South African model dominates present public interest in truth commissions. It is worth recalling that previous commissions have not included conditions of amnesty set out before the commissions began their work.

40. See Boraine, "The Third Way," in this book; Martha Minow, "The Hope for Healing: What Can Truth Commissions Do?" also in this book (quoting Archbishop Desmond Tutu, the chairman of the South African commission). Elizabeth Kiss writes of recognition as a distinct form of justice (Elizabeth Kiss, "Moral Ambition within Political Constraints: Reflections on Restorative Justice," in this book). For views of the commissioners, see TRC, *Final Report* (Cape Town, 1999), I, 125–134, 17–19 (foreword by chairperson).

41. See Minow, "The Hope for Healing."

42. But see Kiss, "Moral Ambition." She says that "there is nothing wrong in principle, with a policy of forgiveness" so long as "those who refuse to forgive are treated with appropriate respect."

43. However, this classification does bring us back to the issues about deontological constraints and favorable consequences, issues that have substantive implications. Someone who claimed that the benefits of truth commissions do not concern justice might then proceed to accord those benefits a lower significance than matters of justice.

44. See Kiss, "Moral Ambition." The *Final Report* of the Truth and Reconciliation Commission, note 40, above, emphasizes the traditional African concept of *ubuntu*.

45. See Gutmann and Thompson, "Moral Foundations" (in this book), claiming that justifications for truth commissions should rest on public reasons. See Kent Greenawalt, *Private Consciences and Pubic Reasons* (New York, 1995), and Kent Greenawalt, *Religious Convictions and Political Choice* (New York, 1988). I am not at all confident that what I say about the United States holds for South Africa; the religious perspectives of many involved in the TRC pose an important and interesting "test" about the proper role of religion in the political life of liberal democracies.

46. As in previous sections, I skip over the intermediate possibility that whether they get amnesty is a matter of indifference from the standpoint of justice.

47. I put aside the numbers argument that the limited justice of "truth" for many cancels the injustice of amnesty in regard to those who might have been convicted.

48. The relation of forgiveness and results is difficult. Forgiveness may be a matter of grace, not something wrongdoers ever quite "deserve." And perhaps forgiveness is never inappropriate; it may be good to forgive regardless of how an offender behaves. (But see Rajeev Bhargava, "Is the Idea of a Truth Commission Justified?" in paper presented at the South African TRC conference at Somerset West (1998), note 51: "A perpetrator cannot be forgiven if he neither acknowledges or repents his crime.") Nevertheless, there are various steps offenders may take that make it more appropriate to forgive than it would otherwise be. See Jeffrie G. Murphy, "Forgiveness and Resentment," in Jeffrie Murphy and Jean Hampton (eds.), *Forgiveness and Mercy* (New York, 1988), 24–25. One should be more ready to forgive someone who expresses genuine remorse and offers compensation than someone who keeps trampling on one's rights without regret.

49. TRC had a separate committee dealing with reparations.

50. Many more people will benefit from reparations than ordinary civil liability, because recipients will not need to establish which individuals were responsible. The outcomes of crimes will be established as a result of confessions produced by amnesty, and because recovery will not depend on offenders' pocketbooks.

51. It might be answered that deterrence is a more central element for punishment of ordinary crimes; but deterrence remains of importance in respect to political crimes (although the connection between punishment of former officials in one country and era to behavior in another country or era is highly conjectural).

52. I do not mean to dismiss out of hand the possibility that the restorative model is one that warrants much broader use. Our standard thinking about justice may be crippled by a lack of imagination.

53. It might be answered that ideally the victims and survivors would forgive and that those closer to the offender would express disapproval and reject. But it is a somewhat strange model that counts on victims having a less condemnatory attitude toward those who have wronged them than those whose lives are intertwined more regularly with the lives of offenders.

54. In his interesting discussion of forgiveness, Bhargava writes that forgiveness does not entail amnesty and should not be equated with mercy. Bhargava, "Idea," note 41 and note 51. An employer could both forgive dishonest employees and fire them for their dishonesty, but usually forgiveness involves restoring the person forgiven to relations that existed before the offense. Of course, the government could treat people as unsuited for official positions while encouraging members of society to forgive them for their past offenses. The TRC did not recommend automatic disqualification from office, but it did suggest that those making appointments and recommendations consider disclosures made before the commission (*Final Report*, I, note 41, at 3).

55. In some political orders there may be very few who are really in between, although support of the government or its opponents may be more or less active.

56. In some countries, some opponents of the oppressive regimes commit grave crimes; in other countries, they do not.

57. People often speak of "victor justice" as if it is not real justice. Just how fair trials under a new regime will be will depend very greatly on the society involved. If, as in South Africa, the new regime does not replace judges from the old regime, one might have considerable confidence that trials of former officials would be fair.

58. Of course, the argument for social healing is strong only in countries where the argument's factual premises are well grounded.

59. One of the criteria for amnesty in South Africa is the proportionability of the act to the objective pursued; but it is understood that many murders and serious tortures are not going to be treated as disproportionate.

60. See Levinson, "Investigating Bodies."

61. In some societies, private revenge constitutes a serious danger.

62. In South Africa, only those who confess get amnesty, so someone mistakenly named will definitely not receive amnesty (unless he or she has made a false confession).

63. Commissions that operate confidentially also cannot have such cross-examination. See the discussion of standards of evidence in Burgenthal, "Truth Commission," in Kritz, *Transitional Justice*, I, 301.

64. Ibid.

XI

Trials, Commissions, and Investigating Committees

THE ELUSIVE SEARCH FOR NORMS OF DUE PROCESS

SANFORD LEVINSON[1]

Introduction Truth Commissions and "Due Process of Law"

At least some of the debate about truth commissions, including, most certainly, the South African Truth and Reconciliation Commission (TRC), concerns their fidelity to the norms of due process of law in regard to those accused of perpetrating immense wrongs against the victims whose stories are the primary focus of the commissions. An implicit (and sometimes explicit) critique of truth commissions is that to the extent that they represent a deviation from—sometimes only a *complement to*, other times a *substitution for*—the regularized formal procedures of criminal law, or even civil litigation, they are deficient, a distinctly second-best way either of ascertaining the truth about the past or of rectifying, through corrective justice, the injustices that occurred then.[2]

One version of this critique can be found in the work of Ackerman. Writing in particular of the aftermath of Communism in Eastern Europe, Ackerman severely criticizes those who would "squander moral capital in an ineffective effort to right past wrongs—creating martyrs and fostering political alienation, rather than contributing to a genuine sense of vindication." Indeed, he says, "Moral capital is better spent in educating the population in the *limits* of the law" rather than engaging in "a quixotic quest after the mirage of corrective justice." Ackerman is not simply making a political point about the effective expenditure of political capital. Rather, he also cautions that any attempts to engage in corrective justice will generate "the perpetuation of moral arbitrariness and the creation of a new generation of victims" because of the inevitable deviations from due process that would attach to trials.[3]

Most of the discussion of such issues has involved self-consciously "transitional" regimes, whether in Central or South America, Eastern Europe, or South Africa.[4] An implicit assumption of such discussion is that one can distinguish clearly between such transitional regimes and presumably "mature" liberal regimes where the trade-offs between certain norms of due process and the achievement of social justice are not so glaring. This chapter calls that distinction into question, by looking at one particular case involving the great transition in the United States, in the 1950s (and thereafter) from its own version of racial apartheid to a more genuinely inclusionist society.

The American Dilemma, the United States Commission on Civil Rights, and "Due Process of Law"

In 1957, one of the chief legislative battles within the Congress of the United States concerned a civil rights bill, which would become the first such bill to be passed in the twentieth century. Slowly but surely, what Myrdal labeled the "American Dilemma"—the patent conflict between an "American creed" organized around aspirations of equality and freedom, on the one hand, and the realities of the treatment of American blacks, on the other—was capturing national attention.[5] The reasons, of course, were many, ranging from the defiant response of southern states to the Supreme Court's decision three years earlier in *Brown v. Board of Education*, which invalidated the mandated separation of the races in public schools, to the pasting the United States was taking in the Cold War debates with the Soviet Union about the treatment of its black population. Indeed, the United States, in its brief to the Supreme Court in the *Brown* case, referred to "the problem of racial discrimination . . . in the context of the present world struggle between freedom and tyranny" and noted segregation's "adverse effect" on America's winning that struggle.[6]

Although the 1957 legislation pales in comparison to the far more significant statutes passed in the 1960s, when the Civil Rights movement was at its height, one of its more important features was the creation of the United States Commission on Civil Rights that would be charged with investigating the situation and preparing a series of reports to Congress, which would presumably act on its recommendations.[7] Southern members of Congress opposed the creation of the commission and then took umbrage at the appointment of some of its members, charging them with being biased against the South (by which was meant southern whites) and with having an undue commitment to civil rights.

Acting under its mandate to ascertain (and then spell out) the often harsh truths of American society, the commission held a variety of hearings throughout the South, including hearings in Shreveport, Louisiana, concerning voting discrimination. Although the Fifteenth Amendment in 1870 had purported to deny exclusion to the ballot on grounds of race, it represented a hollow aspiration so far as most southern blacks were concerned. The commission heard testimony from a number of blacks complaining that they had unjustifiably been denied the right to vote. These witnesses had often named specific Louisiana officials as those placing hurdles in their way. The commission then subpoenaed a number of these officials to explain why so few black citizens were actually registered to vote in that state. Several of these officials objected, offering among their grounds that the complaints against them had been made in "confidential" testimony before the commission, a procedure defended by the commission as absolutely necessary, given the entirely reasonable black fears of retaliation.

A suit was filed by these Louisiana officials, complaining that the commission's procedures constituted a violation of their rights, as guaranteed under the Fifth Amendment to the United States Constitution, which states that no person shall be "deprived of life, liberty, or property, without due process of law." To be subjected to official interrogation by a federal investigatory body—and the possibility of being publicly identified as malefactors in subsequent reports of the commission—without an opportunity to learn the identity of their accusers and to cross-examine them, they argued, violated basic tenets of due process, including "their right to be confronted by their accusers, to know the nature and character of the charges made against them," and to be effectively represented by counsel who could interrogate their accusers.[8]

The case ultimately made its way to the Supreme Court, which, through an opinion written by Chief Justice Earl Warren, ruled against the officials. Beginning his analysis by noting that "the requirements of due process frequently vary with the type of proceeding involved," Warren went on to to hold that the specific procedural rights, however "desirable in some situations," were not constitutionally mandated in the context of the Civil Rights Commission. In particular, "when governmental action does not partake of an adjudication," an authoritative determination of legal rights and obligations, procedural rights can be relaxed. Although lower courts had implied that additional protections were required "since the commission's proceedings might irreparably harm those being investigated by subjecting them to public opprobrium and scorn, the distinct likelihood of losing their jobs, and the possibility of criminal prosecutions," Warren dismissed these points as "conjectural." Morever, even if they occurred, "they would not be the result of any affirmative determinations made by the Commission."[9] No one would be ordered to ostracize or otherwise take action against those described as having engaged in the suppression of blacks' civil rights. Any negative social or legal consequences would, presumably, be merely indirect results of otherwise legitimate governmental activity.

Not the least persuasive part of the majority opinion was a thirty-two-page appendix that followed it, which listed many different examples of federal congressional and administrative procedures that similarly failed to grant the full panoply of rights that a criminal defendant might have. There was nothing particularly unusual about the Civil Rights Commission, save, perhaps, the volatility of the issues that it was charged with studying. To identify the hearings of the commission or of a congressional investigating committee with a judicial trial was to engage in a category mistake.

The Court was not unanimous in its approval. Significantly, a dissent was filed by William O. Douglas, the most fiercely civil libertarian judge on the Court, joined by another great civil libertarian, Hugo Black. Douglas noted that the named individuals who were the focus of the hearings were subject to de facto adjudication, even if the commission could not formally punish. The key word here may be "formally," since the "court of public opinion" could certainly work its ways against those criticized by the Civil Rights Commission.[10] Interestingly enough, Douglas conceded that congressional committees could operate under rules similar to those of the commission, but he distinguished "a Congressional Committee composed of Senators or Congressmen" from the executive-branch agency that was the Civil Rights Commission.[11] The basis of this distinction was left unexplained. It may be, as a practical matter, that Douglas may have thought that the Court would have more success in affecting the Civil Rights Commission than Congress.

This thirty-five-year-old Supreme Court case, dealing with the the United States Commission on Civil Rights, can help us assess the work of the far more recent (and far more politically important) South African TRC. The reasons are twofold. First, and more easily, I want to underscore a major theme of this chapter, the complexity of defining "due process of law" and the lack of any uniform set of criteria that must be complied with whenever a state agency investigates alleged misconduct by named persons. "Due process" is a highly flexible concept whose definition is subject to all sorts of contextual considerations, and any analysis that ignores this flexibility will be profoundly misleading, especially in terms of understanding the positive law. (One might criticize the positive law as being insufficiently respectful of individual rights.)

My second reason for examining the experience of the Civil Rights Commission has less to do with law as such than with the way we conceptualize the entire issue of "truth commissions" and the occasion for their appearance. Ash notes, "The question of what nations should do about a difficult past is one of the great subjects of our time."[12] Although he is specifically referring to a variety of "transitional" countries, especially those in Eastern Europe, as well as South Africa, it should be crystal clear that coming to terms with "difficult pasts" is scarcely limited to these societies. We ought to guard ourselves against the temptation to deny important commonalities between the "transitional" societies and ostensibly nontransitional ones.

No citizen of the United States, for example, should be complacent about the country's own willingness to confront the difficulties attached to the most important single feature of its own past, race-based chattel slavery and its aftermath. Rosenberg, in her invaluable book on the Eastern European response to the collapse of Communism, reveals that she may know more about Eastern Europe (and Latin America, about which she has also written sensitive analyses) than her native country when she suggests that because Americans "worship the self-made man and constantly reinvent ourselves," they do not "understand the importance of the past."[13] More telling is the title of a book by Horowitz, *Confederates in the Attic: Dispatches from the Unfinished Civil War*.[14]

American newspapers are filled with articles detailing debates about whether the nation should "apologize" for its 250-year-long toleration of chattel slavery (and subsequent segregation and other forms of racial discrimination); contemprary American politics also feature remarkably heartfelt and bitter clashes about the propriety of southern states continuing to fly over their capitols flags commemorating the Confederacy and attempted dissolution of the Union, which cost the lives of one of every fifty Americans. As Faulkner, one of America's greatest novelists (who, not at all coincidentally, was from Oxford, Mississippi, and took as his subject the deepest of the Deep South) put it, "The past is never dead. It's not even past."[15] Moreover, one might well argue that the inability of the United States to put slavery and the Confederacy firmly in its past is precisely the result of failing fully to come to terms with their realities in the immediate aftermath of the 1861–1865 Civil War.[16] Or, perhaps as much to the point, by 1877 "reconciliation" took complete precedence over grappling with the "truths" of postbellum society and polity. The "Compromise of 1877" meant the acquiescence by northern political elites in the return to political power, albeit without the formal structure of slavery, of the white elites who had formerly dominated politics; and American politics have been shaped by that decision ever since.

The United States Commission on Civil Rights arose during an important moment of transition within American society. It involved, among other things, an attempt to address the systematic and widespread misconduct of public officials, elected and appointed, who refused to recognize the legal rights possessed by their black fellow citizens. Although the courts were not in fact closed to black citizens who might want to protest their treatment, much of the relatively infrequent litigation that did occur ended unfortunately, with acquittal (by all white juries) of the indicted officials. Indeed, one of the major fights over the 1957 Civil Rights Act involved the right to a jury trial on the part of those accused of violating the rights in question. Southern legislators fought hard for jury trials, invoking not only the traditional rights of freeborn Americans, but, no doubt, making certain assumptions about the racial composition of the juries.

As already suggested, one need not deny the special circumstances of "transitional" countries to be skeptical about the assumption sketched above. Or perhaps we should simply say that almost all countries are always undergoing one or another kind of transition, and one can always ask if established legal institutions respond well. Consider Hayner's "generic" definition of truth commissions as "bodies set up to investigate a past history of violations of human rights in a particular country—which can include violations by the military or other government forces or by armed opposition forces."[17] It is not,

I think, an unacceptable stretch to include the Civil Rights Commission within this broad definition.

Let me emphasize the following simple point: the United States scarcely engages in exclusive reliance on formal judicial procedures as a means to ascertain the truth about past events. Moreover, as a practical matter, the decision to use nonjudicial institutions often means that identified wrongdoers will escape any punishment, at least as defined in traditional terms such as serving time in jail or paying fines (as against public opprobrium attached to having been identified as a malefactor). It is true that we do not make use of explicitly titled "truth commissions." Their functional equivalent can be found in investigatory hearings held by certain administrative agencies, but also, and far more significantly, in the quite frequent occurrence of congressional investigations—including the many cited by the Supreme Court in its decision on the Civil Rights Commission—of alleged official misconduct. I strongly suspect (but have not done the comparative work to prove) that the role of the congressional investigating committee is far more important within the American polity than practically anywhere else in the world, not least because of the institutional separation of powers that, as a practical matter at least over the past quarter-century, has resulted in Presidents and Congresses being of different political parties.[18] It is also worth mentioning that congressional investigations on occasion directly compete with, and may undercut, judicial proceedings, as when a congressional committee, by voting to grant immunity to witnesses, makes it far more difficult, as a practical matter, successfully to prosecute the persons involved.[19]

Some (American) readers may be unhappy at the invocation of congressional hearings as a potential model for truth commissions. More than once congressional investigations within the United States have been denounced as little more than "witch hunts" dominated by political partisans interested in presenting only the most partial versions of the truth and disdainful of the due process rights of the targets of their investigation. There is surely truth to such charges, yet it is also true that many congressional investigators have behaved quite honorably, bringing to public attention important information about the governmental behavior that the agencies in question would certainly have preferred to remain buried.

Due Process(es) of Law, Truth, and Political Justice

A basic question facing any designer of political-legal institutions is to decide how we can best find out the truth about past events and bring to some closure disputes based on those events. According to Ash, "If you ask, 'Who is best equipped to do justice to the past?' the answer is, or at least should be, historians." Part of the reason is, as he points out, the complexity of the materials that the ascertainer of truth must deal with, especially the "official" files of the state about whom truth is being sought. "To use them carefully tests the critical skills that historians routinely apply to a medieval charter or an eighteenth-century pamphlet."[20] Even if one accepts Ash's rather optimistic depiction of the professional historian, it is clear, for both better and worse, that ongoing political institutions scarcely can afford the passage of time necessary to amass the relevant historical materials and gain the perspective that the passage of years often brings; nor, just as importantly, are they likely to cede to private historians the task of making legally authoritative judgments about past (mis)conduct.[21] The issues likely to be presented to truth commissions inevitably raise what Kircheimer many years ago labeled the problem of "political justice," which must ultimately be confronted by political entities.[22] How, then, should we design political institutions to meet such responsibilities?

Why Are Commissions Necessary?

Why *should not* the work of truth commissions be done by "ordinary" judicial institutions in the form of criminal or civil suits? This would mean, among other things, that by definition there would be no difference between the "ordinary" due process found within any given society and the specialized "due process of commissions" since, as a matter of fact, there would be no special commissions. One answer to the question may be that trials are impossible because a political condition of the transition from one regime to another is the agreement by the de facto winners that they will not engage in formal punishment of the losers. Sometimes the losers, in their last moments of power, pass a self-amnesty, as in Argentina; other times, as in South Africa, the displaced Nationalist regime relied on the promise of the African National Congress (ANC) winners that they would not be sent to jail. The TRC is an explicit response to the promise of amnesty, though the great South African innovation is to reject "wholesale" amnesty in favor of a "retail" version whereby each individual in effect gains amnesty at the not inconsiderable price of testifying candidly to the TRC about the injustices that he or she committed. In any event, the decision to forgo ordinary legal process is not the result of a detached comparison of the merits of one institutional structure against another.

But regime change is not necessarily accompanied by such guarantees, and the question remains whether truth commissions have any advantages over ordinary judicial process, perhaps even for countries that are not undergoing the kind of dramatic changes that are occurring in Eastern Europe, Latin America, or South Africa. Is it sufficient to count on public prosecutors to charge miscreants and present their misdeeds in open court, covered by journalists or, indeed, presented on television? Consider an article in the *New York*

Times concerning the exposure, in a German court, of "some of the most closely guarded secrets" concerning the East German athletic programs and their reliance on the massive use of drugs regardless of the harms caused the individual athletes. The trial apparently "provoked nationwide anger and embarrassment," which might well be major purposes of a truth commissions.[23]

The specific victims could also presumably engage in civil suits against alleged wrongdoers and, through the artful use of discovery procedures, presentation of evidence in open court, and examination of relevant witnesses, bring to the public's attention the truth about the past.[24] Indeed, it is worth noting that civil suits, in contrast to criminal prosecutions brought by the state itself, offer real advantages to those seeking the truth and some measure of corrective justice. As to the first, for example, the United States allows full-scale pretrial interrogation of defendants in civil suits, including the power to subpoena almost all relevant records. Moreover, these defendants can often be forced to testify, not only prior to trial but during the trial itself (even if the "testimony" is a statement that they refuse to testify on grounds of the possibility of self-incrimination), whereas criminal defendants in the United States have a constitutional right to refuse to take the witness stand. And as to infliction of sanctions, a plaintiff in the United States need demonstrate only a "preponderance of the evidence" in order to prevail; there is no requirement to prove one's case "beyond a reasonable doubt," a requirement that may well pose significant stumbling blocks in the way of those seeking redress in situations where the evidence might be murky. Finally, at least in the United States, juries are authorized to award "punitive damages" for particularly outrageous conduct, which obviously imports into the ostensibly noncriminal process the possibility of criminal-sanction-like punitiveness, at least financially.[25]

Criminal prosecutions are triply disadvantageous, from the perspective of many litigants: They not only require a far higher burden of proof, but they are also under the control of public prosecutors, who may have their own agendas. Moreover, at least in the United States, prosecutors are not allowed to "discover" the evidence that the defendant will offer in answer to any charges; nor can they call the defendants to testify (or even comment on their failure to testify). The most serious bar in the way of using civil litigation as a mechanism for exposing—and seeking damages from—official wrongdoers may be the existence of various "immunity" doctrines that shield public officials from an ordinary civil suit.[26]

One might also note the possibility of *international* response—either by another state or by an international entity—to claims of legal misconduct, particularly if the conduct in question is thought to have violated basic human rights. That is, it may be that individuals could be tried in country *B* for human-rights offenses committed in country *A*, if we read international law as placing authority in *any* member of the state system to enforce the norms.[27] It is probably not worth spending more space here on this possibility, insofar as we are really interested in the capacity of a given polity to come to terms with its own history, as opposed to the far easier task of condemning someone else's history. The key question is surely whether *local* institutions, judicial or otherwise, prove willing to address the kinds of issues that are the staple of truth commissions.

A basic difficulty with using local *courts*, even assuming that they are open to relevant actions, is that the defendants might be able to respond by plausibly pleading that the activity in question was "legal," at least in a positivist sense, at the time of its commission. Should this be the case, or even seriously arguable, then standard-form legal actions could provoke charges of *ex post facto* law, which were effectively raised by some of the critics of the Nuremberg trials in regard to the charge of waging aggressive war. One of the purposes of the trials, of course, was to ascertain the truth about the decision-making process of Nazi Germany, even as another purpose was to impose just punishment on the leadership of that state. Similar charges, of course, were raised in regard to the Israeli prosecution of Adolf Eichmann. Again the central purpose of that trial, beyond the infliction of retributive justice, was to teach the Israeli (and world) audience the truth about the Holocaust.[28]

One should not be too quick to assume the presence of *ex post facto* defenses, at least at the formal level, on the part of those charged with offenses.[29] Most regimes, after all, resolutely deny that they engage in monstrous conduct such as the use of torture or of "death squads" to eliminate political opponents. Indeed, they often point to laws on their books prohibiting such conduct. It would be surprising if *any* of the various truth commissions around the world have not addressed at least some situations where the conduct complained of was clearly illegal under the law even of the displaced regime. Ironically enough, this is probably clearest in regard to the examination by the TRC of charges levied against members of the now-ruling ANC, such as Winnie Mandela. It appears, though, to be true as well of at least some of the complaints brought against low-level functionaries accused of conduct that violated the formal rules of the previous apartheid regime.

Of course, many of those accurately accused of having engaged in prohibited conduct have, even without formal education in legal sociology, learned to differentiate between what Pound and other American legal theorists of the early twentieth century termed "law and the books" and "law in action."[30] Perhaps the most exquisitely difficult problems are presented by low-level functionaries who accurately describe the law-in-action as being X even if the written (and ignored) law demanded *not-X*. Still, even such persons, let alone those higher in the bureaucratic order, however much they might well have felt as a practical matter immune from punishment, can scarcely be heard to say that it is "unfair" to hold them to the formal law that had been trumpeted to the world in answer to the accusations of just such conduct as in fact was occurring.

Let us assume for the moment, then, that the conduct complained of was indeed criminal, even under the old regime. If that is the case, then to some extent a truth commission can be viewed as the forum for a peculiar form of "plea bargain."[31] This is especially true if the new regime is able to exercise legal control over the commission and can authorize it to grant immunity from further legal liabilty in return for the perpetrator's willingness to spell out fully and accurately the extent of his or her misconduct.[32] What, if anything, is wrong with this result? The United States is famous (or notorious) for making plea bargaining the central procedural mechanism of its criminal justice system in a way that is apparently true of no other legal system. That is, criminal defendants regularly agree to waive their constitutional right to a trial by jury (and, often, their right to object to procedural irregularies in the gathering of evidence) in return for a level of punishment far reduced from what might be obtained following conviction. It is clear beyond argument that the presumptively "mature" legal system within the United States would collapse in an instant if every criminal defendant insisted on full compliance with his or her ostensible set of due process rights.

Perhaps even more to the point is the fact that it was equally clear, following the rupture in the United States between 1861 and 1865 of the North and the South and the so-called "reconstruction" that followed, that it was impossible to bring more than a slight fraction of wrongdoers to trial and punishment, whether the wrongdoers were the Confederate leaders themselves or the leaders of the Ku Klux Klan who organized to repress the newly freed blacks.[33] Courts were open, and there was certainly no formal guarantee of amnesty. Yet political "realities" seemed to dictate a very limited response by federal authority. This simply underscores the fact that the formal legal system has a problem with high numbers: If the numbers of miscreants is high, and one wishes to acknowledge their existence and try to engage in at least some organized social response, then alternatives to formal trials and punishment *must* be created, lest the formal legal system simply be swamped and, perhaps what is even worse, its practical impotence as a mechanism of social control be revealed to the world (including, of course, potential opponents of the regime in power).[34]

As Osiel suggests in his important *Mass Atrocity, Collective Memory, and the Law*, the Durkheimian assumption of an underlying moral consensus that merely need be evoked by the formal criminal law is belied by the circumstance that, as a practical matter, generates the need for truth commissions in the first place, which is the presence within a given social order of deep divisions over basic political questions.[35] The very depth of the division often ensures the presence of such large numbers of alleged wrongdoers that use of "regular" legal forms is simply impossible, and the creation of alternative structures becomes necessary.

Composing Commissions

However, what if the number of potential defendants is relatively small, so that institutional breakdown through sheer force of numbers is not a genuine threat? Should one always prefer formal trials, conducted by the judiciary, at least in these instances, and therefore lament their unavailability if, as in South Africa and elsewhere, the new regime has agreed to forgo such trials?[36] To the extent that the trial would be politically freighted, with ramifications for the polity at large, then the answer may still be no. It is an issue of political debate in the United States whether a sitting President is even liable to criminal indictment, or whether the sole available procedure in regard to alleged misconduct is the impeachment process, which involves the equivalent of indictment by the House of Representatives and then trial by the Senate. It is not, of course, that the President is "above the law"; rather, there is, for good reason, an extraordinary way of handling allegations of presidential misconduct.

One reason to look to extraordinary processes, including truth (and reconciliation) commissions, instead of the ordinary judicial process, may be the identity of the officials concerned, as with presidents or generals. But another, equally important factor may be a relative lack of public stature of those ordinarily assigned judicial duties. It is crucial to note that this is a separate issue from whether they are professionally competent as law enforcement officials. Sometimes, of course, the judges are so identified with now-discredited regimes that they are not given any benefit of doubt.

The two goals of ascertaining truth and persuading the relevant publics that truth has in fact been ascertained may on occasion be in tension. Thus, for example, one might believe that the best way to ascertain the truth about a disputed matter is to have professionally trained persons, independent from any political party or partisan identification, engage in basically unfettered investigation and then report their findings to the public. But one might also believe that the best way to have any given findings *accepted* is to make sure that they have been endorsed (and thus socially validated) by a group of public personages representing a wide spectrum of opinion. As Thomas Nagel has famously observed, there is a "difference between knowledge and *acknowledgement*. It is what happens and can only happen to knowledge when it becomes officially sanctioned, when it is made part of the public cognitive scene."[37] It must be recognized that "official sanction" is a function not only of formal position in a legal order, but also, and probably more importantly, of the general status of the persons offering the acknowledgment. The kinds of "performative utterances" that Nagel refers to, whether they be "acknowledgment" of suffering and the acceptance of responsibility or the grant of amnesty and forgiveness, can be successfully performed only by certain (kinds of) persons possessing (certain kinds of) legal authority. Although logicians might criticize the "genetic fallacy," by which the validity of a proposition is treated as a function of the person asserting it, one could scarcely get through life without relying on the provenance of speakers in lieu of taking the unimaginable responsibility of checking any and all arguments oneself.

As political theorist Friedrich argued many years ago, what we mean by "authority" is precisely the willingness of others to place trust in what someone labeled "an authority" says in regard to his or her field of expertise, secure in the belief that "the authorities" could in fact—and, if pressed, would be willing to—offer "reasoned elaboration" of their views.[38] Someone whose every assertion is "checked out" prior to acceptance is scarcely an authority, whose function is really to foreclose further discussion by allowing persons to rely on the pronouncements of those persons deemed epistemically "authoritative." "Authority" may flow from professional training, as Ash suggests is the case with historians, and as is often suggested with regard to legal officials. But, politically, any one concerned with maximizing the authority of a particular institution must pay careful attention to the composition of a group charged with making especially controversial determinations.

José Zalaquett, discussing the truth commission in his own country of Chile, emphasized, "The commission's composition is very important. Of eight members of the Chilean commission, four had supported General Augusto Pinochet's regime." (The unspoken negative pregnant is that the remainder had not, and that fact is relevant.) The point is, "It would have been impossible for a single person [or, one suspects, a single group of four ideological kindred spirits] to dominate the drafting of the report. The fact that the commissioners were representative of broad sectors of the community made their findings more credible."[39] The unsurprising nature of Zalaquett's point—anyone concerned with establishing a successful truth commission must be extremely attentive to the actual sociopolitical distributions within the relevant country and the implications of these distributions for the likelihood of the general public's being willing to accept a commission's declarations as "authoritative"—does not lessen its importance or its potential challenge to certain models of the rule of law that emphasize the "blindness" of justice as a metonymy for the presumed irrelevance of the actual identity of the legal decision makers.

One might well assess different adjudicative institutions by reference to the extent to which what might be termed "political demographics" are taken into account in their constitution. For example, important congressional investigations within the United States, particularly "special" or "select" committees, on occasion play at least a quasi-adjudicative role in the sense of seeking to determine exactly what the truth is among conflicting assertions; they are often structured on an explicitly "bipartisan" basis. Presumably, the hope is that any committee report joined by both Democrats and Republicans would, simply by virtue of that fact, be more likely to be accepted by the public than an identical report, containing the very same language, signed only by recognized partisans.[40]

Composition counts. The actual identity of decision makers, including those charged with deciding the truth of contested matters and the consequences that should follow, matters. The most explicit legal discussions of such issues within American constitutional law have arisen in the context of juries. Some have criticized the American system of criminal justice, which is now almost unique in the world in placing adjudicative authority in the hands of lay juries, for its formal inattention to the actual demographics of the jury. As a formal matter, no attention can be paid to the composition of a judicial panel or lay jury, in the sense of adopting procedures that will ensure, say, a politically mixed panel or a racially mixed jury. A "jury of one's peers" is better understood within the categories of medieval England, so that *any* "commoner" is by virtue of that status the "peer" of any other commoner, as against a more contemporary sociological understanding that one identify "peerness" with shared social identity. Similarly, whatever the jurisprudential success of American legal realism in teaching the importance of judges' backgrounds and ideological commitments to their legal decisions, no recognition is taken, formally, of such differences, though most multimember federal courts have adopted "randomized" methods of selecting single-judge or three-judge panels in an effort to avoid any political selection bias by judicial administrators themselves.

Although the United States Supreme Court has, since 1880, interpreted the United States Constitution to prohibit exclusion from juries on grounds of race (extended in the 1970s to include gender), the Court has gone out of its way to hold that all this means is that members of the relevant groups must have an *opportunity* to serve on juries. Most definitely, though, this does not mean that they must necessarily be present in any given jury. One might contrast this with the British institution of the jury *de medietate linguoe*, which ended only in 1870, by which aliens were assured of a jury in which one-half of the members would consist of fellow nationals.[41] The lack of any principle of "proportional representation" in regard to jury membership has, of course, become a nationally debated issue following racially sensitive trials where the juries ostensibly lacked "sufficient" representation of a particular minority group.

To expect that jurors will be able to transcend their inevitably partial perspectives on the world seems naive; on the other hand, intentionally to structure juries so that they will "represent" or "mirror" the general demographics of a given locality has struck most observers as ultimately dangerous.[42] To the extent that the formal legal system deemphasizes, or even bars, explicit regard for the political or social status of various decision makers—prosecutors, jurors, and judges—one might seek an alternative institutional structure that can pay more attention to "demographics" of membership. Several American administrative agencies, which include among their powers quasi-judicial roles, by statute must include members of both the Democratic and Republican parties. There are obvious costs to the sacrifice of pure professional competence (assuming, in these postrealist, postmodernist times, that one can really believe in that concept). But it is equally obvious that the sacrifice, if such it is, often is worth the price. It is surely naive to believe that there is "one best way" to select those who will investigate the kinds of conduct brought before truth commissions, and the costs may especially be worth paying if the result is significantly greater political legitimacy for the findings themselves.

Presumably the most important virtue of ordinary trials is the range of protection afforded defendants against unfounded accusations (or, somewhat more controversially, protections afforded defendants against even well-founded charges where the evidence of the misconduct has been gained through improper means). But, as we have already seen, most American criminal defendants are in fact "encouraged" (critics would, of course, say forced) to waive such rights as part of the plea-bargaining process. Recall as well that some of these protections are (properly) unavailable in civil trials. And, as one looks at the panoply of American legal institutions, including legislative investigations, one continues to find often remarkable variation in what is deemed to be "due process of law."

Most lawyers would be tempted to say that the most important protection, practically speaking, is the right to be represented by counsel, who presumably is far more aware of the actual scope of legal rights than is the lay (and often scared) client. Thus Zalaquett includes "the right to counsel" as one of his basic list of requirements of any legitimate legal process.[43] There is, of course, an ambiguity in the term "right to counsel," as revealed in the history of American constitutional law. Although the right to counsel is specified by the Sixth Amendment, added to the Constitution in 1791, for well over a century it was interpreted to mean only that a defendant had the right to hire a lawyer; that is, the state could not force a defendant to undergo trial without a lawyer being present. This did not mean, however, that the state had any duty to provide a lawyer to anyone unable to afford one. It took until 1963 for the United States Supreme Court to interpret the Constitution to require state-provided counsel to indigent criminal defendants. Lest Americans feel too self-congratulatory, though, it must be emphasized not only that much controversy surrounds the actual quality of assistance provided for many indigents—accusations of "ineffective assistance of counsel," especially in complex trials, are rife—but also that the Supreme Court has been strikingly unwilling to find any similar guarantees in regard to civil litigation. The Court has ignored the practical reality that the consequences to a particular individual can be as serious in a civil as in a criminal context; it has held, for example, that death-row inmates are not entitled to counsel in habeas corpus challenges in federal courts to the fairness of their trials in state courts because, as a technical matter, habeas corpus claims that are "post-conviction" rather than "direct appeals" are labeled "civil" rather than "criminal."[44]

There is, of course, something misleading in focusing only on the rights of indigent defendants, as important as that issue may be. At least in the United States, no one who does not possess significant independent wealth can easily afford the costs of becoming enmeshed in legal controversy. Those brought before grand juries as witnesses, for example, are never entitled to counsel, though they are often well advised to retain counsel. Learned Hand, often described as the most important American judge never to have been named to the Supreme Court, once said that "I should dread a lawsuit beyond almost anything else short of sickness and death."[45] Today, one suspects that Hand would expand his qualms to include the entire legal system, and not only a formal "lawsuit."

Surely at least some persons summoned before truth commissions lack significant financial resources. As already suggested, though, one ought not be cavalier in regard even to those who can afford attorneys. If they are in fact innocent of the allegations that bring them to the attention of the authorities in the first place, then one should take no comfort in the often ruinous costs attached to the proof of innocence. Although the so-called English rule requires losers to pay the legal costs of the winners in civil litigation, I do not know of any legal systems that reimburse for their legal expenses those who are acquitted of charges or, even more to the point, never indicted by grand juries before which they are forced to testify.

In any event, are those less well off provided legal counsel, or are they, instead, left to the vagaries of the marketplace or to the charity of private organizations in regard to enjoying the assistance of lawyers? If the former is the case, then an obvious host of questions open up concerning the extent of the funding. The United States Supreme Court, even as it requires court-appointed counsel for indigent defendants, has taken pains to note that this does not at all require providing the same level of legal services that a person with means could purchase through the market. A crucial practical issue, for example, is the extent to which funds will be provided to engage in significant investigation of the factual surround of the allegations, an issue likely to be of special importance in the case of truth commissions.

To focus only on defendants as potential recipients of public subsidy may be problematic. After all, the practical protection of one's rights might require that one assume the role of a plaintiff, and the failure of the state to make it possible for persons of modest means effectively to assume that role by retaining an attorney capable of navigating the legal shoals may itself raise questions about the practical justice of the legal system. This point takes on special meaning in regard to truth commissions, where it is, justifiably, the victims of past oppression who often take center stage and who may be able to benefit from the assistance of attorneys, especially in regard, as in South Africa, to testimony proferred by perpetrators about the events in question. Indeed, South Africa provided funds to both victims *and* the alleged perpetrators brought before the TRC, though, apparently, the sums available to those attorneys representing the latter were significantly greater than those given to the victims' lawyers.[46] From one traditional liberal perspective, this is as it should be, for it is the perpetrators who are, after all, defending their reputations before state agencies. From another perspective, though, this unequal treatment is itself a bitter reminder of the structures of power within the old regime.

In any event, one can always ask if the state is willing to provide counsel. One can imagine at least two different structures of justification for a refusal to do so. The first would direct us to the formal legal doctrines within the polity concerning the circumstances under which indigents have an entitlement to counsel and would point out that truth commission "defendants" are treated no worse. After all, perhaps *no* defendants get counsel, or at least no one outside the formal system of criminal justice, and if the truth commission does not impose traditional punishments—that is, jail or fines—then it could easily be analogized to civil litigation. Thus, the argument might run, those appearing (and, especially, those forced to appear) before truth commissions are being treated "equally" with standard-form participants within the legal process. A second, quite different, argument would assert that appearances before truth commissions are so different, presumably in a benign direction, from ordinary criminal or civil trials that any guarantees of representation present in the latter need not be offered—is it conceivable that one would ever want to say "allowed"?—in the former.

Although I would be upset about a regime that offered counsel to no one at all, as was the case in the United States for noncapital criminal defendants until some thirty-five years ago, the truth commission "defendant" is being treated no worse by a truth commission than would have been the case had he or she become the subject of formal criminal charges. If the basis of provision of representation, on the other hand, is an attempt to differentiate between ordinary trials and truth commissions, that obviously requires the justification of an inequality. Whether the differences between truth commissions and ordinary tribunals can support the denial of state-provided counsel (or the funds to hire counsel from the private market) in the latter and not the former case is a complex question, depending for its answer on close examination of the particular powers of the commissions. Still, no one subpoenaed to appear before a congressional committee is ever provided with counsel, and that has not been viewed as a denial of due process.

What a lawyer does, at least ideally, is to increase the likelihood of adherence to the various procedural devices or laws of evidence that, taken together, constitute the norms of "due process of law." These are, most lawyers believe, essential, for at least two reasons. The first is instrumental: To guard against wrongful conviction of the innocent. It may well be that the price of protecting the innocent is allowing at least some factually guilty persons to escape legal liability. But, most liberals would presumably argue, it is better that some number X of factually guilty people, including, presumably, torturers and similarly barbaric wrongdoers, go free than that some other number of factually innocent people be wrongfully labeled as criminals (even if, because of amnesty provisions, no formal punishment ensues as a result of being so labeled). Protections against wrongful convictions can range from prohibiting the kind of police misconduct likely to lead to inaccurate confessions to limitations on hearsay or "prejudicial" evidence because of fears about its reliability. The second reason is less focused on consequences and more on the expressive importance of paying homage to the dignity interests of all persons (including the guilty) in being treated with the respect that all human beings deserve.

American lawyers no doubt overestimate the particular virtues of the (idealized) American criminal justice system, about which there can in fact be much legitimate debate.[47] The more important point, though, is that it is profoundly misleading to take as our "baseline" of due process the decidedly unusual situation of formal criminal trials, instead of looking at the vast array of institutions that attempt to ferret out truth. One should ask if truth commissions *ought* necessarily to accord the same kind of due process protections that are available before criminal (or even civil) courts. Even if one is critical, as I am, of the United States Supreme Court for exaggerating the difference between formally criminal and civil trials, one can easily accept the proposition that what constitutes "due process" in a particular situation is the product of a complex balancing test.

Conclusion

American lawyers have often proved unable to resist the temptation to advise transitional political regimes in regard to the kinds of constitutional structures they should adopt. All too often, these lawyers assume that the best solution is to adopt the structures found in the United States Constitution. But it should now be clear that interpreters of the Constitution have most definitely not read it to require what might be termed a unitary notion of due process that applies across the board to all legal institutions that threaten persons with untoward consequences. Grappling with the institutional pluralism even within our own, presumably "nontransitional," political order, should reinforce the realization that it is painfully misleading to suggest to those actually engaged in the operation of "truth commissions" that there is one model of due process that they must adopt on pain of chastisement. It is not simply that political structures appropriate for one country, with its particular history, culture, and economy, may be inappropriate for another. Rather, and far more importantly, one discovers that any reasonably developed political and legal culture itself presents a complex array of institutions and attendant notions of "due process" that belie any simplistic reduction to one norm of practice or procedure.

One wants to believe, of course, that there are strong transnational or transcultural universals of political practice; such beliefs, after all, are at the heart of the international human rights discourse that often underlies the specific mandate of a truth commission. I do not mean to dismiss this discourse or to gainsay its sometime practical importance in rectifying some very bleak situations. Facile relativism is no more attractive than facile universalism. But it remains a central question whether any universals can be stated in other than such abstract or general terms that they are relatively useless when deciding what precise procedures are due in any specific context.

Notes

1. I am grateful to Dennis Thompson, Robert Post, and Steven Ratner for comments on earlier drafts of this essay.

2. Whether the truth commission is envisioned as a complement to other existing legal institutions or as a substitute for them is obviously important, as a matter of both theory and practice, though one should also note that theoretically complementary truth commissions, as in Argentina and El Salvador, ended up becoming substitutionary inasmuch as general amnesties negated the possibility of ordinary trials. Carlos Santiago Nino writes, "If a truth commission replaces the criminal system . . . , it will be a second-best solution because the public inquiry into the truth is much more precise and much more dramatic when done through a trial, with the accused contributing to the development of the story. In fact, the quality of narration in an adversarial trial cannot be fully replicated by other means. Even when pardons are issued at the end of a trial, they do not counteract the initial effect of such emphatic public disclosure." See Nino, *Radical Evil on Trial* (New Haven, 1996), 146.

3. Bruce Ackerman, *The Future of Liberal Revolution* (New Haven, 1992), 72, 73 (emphasis added). What, for example, should be the fate of the various files that detail the manifest injustices visited by—and the identities of—the officials of past regimes on their citizenry (or, somewhat more accurately, those they deem their subjects)? Ackerman's answer is remarkably forthright: "Burn them, I say." Only such a suppression of even truthful materials about the past will prevent a "spiral of incivility, which will poison the political atmosphere by leading to charges and countercharges, public and private, over past collaboration" (81). "In warning against factfinding," Ackerman does not denigrate the legitimacy of criminal punishment. Instead, he believes it is essential to dampen all urges toward retribution that might be felt by the new political winners gainst their former oppressors. "There is enough pain in the world without our creating more in the hope that it will somehow ease our collective confrontation with the past—especially when the demand for retribution endangers the community-building process

central to constitutional legitimation." The task for "liberal revolutionaries" is "to shape retributive urges into manageable forms," and one mode of such shaping, apparently, is suppression of the past (98).

4. See Sanford Levinson, "Transitions," *Yale Law Journal* CVIII (1999): 2215. The leading collection of materials is Neil J. Kritz (ed.), *Transitional Justice: How Emerging Democracies Reckon with Former Regimes* (Washington, D.C., 1995), 3 volumes. See also the important article by Ruti Teitel, "Transitional Jurisprudence: The Role of Law in Political Transformation," *Yale Law Journal* CVI (1997): 2009.

5. Gunnar Myrdal, *An American Dilemma* (New York, 1964; orig. ed. 1944). The "American Creed" is the topic of chapter 1, "American Ideals and the American Science."

6. Quoted in Eric Foner, *The Story of American Freedom* (New York, 1998), 239.

7. See Foster Rhea Dulles, *The Civil Rights Commission: 1957–1965* (East Lansing, Mich., 1968), 115.

8. The complaint is described in the Supreme Court case that ultimately considered the matter, *Hannah v. Larche*, 363 U.S. 420, 427 (1960). I note that identical concerns were expressed in regard to the procedures of the South African Truth and Reconciliation Commission. See *Truth and Reconciliation Commission v. Du Preez and Another*, 1996(3) SA 997 (1996)(Cape Provincial Division), overruled in *Du Preez and Another v. Truth and Reconciliation Commission*, 1997 (3) SA 204 (Appellate Division), which come to conflicting conclusions concerning the meaning of "fairness" in regard to persons identified by ostensible victims as the perpetrators of the injustices against them. In particular, the Appellate Division held that alleged perpetrators are entitled to prior notice "of the substance of the allegations against him or her, with sufficient detail to know what the case is all about," 1997(3) SA 204, 234, though the court acknowledged the ability of the TRC, when necessary, to withhold disclosing the identity of particular witnesses (235, 236).

The various legal challenges to the TRC are set out in the TRC *Final Report*, I, chap. 7 (available at www.polity.org.za/govdocs/commissions/1998/trc/1chap7.htm) The TRC noted, in paragraphs 50–58, the "implications" and "impact" of these rulings. It noted, for example, the "administrative and logistic burden" imposed on the commission (53). More interesting, perhaps, is the commission's comment that it "had to contend with perpetrators demanding to be heard at the same hearings as victims and requesting that they be allowed to cross-examine witnesses. This had a traumatising effect on many victims who had finally found the courage to testify" (54). Finally, and most importantly, after the public hearings had been completed and the report was being drafted, "the full impact of the judgement became clear. Where the Commission contemplated making a finding against a person to their detriment in the report, the person would need to be notified of the decision contemplated as well as afforded the opportunity to make written representation to the Commission" (55). "In essence, the Commission found itself in a position in which it was obliged to give alleged perpetrators a prior view of its report—a highly unusual circumstance for a report on a commission of enquiry" (56).

9. *Hannah v. Larche*, 440, 442, 443.

10. It might be noted, incidentally, that many of the particular individuals bringing suit would probably not be punished by the "court of public opinion" inasmuch as they were the foot soldiers of the attempt to maintain the traditional racial order. Perhaps

this helps to explain why Chief Justice Warren, perhaps especially sensitive to the southern "massive resistance" against any attempts to implement *Brown v. Board of Education*, the school segregation opinion written by him, found the claims of harm merely "conjectural."

11. *Hannah v. Larche*, 497.

12. Timothy Garton Ash, "The Truth about Dictatorship," *New York Review of Books*, 19 February 1998, 35.

13. Tina Rosenberg, *The Haunted Land: Facing Europe's Ghosts after Communism* (New York, 1996), xvi.

14. Tony Horwitz, *Confederates in the Attic: Dispatches from the Unfinished Civil War* (New York, 1997).

15. William Faulkner, *As I Lay Dying* (New York, 1930), quoted in Horwitz, *Confederates*, 352.

16. Indeed, the "lustration" controversy within the Czech Republic has echoes in the debate about disqualifying from public office, including the practice of law, those who had supported the rebellion against the authority of the United States government. See Charles Fairman, *Reconstruction and Reunion, 1864–88 (Part One)* (New York, 1971), 240–248 (Vol. VI of the Oliver Wendell Holmes Devise History of the Supreme Court of the United States).

17. Quoted in Priscilla B. Hayner, "Fifteen Truth Commissions—1974 to 1994: A Comparative Study," in Kritz, *Transitional Justice*, I, 225.

18. It would be foolhardy in the extreme to imagine the British Parliament (or the Israeli Knesset) as a vigorous investigator of alleged misconduct by the government in power, and this is probably true of any parliamentary system where the government is defined as the representatives of the parliamentary majority (including, of course, coalitions). This, as much as anything else, explains why Israeli investigations of alleged governmental failings have always utilized extraparliamentary commissions, usually headed by a distinguished judge. See, e.g., Pnina Lahav, *Judgment in Jerusalem: Chief Justice Simon Agranat and the Zionist Century* (Berkeley, 1997), 233–243, for a detailed review of the work of the "Agranot Commission" examining the circumstances by which Israel was vulnerable to the Yom Kippur attack in 1973. Similarly, the Kahan Commission wrestled with the liability of the Israeli military, particularly Ariel Sharon, for the 1982 massacres in Beirut conducted by Falangists allied with Israel.

19. The Court of Appeals for the District of Columbia reversed convictions of Oliver North and John Poindexter, the latter the former national security adviser to President Ronald Reagan, because, it held, their testimony to Congress, procured under a grant of immunity, inevitably tainted the judicial proceedings. (The special prosecutor insisted that the prosecutors maintained a relentless ignorance of what North and Poindexter had said to Congress.)

20. Ash, "The Truth," 40. See, for a somewhat more pessimistic account, Mark Osiel, *Mass Atrocity: Collective Memory and the Law* (New Brunswick, N.J., 1997), 197–198 (detailing circumstances of the "historians' debate" in Germany concerning Hitler). See also Charles S. Maier, *The Unmasterable Past: History, Holocaust, and German National Identity* (Cambridge, Mass., 1988).

21. An independent paper could be written about the phenomenon of "private truth commissions." Priscilla Hayner notes the existence of such nongovernmental commissions, though she denies them the appellation "truth commissions . . . because they are

not authorized in some way by the government or other official body." See Kritz, *Transitional Justice*, I, 258. It is certainly not an analytical truth that a "truth commission" should be a public body, though there are all sorts of reasons why public truth commissions may be more successful, in the court of public opinion, than private entities. (We ought to recognize, though, that at least on occasion the opposite could be true, and political scientists might profitably investigate the circumstances under which that would be the case.)

22. See Otto Kirchheimer, *Political Justice: the Use of Legal Procedure for Political Ends* (Princeton, 1961).

23. See Alan Cowell, "Little Blue Pills and a Lot of Gold," *New York Times*, 5 April 1998, A25.

24. Robert Post has noted, in private communication, that the civil libel trials filed by William Westmoreland against the Columbia Broadcasting Company and by Ariel Sharon against *Time* magazine were viewed by Westmoreland and Sharon as ways of establishing fundamental truths, not so much about the carelessnessness of the media in question but, rather, about the underlying events in Vietnam and the Lebanese invasion by Israel, respectively.

25. The Supreme Court, in spite of repeated invitations to do so, has not interpreted the due process clause of the United States Constitution significantly to limit the freedom of juries to award punitive damages.

26. A dramatic such example in the United States is *Nixon v. Fitzgerald*, 457 U.S. 731 (1982), which held that a President enjoyed absolute immunity from having to pay damages for official misconduct. The Court emphasized that the "president occupies a unique position in the constitutional scheme" and, therefore, could not be sued for acts done as part of his official duties. It was, incidentally, this case upon which President Bill Clinton relied in his recent attempt to avoid having to respond to sexual misconduct charges by Paula Jones, though the Supreme Court rejected his argument in part because the conduct that was complained of, which occurred well before Clinton's election to the presidency, had nothing whatsoever to do with his official duties. For a lawyer, perhaps an even more dramatic example of immunity doctrine is *Stump v. Sparkman*, 435 U.S. 349 (1978), in which the Supreme Court upheld the immunity of an Indiana state judge who had ordered the sterilization of a fifteen-year-old girl who was told that the operation was an appendectomy. As two commentators have written, "The effect of absolute immunity is to vindicate fully the public's interest in unintimidated decision making by its officials, but only at a correspondingly complete sacrifice of the interests of those who may be disadvantaged by abuse." See Peter W. Low and John C. Jeffries, Jr., *Civil Rights Actions: Section 1983 and Related Statutes* (Mineola, N.Y., 1988), 29. Presumably one's support for extensive immunity will be a function of the confidence one has in public officials, and the Supreme Court, generally speaking, has expressed high faith indeed.

27. See Steven R. Ratner and Jason S. Abrams, *Accountability for Human Rights Atrocities in International Law: Beyond the Nuremberg Legacy* (Oxford, 1997), 139–192. See also John Dugard, "Retrospective Justice: International Law and the South African Model," in A. James McAdams (ed.), *Transitional Justice and the Rule of Law in New Democracies* (Notre Dame, Ind., 1997), 280. Whether enforcement of international human rights norms should be subordinated to political exigencies within particular states is, as one might expect, a major issue surrounding the grant of amnesty to officials

of displaced regimes, including, of course, those whose amnesty is conditioned on cooperation with truth commissions.

28. The best recent analysis of the Eichmann trial is in Lahav, *Judgment*, 145–162.
On the Eichmann trial's status as a "show trial," see Osiel, *Mass Atrocity*, 60–63, 80–82.
Key to Osiel's book is understanding that the description as a "show trial" is not neces-
sarily meant to be a criticism.

29. As a matter of United States constitutional law, the *ex post facto* clause has been
interpreted as applying only to formal criminal liability. Thus, it has been held not to
violate the clause when, for example, Congress changes tax rates retroactively or, far
more ominously, changes the list of deportable offenses, in regard to resident aliens, and
applies the new list retroactively. The Supreme Court has solemnly held that deporta-
tion is not "punishment," which therefore takes the case out of the *ex post facto* clause.

30. See Roscoe Pound, "The Law in Books and the Law in Action," *American Law
Review* XLIV (1910): 12–36.

31. See José Zalaquett, "Confronting Human Rights Violations Committeed by
Former Governments: Principles Applicable and Political Constraints," in Kritz, *Transitional Justice*, I, 7–8. I am told that South African Justice Albie Sachs had earlier
analogized the amnesty function of truth commissions to plea bargaining.

32. One of the most controversial aspects of the South African amnesty process is
that the amnesty extends to *civil liability*, which deprives the victims of the perpetrators'
misconduct of any legal redress at all. It is one thing to say that the state, which speaks
in the name of the generalized people, will forgo legal redress. It is, in its own way, far
more drastic for the state to waive any legal rights possessed by discreet individuals.
Needless to say, the explanation for the extent of the amnesty lies in the political exigencies of the moment of transition, and the justification depends on one's assessment
of the values at stake in regard to a less peaceful transition. See the chapter by Amy
Gutmann and Dennis Thompson in the present volume for further discussion of this
point.

Of course, not all truth commissions have had amnesty power, and the obvious question arises as to what incentive malefactors have to confess if they in fact make themselves more vulnerable to future punishment by providing evidence against themselves.
The issue of incentives is discussed in the decision of the South African Constitutional
Court upholding the legal right of the TRC to grant amnesty from both criminal and
civil liability for the wrongs confessed to:

> Central to the justification of amnesty in respect of the criminal prosecution for
> offences committed . . . is the appreciation that the truth will not effectively be re-
> vealed by the wrongdoers if they are to be prosecuted for such acts. That justification
> must necessarily and unavoidably apply to the need to indemnify such wrongdoers
> against civil claims for payment of damages. Without that incentive the wrongdoer
> cannot be encouraged to reveal the whole truth which might inherently be against his
> or her material or proprietary interests. *AZAPO & Others v. President of the Republic
> of South Africa*, 1996 (4) SA 671, 693 (1996)

33. See, for example, the excellent book by Lou Falkner Williams, *The Great South
Carolina Ku Klux Klan Trials, 1871–1872* (Athens, Ga., 1996). One might, of course,
well regard the United States at that time as "transitional," though many of the same
problems occurred in the 1960s, when much of the South was engaging in "massive

resistance" against not only the Civil Rights movement of the time, but also, and for our purposes more significantly, against federal law. Again, this demonstrates that the division between transitional and nontransitional societies may be more porous than first believed.

34. Alex Boraine spoke eloquently to those of us attending the Somerset West conference (1998) about what he had observed in Rwanda, where literally thousands of persons accused of violations of human rights were incarcerated in unimaginably horrendous prisons without any realistic hope of being subjected to formal trials for years and years. Unless one has an unwarrantedly high confidence in the culpability of all of those who are confined, it seems inadequate (and utopian) to insist on full-scale trials and punishment rather than to adopt some alternative procedures, including those instantiated by the TRC.

35. See Osiel, *Mass Atrocity*, 24–35, discussing Emile Durkheim, *The Division of Labor in Society* (Glencoe, Ill., 1964).

36. One should note that prosecution appears available in South Africa if alleged perpetrators, identified by victims, refuse to ask for amnesty or otherwise refuse to disclose fully their participation in past injustices. It is not clear to what extent the new government will take advantage of this theoretical possibility. The most delicate cases are presented by former presidents Pieter W. Botha and Frederik W. de Klerk (who, of course, shared a Nobel Prize with Nelson Mandela for his willingness to dismantle the Nationalist hegemony in South Africa).

37. Quoted in Lawrence Weschler, *A Miracle, A Universe: Settling Accounts with Torturers* (New York, 1990), 4.

38. See Carl J. Friedrich, *Authority, Reason, and Discretion*, in Friedrich (ed.), *Authority* (Cambridge, Mass., 1988), 28, 35–36.

39. Quoted in Henry J. Steiner (ed.), *Truth Commissions: A Comparative Assessment* (Cambridge, Mass., 1996), 19.

40. The importance of the actual identity of investigators has been crucial in regard to several inquiries involving alleged misconduct by President Clinton and his associates. Special prosecutor Kenneth Starr is viewed by many (with justification, I believe) as a partisan opponent of the President. Interestingly enough, part of the controversy surrounding the conduct of his investigation involved the limited standards of due process surrounding grand jury investigations and the special prosecutor's propensity to take full advantage of the latitude offered prosecutors, including the power to offer immunity from prosecution in return for useful testimony. Moreover, Starr took full advantage of his statutory duty to notify the House of Representatives of his conclusion that there was some basis to consider impeachment of the President in order to lay out, with remarkable vividness, the case against the President without giving his lawyers an opportunity to scrutinize (and respond to) the arguments prior to submission. No more profoundly important an exercise of political justice (and judgment) could be imagined. And, needless to say, the subsequent inquiry by the House Judiciary Committee, considering whether to impeach the President, and then the Senate, considering whether to convict, were widely (and justifiably) viewed as partisan and thus were unable to bring true closure to the controversy.

41. See, generally, Marianne Constable, *The Law of the Other: The Mixed Jury and Changing Conceptions of Citizenship, Law, and Knowledge* (Chicago, 1994). The demise of this mixed-jury system is treated at 144–145.

42. See, e.g., Jeffrey Abramson, "Jury Selection and the Cross-Sectional Ideal," a chapter in Abramson, *We, the Jury* (New York, 1995), 99–141.

43. Kritz, *Transitional Justice*, I, 10.

44. See *Murray v. Giarratano*, 492 U.S. 1 (1989). Justice Sandra Day O'Connor, concurring, emphasized that "[a] postconviction proceeding is not part of the criminal process itself, but is instead a civil action designed to overturn a presumptively valid criminal judgment." Justice John Paul Stevens, joined by three other justices in dissent, noted, "The success rate in capital cases ranged from 60% to 70%. Such a high incidence of uncorrected error [at the ordinary appellate stage within state systems of criminal justice] demonstrates that the meaningful appellate review necessary in a capital case extends beyond the direct appellate process." Since, in the United States, direct appeals from the highest state courts can be taken only to the United States Supreme Court, which rarely in fact takes an appeal, collateral habeas actions are the only effective way of providing a federal-court check on state courts that are sometimes resistant to federal constitutional guarantees.

45. Learned Hand, "The Deficiencies of Trials to Reach the Heart of the Matter," *Lectures on Legal Topics*, III (1926), 89–106, quoted in Fred R. Shapiro, *The Oxford Dictionary of American Legal Quotations* (Oxford, 1993), 304.

46. I was told by a South African lawyer that "defendants'" attorneys received up to 4000 rands/per day (about $650 in 1999), whereas victims' representatives were paid a maximum of only 400 rands.

47. The tension between ascertainment of truth and protection of general public order, on the one hand, and the particular protections accorded criminal defendants, on the other, is the subject of an important book, Akhil Reed Amar, *The Constitution and Criminal Procedure: First Principles* (New Haven, 1996).

XII

The Hope for Healing

WHAT CAN TRUTH COMMISSIONS DO?

MARTHA MINOW[1]

> Ignorance about those who have disappeared /
> undermines the reality of the world.
>   *(Zbigniew Herbert)*[2]

> I feel what has been making me sick all the time is the
> fact that I couldn't tell my story. But now I—it feels
> like I got my sight back by coming here and
> telling you this story.
>   *(Lucas Baba Sikwepere)*[3]

THE mass atrocities of the twentieth century, sadly, do not make it distinctive. More distinctive than the facts of genocides and regimes of torture marking this era are the search for and invention of collective forms of response. This is especially noteworthy given that no response to mass atrocity is adequate. The sheer implication of adequacy is itself potentially insulting to the memory of those who were killed and to the remaining days of those who were tortured, and to those who witnessed the worst that human beings can do to other human beings. Yet, during the twentieth century, a particular hope, or ideology, has inspired specific efforts to use law and state power to address and redress episodes of collective violence.

The basic idea is that public power—through prosecutions, reparations, and commissions of inquiry—can locate the violations on maps of human comprehensibility, deter future violations of human dignity, and ensure that the ambitions of the agents of violence do not succeed. The novel experiment of the Nuremberg and Tokyo tribunals following World War II reached for a vision of world order and international justice, characterizing mass violence as crimes of war and crimes against humanity. Individual states also prosecuted their own citizens and citizens of other states for participation in mass murders and torture. These trials have inspired the international movement for human rights and represent in many people's minds the "gold standard" for any public response to mass violence. The use of criminal trials holds out the rule of law as the framework for rendering accountability for unspeakable conduct, for deterring future violations, and for gathering a formal public record so that the attempts to destroy groups of people cannot succeed in destroying their memory.[4]

Each of these goals is admirable. They are also exceedingly difficult to achieve. The trial process does not always work, and even when it does, it is marked by sharp constraints. Trials and the framework of the rule of law also miss another collection of purposes that are at least of equal importance for individuals and societies emerging after large-scale violence and brutality. These purposes center on rectifying the damage to human dignity that so often endures even for those who survive violence and on healing societies torn by hatred and brutality. Failure to address damage to individual dignity and to the very idea that members of targeted groups are persons with dignity ensures that the consequences of mass violation will persist and may give rise to new rounds of revenge.

One woman who was raped while in police detention for her political opposition to apartheid recalled how she forced herself to survive by putting her sense of herself or her soul in the corner of the room, outside of her body, while the rape occurred. She survived, but tells Bill Moyers during an interview for his 1999 documentary film, *Facing the Truth*, that what she longs for is to return to that room and find herself again. Multiply this utter sense of violation across all those wounded physically and spiritually by mass violence.[5] Trauma alters people's abilities to sleep, eat, hope, and work; trauma alters people's brain scans and capacities to care for others. Can collective responses to mass violence redress trauma, or at least do so with the same acknowledgment of ultimate inadequacy that must accompany any other public response to genocide, torture, and mass rapes?

This question is posed most vividly through the development of truth commissions in the closing decades of the twentieth century.[6] Investigation and exposure of gross human rights violations have been "the stock in trade of international human rights organizations and the international press for some decades."[7] More recently, though, national legislatures and executives, and international institutions, have authorized such investigations, giving official acknowledgment to the issues and to the truths ultimately gathered. These official bodies are established to investigate and publicly report on human rights violations and collective violence. They emphasize both truth finding and truth telling. If the goals of repairing human dignity, healing individuals, and mending societies after the trauma of mass atrocity are central, truth commissions offer features that are often more promising than prosecutions. Even in light of the basic goals of prosecutions, truth commissions can afford benefits to a society. Thus, any evaluation of legal responses to mass violence must acknowledge the specific goals sought as well as their shortfall in practice. Because attention to the victimized should rate highly among the goals, truth commissions should be an important part of the national and international repertoire of responses to mass violence.

Second Best or Independently Valuable?

A truth commission looks like a second choice if prosecutions for human rights violations serve as the model for institutional responses to state-sponsored violence. Commentators argue that prosecuting human rights violations can substantially enhance the chance of establishing the rule of law. Doing so signals that no individual stands beyond the reach of legal accountability.[8] Prosecutions also provide a legitimate means for punishing wrongdoers. The threat of such punishment in turn is the chief method for deterring future human rights violations. Prosecutions set in motion an official process for gathering and testing testimony and documentary evidence that can disclose hidden truths about the atrocities and prevent future cover-ups or denials.

In comparison, a commission of inquiry charged with investigating and reporting human rights violations may seem a pale and inadequate substitute. International human rights activists and scholars argue that criminal prosecution is the best response to atrocities and that truth commissions should be used only as an alternative when such prosecutions are not possible.[9]

In this view, truth commissions become an important alternative only because practical reasons do often interfere with or prevent prosecutions. There may simply not be enough courtrooms, lawyers, witnesses, or time for prosecuting all who deserve it in places like Kosovo, Rwanda, Cambodia, East Germany, East Timor, and Brazil. There may be an inadequate number of skilled people who were not participants in the offending regime to administer the justice system. When the offenders are part of a military regime that remains in force, the government usually lacks the clout to proceed with prosecutions.

Even when a successor regime is in charge, and not under the pervasive powers of the military command that participated in or permitted atrocities, the new leaders may hope to avoid the confrontational atmosphere generated by trials. They may also conclude that prosecutions that would be perceived as politically motivated or politically tainted could not advance the rule of law. Prosecutorial decisions may be foreclosed by political realities. Negotiation of a peaceful transfer of power often involves measures to ensure immunity from prosecutions against outgoing leaders as a crucial condition.

Prosecutions may be hampered alternatively by the ability of high-ranking officials to flee to other countries or to retain sufficient political or economic power to render prosecutions difficult. If only low-ranking participants can be found and prosecuted, the resulting trials could create martyrs while leaving the important decision makers untouched.[10] Or only high-level officials may be prosecuted, leaving the impression that those lower in the chain of command are excused or free to act. Selective prosecutions jeopardize the ideals of accountability and the hopes for deterrence; in these circumstances, those newly in charge may prefer to avoid any prosecutorial effort and develop an alternative response.

Yet arguments for alternatives may be founded not just in search for a substitute when trials are not workable. The trial as a form of response to injustice has its own internal limitations. Litigation is not an ideal form of social action. The financial and emotional costs of litigation may be most apparent when private individuals sue one another, but there are parallel problems when a government or an international tribunal prosecutes. Victims and other witnesses undergo the ordeals of testifying and facing cross-examination. Usually, they are given no simple opportunity to convey directly the narrative of their experience. Evidentiary rules and rulings limit the factual material that can be included. Trial procedure makes for laborious and even boring sessions that risk anesthetizing even the most avid listener and dulling sensibilities even in the face of recounted horrors. The simplistic questions of guilt or innocence framed by the criminal trial can never capture the multiple sources of mass violence. If the social goals include gaining public acknowledgment and producing a complete account of what happened, the trial process is at best an imperfect means.

If the goals extend to repairing the dignity of those who did survive and enlarging their chances for rewarding lives, litigation falls even farther short. Trials focus on perpetrators, not victims. They consult victims only to illustrate the fact or scope of the defendants' guilt. Victims are not there for public acknowledgment or even to tell, fully, their own stories. Trials interrupt and truncate victim testimony with direct and cross examination and conceptions of relevance framed by the elements of the charges. Judges and juries listen to victims with skepticism tied to the presumption of defendants' innocence. Trials afford no role in their process or content for bystanders or for the complex interactions among ideologies, leaders, mass frustrations, historic and invented lines of hatred, and acts of brutality.

For truth telling, public acknowledgment of what happened, and attention to survivors, a commission of inquiry actually may be better than prosecutions. When the commission is authorized or taken seriously by the government, and is capable of producing a report with wide public reception, public acknowledgment can be dramatic and effective. The daily broadcast of proceedings of the South African Truth and Reconciliation Commission (TRC) marked this kind of public acknowledgment and made preexisting, widespread denial—especially within white communities—less and less tenable. It reflected a deliberate policy of maximum publicity. The TRC developed partnerships with community-based organizations to communicate its work, developed an advertising campaign to inform the public about its activities, and worked with newspaper, television, and radio professionals to communicate its message.

A truth commission can be set up to hear from victims for their own sake, and it can be designed to try to restore their dignity. Being able to giving a full account of their suffering can be meaningful for survivors, even if perpetrators are never found or punished. In South Africa, where courtrooms had so often been used to reinforce the power of the apartheid regime and deny rightful claims by its victims, the creation of a setting quite distinct from courts held a special value. A truth commission also can offer bystanders the roles of listeners, while also turning at times to focus on what bystanders failed to do to prevent or stem the violence.

The aspiration to develop as full an account as possible requires a process of widening the lens, sifting varieties of evidentiary materials, and drafting syntheses of factual material that usually does not accompany a trial. Yet truth commissions typically undertake to write the history of what happened in precisely these ways. Putting together distinct events and the role of different actors is more likely to happen when people have the chance to look across incidents and to connect the stories of many victims and many offenders. A truth commission can examine the role of entire sectors of a society—such as the medical profession, the media, and business—in enabling and failing to prevent mass violence. The sheer narrative project of a truth commission makes it more likely than trials to yield accounts of entire regimes. Trials in contrast focus on particular individuals and their conduct in particular moments in time, with decisions of guilt or nonguilt, and opinions tailored to these particular questions of individual guilt.

Truth commissions still face enormous barriers in gathering facts and producing comprehensive accounts. Especially in regimes that operate through terror, secrecy is the ground rule. Some of the story can never be known without grants of immunity to those who can tell it. Here, the innovative South African approach to amnesty is especially noteworthy. The TRC applications from individuals for amnesty were to be approved only if those applicants recounted truthfully and fully their roles in committing human rights violations, and also only if their conduct were motivated by politics and was not disproportionately heinous.[11] Although borne of the political compromise necessary to ensure peaceful transition of power, this method for granting amnesty also reflected the experience of leaders in the African National Congress (ANC) with their own commissions of inquiry exposing hidden human rights abuses. The ANC had previously conducted two inquiries into its own human rights violations, and found the value of disclosures by insiders.[12] This experience contributed to the design of the Amnesty Committee of the TRC, which also gave victims the right to cross-examine applicants.

The trade of amnesty for testimony allowed the TRC to use the participation by some to gain the participation of others. Five mid-level political officers sought amnesty and in so doing implicated General Johan van der Merwe as the one who gave the order to fire on demonstrators in 1992.[13] The general then himself applied for amnesty before the commission and confessed that he had indeed given the order to fire. He in turn implicated two cabinet-level officials who gave him orders.[14] Evidence of this kind, tracing violence to decisions at the highest governmental levels, is likely to be held only by those who themselves participated in secret conversations, and the adversarial processes of trials are not likely to unearth it. Combining information from amnesty petitions and hearings with victim testimony and independent investigations, the TRC had the chance to develop a much richer array of evidence than the courts would have had in expensive and lengthy criminal prosecutions.

Practical limitations will mar truth commission work just as they prevent actual trials from achieving their ideal. The patterns of secrecy, misinformation, and rumor that accompany oppressive regimes and reigns of terror make the task of finding and reporting the truth daunting if not impossible. Crucial evidence is destroyed. Mass graves do not disclose who performed the murders, much less who gave the orders. Mass atrocities explode the frames of reference usually available for historical investigations. Any report that claims to be comprehensive will be defective precisely on those grounds.

Even if a report is issued with governmental endorsement, the public may not become engaged with it. Many victims and many perpetrators will prefer not to participate, and this will invite charges that the report is unfair or unrepresentative. The commission may take too long to do its work. Or it may work under tight deadlines and simply be unable to meet the challenge of reporting fully on what happened.

Yet the process of testifying before and being heard by the official human rights committee at a truth commission potentially holds independent value for the individual victims and for the nation. This is what makes truth commissions a notable innovation. The process of engaging official listeners in hearing from victims, and broadcasting that process before a listening public, accomplishes some important healing for individuals and for societies. If this goal is taken seriously, truth commissions are not a second best, but an admirable alternative to prosecutions.

The Aspiration of Healing

Putting the affirmative case for truth commissions at least in part in terms of the goal of attending to the trauma of victims and the larger society raises further questions. What does it take to attend effectively to individuals after mass trauma? Are the same methods that offer some help to individuals useful at a societal level, or is it a big mistake to analogize individual trauma to the difficulties at a national level following mass violence? Are truth commissions equipped either for helping individuals or for helping a nation?

The notion of healing seems foreign to the legal world underpinning prosecutions. Emotional and psychological healing did not figure largely in the national and international responses during the first decades after the Holocaust. Yet healing recurs in contemporary discussions, perhaps reflecting the popularization of psychological ideas over the course of the twentieth century.[15] Another source is the experiences of survivors of atrocities and their family members. From the vantage point of passing decades, survivors and their families and friends often emphasize the need to heal and to learn to live again.

Echoing the assumptions of psychotherapy, as well as religious confession and journalistic muckraking, advocates of truth commissions argue that telling and hearing narratives of violence in the name of truth can promote healing for individuals and for society. Supporters hope that watching and listening to others may help even those victims who do not speak up. A report that overcomes denial and secrecy, it is hoped, will create a platform and framework for the nation to deal with its past. Some support for these assumptions appears in the counterexamples of nations that undertook no deliberate efforts at truth telling and suffered decades and even generations of festering distrust.[16]

Whether the process for individual healing matches what an entire nation must undergo is difficult to prove. There do seem to be compelling analogies. Rosenberg finds parallels between truth commissions and the therapeutic process that helps individual victims deal with post-traumatic stress disorders.[17] She notes how, in both contexts, individuals need to tell their stories to someone who listens seriously and who validates them with official acknowledgment. In both settings, individuals must be able to reintegrate the narrative of atrocity into their entire life stories. She adds, "If the whole nation is suffering from post-traumatic stress disorder, this process would be appropriate for the whole nation."[18]

On the contrary, some may say that individuals and nations can have too much memory. Perhaps this happens only when it is the wrong kind of memory, when it is superficial, or unincorporated in the tasks of everyday life. Too much memory may result from dwelling in the conflict between competing accounts that cannot be reconciled. "Either the siege at Sarajevo was a deliberate attempt to terrorize and subvert the elected government of an internationally recognized state or it was a legitimate preemptive defense of the Serbs' homeland from Muslim attack." It cannot be both, Ignatieff reminds us.[19] Perhaps the problem is not too much truth but too little; the truth can never be full enough, or sufficiently embracing, to overcome intergroup divisions so deep that members see the world differently.

Or perhaps truth-telling seems unavailing when it attends to a past without affording a bridge to the future. Weschler invoked Merwin's prose poem,

"Unchopping a Tree," as a warning about the limitations of truth commissions.[20] In the poem, Merwin examines step-by-step how one would reassemble a tree that has been destroyed so completely that its leaves, branches, and twigs have all come apart. After the painstaking steps to reassemble the tree, part by part, it stands; but the breeze still can touch only dead leaves. Healing is an absurd or even obscene notion for those who have died. Survivors of mass atrocity often feel as though they themselves died, or are living among the dead. Then endurance, not healing, is what survivors come to seek.[21]

Nonetheless, scholars and therapists have explored the dimensions of healing that can emerge for individuals and perhaps for societies, after collective violence.[22] Lifton emphasizes that the victims of violence experience trauma that breaks the lifeline and leaves to the survivor the task "of formulation, evolving new inner forms that include the traumatic event."[23] Others recount the effects of chronic fear and unspoken terror on survivors of totalitarian regimes. Hopelessness, emotional breakdowns, and recurrence of traumatic events in the guise of personal problems persist for many individuals who may then turn to psychotherapeutic help.[24]

Conventional therapeutic methods are inadequate unless they acknowledge the larger contexts of such traumas. Herman develops a theory of trauma and recovery that connects the experiences of Holocaust victims, U.S. soldiers in Vietnam, battered women, child abuse victims, and survivors of rape and incest.[25] She finds that the initial injury for such victims follows two stages. First, they relinquish their autonomy, their connections with others, and their moral principles in the face of terror and domination. Second, they lose the will to live.[26] Herman argues, "Denial, repression and disassociation operate on a social as well as individual level," and that the fantasies about revenge are aspects of trauma that can be worked through.[27]

Herman's theory of trauma and recovery connects healing and justice in subtle ways and implies questions to test an innovation like a truth commission. Herman stresses the importance of learning to recover memories and to be able to speak of atrocities in order for individuals to heal. Survivors need to find ways to incorporate the memories of the self "who can lose and be lost to others," and the self who learned firsthand about the capacity for evil, within others and within oneself.[28] Through a process of truth-telling, mourning, taking action and fighting back, and reconnecting with others, Herman argues, even individuals who have been severely traumatized by totalitarian control over a prolonged period can recover.[29] Political action can assist the recovery of a sense of power and community that are themselves building blocks for healing. Political and legal action can support a healing sense of mission for some survivors, although the direct relationship between a trauma survivor and a therapist remains critical to the recovery process, according to Herman.[30]

No one should pretend that the process of testifying before a truth commission involves the establishment of trusting relationships called for by the model of therapy. Pumla Gobodo-Madikizela noted that although the TRC provided assistance to victim-witnesses before and after their testimony, it fell short of full therapeutic services.[31] The question is whether, nonetheless, the activities of a truth commission can afford some assistance in the complex and arduous healing process. The restorative powers of truth-telling, of being heard by sympathetic listeners and forging a relationship with them, and of establishing potentially affirmative roles for bystanders and perpetrators are key elements of the recovery for trauma survivors. The promise and limitations of truth commissions in the pursuit of healing for individuals and society as well can be framed in terms of these three dimensions.

The Restorative Power of Truth-Telling

"The fundamental premise of the psychotherapeutic work is a belief in the restorative power of truth-telling," reports Herman.[32] The same premise undergirds a truth commission that affords opportunities for victims to tell their stories. In both settings, the goal is not exorcism but acknowledgment, and the story of trauma becomes testimony. Know the truth and it will set you free; expose the terrible secrets of a sick society and heal that society. Are these assertions that can be tested, or instead are they articles of professional, cultural, or religious faith? Without answering these questions fully, anecdotal evidence suggests the healing power of speaking about trauma.

Mzykisi Mdidimba told Rosenberg that testifying before the TRC about being tortured at age sixteen "has taken it off my heart." He continued, "When I have told stories of my life before, afterward, I am crying, crying, crying, and felt it was not finished. This time, I know what they've done to me will be among these people and all over the country. I still have some sort of crying, but also joy inside."[33]

Therapists who work with refugee survivors of persecution emphasize the significance of testimony both in the private, confessional sense and in the public, juridical sense.[34] Mollica explains that the trauma story is transformed as testimony from a telling about shame and humiliation to a portrayal of dignity and virtue; by speaking of trauma, survivors regain lost worlds and lost selves.[35] Therapists who work with trauma survivors agree that helping their patients to face rather than forget trauma is crucial to avoid reproducing trauma through emotional disturbance.

A group of Chilean therapists conclude: "We have found that the person or the family needs to recount the traumatic experience in detail, and express the emotions it produced. This permits integration into a coherent history of events that were necessarily disassociated, allowing the person to feel the pain of the losses experienced. It opens up the possibility for grief and mourning, and facilitates the development of a more coherent self-image."[36] By confronting the past, traumatized individuals can learn to discriminate between past, present, and future. When the work of knowing and telling the story comes to an end, the trauma then belongs to the past; the survivor can face the work of building a future.[37]

The clandestine nature of torture and abuse by repressive governments or insurgent groups compounds the physical pain with disbelief by the community, and at times by victims themselves. Testifying publicly before an official body can transform the seemingly private experience into a public one. Manour Muttetuwegama chaired the Presidential Commission on Disappearance in the southern provinces of Sri Lanka. She reported how eager people were to testify and provide vivid accounts of their tragic experiences.[38] Gobodo-Madikezela, a psychologist who served on the Human Rights Committee of the TRC, recounts how one mother testified about her pain of losing a child to torture and then death. She said later that she did not intend to cry before the commission, but nonetheless she did cry. Knowing that the testimony was broadcast, she concluded: "I wanted the world to see my tears." There is pride and strength in seeing oneself as an actor on a world stage, and as one who can educate the world while also exposing personal suffering in a public way. Tears in public will not be the last tears, but knowing that one's tears are *seen* may grant a sense of acknowledgment that makes grief less lonely and terrifying.

Preserving choice about how public to make the testimony is an important feature of respect for victims. Some people may feel exploited by media coverage of their grief. Also, there is often simply not enough time or media for oral hearings and media coverage for every victimized survivor. Many more can participate by offering written statements. More than 22,000 people presented their stories to the TRC, most in statements recorded by statement takers rather than through public hearings.

Speaking with or without a public broadcast to an official inquiry can be affirming if there is a sense of being heard and believed.[39] Some individuals may find it helpful to testify even when they personally dislike or refuse a psychological framework for their suffering.[40] A truth commission could help individuals who testify, and even those who do not, to locate their experiences within the larger setting of political violence. Coming to know that one's suffering is not solely a private experience, best forgotten, but instead an indictment of a social cataclysm, can permit individuals to move beyond trauma, hopelessness, numbness, and preoccupation with loss and injury. Even those who are too afraid or too much in pain to testify can gain some benefit from hearing the testimony of others that may parallel their own experiences. Integrating personal devastation within the larger context of political oppression can be crucial to a therapeutic result. One mother in Chile felt guilty about the death of her young son, who was shot by police after she had let him cross the street to watch television with neighbors. In therapy with professionals committed to acknowledging the context of political terror in Chile, the woman learned that her son was shot as part of mass political repression. The process helped her attain "an emotional understanding of the fact that the police, and not she, had killed her son."[41]

To be healing, the act of narrating an experience of trauma needs to move beyond a plain statement of facts to include also the survivor's emotional and bodily responses and reactions of others who mattered to the individual. For healing to occur, testimony must include the accompanying emotions and work toward reintegration with the individual's values and hopes.[42] The elements are likely to exceed the time, attention, and expertise of members of a truth commission. Yet unless the commissioners and staff attend to these dimensions, the therapeutic effects for testifying victims will be limited. A truth commission cannot conduct the arduous process of working through trauma with a therapist, but a commission may offer therapeutic moments and afford links to more continuous services and supports.

The Presence of Sympathetic Witnesses

The benefits of truth telling depend in no small measure on the presence of sympathetic witnesses. The speaker who recounts the painful stories then may establish trusting relationships and receive acknowledgment and validation from others.[43] Many who came forward to speak before the South African TRC explained how they wanted the commission to witness their pain or the evidence of their lost loved ones.[44] Are there therapeutic, healing benefits potentially available to individuals who do speak to sympathetic listeners in the official setting of the commission?

One clue emerges from the insights of therapists about the importance of a moral, politically committed stance to the listening that happens even within patient-psychologist relationships. Therapists who work with survivors of traumatic violence have discovered how crucial a moral, sympathetic, and politically attentive stance is to the therapeutic relationship. The therapist should not be merely neutral or focused solely on the subjective sphere.[45] Thus, therapists working with survivors of political repression have concluded that the "primary challenge to the therapist, in fact, is to maintain the link between psychotherapeutic work and the sociopolitical phenomena in which the symptoms are rooted."[46] The therapist and the patient need to build a bond of commitment premised on an explicit political, social, and psychological alliance.[47] Therefore, it is "taken for granted that the patient's disturbance is the result of a traumatic experience inflicted purposefully and criminally for political reasons."[48]

Acknowledgment by others of the victim's moral injuries is a central element of the healing process.[49] "The therapist is called upon to bear witness to a crime. She must affirm a position of solidarity with the victim."[50] When survivors speak of their relatives who "died," one psychologist instead emphasizes the fact that they were murdered.[51] Reestablishing a moral framework, in which wrongs are correctly named and condemned, is crucial to restoring the mental health of survivors.

Similarly, recognizing the indignity of the abuses is vital in order to communicate to the victimized, and to the rest of the nation, that individuals do matter. Although it may not be easily demonstrated that the simple gathering of testimony accomplishes this task, failure to take such steps would most likely convey the message that individuals and their pain do not matter. That indifference would compound the victimization.[52]

The very establishment and structure of a truth commission that receives testimony from survivors can accomplish some of these goals. The TRC Human Rights Committee hearings, for example, gave victims the chance to tell their stories before sympathetic listeners, and created a public setting devoted to documenting the atrocities and locating individual trauma in the larger political context. Such opportunities can afford chances for individuals to feel heard and respected. By identifying individual suffering as an indictment of the social context rather than treating it as a private experience that should be forgotten, a commission can help an individual survivor make space for new experiences.[53] Although a commission cannot create the bond of commitment that exists between therapist and client, it can enable public acknowledgment of the horrors. This acknowledgment, in turn, is a basic precondition before individual survivors can reestablish the capacity to trust other people and to trust the government.

To create such trust, the TRC tried to present its hearings with a tone of caregiving and a sense of safety. This meant departing from the neutral and remote tone of a court. Where courtrooms carry memories of repression and indifference, a truth commission carries the burden of creating an immediate sense of a different, welcoming setting. The Human Rights Committee of the TRC particularly avoided giving chilling reminders to victimized people of the hostility and insensitivity of the courts under apartheid. Its task was to treat those who testified about human rights abuses as persons to be believed, rather than as troublemakers or even people with a burden to prove their stories. In trying to meet this task, the TRC experience offered a stark contrast with adversarial hearings and inquests.[54]

Yet, in order to encourage amnesty applications from perpetrators, the TRC had to appear fair and sufficiently neutral. It helped to separate the amnesty review from the collective testimony of victims and survivors—dividing the commission into distinct teams.

Daily broadcast of the TRC hearings, with a weekly show recapping the sessions, extended the arena of witnesses to hear the testimony of survivors. In one televised session, Singqokwana Ernest Malgas, using a wheelchair because of injuries from torture, tried to describe the techniques of torture he had endured; and he broke down in sobs, which he tried to hide with his hands. Malgas was an ANC veteran who had been imprisoned in Robben Island for fourteen years. During that time, his house had been repeatedly firebombed and police had burned one of his sons to death with acid.[55] As Malgas hid behind his hands before the TRC committee, family members and a staff person tried to comfort him and help him recover the ability to speak. Seated across the room was Archbishop Desmond Tutu, chair of the commission. Hearing the man testify and cry, Tutu buried his head in his hands and then bowed, prone, before the table between them. Perhaps he was carefully holding his own horror from view, or seeking to prevent his own sympathetic pain from displacing attention from the testifying victim. In either case, this moment, caught in a television broadcast, exemplified the complex and deep process of acknowledging, bearing witness to, and mourning the atrocities committed under apartheid. It also restored dignity to those whose very being had been so deeply violated. The public process of acknowledgment brought recognition even to stories that were already known by those who testified and those who listened.

Justice Albie Sachs of the South African Constitutional Court noted: "Tutu cries. A judge does not cry."[56] At the close of his introduction to the final report, Tutu wrote,

> It has been a grueling job of work that has taken a physical, mental and psychological toll. We have borne a heavy burden as we have taken onto ourselves the anguish, the awfulness, and the sheer evil of it all. . . . The chief of the section that typed the transcripts of the hearings told me: As you type, you don't know you are crying until you feel and see the tears falling on your hands. . . . Some of us already experienced something of a post traumatic stress and have become more and more aware of just how deeply wounded we have all been; how wounded and broken we all are. . . . We have been called to be wounded healers.[57]

During public hearings, at times the commissioners joined witnesses in singing, or in bowing their heads in prayer. Some observers were put off by the religious tone of many TRC sessions, which often elevated suffering and victimhood and called for confession and common prayer. Many antiapartheid activists believed that they had engaged in a war and had won. Accordingly, the invitation to testify as victims did not fit their sense of themselves or what had happened. Sympathy by listeners can sometimes take a form that does not support those who were victimized. The choice to testify itself must reflect the individual's perception about whether the format that is offered seems supportive and appropriate.

Tasks for Perpetrators and Bystanders

Therapists who work with victims of collective violence emphasize the need for social repair. "Victims need to know that their society as a whole acknowledges what has happened to them."[58] Such general, social acknowledgment is needed also for bystanders, who often experience guilt in their avoidance of harm or else participate in ignorance and denial of collective violence.[59]

Sources such as the *New York Times* asserted during the TRC hearings that watching the testimony of victims on television offered white South Africans a therapeutic opportunity. "The hearings are therapeutic not only for the victims. The televised statements of victims and criminals can open the eyes of whites who ignored or justified apartheid's crimes, a crucial ingredient of reconciliation and for creating a democratic culture."[60] Whether this is true, or instead simply a belief circulating among commentators, remains to be seen.

The fact of the broadcasting on television and radio may enable the audience to share in the process of acknowledgment, mourning, and sympathetic listening. It may also add dimensions of voyeurism, and it is not clear how the televised aspects of the hearings affected viewers or, for that matter, participants. Sometimes people from different quarters see the same thing and empathize with the same witnesses and sometimes they line up with those whose positions most resemble their own. Yet, if the public audience can acknowledge suffering and wrongdoing, televising is valuable. If broadcasts can extend across a nation, at least in those moments they can create a shared experience in a nation of segregated and divergent experiences. The sheer fact that hearings are held and publicized triggers countless discussions and provides points of reference for a nation that widely denied the underlying atrocities. No longer can the denial persist.

Other mechanisms can involve bystanders more directly in the process of creating a shared national narrative. The TRC created the Registry of Reconciliation to enable people to write their reactions even if they were not victims or had no reason to seek amnesty. The flood of comments ("I didn't know . . ." or "I should have done more to help resist . . .") received in an initial wave suggests that the commission's process provided a beacon for bystanders as they reoriented themselves with the new national agenda. The TRC steered the victims toward reconciliation. It officially described the register as a means of granting "members of the public a chance to express their regret in failing to prevent human rights violations and to demonstrate their commitment to reconciliation."[61]

The TRC invited members of the business, religious, legal, and media communities to offer submissions for amnesty for their complicity with the apartheid regime, but it obtained minimal responses. No individual members of the judiciary came forward to seek amnesty for acts performed in the apartheid courts, but leading judges as a group signed and submitted a document acknowledging judicial enforcement of apartheid and judicial failures to protect people from torture.[62] Nonetheless, the commission undertook its own investigation into the role of these sectors. One volume of the TRC's final report summarizes the institutional and special hearings that included inquiries into the roles of businesses and labor, faith communities, legal professionals, the health sector, and the media both as beneficiaries of and at times enforcers of apartheid. Its explicit goal was to engage representatives of leading institutions in the process of accountability and the process of transition from oppression to democracy.

Perhaps the most crucial acknowledgment of the wrongs must come from perpetrators,[63] yet sincere acknowledgment cannot be ordered or forced. The South African legislation did not require those seeking amnesty to show contrition.[64] Still, the amnesty available to perpetrators on the condition that they testify fully before the TRC about their politically motivated crimes and misconduct elicited confessions, with details, of acts of torture, shooting, and bombings.

Consider the story of General Magnus Malan, army chief and later defense minister. Charged with authorizing an assassination squad that mistakenly killed thirteen women and children in 1987, Malan was the subject of one of the few prosecutions before the completion of the work of the TRC in South Africa. The prosecution grew from nine months of investigation and took nine more months, costing 12 million rand. In 1996, Malan was found not guilty, despite numerous allegations that continued to be made after the trial ended. Then, in 1997, Malan volunteered to speak before the TRC. He expressly did not seek amnesty but instead seemed to want the chance to tell his own story. He acknowledged cross-border raids; he described how he had set up a covert unit to disrupt Soviet-backed liberation movements. He denied giving approval for assassinations or atrocities. He also made clear his opposition to the operation of the TRC itself, as a witch-hunt, but said that he had come forward to take moral responsibility for the orders he had given.[65]

On occasion, those seeking amnesty acknowledge their wrongdoing and seek forgiveness. When General Johan van Merwe confessed that he was the one who had given the order to fire on demonstrators in 1992, he cracked the secrecy and anonymity of the apartheid regime. When he confessed to his order to fire on the demonstrators, he said he was sorry. Tutu said later, "It was an incredible moment. I said we should just keep quiet a bit and put our heads down for a minute."[66]

Other moments for the TRC do not have this quality. A police captain admitted his role in the shooting of thirteen people, and asked the victims' family for forgiveness. Instead, he was met by what a *Times* reporter described as "low grumbling," clarified later as a clear resistance to the notion that amnesty and truth could heal wounds.[67] Other alleged perpetrators lied to the commission, distorted their actions, responded with arrogance and adversariness, or admitted their crimes in monotones, with no embarrassment.

The healing sought by the TRC did not require apologies or forgiveness. On behalf of bystanders and perpetrators, as well as victims, it sought to reestablish a baseline of right and wrong, to humanize the perpetrators, and to obtain and disclose previously hidden information about what had happened, who had given orders, and where missing persons had ended up. Commissioner Dumisa Ntsebeza of the TRC explained that victims of apartheid were not only those on the receiving end of gross violations of human rights, but so also were family members who learned of the offenses committed by their loved ones. Even perpetrators had been warped and sometimes broken by their conduct as spies, torturers, and murderers.[68]

Cynthia Ngewu, mother of one of the individuals known as the Guguletu Seven, expressed the vision beautifully: "This thing called reconciliation . . . if I am understanding it correctly . . . if it means the perpetrator, this man who killed Christopher Piet, if it means he becomes human again, this man, so that I, so that all of us, get our humanity back . . . then I agree, then I support it all."[69] This generosity of vision that extends to perpetrators the hope for healing was a distinctive feature of the TRC.

Yet that generosity does alter the central task of articulating what had been wrong and had never been justifiable. This assertion of moral judgment frames the events in a new national narrative of acknowledgment, accountability, and civic values.[70]

Healing and Reconciling a Nation

How might therapeutic processes work for collectivities? Are truth commission mechanisms, which already fall short of the elements necessary for full therapeutic benefits for individuals, able to promote reconstruction of whole societies? It would be wrong to imagine that the commission by itself could accomplish the reconstruction of societies devastated by violent and hostile divisions. Yet there are promising roles that a commission could play.

A truth commission can cut through myths, rumors, and false pictures of the past even if it cannot erect one picture that will be full and true for all time. The truth commission report on El Salvador confirmed what some suspected, and what others refused to believe, while separating truth from rampant lies and rumors.[71] According to one of its drafters, the report put an end to inflammatory charges and countercharges, overcame denial of terrible truths, and allowed the nation to focus on its future.[72] Crucial here was the credibility established by the commission through its process and its apparent honesty.[73]

It remains an open question whether a truth commission can also help to reconcile groups that have been warring or have otherwise engaged in animosities. Reconciliation could mean minimal agreement to coexist and cooperate, or a stronger commitment to forgive and unify. Some want to forgive but lack the basic information about whom to forgive; here, a truth commission may help identify names. A teenaged daughter of a murdered South African activist indicated that she wanted to forgive but did not know who had committed the murder; and then her father's murderers applied for amnesty.[74] Others do not want to and certainly do not have to forgive perpetrators. Omar, former

South African Minister of Justice, emphasized that "forgiveness [was] a personal matter. However bitterness can only exacerbate tensions in society. By providing victims a platform to tell their stories and know the destiny of their loved ones, one can help to achieve a nation reconciled with its past and at peace with itself."[75]

The TRC was committed to exposing abuses by the liberation forces as well as by apartheid officials and supporters, and perhaps this commitment to the injuries on both sides can support reconciliation over time. Yet the very effort to articulate the moral baseline was bound to treat the crimes of apartheid as worse than the crimes of the ANC or other antiapartheid activists.[76] Those who abuse government power do something worse than those who resist it, even when each side uses similar, unacceptable means. When former president Frederik W. de Klerk withdrew his cooperation with the TRC, he cited what he perceived to be unequal treatment; he claimed he had been badgered and disbelieved in his testimony while ANC officials who testified about their misconduct had not been probed or seriously questioned.[77] Some observers objected that the entire TRC operated as a political witch-hunt designed to discredit the former National Party government.[78]

This very dissension, ideally, could be part of the story narrated by a truth commission. An investigatory commission can expose the multiple causes and conditions contributing to genocide and regimes of torture and terror, and distribute blame and responsibility across sectors of society. It need not be a victors' report. Instead, close historical analysis of testimonies and documents can expose the influences of politicians; totalitarian structures; passive bystanders who feel ineffective, disengaged, or panicked; leaders and cultural practices dehumanizing particular groups of individuals; and military and police practices with no accountability to the public.[79] The issues of justice are unavoidable in the search for truth; the wager of the TRC was that reconciliation can be better reached if the emphasis is on truth, rather than justice.

Although the very trappings of therapy may disturb many who seek justice, a truth commission can clear the air with acknowledgment of the casualties of collective violence and causal chains behind them, especially when crimes have been covered up or officially denied. Thus, tensions between therapeutic goals and aspirations for justice do not demand abandonment of truth commissions.

Many in South Africa proudly embraced the TRC's search for nonviolent responses to violence.[80] From this vantage point, it is an act of restraint not solely to pursue criminal sanctions, and an act of hope not to strip perpetrators of their political and economic positions. When a democratic process selects a truth commission, a people summon the strength and vision to say to one another: Focus on victims and try to restore their dignity; focus on truth and try to tell it whole. Redefine the victims as the entire society, and redefine justice as accountability. Seek repair, not revenge; reconciliation, not recrimination. Honor and attend in public to the process of remembering.

These are bold ambitions.[81] They may be doomed to create such high expectations as to invite disappointment. A report that recounts the process that produced it and makes the testimony available for others to interpret can assist a spirit of open inquiry. The TRC's *Final Report* is exemplary in this respect as it provides both a full account of its own methods and limitations and summaries of its hearings and investigations. By locating its work explicitly as part of the struggle to move from oppression to democracy, a truth commission such as the TRC can model the virtues of openness and fairness to all sides that it hopes to help usher into the society.

Setting open inquiry and reconciliation as goals, a highly visible public process of investigation into past atrocities redirects at least to some degree people's understandable desires for vengeance and recrimination. The democratic origins of the TRC helped to consecrate that redirection through a process of broad participation. A truth commission imposed by the nation's executive or an international body may have more difficulty conveying the messages of reconciliation. It might instead seem merely an insincere or ineffective sop to those who demand some response to the atrocities. No truth commission can accomplish fully the goals of accountability and reparation. Articulating modest goals—such as gathering names and accounts of victims and documenting the scope of killings, torture, and other atrocities—could save truth commissions from generating cycles of high hopes and bitter disappointments.

The TRC's pursuit of restorative justice in South Africa is also in jeopardy if it presages no changes in the material circumstances of those most victimized. Characterized as only one step in the process of reconciliation, the TRC was designed to propose specific reparations and also to assist the development of a society stable enough to pursue land reform, redesign of medical and educational systems, and other reforms to redress the massive economic imbalances in the country. The TRC committee on reparations recommended to the president specific acts requested by the victimized, such as funds for gravestones, as well as collective reparations in the form of monuments, parks, and schools named for victims and survivors. By the end of 1999, nothing much had happened. The new government had not even bothered to respond to the TRC report, although the government seems generally committed to economic fairness and social reconstruction. The longer term vision of social transformation offers the idea of redemption for suffering. Yet if progress toward this vision is not made, skepticism about the goals of healing and reconciliation will mount in South Africa.[82]

The Spectrum of Goals

Perhaps, as some say, there are simply two purposes animating societal responses to collective violence: justice and truth.[83] Then the question becomes, which of these two purposes should take precedence? One answer calls for "[a]ll the truth and as much justice as possible";[84] another would stress punishment for wrongdoing, especially horrific wrongdoing. We should make prosecution a duty under international law to ensure that new regimes do not avoid hard tasks and overstate the obstacles they face, argues Orentlicher.[85] Yet, only if we acknowledge that prosecutions are slow, partial, and preoccupied with the either/or simplifications of the adversary process can we recognize the independent value of commissions. They can investigate the larger patterns of atrocity and complex lines of responsibility and complicity.

Yet, as this chapter has explored, even to do so captures but a narrow portion of the potential goals for societal responses to collective violence. Truth and justice are not the only objectives, or at least they do not transparently indicate the range of concerns they may come to comprise. After mass violence, a nation or society needs to address at least eight goals:

1. Overcome communal and official denial of the atrocity; gain public acknowledgment.

2. Obtain the facts in an account as full as possible in order to meet victims' need to know, to build a record for history, and to ensure minimal accountability and visibility of perpetrators.

3. Forge the basis for a domestic democratic order that respects and enforces human rights.

4. Promote reconciliation across social divisions; reconstruct the moral and social systems devastated by violence.

5. Promote psychological healing for individuals, groups, victims, bystanders, and offenders.

6. Restore dignity to victims.

7. Punish, exclude, shame, and diminish offenders for their offenses.

8. Accomplish these goals in ways that render them compatible rather than antagonistic with the other goals.

In light of this list, truth commissions are not a second-best alternative to prosecutions, but instead a form better suited to meet many of the goals. Indeed, to better serve the goals of promoting healing for individuals and reconciliation across social divisions, truth commissions would need to diverge even more than they usually do from prosecutions, and offer more extensive therapeutic assistance and relief from threats of prosecution.

When the societal goals include restoring dignity to victims, offering a basis for individual healing, and promoting reconciliation across a divided nation, a truth commission may be as or more powerful than prosecutions. The commission can help set a tone and create public rituals to build a bridge from a terror-filled past to a collective, constructive future. Individuals do and must have their own responses to atrocity, but the institutional framework created by a society can either encourage desires for retribution or instead strengthen capacities for generosity and peace.

It is far from clear that a truth commission can achieve therapeutic and reconciliation goals at the same time that prosecutions proceed. Although South Africa permitted prosecutions of those individuals who did not obtain amnesty from the TRC, all of the practical dimensions of prosecutions could work against the goals of healing, reconciliation, and full truth-telling. Nonetheless, healing from atrocity often is enhanced by an operating justice system that prosecutes and punishes perpetrators so long as it does not also unleash new violence and thirst for revenge.

What prosecutions and truth commissions share, fundamentally, is the effort to cabin and channel through public, legal institutions the understandable and even justifiable desires for revenge by those who have been victimized. Prosecutions and truth commissions lie among an even broader range of potential societal responses to collective violence. A society may respond to past atrocity by opening secret police files, removing prior political and military officials and civil servants from their posts and from pension benefits, publicizing the names of offenders and the names of victims, securing reparations and apologies for victims, developing and making available appropriate therapeutic services for victims, promoting commemorations and imaginative renewal through memorials and the arts, and developing public education programs for children and for adults.

Any evaluation of responses to mass atrocity depends upon the goals sought and the distance between the ideal and the real, as implemented. Today, responses to collective violence actually lurch among rhetorics of history (truth), justice (punishment, compensation, and deterrence), theology (forgiveness), art (commemoration), education (learning lessons), politics (building democracy), and therapy (healing). Each goal is desirable, but each also risks failing to attend to those who were victimized. Bearing witness to their deaths, disabilities, and lost hopes; considering what could help those who survived to return to living; and redressing the dehumanization that both presages and endures after mass violence: each of these aspirations calls for a process that focuses on the voices and lives of real individuals. Resisting the destruction of memory and human dignity, responses to atrocity must invigorate remembrance of what happened and prevent any further dehumanization of the victimized.

The repertoire of societal responses to collective violence must include prosecutions, but also must not be limited to them. Investigatory commissions, most fully developed in the TRC, challenge the assumption that prosecutions are the best form of response. Investigatory commissions open inquiry into the varieties of possible responses and the multiple purposes that they may achieve. Truth commissions emphasize the experiences of those victimized; the development of a detailed historical record; and the priority of healing for victims and entire societies after the devastation to bodies, memories, friendships, and politics caused by collective violence. Whether these are counters or instead complementary partners to justice, they are worthy of human effort in the continuing struggles against mass atrocities.

Notes

1. I wrote the first version of this essay for this book; a longer version of some of the ideas presented here then appeared in Martha Minow, *Between Vengeance and Forgiveness: Facing History after Genocide and Mass Violence* (Boston, 1998). Now I have revised this essay in light of the final report of the South African Truth and Reconciliation Commission.

2. Zbignew Herbert (trans. John Carpenter and Bogdana Carpenter), *Report from the Besieged City and Other Poems* (New York, 1985), 67.

3. Testimony to South African Truth and Reconciliation Commission Human Rights Committee, quoted in Antjie Krog, *Country of My Skull* (Johannesburg, 1998), 31.

4. Civil trials—typically seeking monetary damages—can accomplish some of the same purposes, although they are pursued by individuals and involve the state apparatus as arbiter and enforcer of international human rights norms. See Kenneth Randall, *Federal Courts and International Human Rights* (Durham, N.C., 1990).

5. Complicating matters is the fact that particular individuals fairly may be viewed as victims, perpetrators, and bystanders. A student watches his parents being harassed by secret police; the student joins protest groups and then is arrested; the student emerges from prison willing to use terrorist tactics against the secret police, and sets off bombs that kill civilians. See the description of Donocan "Faried" Ferhelst, in *Hearts and Minds: The Burden of Truth* (Soundprint Media Center, Washington, D.C., 1997; audiotape, broadcast on National Public Radio).

6. In addition, after World War II and since, some nations have offered monetary reparations to victims and families of victims following governmentally sanctioned violence. Some have also promoted restitution of stolen objects and monetary support for newly democratizing nations. Reparations acknowledge wrongs and present concrete gestures of remedy, even though they inevitably fail to restore lives, hopes, and opportunities destroyed by violence. Yet reparations risk overemphasizing that which can be given a monetary value or the material losses and risk trivializing the human losses.

7. Joan Fitzpatrick, "Nothing But the Truth? Transitional Regimes Confront the Past," review of Naomi Rhot-Arriaza (ed.), *Impunity and Human Rights in International Law and Practice"* in *Michigan Journal of International Law* XVI (1996): 720.

8. See Richard Lewis Siegel, "Transitional Justice: How Emerging Democracies Reckon with Former Regimes," review of Neil J. Kritz (ed.), *Transitional Justice: A Decade of Debate and Experience* (Washington, D.C., 1995), *Human Rights Quarterly* XX (1998): 431, 454; Stephan Landsman, "Alternative Responses to Serious Human Rights Abuses—Of Prosecutions and Truth Commissions," paper presented at the Law & Society Annual Meeting (May–June 1997), 4.

9. E.g., Mary Albon, "Truth and Justice: The Delicate Balance—Documentation of Prior Regimes and Individual Rights," in Kritz (ed.), *Transitional Justice*, I, 290;

Douglas W. Cassell Jr., "International Truth Commissions and Justice," in Kritz (ed.), *Transitional Justice*, I, 326, 333.

10. Carlos Nino, *Radical Evil on Trial* (New Haven, 1995), viii.

11. See Tina Rosenberg, "A Reporter at Large: Recovering From Apartheid," *New Yorker*, 18 November 1996, 86, 87.

12. See Truth And Reconciliation Commission, *Final Report* (Cape Town, 29 October 1998), I, chap. 4, par. 6–7.

13. Suzanne Daley, "Bitter Medicine: Settling for Truth in the Quest for Justice," *New York Times*, 27 October 1996, 1.

14. Similarly, constructive interaction between trials and the TRC occurred in South Africa. Colonel Eugene de Kock, head of the Vlakplaas police unit, was prosecuted successfully for murder and fraud. He then offered incriminating testimony in the contempt hearing following former president Pieter W. Botha's refusal to respond to subpoenas issued by the TRC. See Suzanne Daley, "Killer Tells of Rewards for Defending Apartheid," *New York Times*, 4 June 1998, 11.

15. Abraham Lincoln, however, also used the notion of healing for America's Civil War.

16. Calvin Sims, "A Killer's 'I'm Sorry' Isn't Enough Any More," *New York Times*, 22 February 1998, 3 (Argentina's reconsideration of amnesties in the face of continuing sense that the truth was being covered up).

17. Tina Rosenberg, *The Haunted Land: Facing Europe's Ghosts after Communism* (New York, 1995), 26.

18. Ibid., 24.

19. Michael Ignatieff, "The Elusive Goal of War Trials," *Harper's* (March 1996); reprinted in "Articles of Faith, Index on Censorship," *Harper's* (September/October 1997): 15, 16.

20. See comments of Lawrence Weschler, quoting William S. Merwin, "Unchopping a Tree," in *The Miner's Pale Children* (New York, 1970), 85–88, in Henry Steiner (ed.), *Truth Commissions: A Comparative Assessment* (Cambridge, Mass., 1997), 15.

21. Lawrence Langer, Panel on Hearing the Victims (comments at "Searching for Memory and Justice: The Holocaust and Apartheid" conference, Yale University, 8 February 1998).

22. Eric L. Santner, "History Beyond the Pleasure Principle: Some Thoughts on the Representation of Trauma," in Saul Friedlander (ed.), *Probing the Limits of Representation: Nazism and the "Final Solution"* (Cambridge, Mass., 1992), 143, 147–148, 153–154.

23. Robert Jay Lifton, *The Broken Connection: On Death and the Continuity of Life* (New York, 1979), 176.

24. David Becker, Elizabeth Lira, Maria Isabel Castillo, Elana Gomez, and Juana Kovaksys, "Therapy with Victims of Political Oppression in Chile: The Challenge of Social Reparation," in Kritz (ed.), *Transitional Justice*, I, 583, 586; Ervin Staub, "Breaking the Cycle of Violence: Helping Victims of Genocidal Violence Heal," *Journal of Personal and Interpersonal Loss*, I (1996): 191–197.

25. Judith Herman, *Trauma and Recovery* (New York, 1992).

26. Ibid., 84–85.

27. Ibid., 137, 229–231.

28. Ibid., 93.

29. Ibid., 157.

30. Ibid., 207–211.

31. Ibid., 114 (discussing therapists with Holocaust survivors, Indochinese refugees, and other victims of violence). In addition, a truth commission typically pays insufficient attention to the psychological needs of commission members and others who listen to victims of torture and violence.

32. Ibid., 181.

33. Rosenberg, "Reporter at Large," 92.

34. See Inger Agger and Soren B. Jensen, "Testimony as Ritual and Evidence in Psychotherapy for Political Refugees," *Journal of Traumatic Stress* III (1990), 115–130.

35. Richard Mollica, "The Trauma Story: The Psychiatric Care of Refugee Survivors of Violence and Torture," in Frank Ochberg (ed.), *Post-Traumatic Therapy and Victims of Violence* (New York, 1988), 295, 312.

36. Becker et al., "Therapy with Victims of Political Oppression in Chile," 587.

37. Herman, *Trauma and Recovery*, 195.

38. Steiner, *Truth*, 16.

39. Thomas Buregenthal, one of three commissioners in the United Nations Truth Commission for El Salvador, reported:

Many of the people who came to the Commission to tell what happened to them or to their relatives and friends had not done so before. For some, ten years or more had gone by in silence and pent-up anger. Finally, someone listened to them, and there would be a record of what they had endured. They came by the thousands, still afraid and not a little skeptical, and they talked, many for the first time. One could not listen to them without recognizing that the mere act of telling what had happened was a healing emotional release and that they were more interested in recounting their story and being heard than in retribution. It is as if they felt some shame that they had not dared to speak out before and, now that they had done so, they could go home and focus on the future less encumbered by the past. (Thomas Buergenthal, "The United Nations Truth Commission for El Salvador," in Kritz, *Transitional Justice*, I, 292, 321).

40. See Agger and Jensen, "Testimony as Ritual and Evidence in Psychotherapy for Political Refugees," 124.

41. Becker et al., "Therapy with Victims of Political Oppression in Chile," 588.

42. Herman, *Trauma and Recovery*, 177–179.

43. See remarks of Tina Rosenberg, in Steiner, *Truth*, 215; José Zalaquett, "Balancing Ethical Imperatives and Political Constraints: The Dilemma of New Democracies Confronting Past Human Rights Violations," *Hastings Law Journal* XLIII (1992): 1425, 1437.

44. For example, Joyce Mtimkhulu brought the TRC a handful of the hair of her then-21-year-old son, who had been imprisoned, poisoned, and then murdered by security police officers. "'This is Siphiwe's hair. I want the commission to witness what I've brought here today so that they should know the effects of the poison that was used on my son. I thought I would make burial of my son through his hair, but by God's will I didn't, as if I knew I would be here today.'" Quoted in Mark Gevisser, "The Witnesses," *New York Times Magazine*, 27 June 1997, 32, 34.

45. See Herman, *Trauma and Recovery*, 178–180.

46. Ibid., 586.

47. Ibid., 587.

48. Ibid.

49. Staub, "Breaking the Cycle of Violence," 193–194.

50. Herman, *Trauma and Recovery*, 135.

51. Ibid. (describing Yael Danieli's work with Holocaust survivors).

52. Justice Pius Langa, "Hearing the Victims" (paper presented at "Searching for Memory and Justice: The Holocaust and Apartheid" conference, Yale University 8 February 1998).

53. André du Toit, in Steiner, *Truth*, 28.

54. A written account appears in Mark Gevisser, "The Witnesses," *New York Times Magazine*, 27 June 1997, 32, 34.

55. Comments at "Searching for Memory and Justice: The Holocaust and Apartheid" conference, Yale University. At the same event, Commissioner Dumisa Ntsebeza of the TRC recounted how the widow of Mapetla Mohapi, a man found hanged with a suicide note in an apartheid jail cell in 1977, had demanded an inquest, which yielded inconclusive results. She then sued the government, with no success, at enormous cost to herself. In 1996, she testified before the TRC and afterward reported that, for the first time, she felt she was treated there with belief rather than hostility. She concluded that she no longer needed to know the details about what happened to her husband. If the TRC's investigative unit found out the information, that would be a bonus on top of the benefit that she had already received. See also Ntsebeza, chapter in this volume.

56. TRC, *Final Report*, foreword by chairperson, par. 87, 88, 89.

57. Comments at "Searching for Memory and Justice: The Holocaust and Apartheid" conference.

58. Becker, "Therapy," 589.

59. See Gevisser, "The Witnesses," 38. (De Klerk's view that the commission was biased toward the liberation movement is "emblematic of most white South Africans, who have been shocked by the evidence ['We never knew!'] but have neither taken responsibility nor displayed remorse for acts committed in their name.")

60. Editorial, "The Truth About Steve Biko," *New York Times*, 4 February 1997, A22.

61. This appears on the TRC home page, www.truth.org.za (visited on 19 March 1998).

62. Albie Sachs, comments at "Searching for Memory and Justice: The Holocaust and Apartheid" conference. The TRC *Final Report* acknowledged that the independence of sitting judges might have been jeopardized if they had appeared at the TRC hearings. See *Final Report*, IV, chap. 4, par. 14. See also *Final Report*, IV, chap. 4, par. 5, 46, 47, 48 (rejecting the claim that appearance before the commission would have jeopardized the independence and collegiality of sitting judges and magistrates).

63. Staub, "Breaking the Cycle," 193.

64. Gevisser, "The Witnesses," 32.

65. See Suzanne Daley, "Apartheid-Era Defense Defends Role in Ordering Raids on Neighboring Countries," *New York Times*, 8 May 1997, 16. "I come here to tell you my story and to face your judgment. . . . I shall be content if what I am saying may spur the slightest of understanding of former adversaries. I shall rejoice if my efforts can contribute in the minutest sense toward reconciliation and if all soldiers may obtain

moral amnesty. . . . It is understanding and forgiveness we really seek, not legal pardons."

66. Suzanne Daley, "Bitter Medicine: Settling for Truth in the Quest of Justice," *New York Times*, 27 October 1996, 1.

67. Daley, "Bitter Medicine."

68. Comments at "Searching for Memory and Justice: The Holocaust and Apartheid" conference.

69. Quoted in Krog, *Country of My Skull*, 109.

70. See comments of Zalaquett in Steiner, *Truth*, 29–31.

71. Buergenthal, "The United Nations Truth Commission for El Salvador," 321.

72. Ibid.

73. See also ibid., 325:

A nation has to confront its past by acknowledging the wrongs that have been committed in its name before it can successfully embark on the arduous task of cementing the trust between former adversaries and their respective sympathizers, which is a prerequisite for national reconciliation. One cannot hope to achieve this objective by sweeping the truth under the rug of national consciousness, by telling the victims or their next of kin that nothing happened, or by asking them not to tell their particular story. The wounds begin to heal with the telling of the story and the national acknowledgment of its authenticity.

How that story is told is less important than that it be told truthfully. Hence, whether the names of the perpetrators are revealed, whether trials are held, sanctions imposed, compensation awarded, or amnesties granted, these are all considerations that may well depend upon the nature of the conflict, the national character of the country, the political realities, and compromises that produced the end of the conflict. But if the basic truth about the past is suppressed, it will prove very difficult to achieve national reconciliation.

74. Gevisser, "The Witnesses," 38.

75. Dullah Omar, "The South African Truth and Reconciliation Commission" (written text of the address of South African Minister of Justice to "Facing History and Ourselves," Twelfth Annual Human Rights and Justice Conference, Harvard University, 10 April 1997), 22–23.

76. See Gevisser, "The Witnesses," 38.

77. Suzanne Daley, "Divisions Deepen on Apartheid Crimes Inquiry," *New York Times*, 8 June 1997, 6.

78. Daley, "Divisions."

79. See, generally, Erwin Staub, *The Roots of Evil: The Origins of Genocide and Other Group Violence* (Cambridge, 1989). See also particular commission reports, reprinted in Kritz (ed.), *Transitional Justice*, III.

80. Dullah Omar, "The South African Truth and Reconciliation Commission," 22–23: "To the majority of victims, . . . the knowledge and full disclosure of what happened to their loved ones has been extremely relieving and satisfying. Indeed, we have had occasions where victims have embraced perpetrators and clearly indicated a commitment to work for reconciliation."

81. See Elizabeth Kiss, "Moral Ambition within Political Restraints: Reflections on Restorative Justice," in this volume.

82. Albie Sachs, lecture to members of the Harvard Law School community, 17 January 1999. In addition, the TRC's charge to investigate gross violations of human rights may prove too narrow to encompass the degradations and humiliations of the pass system, the relocation of homes, and the oppressive living and working conditions of blacks and coloured persons under apartheid.

83. E.g., Stanley Cohen, "State Crimes of Previous Regimes: Knowledge, Accountability, and the Policing of the Past," *Law & Social Inquiry* XX (1995): 7–50.

84. "*State Crimes of Previous Regimes*," attributing it to Zalaquett. See Kate Millett, *The Politics of Cruelty: An Essay on the Literature of Political Imprisonment* (New York, 1994).

85. Diane F. Orentlicher, "Settling Accounts: The Duty to Prosecute Human Rights Violations of a Prior Regime," *Yale Law Journal* C (1991): 2539.

XIII

Doing History, Doing Justice

THE NARRATIVE OF THE HISTORIAN AND OF THE TRUTH COMMISSION

CHARLES S. MAIER

Feasible Justice

The activity of truth commissions challenges historians to reflect on their craft. In turn, the historian can offer some insights into the process of seeking truth and reconciliation. A truth commission is a panel that attempts to establish the facts of human rights abuses under an earlier regime or set of governmental practices, but refrains from prosecuting the perpetrators who testify under its auspices. Measured by the number of hearings, the size of the country, the broad scope of repressive policing to be scrutinized, and the mandate to produce an extensive report, the most notable such panel was the South African Truth and Reconciliation Commission (TRC), which offered former perpetrators the chance to admit to past abuses in return for amnesty. By 1999, twenty comparable national panels have functioned in other postauthoritarian states.[1] In fact, however, this chapter considers not just truth commissions, which refrain from trial and punishment, but political trials held in the aftermath of a regime change or the end of a period of civil violence. This chapter is not designed to make the case for the value of these commissions or trials.[2] At issue are the parallels between historians and the commission or court as they take up the assignment of establishing, explaining, and interpreting a narrative of political violence.

This chapter is based on the varieties of experience reported in a symposium organized by the World Peace Foundation and the Human Rights program of the Harvard Law School, the proceedings of which have now been published; on my own unsystematic reading about such commissions outside Europe, earlier examination of "épuration" controversies (i.e., the purge of collaborators) and war-crimes trials after World War II; and, most recently, my direct research into the trials of East German officials after unification.[3]

Truth commissions are a recent expedient in the search for feasible justice. They have emerged as a widespread feature of the many transitions to democracy that have taken place in the last decades of the twentieth century. As Yael

Tamir observed, the ability of a commission to function is grounded in a sharp discontinuity of a political regime.[4] Political trials and epuration reflect the fact that one side had defeated the other militarily; the truth commission emerges when a settlement is negotiated rather than imposed. Truth commissions have thus come to serve in those cases where criminal trials seem impractical. Although the security or military forces of the former regime may not have been able to negotiate their own immunity, it may still seem prudent not to summon them before a court. As in Chile, they may still hold on to military power or appear potentially threatening. Perhaps so many of the population still believe that the earlier authorities' violent conduct was necessary and justified that forging a new political consensus may recommend silence about past misdeeds. Eminent legal scholars, such as Ackerman, have justified this prudential silence, even though others have argued that denying justice in this way will produce long-term handicaps for democratic development.[5]

Sometimes a successor regime will institute trials and investigative commissions simultaneously. For a while at least, successor regimes respond to intense pressure from victims and their relatives, most poignantly symbolized (and effectively mobilized) by the Argentine "mothers of the disappeared." The Alfonsin government in Argentina tried senior military officials who were considered responsible for the "dirty war," and established an official commission to report on the previous government's atrocities.[6] This bold approach, however, was reversed by the broad amnesty provisions of the Menem government. In unified Germany, officials and border soldiers of the former German Democratic Republic (GDR) were put on trial under the terms of the unification treaty. This provided for criminal trials in the case of conduct that was itself allegedly prohibited under GDR law; the trials have centered on whether East German behavior, including the use of violence in enforcing the border regime, electoral fraud, or judicial abuse, actually violated the extinct state's nominal norms of human rights. The state of Brandenburg also commissioned an inquiry into the possible collaboration with the State Security services (the Stasi) of its Minister President, Manfred Stolpe, a Protestant church administrator before 1990. Doing so required a highly contentious intepretation of the propriety of his conversations with Stasi officials. Working in an even broader fashion, the federal legislature held two series of investigations with witnesses and testimonies about governmental practices in the former GDR.[7] Advocates of such commissions have argued that the whole governing system was authoritarian and abusive enough to warrant a detailed investigation of how it had systematically infringed human rights even when no specific criminal charges were involved.

The experience of united Germany, however, reveals that some fundamentally different types of "truth" are at stake. The post-1990 trials of the border guards addressed open violence by national security officials who were making no effort to conceal what they regarded as law enforcement. The later trials of a few high officials for establishing and tolerating the border regime or for electoral fraud have sought to focus on more systemic abuses, although at the cost of great selectivity in choosing defendants as well as of raising always troubling questions of legal retroactivity. The Enquete-Commission established by the parliament endeavored to provide for national education concerning the overall structure of antidemocratic and unjust procedures that the previous dictatorship had imposed. But the most spectacular post-1989 effort to come to terms with the East German past was neither the trials nor the Enquete-Commission, but the opening of the Stasi, or secret police, records.

The so-called Gauck Authority, established in 1990 by the last, finally democratized East German legislature, was given legal control of the Stasi records and opened them on the demand of citizens who wanted to learn details of the secret surveillance to which they had been subject.[8] In this sense, its mission is somewhat parallel to the effort at public acknowledgment of abuses pursued by the South African TRC. The Gauck Authority [named after Joachim Gauck] has also disclosed the identity of informants to their victims and to government agencies on request. What this process revealed was a large network of informal collaborators with the Stasi who reported on their fellow citizens. The GDR was certainly suffocatingly repressive and sanctioned dissent with loss of job and educational opportunities, blanket restrictions on travel, and sometimes prison, but for the prior three decades it had not been particularly violent or brutal, certainly not in comparison with the earlier National Socialist dictatorship, the Argentinian generals, or the South African security forces. The truth that has proved so problematic is not that of denied violence or unacknowledged murders and torture, but of secret informing.

It is not the subject of this essay, but it is important to note that there are different varieties of truth as well as of disclosure processes. The truth of widespread complicity with an authoritarian regime is a less heroic, indeed far more shameful one than the truth even of widespread secret and unacknowledged government brutality. It brings into question the alleged decency of the society that successor regimes would like to portray as largely arrayed against their unjust rulers. Citizens of the former GDR, like the French coming to terms with Vichy, or the survivors of any regime in which pervasive denunciation played a role, face a different sort of truth. Focusing usually on the trade-off between punishment and disclosure, most of the analyses of the truth commission experience have not taken into account this particular complexity. While truth commissions have certainly sought to cope with cases of secret denunciation and violence, they have still presupposed a confrontation under the old regime between society and its rulers. They document a secret war. Are they a sufficient instrument for delving into the complicitous patterns of many modern dictatorships?

Advocates of the truth commission process recognize that the procedure is problematic, but problematic in terms of politics and justice. The price of

forswearing punishment can be a high one, when officials who behaved brutally walk away scot-free. Alex Boraine claims that the distinction between a
general amnesty, as decreed in some Latin American cases, and the "amnesty
with disclosure" and testimony is great enough to preclude the disenchant-
ment with democracy that the blanket amnesty unleashes. Full and detailed
disclosure, testimony in an open hearing, and restricting amnesty to "political"
abuses, allegedly will guard against the cynicism, fear, and disillusion of the
blanket amnesty.[9] Still, in South Africa, relatives of those brutalized or murdered by the security forces sometimes grew embittered as former sadists
traded their stories for immunity. On the other hand, after a war, providing for
a truth commission may help establish a cease-fire and the ground for political
settlement between opposing forces. It will partially satisfy victims without
excessively frightening those who might have to renounce power. Once the
truth commission begins its work, victims and victimizers allegedly "work
through" their respective anger and guilt, reaching a valuable catharsis and,
perhaps, reconciliation. "We hope that the Commission will contribute to the
process of healing a traumatized and wounded people. We open wounds only
in order to cleanse them, to deal with the past effectively and so to close the
door on that dark and horrendous past forever. Together we can then turn to
the present and the future. Then we will be able to work for a prosperous and
reconciled South Africa."[10] The metaphor of psychiatric transference is sometimes invoked; as Weschler observed, victims are enabled "to move on in their
lives."[11] It is believed valuable to establish the historical truth of past practices
even if some sort of retributive reckoning remains out of reach. The establishing of historical truth may help to deter any relapse into shameful practices.

Teaching History

A truth commission is thus predicated on the idea that establishing the historical record, more precisely, and securing its public acknowledgment, is a requi-
site for successful democratization. But what is the relation of that record to
"history" or to what a historian does? A historian can interact with the truth
commission or political tribunal in several different capacities. First, the evidence gathered by the commission can serve as a source for a historian's own
reconstruction of events. But like any historical source, the truth commission
has to be interrogated. The appearance of former security officers is often negotiated; their testimony is calculated. Issues of motivation are especially likely to
be distorted, above all if the commission is designed to elicit the appearance of
contrition. Claims of acting under orders or compulsion must be carefully
examined. The commission will always be inquiring about states of mind and
motivation: Why was a prisoner in custody? How did an interrogation get out
of control? Who encouraged the use of force and torture? Why did minimal

restraint fail? Who had given orders to do what? No matter how clear-cut the exposed abuse may seem—how brutal and violent and clearly established—there are no unproblematic issues about violence and power, certainly not when hierarchies of command exist. This means that historians must interpret, indeed must often implicitly raise questions, that the commission itself failed to ask. A truth commission is not a magic source, any more than are the files of the secret police a magic key to the operation of a totalitarian system.

Second, the commission and its work are themselves subjects for historical investigation. Posttransition political justice has emerged as a compelling field for research. A historian asks whether the commission was part of a negotiated pact or just the uneasy recourse of a fragile government, caught between countless victims of injustice and the still threatening possibility that former rulers might intervene in politics once again. What forces urged its establishment? Who resisted? Was its establishment possible only because of divisions among the former rulers or their collective powerlessness? Does the investigation really close the door on the past or leave it subject to continued conflict and strife?[12] Is it called upon to investigate the abuses of former power holders, or, as in the South African case, to consider the abuses conducted by both sides (or more than two sides) in a period of long civil and political struggle? But the issue that claims attention is somewhat different: namely, the relationship between a version of the past that the truth commission or trial generates and that about which a historian writes.

Not all truth commissions set so ambitious a task as the South African TRC. Reflecting on the Chilean experience, "The distinction between fact and interpretation has become very important in the working of truth commissions," Zalaquett reported. "They should concentrate largely on facts, which may be proved, whereas differences about historical interpretation will always exist." Steiner largely concurred, lest the commissions' reports lose "distinctiveness and a sense of objectivity."[13] But the South African TRC has from the outset declared that it was interested in political violence and wished to illuminate the role of violence in the maintenance of a system that it construed as long-term entrenched racist domination. The TRC sought to have political leaders seek amnesty for their responsibilities in enforcing a regime of state segregation. Like United Germany, with its Enquete-Commission, the TRC attempted to add a project of national pedagogy to an effort at rendering individual justice.

Still, some distinction between these two goals is needed. Certainly a trial, as Osiel rightly observes, will lose credibility or acceptance if it seeks to promulgate an official version of events. The history a trial teaches must emerge integrally from its agonistic dramaturgy.[14] The trial of the major war criminals at Nuremberg, of Adolf Eichmann at Jerusalem, and of Klaus Barbie decades later, were designed to expose and explain the monstrous aspects of National Socialism or Vichy collaborators. The pedagogic purpose was supposed to emerge as a by-product of a riveting drama about guilt and punishment, although the prosecution freighted the trials with a didactic agenda that may in fact have weakened the impact of the extended judicial proceedings. The line remains at best a fine one: the "lessons" must be immanent in the process, not superimposed by the prosecution's rhetoric or history lessons. In assessing the procedure, the historian has to ask who is the intended audience or subject of the didactic: the mass of citizens who supported or tolerated the abusive system being exposed by means of the perpetrators' crimes, the righteous victims who must not be allowed to forget how they suffered, or the outside world being shown why the victims have claimed new rights of statehood and political power intimidation; they reveal how the security forces operated. When repentant or at least confessing members of the police or military seek to explain or justify their action, they often reveal the reigning assumptions of the rulers: victims were seen as the agents of imperialism, for example, by Communist police, or of Communists as the policemen of apartheid. A historian gains insights specific to the regime under investigation, but also learns important lessons about political conflict and police power more generally: how victims are divested of their individuality, how perpetrators shed moral compunctions in an ambiance where they face no criticism. Many of these lessons are depressingly familiar, others are new and specific.

Serving Justice, Serving History

There is a further issue, that is not usually raised, and that is to what sort of historical narrative the trial or truth commission can aspire. Is serving justice tantamount to serving history? What relationship does a historian's work have to that of a truth commission or, alternatively, to a political trial? To what extent are these enterprises analogous, and what are the lessons of any such analogies? Consider, first, the differences from the perspective of the historian (and of the citizen more generally) between the truth commission and the political trial. The trial is the more exhaustive procedure, but it presents risks for those who stage it. (For the current Hague Tribunal, gaining custody of defendants has proved difficult.) The defendants in custody who once strutted and terrorized often appear withered and implausible avatars of their earlier selves; their identity with the violator appears as tenuous as if they were Alzheimer victims. Part of their defense will consist of arguing that the authority putting them on trial has committed equivalent violations. If not at the very apex of a command structure, the defendants will frequently describe themselves as cogs in a larger machine, and acting under orders or compulsion. Conversely, if the crime were carried out by people subject to their command, they may deny knowledge or responsibility for events that took place within areas nominally subject to their command. The prosecution will seek to estab-

lish the freedom of decision of the defendants, their capacity to have said no
to superiors, or their responsibility for controlling their subordinates. They
will fill in the mise-en-scène of the crime to emphasize its horror or its gratu-
itous nature. Each defendant must calculate whether contrition or denial is a
more plausible strategy. Ultimately, the judges or jury must aggregate all the
factors involved—the nature of the offense, the nature of the command system
in which the defendants operated, and such factors as their potential autonomy of action, ideological motivation, and ambient circumstances of war or
terror—to pass judgment. The court must thus weigh many complex circumstances to produce a single outcome. It must vastly simplify and simultaneously render justice.

Perhaps it is just an artifact of language, but the aims involved in the exercise all involve some sort of recuperative trope signified by the "re-" prefix:
*Re*tribution remains out of reach (at least within the commission itself); but in
compensation, *re*covery from a psychic damage seems possible for victims;
*re*habilitation is offered to perpetrators; *re*conciliation beckons as a basis for
civic reconstruction; and *re*cording the historical truth at last seems possible.
To what extent can these promises be redeemed? To what degree must they
remain out of reach? The truth commission had to listen to the narration of a
fact. It may wish to contextualize the abuse of power in a larger system, but it
need not. And victims appear as well as defendants. The commission is designed as much to hear their stories as to record the confessions of perpetrators, in order to provide an audience that certifies the pain of those whose
suffering has hitherto been denied or suppressed. Its advocates point out that
without the truth commission's power to bestow amnesty, these stories would
not emerge. The historical record would remain silent; perpetrators would not
take the opportunity of even a partial unburdening of conscience and acceptance of responsiblity; victims would not find even the partial satisfaction of
having an audience that listened to their hurt. The truth commission may not
be able to provide justice in the sense of rendering retribution, but it at least
avoids the accumulated injustice of denying recognition of suffering. It is a
step toward acknowledgment.

Acknowledgment of group suffering, however, is relatively easy; acknowledgment of someone else's historical interpretation of the suffering is far less
so.[15] Rendering a historical verdict—that is, addressing the moral questions
that history inevitably poses as the story of agents who at least believe themselves free—requires drawing a moral bottom line, much as the trial does.[16]
Even if the historian wishes to avoid judgment, it is hard, for example, to
narrate the destruction of Dresden in February 1945 or Hiroshima in August
1945 without asking about reasons and whether they were "good" or "bad,"
flawed or well grounded, justified or captious. The Japanese find it difficult to
acknowledge the degree of responsibility for the East Asian war that their
former enemies, including, but not only, the United States, believe they should

admit to. Israelis will not acknowledge the Palestinians' claims of expulsion in 1947–1948. Benjamin Netanyahu and Edward Said are unlikely to be able to write a common history of the Palestinian question. In this sense, agreeing on a historical version of events requires a moral sifting closer to the aggregation of the trial than just the testimonies of the TRC.

Let me distinguish between strong retributive justice, which can punish, and weak retributive justice, which can shame or extract contrition. By punishing a perpetrator, the political or ordinary criminal trial renders strong retributive justice. It endeavors to restore a balance of pain, no matter how imperfectly. It seeks to even the score. Although a truth commission does not have the authority to even the score by means of punishment, it can at least provide what we might term weak retributive justice by helping to reequilibrate the perceived power between perpetrator and victim.[17] A truth commission can mobilize belated public opprobrium against the perpetrators. It may keep them from any further positions of dignity or power. It publicly acknowledges the suffering of the victim, which constitutes a contemporary form of justice in its own right. Increasingly, the fabric of civic life in modern democracies involves a politics of recognition, and at the basis of this politics in modern democracies, for better or worse, is usually the acknowledgment of collective suffering.[18]

Pluralist democracies often involve competing and overlapping claims to having been badly treated; the groups that compete for civic status demand acknowledgment of victimhood. This acknowledgment often brings a modicum of political influence and material or symbolic compensation: a parliamentary seat, monetary reparation, a monument or memorial, and perhaps a national holiday or a moment of public silence and reflection. To exaggerate, modern democracy means eventually having to say that you are sorry. This is hardly a sufficient basis for politics, but it may be a necessary one, and it is better than never being willing to say you are sorry. In an age when the modern state is perceived as vulnerable and unable to ensure the collective destiny of its citizens, it is a historically logical development. Founding or reestablishing a democracy after a period in which politics was based on coercion over, repression of, or violence inflicted on a large number of citizens requires having to process and acknowledge many such claims in a short period of time. To use a financial metaphor, the weak justice of a truth commission in effect clears the moral accounts for the emerging democracy. It does not itself restore the wealth wrested from the account of the victimizers to the victims, but it reveals how some groups accumulated ill-gotten gains, while others were expropriated. In contrast, to prolong the metaphor, the strong justice of the political trial endeavors at least to remove the ill-gotten wealth of those who used earlier power to accumulate it.

But the metaphor reveals that retribution and even reparation must be imperfect. Strong justice is only relatively strong. Previous wrongs have not involved just the forced transfer of an asset that can be restored. The prior abuses have inflicted blighted careers, the deprivation of liberty, bodily pain and mental anguish, the cruel rupture of family relationships, and the outright loss of life—pain and suffering that can never be compensated. Deaths cannot be reversed, suffering really cannot be compensated, and revenge proves unsatisfactory. Executing six million Germans would not have resuscitated six million Jews. The fabric of people's lives has been rent; even if resewn, the seam remains to scar the tissue. We cannot undo history. Yet, only punishment and retribution seem available to at least partially balance moral accounts, but truth commissions forswear these instruments. Perhaps a commission mobilizes public opprobrium, but this seems a weak punishment.

Still, the available choice is usually not between the weak justice of a truth commission and the strong justice of political trials—assuming that the latter can be conducted under conditions of justice. Trials, after all, present many problems—most often the fact that indictments must often be for offenses against common or natural law, since prior statutory law never envisaged the repressive conditions that came to pass. Even assuming that most of a population accepts the justice of suspending the normal strictures against *ex post facto* trials (i.e., suspending the precept of *nulla poene sine lege*), many other problems afflict the choice for trials. They take a long time; they are exhausting. It is often easier to try relatively minor offenders, rather than those higher up; the gradations of choice and responsibility are hard to establish; there will be inequities of punishment and exoneration; the population will grow sick of the spectacle. The post-1945 experience in Europe reveals how imperfect an instrument political épuration was.[19] But these difficulties are not usually the reason that postauthoritarian societies have chosen truth commissions instead. The fact is that a trial was deemed too risky or impossible. The choice is not between a truth commission and highly imperfect trials, but between a truth commission and silence, or worse than silence: between the commission and the often unbearable sight of seeing earlier abusers of power continue in office and enjoy the wealth they may have accumulated.

Each of these processes has some kinship with the task of historians. Most historians might likely admit that their effort to establish a record of what happened parallels that of truth commissions. Contemporary historians are uncomfortable with the idea of serving as judges and seeking to establish guilt or innocence. Such a determination might have fitted a magisterial nineteenth-century concept of their role. But even before contemporary poststructural critiques of narrative and explanation recommended skepticism about narrative itself, academic historians had long since disavowed the function of rendering judgment. Trials are about guilt or innocence, and this language makes historians uncomfortable. Most obviously, a trial must also establish a penalty (in the case of guilt) or assess damages (in the case of liability), which is not a task for the historian.

Nonetheless, historians follow an intellectual process more akin to that of a trial than a truth commission. Trials are about responsibility (which may or may not open a defendant to punishment or civil damages) as well as guilt. And historians do use—and must use—the concept of responsibility. The historian confronts responsibility precisely because it helps to measure the degree of freedom of choice within a given institutional context. Historians tell a story of agents who, it is presumed, might have acted differently. She or he, in effect, cross-examines witnesses and seeks to embed the protagonists' actions within a context of influences, compulsion, and alternative possibilities. A truth commission presupposes choice, but need not ask how extensive or circumscribed it might have been. The victim demonstrates an injury; the perpetrator admits to committing an abuse. The truth commission presupposes that the witness appearing before it has crossed a certain threshold of contrition or repentance, but a trial does not. A trial takes place to determine the responsibility and/or guilt and to assess a remedy that in effect aggregates all the contending motivations, ambient conditions, cross-cutting pressures, and, finally, the state of mind of the defendant. In this sense, a historian, like a tribunal, yearns to reach an aggregate judgment about responsibility, if not penalty. Historians, like tribunals, are asked to answer questions of why; they are also summoned to explain the significance or importance of the transgression being examined.

I have suggested elsewhere that "doing justice" and "doing history" are related activities. A historian endeavors to "do justice" in several senses, first of all in the simplest sense of giving his protagonists their due; that is, by voicing their aspirations and exploring their choices. This act of giving voice to sometimes otherwise silent or silenced actors is, of course, a minimum—the least historians can or must do. This does not mean that historians can render justice in the same way a judge can, for a historian is not equipped with the force of law. Nevertheless, doing justice and doing history are akin by virtue of their aspiration to a narrative that is, on the one hand, synthetic, and, on the other, open to conflicting testimony.[20] Synthesis threatens, of course, to silence dissidents, to impose an authoritative orthodoxy or an authoritative version of what happened. But a verdict must finally involve a summation and must assess choices made and damages done, or damages that were allowed to take place. A national society or another voluntarily accepted legally binding association presupposes that sufficient community exists to write a single history or render a legitimate verdict, and that this community of citizens (or of readers) asks for a bottom line.

A judge and a historian, moreover, at least insofar as they act as liberals, both exhibit a quality that I call jurisprudential wisdom.[21] They must judge specific cases on individual bases; general principles and even precedents offer guidelines but always need application. Both must have a sense of how normal people—neither saints nor those disposed to cruelty—are expected to behave.

Each must have had enough experience of life to understand the context of historical or brutal actions. Each must judge outcomes not in terms of perfection but of normative plausibility. But each, I would submit, must also believe that some capacity for decency can or should persist throughout political contention. All these are preeminently Aristotelian approaches to civic virtue. They tend to exclude a utopian perfectionism or Schmitt's famous view of politics as war.[22] Their standards are grounded less in universal principles than in history. And for that reason, I argue that the trial, like the writing of history, and the judge along with the historian, both preeminently aspire to produce a coherent narrative: one that explains and interprets as well as records.

Narratives, Partial and Shared

Why focus on narrative?[23] Because both history and the trial are based on a highly ordered recitation of reports that makes sense of "events" by placing them in a sequence structured by time. Witnesses have stories to tell. The narrator—single or collective—arranges testimonies in an order that seems self-evident, but is necessarily artful. Until the narrative is constructed, causality is vague and diffuse. Perhaps it has little meaning. Causality, after all, is the assertion of influence of earlier on later events; it makes no sense the other way around. History, unlike supposedly the laws of physics, cannot by definition be construed as time symmetric—plausible no matter which way the film of events is run.

The narrative seems particularly important for understanding cases of otherwise "senseless" violence. Society devotes great effort to reconstructing the stories of its violent episodes; otherwise they remain disturbing and a source of unease like the unburied bodies of Greek mythology. Whether at Nuremberg or after Oklahoma City, the trial becomes crucial. And while part of the point of the trial is the determination of guilt and punishment, part of its function is just to provide an adequate narrative, so that the violence that shatters lives and bodies can be comprehended. By establishing a before and an after, that minimal scaffolding of historical and jurisprudential causality, events are sorted out: outsiders arrive, commit an outrage, shatter lives, and leave. If the narrative is complex, the narrative explains why some people side with the perpetrators and others are condemned to be victims. For a consistent pattern of atrocities, the narrative is only one of a series of massacres or crimes. The narrative establishes individual roles within an institutional context. It postulates reasons for violence and for resistance that can be explained. Both a trial and a history presuppose a narrative; that is, a coherent account in which earlier events are cited to account for later ones. The narrative thus involves temporal causal sequencing, what political scientists have been discovering as path dependency. The narrative makes sense of action. What a truth commission is seeking, what a political trial asserts, and what historians want to convey is not just violence or repression or conflict, but a reason for even the most brutal confrontation.

But the narrative, as literary theorists remind us, is also a political act. It can be an instrument of control. Postmodern and postcolonial critics have stressed its potential for domination and hegemony. Production of a written record from diverse oral testimonies is crucial for an authoritative trial. Above all, in cases of alleged subversion or terrorism (as earlier in cases of heresy or witchcraft), the tribunal works to unite diffuse testimonies into a master narrative that alone reveals the magnitude of conspiracy. More generally, a written narrative seems to be the key to dominating truth and extracting the magistrates' authoritative version from a confusing welter of oral reports. Bhaba (quoting Derrida) has argued that colonial rulers also required narrative to manufacture coherence and assure domination: "This need is addressed in a vigorous demand for narrative, embodied in the utilitarian or evolutionary ideologies of reason and progress: a demand which, nonetheless, in Derrida's words, is a matter for the police: . . . 'To demand the narrative of the other, to extort it from him like a secretless secret something that they call the truth about what has taken place, "Tell us exactly what happened."'"[24] Written narrative, in this perspective, is contrasted with exercising political voice—an oral act that involves speaking out, whether in parliaments or political meetings. Again, Bhabha contrasts Mill's defense of written "recordation" as a guarantee of legality for colonial subjects with the oral debate crucial to mature self-government; that is, the citizen's "'steady communal habit of correcting his own opinion and collating it with those of others.'"[25]

This writer does not accept the idea that the written narrative must remain the strategy of the master class or else deconstruct entirely. Too many colonial subjects, enfranchised slaves, and individuals struggling for freedom have transformed their narratives into liberating acts for historians to "write off" the written narrative as a merely a tactic of repression. The experience of the TRC, moreover, encourages us to believe that the narrative need not remain in the hands of the colonial master or the police. Postmodern theorists, including Derrida, may contrast the authoritarian potential of the narrative with the emancipatory potential of oral participation, but narrative is not per se politically biased.[26]

Nevertheless two questions must be addressed. The first is whether a truth commission can in fact construct a narrative. It can certainly collect the material for a narrative. That may be emancipatory and help to render justice in its own right, but by itself it stops short of an encompassing history. The same holds for opening up the political files of an ancien régime. Rosenberg argued that the opening up of the files of the former security forces or secret police itself created a sufficient basis for political reconstruction.[27] Opening the files, like taking the testimony of victims or hearing the confessions of perpetrators, demonstrated how and when injustice may have been committed; it also revealed who was collaborating. But by itself this information cannot guarantee democratic praxis. To judge from the German experience with the Stasi files, one might ask whether the preoccupation with unveiling earlier secrets did not, in effect, divert some of the effort needed for civic reconstruction into a preoccupation with uncovering collaboration? The Stasi could become almost an alibi for a wider acceptance of a shabby authoritarianism. I would not favor closing the files, but a certain dose of realism about what such revelation accomplishes seems necessary. Opening the Stasi files, learning who collaborated in secret, may serve perhaps as a precondition for reconstructing civic trust following upon a regime in which trust was systematically perverted. (On the other hand, West Germans managed to construct a democratic regime after 1945 despite a great deal of effort that went into suppressing or forgetting individuals' pasts. It could be argued that the issue after 1945 was not distrust: since so many Germans had openly and willingly embraced the regime, knowledge about past behavior did not have to be revealed.) But opening the files of the secret police by itself cannot substitute for experience with debate, argument, and competitive political organization.[28]

A truth commission thus suggests that societies and historians can establish narratives that are emancipatory and not simply efforts to control history or to channel the transition from one dominating elite to another. *But a truth commission itself does not complete this narrative task; it only offers us the possibility— an advance, to be sure, but hardly a guarantee either of justice or democracy.* A truth commission helps to establish a narrative, but a narrative of coercion and abuses of power. It presents to the public the dark side of a national project that could not earlier be disclosed. Historians, I believe, will have to use this material, but integrate it into a different framework. Which is not to say that a historian must simply try to justify the brutality in terms of some deformed aspirations or supposedly higher purpose; nor that a historian simply aggregates different stories. A historian, rather, must also evaluate to what degree the earlier authoritarian project enjoyed consensus (if only among the dominating minority), and to what extent it remained contested or opposed. He or she has to evaluate the elusive issues of complicity and denunciation that society will try to cover with collective reticence and taboo. Then, a historian must further evaluate to what degree the use of fear and force was integrated with other nonviolent mechanisms of domination, such as the formal stipulations of the legal system and the networks of economic power.

For Boraine, the TRC apparently was intended to expose the use of violence within the overall system of apartheid and racial domination. The findings of the TRC alone cannot historically reconstruct that sort of system as a whole, since it rested on the control of the economy and the media and the courts and the totality of "legal" institutions. And even if one establishes an encompassing narrative—whether in the form of a trial or of a history, or sometimes through an exemplary work of fiction—this provides no guarantee of civic reconstruction either. Indeed, the preoccupation with judicial épuration or with writing a history of victims can also serve as a diversion from institutional reform and civic reorientation. Despite the heartfelt commitment of the intellectual, it is not certain that justice makes a better foundation for stable democracy than amnesia. But perhaps we must ask for justice in its own right regardless of its political implications: *Fiat iustitia, et pereat mundus* (Let justice be done, even if the world should perish).

If we remain committed to the judicial and/or historical narrative, and perhaps even optimistic that such a narrative will ultimately strengthen liberal-democratic practice, the second preliminary question must be confronted: how do historians ensure a procedure that protects the new narration from simply degenerating into a new strategy for domination? Trying to "synthesize" a narrative from diverse sources and voices is a dangerous exercise: reduction of many voices to one coherent story line means valuing some testimonies more than others, or privileging the significance of some stories more than others. The temptation for the postmodern historian is to say the task is impossible—to fall back upon Benjaminian tropes of fragmentation and epiphany, to deny the possibility of narrative as well as metanarrative.[29] Nonetheless, just as a trial must produce some verdict—some aggregation of testimonies to acquit or convict and punish—a national public demands some overall assessment. If historians shun doing it carefully, there will be no shortage of calculating or naively apologetic versions. Winners and losers always have their own story to tell. Of course, historians are not disinterested in the outcome of their craft (or the public recognition it receives), but this particular historiographical interest should be consonant with the most encompassing narrative, not an apparently partisan one. In this respect, the truth commission does suggest the possibility of an adversarial or contrapuntal history. At the least, it has granted those previously deprived of a voice to have a voice that brings to light those facts earlier suppressed. But neither can the historian rest content with merely writing a counternarrative: good history cannot remain simply ex parte even if the historian is rescuing worthy subjects hitherto forced into silence. Ultimately, the historian must create a narrative that allows for contending voices, that reveals the aspirations of all actors, the hitherto repressed and the hitherto privileged.

Perpetrators have a history as well as victims, but in what sense do they share a narrative? In fact, their narratives intertwine just as all adversarial histories must. To return to an example proposed above, Said and Netanyahu will never write the same narrative, but historians of Israel and the Palestinian question must render them both justice within a single story. This does not mean banally insisting that both have a point, or "splitting the difference" (which is a political strategy). It means listening to, testing, and ultimately making public their respective subnarratives or partial stories. To resort to a musical analogy: written history must be contrapuntal, not harmonic. That is, it must allow the particular histories of national groups to be woven together linearly alongside each other so that the careful listener can follow them distinctly but simultaneously, hearing the whole together with the parts.

A historical public can legitimately ask for a national history—a history of the different peoples in a political territory; a history of the United States, Germany, or South Africa. Insofar as it answers the community's demand for "synthesis," that synthesis must remain multivocal. United States history has to trace the conditions of the different peoples—whether the original indigenous American Indians continually harried and diminished, the diverse immigrant settlers, the aspiring elites of plantation and enterprise, or the African-Americans brought as slaves who built their communities under duress. Each must receive its due and historiographical justice, which means that the aspirations and development of each community has to be taken seriously, researched, and narrated. The same respect must be shown for the diverse peoples in South Africa, and for every society that, if not ethnically so "rainbow-like," comprises multiple communities of faith and work. In an era of pluralist democracy, a historian of the peoples within a circumscribed national territory can no longer just strive for a chordal resolution that obliterates the distinct stories into some higher whole.

Not all histories must aspire to this multivocal quality. But any history that has politics or conflict at its core, that seeks to encompass the story of a society or regime—that is, a history that seeks to do justice to the public experience of individuals—must work to achieve such a contrapuntal narrative. Even if a historian is following only one individual and writing a biography, the story of a life conducted in society cannot be told without some sense of the struggles of the protagonist; and to convey the scope of these struggles requires doing justice to adversarial stories.

Is writing such history a utopian project? Will doing justice by doing history finally prove unfeasible because the adversarial stories fly apart and deconstruct any encompassing community within which the protagonists might be placed narratively? I do not think so, but the historiographical product will always remain contested, because the weight given to different voices, and the evaluation of claims, draw continually on judgmental reasoning and are rooted in a historian's own sense of political decency. No matter how "judicious," such a history will be provisional, which is not equivalent to saying that it must remain partisan or biased. Histories can be both authoritative and provisional: they are authoritative in that they impose what for broad (though not all) segments of opinion can be accepted as a plausible narrative. They are always provisional in that they remain subject to amendment as new evidence is mobilized and as new political values become established and thereby open up new agendas for the humanities and social sciences. Historiography is not diminished by a growing inclusiveness of inquiry.

Theorists of literature have revealed the authoritarian potential of the written narrative. Truth commissions have revealed the possibility for the restoration of justice and empowerment in the collection of stories. Historians can learn from both: the narrative does, momentarily at least, rally the interpretive needs and energies of the community; it seizes the political high ground until dislodged. It aspires to a historiographical hegemony, knowing that it will remain precarious at best; but it can do so on behalf of a more just and more inclusive vision both of the past and future. "Doing justice" is an injunction that is laid upon historians and truth commissions alike.

Notes

1. Timothy Garton Ash, "The Truth about Dictatorship," *New York Review of Books*, 19 February 1998, 35–40; Alex Boraine, "Justice in Cataclysm: Criminal Tribunals in the Wake of Mass Violence. Alternatives and Adjuncts to Criminal Prosecution" (speech at Brussels, 20–21 July 1996; from the TRC website: www.truth.org.za/reading/speech01.intro). The 1994 survey by Priscilla B. Hayner, "Fifteen Truth Commissions—1974 to 1994: A Comparative Study," as excerpted in Neil J. Kritz (ed.), *Transitional Justice: How Emerging Democracies Reckon with Former Regimes* (Washington, D.C., 1997), I, 225–261, would have totaled eighteen, but the German Enquete-Ausschuss (Committee) she discusses was a far more general inquiry into the German Democratic Republic (GDR) dictatorship than an effort to document particular abuses. See the discussion below. Hayner noted commissions just forming and not included in her inventory: South Africa and Guatemala.

2. My own reflections on this topic began with issues raised by the German historians' controversy over normalization of the Holocaust—see Charles S. Maier, *The Unmasterable Past: History, Holocaust and National Identity* (Cambridge, Mass., 1988)—and then took up again in "Doing Justice, Doing History: Political Purges and National Narratives after 1945 and 1989," paper presented at "In Memory: Revisiting Nazi Atrocities in Post-Cold War Europe," an International Conference to Commemorate the Fiftieth Anniversary of the 1944 Massacres around Arezzo, Italy, 22–24 June, 1994, and since published as "Fare giustizia, fare storia: Epurazioni politiche e narrativi nazionali dopo il 1945 e il 1989," *Passato e Presente* 34 (1995): 23–32. In pondering the themes of justice and collective memory, I have benefited preeminently from scholarly exchange with Anne Sa'adah (cited below) and with Mark Osiel, whose *Mass Atrocity, Collective Memory, and the Law* (New Brunswick, N.J., 1997; a revised version of the original in the *University of Pennsylvania Law Review* CXLIV: 505–690) is the most encompassing treatment. Both truth commissions and trials of earlier officials are political in the sense that their taking place at all depends upon the outcome of a struggle for power. That fact alone does not deprive them of justice. For the classic earlier work, see Otto Kirchheimer, *Political Justice: The Use of Legal Procedure for Political Ends* (Princeton, 1961).

3. Henry J. Steiner (ed.), *Truth Commissions: A Comparative Assessment* (Cambridge, Mass., 1997).

4. Cited in Steiner, *Truth*, 17.

5. See Gesine Schwan, *Politik und Schuld: Die zerstörische Macht des Schweigens* (Frankfurt am Main, 1997) for a discussion of the public and private costs of repressing an open confrontation with the past, including the distortions of family relationships. "Guilt splits the person from the society. Silence about guilt prolongs the fracture destructively and with great peril" (219).

6. Comision Nacional Sobre la Desaparicion de Personas, Nunca Mas, *The Report of the Argentine National Commission on the Disappeared* (Buenos Aires, 1986).

7. See Anne Sa'adah, *Germany's Second Chance: Truth, Justice, and Democratization* (Cambridge, Mass., 1998), 190–236; also the published report of the Brandenburg committee, Ehrhart Neubert (ed.), *Abschlussbericht des Stolpe-Untersuchungssausschuss des Landtag Brandenburg* (Cologne, 1994); and the brief discussion of post-1990 jurisprudence in Charles S. Maier, *Dissolution: The Crisis of Communism and the End of East Germany* (Princeton, 1997), 311–325, with citations 415–418; also the published report and materials of the First Enquete-Kommission, Materialen der Enquete-Kommission, *Aufarbeitung von Geschichte und Folgen der SED-Diktatur in Deutschland* (Baden-Baden, 1995), 30 volumes, or (Frankfurt am Main, 1995), 18 volumes. For a survey of post-1989 efforts at political justice in the ex-Communist countries, see Tina Rosenberg, *The Haunted Land: Facing Europe's Ghosts after Communism* (New York, 1995).

8. See Joachim Gauck's own summary, "Dealing with a Stasi Past, *Daedalus* CXXIII (1994): 277–284, and the diverse materials in Kritz (ed.), *Transitional Justice*, II, 593–644.

9. Boraine, "Justice in Cataclysm."

10. "Message from the Chairperson. Interim Report of the TRC," http//www.truth.org.za/reports/rep1–01.htm.

11. Cited in Steiner, *Truth*, 25.

12. For an encyclopedic survey of these issues, although disappointing in its lack of attention to trials and truth commissions, see Juan J. Linz and Alfred Stepan, *Problems of Democratic Transition and Consolidation: Southern Europe, South America, and Post-Communist Europe* (Baltimore, 1996). For an exemplary study of how the burdened past continues to traumatize successor generations, see Henry Rousso (trans. Arthur Goldhammer), *The Vichy Syndrome: History and Memory in France since 1944* (Cambridge, Mass., 1991); Eric Conan and Henry Rousso (trans. Nathan Bracher), *Vichy, an Ever-Present Past* (Hanover, N.H., 1998).

13. Steiner, *Truth*, 15, 16, 71–72. José Zalaquett was recapitulating what he had earlier written in defense of the Chilean National Commission on Truth and Reconciliation: Zalequett, "Balancing Ethical Imperatives and Political Constraints: The Dilemma of New Democracies Confronting Past Human Rights Violations," *Hastings Law Journal* XLIII (1992), excerpted in Kritz (ed.), *Transitional Justice*, II, 495–498.

14. Osiel, *Mass Atrocity*, 79–141.

15. See Steiner, *Truth*, 75–76.

16. I grant that historians can deny freedom of choice, although it is harder to deny that actors seem to behave and talk as if they had it. Postmodern historians might further argue that agency is an illusory concept; historians should not presuppose it. Without arguing the issue here, I reject this approach, in part because of its moral as well as historiographical consequences.

17. The discussion here does not really plumb the problematics of retribution and justice. I have been instructed by an unpublished paper of Anne Sa'adah's, "Elusive

Justice: Retribution, Citizenship, and Democratization" (November 1997), which wrestles with the extensive and troubling literature on this theme.

18. Democratic "recognition" is sometimes traced back to the centrality of "recognition" in Hegel, but as explicated by Alexandre Kojève (trans. James H. Nichols, Jr.), *Introduction to the Reading of Hegel: Lectures on the Phenomenology of Spirit* (Ithaca, N.Y., 1980), 40–49, 58–62. The need for recognition generates the dialectic of man and slave, not the condition of citizenship. It would require a universal state to meet the desire for a recognition of man's universal, rather than specific, characteristics: the so-called end of history (237). The group recognition that is sought and granted in today's democracies would be, in the Kojève-Hegel view, the sign of a quite inferior polity.

19. Klaus Dietmar Henke and Hans Woller (eds.), *Politische Säuberung in Europa: Die Abrechnung mit Faschismus und Kollaboration nach dem Zweiten Weltkrieg* (Munich, 1991); Woller, *Die Abrechnung mit dem Faschismus in Italien 1943 bis 1948* (Munich, 1996). Rousso is currently researching the French épuration; see his article, "L'Epuration," in the Henke-Woller collection, 192–140. See also Peter Novick, *The Resistance versus Vichy: The Purge of Collaborators in Liberated France* (New York, 1968). For the unwillingness to remove ex-Nazis from influence in early postwar Germany, see Norbert Frei, *Vergangenheitspolitik: Die Anfänge der Bundesrepublik und die NA-Vergangeheit* (Munich, 1996).

20. Maier, "Doing Justice."

21. Ibid. Osiel emphasizes the same points, in *Mass Atrocity*, 84–89, 256–268, but stresses that they presuppose a specifically liberal concern with rendering individual justice.

22. Carl Schmitt (trans. and ed. George Schwab), *The Concept of the Political* (New Brunswick, N.J., 1976).

23. Again cf. Osiel, *Mass Atrocity*, 72–78, 283–292.

24. Homi K. Bhabha, "Sly Civility," in Bhabha, *The Location of Culture* (London, 1994), 98, citing Jacques Derrida, "Living On: Border Lines," in Derrida et al (eds.), *Deconstruction and Criticism* (London, 1979), 87. See also Alessandro Portelli's discussion of the trials of Italian red-brigade terrorists: "Oral Testimony, the Law, and the Making of History: The 'April 7' Murder Trial," *History Workshop Journal* XX (1985), 5–35.

25. Bhabha, "Sly Civility," 94, citing John Stuart Mill, "On Liberty," from *Utilitarianism, Liberty, Representative Government* (London, 1972), 99.

26. Jacques Derrida (trans, Gayatri Chakravorty Spivak), *Of Grammatology* (Baltimore, 1976), 167–171.

27. See Steiner, *Truth*, 43–45, for our exchange.

28. The number of books and documentary collections on the Stasi in the first years after unification revealed the obsession with this aspect of the regime, preeminently the disclosures of complicity on the part of "unofficial" informants. I have discussed the phenomena in *Dissolution*, 46–50, 312–317. For some comparative treatments of informing, see Sheila Fitzpatrick and Robert Gellately (eds.), *Accusatory Practices: Denunciation in Modern European History* (Chicago, 1997).

29. See Walter Benjamin's theses on history: "Über den Begriff der Geschichte," in *Gesammelte Schriften* (Frankfurt am Main, 1974–1985), I, 2, 695.

XIV

Constructing a Report

WRITING UP THE "TRUTH"

CHARLES VILLA-VICENCIO AND WILHELM VERWOERD

THE *Final Report* of the South African Truth and Reconciliation Commission (TRC) has contributed to the emergence of a new inclusive heritage and memory on which the nation can draw in its pursuit of a human rights culture. This decidedly does not include the imposition of a single, official "truth."[1] Indeed the report supports the case for the recognition of the depth of past differences. This acknowledgment is an incentive to construct a political dispensation that enables the postapartheid South African nation to negotiate the pitfalls and continuing conflicts associated with past divisions—and eventually even to rise above them.

Suffice it to say, the story of the conflicts in the recent South African past is a story of a multitude of nuances and many layers of truth that capture the motives and perspectives of those who shaped the agony and triumphs of the past. The commission's account of that history is necessarily a partial record. It is only one attempt to capture key aspects of the past. The report will be open to criticism—and will be criticized. At the same time, it is hoped that the report can be a basis for an inclusive recognition that says "yes, that is who we were (and to an extent still are) as a nation." If, having put the inevitable politicking around the report aside, it accomplishes that objective, the report will have served the nation.

Contributing to the shared acknowledgment by all South Africans of what happened in the apartheid years, in both repression and resistance, as well as the recognition that humanity has the capacity to do it again (in one way or another), was surely among the most important legacies that the TRC could bequeath to the nation. This shared acknowledgment thus involves the public recognition of the painful truth about the past *and* about human nature. In the salutary words of President Nelson Mandela, during a speech in the National Assembly on 15 April 1997:

> All of us, as a nation that has newly found itself, share in the shame at the capacity
> of human beings of any race or language group to be inhumane to other human

beings. We should all share in the commitment to a South Africa in which that will never happen again.[2]

The Promotion of National Unity and Reconciliation Act, no. 34, of 1995 (the Act), required the TRC, in presenting its *Final Report*, to contribute to the building of "a historic bridge between the past of a deeply divided society characterised by strife, conflict, untold suffering and injustice, and a future founded on the recognition of human rights, democracy and peaceful coexistence and development opportunities for all South Africans, irrespective of colour, race, belief or sex."[3] Such ideals made the writing process of the *Final Report* an anxiety-filled exercise. The end product was meant to capture the tensions inherent to all that is involved in bridge-building—without avoiding the "hard truths" that needed to be told. To change the analogy, "It was a bit like walking a tightrope, in a bad storm," observed one of the writers in the TRC's research department. At no time did any drafter of any section of the report feel that he or she could say all that (from his or her perspective) needed to be said. The dictates of the legislation needed to guide every step of the writing process. The commissioners, who had to take ultimate responsibility for the report, in turn, brought different perspectives to bear on the interpretation of the data before the commission.

The pressure of writing, while the investigations and findings process were still under way, brought its own set of issues. Unlike most academic exercises, writers could not afford the time to stand back—to distance themselves from the project, test their perspectives, and tease out the hidden nuances that constituted the contested information before the TRC. Time simply did not allow that. It became clear to all involved that the manuscript in production could be no more than the report of a commission that was required to complete its work in a given period of time—rather than a well-rounded, considered delivery, giving expression to all that any serious researcher would have hoped to produce. The outcome of the exercise was, at the same time, one that was awaited by the media and public as the culmination of an important step in the South African transition. Writers were also painfully aware that what they wrote would be an important, if not an indelible, record of this period of history.

The written text is (and must be) challenged, but it also endures. The consolation to those involved in the writing process was that, through its work, the commission had produced an extensive archive of data, which may yet prove to be among its most important contributions to posterity. This is located in the South African National Archives, to which future generations of scholars, journalists, and interested persons can resort in their quest for an understanding of the past.[4] The report needed to be faithful to the material collected during the TRC's existence.

The report was intended to constitute a road map that would enable others to access the resources on which the TRC's conclusions drew. Over 22,000 statements of victims and survivors were generated—making this probably the biggest single human rights survey in the history of the world. Over 7,000 amnesty applications were filed—providing a reservoir of insights into the motives and perspectives of a significant sample of actors in the South African struggle.

The problem faced by researchers and others involved in the writing of the report was how to reduce the huge amount of material collected by the commission into a readable account. Questions of selection and interpretation attained nightmare proportions. Representative cases had to be selected to illustrate the different kinds of gross human rights violations, as well as the complex interplay of racial, ethnic, regional, gender, and age variables at stake. The chairperson's foreword acknowledges such perspectival realities and encourages others to challenge, critique, and correct these limitations.[5]

A Balancing Act

Judge Ismail Mahomed, in handing down the finding of the South African Constitutional Court in a case brought by the Azanian People's Organisation and others against the TRC during its first year of existence, vividly captured the tension central to the amnesty process—a tension that was inherent in every aspect of the commission's work.

> [The granting of amnesty] is a difficult, sensitive, perhaps even agonising, balancing act between the need for justice to victims of past abuse and the need for reconciliation and rapid transition to a new future; between encouragement to wrongdoers to help in the discovery of the truth and the need for reparations for the victims of that truth; between a correction in the old and the creation of the new. It is an exercise of immense difficulty interacting in a vast network of political, emotional, ethical and logistical considerations.[6]

The tensions inherent in the mandate of the commission were always there—and when writers of the report lost sight of them, there were invariably those on the commission who reminded them of those realities. In brief, the task was to focus on past "gross human rights violations" committed by all parties to the conflict of the past; to understand the "motives and perspectives" of those responsible for these violations; and to be even-handed in so doing—without suspending moral judgment.[7] Ultimately, the report of the TRC was meant to uncover painful truths and "promote national unity and reconciliation." The very assignment posed the question, which many of the commission's severest critics have asked throughout the process: *Can the exposing of past atrocities ever lead to reconciliation?* The chapter of the TRC *Final Report* dealing with the principles that governed the work of the commission wrestles at length with this and the other related issues that defined its work.[8]

Problems came, however, not only from the Act itself, but also from sources other than the Act. The TRC, unlike other truth commissions, arose from a uniquely public, democratic process. The South African TRC was appointed by the legislative arm of the state. The passing of the Promotion of National Unity and Reconciliation Act was preceded by extensive negotiations within the Parliamentary Standing Committee. It, in turn, was informed and influenced by an unprecedented process of public debate and scrutiny about the formulation of the commission's objectives and functions, its specific procedures, and the appointment of the commissioners. For example, one of the compromises reached with the former ruling party (the National Party) when the bill was discussed in cabinet was that amnesty hearings would be held behind closed doors. Various nongovernmental organizations, including a number of human rights organizations, strongly opposed this result. Eventually, the principle of open hearings, except where it defeated the ends of justice, was included in the Act—and the vast majority of hearings *were* held in public.[9]

There were in excess of seventy public hearings focusing on the testimony of individual victims of gross human rights violations.[10] There were a series of open hearings on key political events, such as the 1976 Soweto student uprisings, chemical and biological warfare, secret state funding, and the exhumations of the bodies of executed activists.[11] Institutional hearings on the health sector, the media, business, and the faith communities, and special hearings on women and children and on compulsory military service, were also held.[12] Attempts were made to incorporate the richness and multidimensionality of these hearings into the report, subjected as they were to public scrutiny.

Process and Product

The actual writing of the *Final Report* was a consultative, complex process. Two steps marked the beginning of the work of the research department, whose primary responsibility was the production of the report. One step was to assist in the design and implementation of the database that provided for the accessing and recording of information from the widest possible sources. The other was to hold consultations in different parts of the country with a view to establishing chronologies of gross human rights violations. From these chronologies of events (which were refined and published in the report), a number of strategic research themes were identified on the basis of wide consultation with academic historians and social scientists, journalists, activists, politicians, and others who had a knowledge of past events.[13] These themes were developed either by TRC or contracted researchers. They were often debated and frequently made the subject of research seminars organized by the research department.

As a result of the hearings of the commission and the investigation process, the themes were further refined (and at times reconstituted) to become chapter outlines for the report. The titles of proposed chapters were shared widely and extensively reported in the several newspapers. Several contributions to various chapters were written by leading scholars—while all this material was received strictly as "information only" by the TRC. This ensured that the ultimate responsibility for the report rested in the hands of a commission that was by law required to function independently in reporting to the president. Each chapter that ultimately formed part of the report was discussed as much as possible by the commission. Revisions were frequently made and compromise positions adopted to ensure as wide a consensus as possible. This resulted in the basic structure of the report being formally revised by the TRC on seven different occasions. Despite pressure resulting from revisions to the final text until the very day that the report was being transported to Pretoria for presentation to the president, the full commission, with the exception of one commissioner, adopted the report.[14]

This entire process was directly influenced and controlled by the data before the commission. Every attempt was made, often through vigorous disagreement, to be loyal to the data before the TRC, recognizing that to a significant extent the vast archive of transcripts of oral testimony, press clippings, video recordings, and hundreds of submissions left behind by this commission makes the report less than "final." The handing of the five-volume written report to the president in October 1998 was an important event, but in many ways not the end of the process. A codicil will have to be added to the report once the work of the Amnesty Committee is completed, later in 2000.

More important is the fact that the publication of the report signaled the beginning of the very important process of digesting the report and the other information gathered through the work of the TRC. It is the nation as a whole (and not least those who shape public opinion) that has the "final" word. The impact of the commission has reverberated throughout society. There are few informed people who do not have an opinion on the commission and its work. The ultimate result was a proliferation of inquiries from individual, scholarly, journalistic, and civil societies into what the TRC achieved or failed to achieve, plus a range of suggestions as to what should come in its wake.

The Double-edged Media Sword

In contrast to other truth commissions, which concluded their work behind closed doors (Chile) or even in secret (Brazil) before presenting their findings to the public, the TRC worked not only in the public eye but consciously engaged the public as well.[15] It held regular press briefings, encouraging public debate on what was happening in its public hearings.

Understandably, the mass media thus played a powerful and often ambiguous role in the work of the commission. Given the politically contested and emotionally charged nature of South Africa's past, different sections of the media (not least sections of the Afrikaans media that supported the former state) used the public hearings of the commission to pursue their own political agendas. Other sections of the media, so long silenced by the former state, understandably used the occasion of the commission to settle former disputes. Inevitably, there were misconceptions and even deliberate distortions that formed part of the mass media's handling of the commission's particularly complex process of "dealing with the past." The question remains unanswered to what extent the legitimacy of the report and the positive potential of the recommendations contained in it were undermined by this process. What is clear is that the impact of an increasingly media-savvy public on the TRC tended to be neglected, even by some of those emphasizing the importance of the public, democratic nature of this kind of institution.[16]

For journalist and poet Krog, the "definite starting point" of the TRC was the "unforgettable wail of Nomfundo Calata" at the first hearing of the commission in East London in April 1996.[17] In brief, the dominant public perception of the commission was one where people (mostly black, mainly women) wept on stage, struggled to tell what had happened to them or their beloved ones, and often identified members (mostly white, male Afrikaners) of the apartheid security forces as the perpetrators of crimes against them.

This perception played into the hands of those who described the TRC as an "ANC witch hunt." Conversely, it also fueled the fires of those who saw the TRC as a "talk shop" that required victims and survivors to be exposed to television cameras as a means of dramatizing the past—without any real commitment by the commission to ensure that "justice would be done."

The problem is that many of the other activities of the commission were less visible, and therefore less accessible to outsiders. Policy workshops, statement analyses, corroboration of statements, paper-based research, archival searches, and routine investigations do not make good TV news. After more than two years of constant scrutiny, the media began to experience what a journalist described as "TRC fatigue." People became tired of the commission.

To a significant extent the "double-edged sword" was corrected by the *Final Report*. The "tough findings" of the commission against the liberation movements and the apartheid state silenced many of its fiercest critics—not least the Afrikaans media, who had seen it as an "ANC commission." Major Afrikaans newspapers, like *Die Burger* and *Die Rapport*, however, had from the start engaged in a sustained campaign to undermine the legitimacy of key commissioners, the institution itself, and its findings—presumably in anticipation of what it would have to say about a period of history within which these newspapers supported most actions of the state. With repeated refrain, they referred to the TRC as a "commission of lies and revenge." In failing (perhaps deliberately) to grasp the purpose of victims' hearings—these wide-circulation newspapers accused the TRC of listening "to untested evidence." They complained about there being "no cross-examination" of victims. "Evidence," it was suggested, "from those victims who were tortured by the ANC is cut short." "The TRC chairman," the public was told, "cries when a black person tells of maltreatment at the hands of the police. He does not cry when a white man tells how his family was wiped out and mutilated by terrorists."[18]

The importance of creating a space in which victims and survivors could freely and publicly unburden themselves, telling their story to the nation, was ignored. Pumla Gobodo-Madikizela, a member of the TRC's Human Rights Committee, observed:

> The kinds of statements that are submitted to the Commission come from people who are deeply hurt by the past. These are people who are looking for someone, somewhere, to unburden themselves and to validate their experience of pain and hurt. People who reflect more favorably on the past have tended to steer away from the Commission, setting in motion a vicious cycle of self-exclusion and attack on its credibility.[19]

It was not easy to persuade those committed to a particular interpretation of the TRC to concede these points. The repeated attempts by the commission to include the voices of white (and Afrikaans-speaking) people who had suffered at the hands of the liberation movements were not acknowledged—partly, perhaps, because there were decidedly fewer whites who had suffered than blacks. Suffice it to say, it is difficult to correct entrenched views on the commission in a report that was required to produce a "difficult, sensitive . . . balanced" message.

Between Even-handedness and Moral Integrity

The report needed to be impartial and objective. All gross human rights violations—whoever the alleged person or organization happened to be—were scrutinized and assessed in an unbiased and thorough manner. Where sufficient evidence existed and after due corroboration, a finding had to be made on the basis of accepted principles of due process as agreed on for commissions of inquiry. First, these principles allowed decisions to be made on the "balance of probability," rather than "beyond all reasonable doubt," as in the conventional criminal justice system. This means that, when confronted with different versions of events, the TRC had to decide which version was the more reasonable or likely, after taking into account all the available evidence.[20] Second, even with sufficient evidence available, perpetrators could be named only after affording the person or organization against which a finding was being contemplated a fair and unbiased opportunity to respond to allegations.[21] One result of this process was the much publicized removal of a finding against former president Frederik W. de Klerk less than twenty-four hours before the release of the report.[22]

Again a tightrope had to be walked. The lives of those against whom a negative finding was made would irrevocably be affected. Every care had to be taken to ensure that due process was honored before such a finding was made. On the other hand, to fail to name organizations and individuals involved in gross human rights violations would have reneged on the responsibility imposed on the TRC by the Act. The balance was between the public interest (and the requirement of the Act) to expose wrongdoing and the need to ensure fair treatment of the individuals involved. It was between the rights of victims of gross violations of human rights to know who was responsible and the fundamentally important question of fairness to those who were accused of crimes or serious wrongdoing.[23]

To be unbiased and impartial in the hearing, investigation, and finding process did not, however, imply moral indifference. To "establish as complete a picture as possible" involved holding up a mirror on the past, thereby helping the nation to acknowledge what had happened. This acknowledgment implies owning the past, in the sense of accepting what went wrong, rather than denying or rationalizing what happened. The overall goal of the TRC was to promote "national unity and reconciliation" on the basis of truth (about certain categories of gross human rights violations) and acknowledgment. If the TRC ignored or failed to acknowledge the extent to which an individual, the state, or a liberation movement, either legally or illegally, deployed its resources systematically to violate the rights of others, it would have failed to give a full account of the past. The past assaults on human rights could not be adequately acknowledged if the report sidestepped this moral challenge through the use of ambiguous language or moral indifference.[24]

The standard response to this kind of argument is, By whose standards was this judgment made? The short answer is that, having left the laager of global isolation, we are obliged to acknowledge the existence of international human rights standards. We could not both have our cake and eat it. To rejoin the world is to accept those values and norms of decency that sustain it. International instruments, protocols, and conventions therefore provided the prism through which the TRC viewed and assessed the past. By using this prism, the report gave expression to the importance of our new nation's acknowledgment that racism and authoritarianism were dismal failures.

If we are going to succeed as a newly reformed nation, this awareness *must* grow in the minds of all South Africans. For this to happen the TRC had to make moral judgments as a basis for ensuring a new beginning, within which the possibilities of both structural inequalities and the kind of gross human rights violations of the past reoccurring in the future are kept to a minimum. This is why the commission was obliged to make moral judgments about the

past, involving *just cause* in the fight for and against apartheid. It also needed
to distinguish, in an even-handed way, between just and unjust *ways* of pursuing that cause.

The report's chapter on the mandate of the commission seeks to address
this concern at some length.[25] It is one thing to distinguish between a just and
an unjust cause; clearly, those fighting against apartheid had international law
on their side, whereas those who fought to uphold apartheid could scarcely
claim that their cause was just. The TRC, at the same time, applied the principles of the Geneva Convention equally to both the former state and the liberation movements as a basis for identifying acts that were judged to contravene
the acceptable means of war. In so doing, the commission identified agents of
both apartheid and the liberation process as perpetrators where they failed to
uphold international standards of war, without losing sight of which side was
engaged in fighting for the cause of what was judged internationally to be right
morally. The criticism of the TRC's use of the Geneva Conventions by Deputy President Thabo Mbeki, in the parliamentary debate on the TRC Report
on 25 February 1999, is a matter that could merit more debate. Mbeki took
issue with the commission on specific judgments it had made regarding civilian victims of ANC land mines and bombings. The TRC labeled them "gross
violations" of human rights. Mbeki believed them to be unfortunate casualties
of a kind not prohibited by the Geneva Conventions. He spoke of the TRC's
"erroneous logic . . . including the general implication that any and all military
activity which results in the loss of civilian lives constitutes a gross violation of
human rights." He suggested that the TRC's findings were "contrary even to
the Geneva Conventions and Protocols governing the conduct of warfare."[26]

Suffice it to say, every reasonable attempt was made by the TRC to deal in
an even-handed manner with the material at its disposal, within the time constraints it experienced. Its work, nevertheless, was challenged by both de Klerk
and the ANC leadership. This dual challenge from opposing sides of the political spectrum did much to counter the accusations that came from some
quarters to suggest that the TRC was biased against the former regime and
had covered up gross violations of human rights by the ANC. Indeed, few in
the media and elsewhere have challenged the broad findings of the TRC,
agreeing that it *was* unbiased in its assessments of past atrocities.[27]

Understanding, without Excusing

Moral judgment, of course, is never helpful when it degenerates into single-
minded arrogance. Anne-Louise-Germaine de Staël (the late eighteenth-
century French intellectual) suggested that "to understand all is to forgive all."
Louis de Broglie observed later, "We should beware of too much explaining,
lest we end up with too much forgiving."[28] Neither aphorism is satisfactory,
although both deserve thought. One of the TRC's tasks was to establish the

"antecedents, circumstances, factors and context of [gross human rights] violations as well as the causes, motives and perspectives of persons responsible."[29] We had to explain why and how gross human rights violations of the most horrific kind could have happened. We were obliged to do so not as a basis for wallowing in the macabre, but as a way of knowing the depths to which human nature is capable of descending, and as a basis for contributing to the process of seeking to ensure that similar atrocities do not recur in the future.[30]

If we do not understand why and how the past happened, we are likely to repeat it in the future. History is cluttered with the wreckage of past victims rising above their past only to the extent of appropriating the patterns of abuse of their oppressors. Camus (perhaps too pessimistically) warned that "revolutionaries of yesterday too frequently become the hangmen of tomorrow."[31]

To acknowledge the truth about the past involves more than to discover what many others already know. It involves accepting responsibility for the past, while recognizing that there are different levels of culpability and involvement. Craig Williamson, the former South African spy, made the point clearly at a commission hearing in Cape Town, in October 1997:

> It is therefore not only the task of the members of the security forces to examine themselves and their deeds. It is for every member of the society we served to do so. Our weapons, ammunition, uniforms, vehicles, radios and other equipment were all developed and provided by industry. Our finances and banking were done by bankers who even gave us covert credit cards for covert operations. Our chaplains prayed for our victory and our universities educated us in war. Our propaganda was carried by the media and our political masters were voted back into power time after time with ever increasing majorities.[32]

The Tip of an Iceberg of Truth

The *Final Report* was required to do justice to the Act's requirement to "establish as complete a picture as possible—including the antecedents, circumstances, factors and context of such violations as well as the perspectives of the victims and the motives and perspectives of the persons responsible for the commission of the violations, by conducting investigations and holding hearings."[33]

What was seen to be possible during the early life of the TRC turned out to be impossible later on. Various factors limited the possibility of a "complete picture" emerging through the report. In a number of areas, our investigations only managed to scratch the surface. A simple lack of resources, for example, allowed the TRC to exhume only fifty bodies out of more than two hundred that probably could have been identified.[34] A large quantity of documentation had been deliberately destroyed by agents of the former state.[35]

The mandate, too, imposed limitations on the report—requiring the TRC

to focus on a narrow range of "gross human rights violations" that had occurred within a relatively short period of thirty-four years. These acts of torture, abduction, killing, and severe ill-treatment clearly represent only the tip
of the iceberg of truth about apartheid and the preceding decades of segregation and exploitation of black people. Mamdani observed:

> Victims of apartheid are now narrowly defined as those militants victimised as they
> struggled against apartheid, not those whose lives were mutilated in the day to day
> web of regulations that was apartheid. We arrive at a world in which reparations are
> for militants, those who suffered jail or exile, but not for those who suffered only
> forced labour and broken homes.[36]

Mamdani's analysis is only partly true. The vast majority of victims who
chose to give testimony to the TRC were hardly "militants." They were ordinary women and men who wanted to know what had happened to their loved
ones. His essential point must nevertheless not be overlooked. Numerous
other voices could not be heard by the TRC, which was only one of several
initiatives designed to redress past injustices. The large majority of victims of
human rights violations during the apartheid era were excluded from testifying
by the TRC's narrow mandate and short life span. Therefore, only a limited
amount of the truth about certain gross violations of human rights could be
exposed by *this* commission.[37]

The limited nature of this exposure does not undermine the unique contribution of the TRC. The fact that this exposure was done by an official and
uniquely public institution remains highly significant. The report offers crucial
insights and makes important findings. However, given the inherent limitations of this kind of document, it is now the time for investigative journalists,
scholars, politicians, critics, poets, writers, and everyone else to use it as a map
to access the huge body of material gathered during the life of the commission.
Others need to address many of the issues that the TRC could not or were not
mandated to address.[38]

This limitation of the report is ironically salutary. It militates against what
some have described as "Orwellian spectres of political show trials and the
imposition of a 'true' perspective on history."[39] Comfort can be taken in the
(probably too pessimistic) words of Ignatieff: "All that a truth commission can
achieve is to reduce the number of lies that can be circulated unchallenged in
public discourse."[40]

The understanding of the report as a "road map" reflects the close link
between process and product in the case of the TRC. The commission sought,
however imperfectly, to implement and manage an inclusive, accessible, and
transparent process in order to facilitate a pluralistic public account, generated
by diverse individuals "telling their own stories" and a variety of individuals
and institutions making submissions. The alternative would have been a more
typical, "elitist" commission of experts attempting to produce an authoritative
version of the "truth."

Unchopping a Tree

To tell the truth is both subversive and not always politically correct. Sometimes it is not advisable to tell the "naked truth" when a democracy is still being consolidated (in the wake of repressive and authoritarian rule), in a situation where its future existence and growth cannot be taken for granted. A strong case can be made for why the politics of compromise that gave rise to the commission needed to shape the writing of the report. This sensitivity did not, of course, mean that the findings of the TRC were to be compromised in order not to offend. But it did mean that the tensions inherent in the life of the TRC, which is the burden of this chapter, needed to be addressed responsibly. At the same time, it must be remembered that the mandate of the TRC was based on the assumption that truth ultimately *could* heal. However painful the process, it was the underlying principle of the Act that there was simply no way of avoiding the past. It had to be confronted.

Merwin's prose poem, "Unchopping a Tree," provides a powerful metaphor for the healing of a nation. It reminds us of the limitations of any human endeavour. The author describes the difficult process of reconstructing a tree—placing each fallen branch, withered twig, and dried leaf in its appropriate place. The final lines of the poem are:

> The first breeze that touches its dead leaves. . . . You are afraid the motion of the
>   clouds will be enough to push it over.
> What more can you do? What more can you do?
> But there is nothing more you can do.
> Others are waiting.
> Everything is going to have to be put back.[41]

Have the leaves been placed in the correct place? How many twigs are missing? Will the birds recognize their nests? Will the tree take root and grow? Perhaps endurance, not restitution, never full recovery, not even full healing, is all that survivors can strive for. Some even hope—as they remember the great tree that once was.

The work of the TRC, described as fully as possible in its *Final Report*, obviously, does not guarantee reconciliation. It was neither possible nor the expectation of the commission that this could happen.

- There are too many conflicting memories. Distorted, one-sided, contested memories drive people apart. Old myths and dated histories are strangely impervious to new insights. Former president Pieter W. Botha and his supporters clung to their way of seeing things.
- Newly disclosed information and irrefutable evidence of past atrocities at times produced a level of public acknowledgment. The legitimacy of those responsible

may in the process be undermined, but often their power survives. There is a semblance of reconciliation, while the forces that contributed to past suffering, often in different guise, continue to defend past privilege. The more than 3.5 million people forcibly removed by apartheid bosses continue, despite several gains, to be marginalized and exploited.

- The pursuit of truth is the beginning of justice—both retributive and restorative. It does not, however, necessarily produce justice of either kind. Truth and power are intertwined. Buoyed by privilege, the wealthy cling to what they have. Old privilege is too precious to lose. Newly found privilege is too enticing to turn away from. The new South African divide is boldly economic and increasingly of a class nature.

- Truth can disclose the reality beneath the celebration of democracy without providing an incentive to healing. The great nations of the world, driven by democratic and human rights values, have long endured the exposure of human suffering, human rights violations, and exploitation in the midst of prosperity. Why should South Africa be any different?

It is going to take much more than *truth*, however partial or fully it was revealed by the TRC, to heal the South African nation. Truth is truth. It is not, in and of itself, social reform, institutional transformation, or political reconciliation. It all depends on what we do with "the truth." This was emphasized in a submission to the health sector hearing:

> There has been far too little genuine debate about the nature of social healing and what surely promotes it. Truth is one essential component of the needed social antiseptic which could cleanse the social fabric of the systematised habit of disregard for human rights, but it needs to be an examined truth; it needs to be considered, thought about, debated and digested and metabolised by individuals and by society. Failure to comprehend recent suffering is too often, in the studies I have made, the seed of future suffering.[42]

Despite its many flaws, the TRC facilitated a process within which:

- Different stories and memories told a story of a common commitment by different people, often locked in conflict. There was a choice between enduring conflict and mutual coexistence.
- Suffering by both blacks and whites, some of whom were bystanders caught in the cross fire, spoke of shared (although often hostile) sadness.
- The motives, perspectives, and ideals of those who inflicted suffering on others were slowly unraveled. The revealed hopes and fears of many of the nations' worst perpetrators were not vastly different from those of most other protagonists in the South African conflict. There is a potential perpetrator in each one of us—requiring that the humanity of both the abused and the abuser is ultimately regained.

- The realization that the will to take charge of one's own destiny and to enjoy material, cultural, and spiritual well-being is a basic ingredient of humanity itself. Over this not even the most repressive regime can triumph.

Notes

1. See the distinctions between "factual or forensic truth," "personal and narrative truth," "social truth," and "healing and restorative truth," in TRC, *Final Report* (Cape Town, 1998), I, chap. 5, 110–114.

2. Republic of South Africa, *Debates of the National Assembly (Hansard)*, First Session, Second Parliament, 1099–1100.

3. This section, like the rest of the preamble to the Act, is based on the influential "postamble" of the Interim Constitution, Act 200 of 1993.

4. See *Final Report*, V, chap. 8, 343–345.

5. Ibid., I, chap. 1, 1–4.

6. *AZAPO and Others v. the President of the RSA and Others*, 1996 (8) BCLR 1015 (CC) at paragraph 21.

7. The Act defines a "gross violation of human rights" as "the violation of human rights through (a) the killing, abduction, torture or severe ill treatment of any person; or (b) any attempt, conspiracy, incitement, instigation, command or procurement to commit an act referred to in paragraph (a), which emanated from conflicts of the past and which was committed during the period 1 March 1960 to 10 May 1994 within or outside the Republic, and the commission of which was advised, planned, directed, commanded or ordered, by any person acting with a political motive," Section 1(1)(x).

8. See *Final Report*, I, chap. 5, 103–135.

9. On the legislative and historical origins of the TRC, see *Final Report*, I, chap. 4.

10. See *Final Report*, V, chap. 1, 24–25.

11. Ibid., II, chap. 6, 488–576.

12. Ibid., IV.

13. Ibid., III, chap. 1, appendix, 12–33.

14. See Minority Position submitted by Commissioner Wynand Malan, *Final Report*, V, 436–456.

15. See *Final Report*, I, chap. 4, 54–55; chap. 5, 104–105.

16. John Thompson, *Ideology and Modern Culture: Critical Social Theory in the Era of Mass Communication* (Stanford, 1990). He defines the "mediazation" of modern culture "as the rapid proliferation of institutions of mass communication and the growth of networks of transmission through which commodified symbolic forms were made available to an ever-expanding domain of recipients" (11). He argues that these institutions of mass communication are central to modern social and political life: "Today the activities of states and governments, of their organizations and officials, take place within an arena that is to some extent *constituted by* [the] media of mass communication" (95) (emphasis in text). See also Amy Gutmann and Dennis Thompson, "The Moral Foundation of Truth Commissions," in this book; "Media and the Truth and Reconciliation Commission," special edition of *Rhodes Journalism Review* (Grahams-

town, 1997); Wilhelm J. Verwoerd, "Continuing the Discussion: Reflections from within the TRC," *Current Writing* VIII (1996): 66–85.

17. "Truth Trickle Becomes a Flood," *Mail & Guardian*, 1–7, November 1996, 14. See also Antjie Krog, *Country of My Skull* (Johannesburg, 1998), 36–37.

18. "Kommissie van Wraak" (Commission of Revenge), *Die Burger*, 26 September 1996, 18; "Waarheid en Wraak" (Truth and Revenge), *Die Burger*, 1 October 1996, 10; "Die Nuwe Slagoffers" (The New Victims), *Rapport*, 27 October 1996. See also Willie P. Esterhuyse, "Cartoons and the Afrikaner community," in Wilhelm J. Verwoerd and Mahlubi Mabizela (eds.), *Truths Drawn in Jest: Commentary on the TRC through Cartoons* (Cape Town, 2000).

19. See transcript of TRC Special Hearing on Compulsory Military Service in Cape Town, 23 July 1997; *Final Report*, IV, chap. 8.

20. The kinds of evidence that guide the commission in this regard included (a) identification through court records, confessions or statements implicating someone in police dockets, and/or previous rounds of indemnification; (b) a high degree of corroboration produced by the commission's own investigations (e.g., a victim's statement supported by other witnesses present at the time); and (c) a consistent recurring of names in the statements of people making allegations concerning gross human rights violations. See *Final Report*, I, chap. 4, 90–92.

21. Section 30 of the Act required the TRC to send a notice to those that it intended to name and to allow them an opportunity to respond.

22. See *Final Report*, V, chap. 6, 225–226.

23. See Louis Blom-Cooper, "Public Inquiries," *Current Legal Problems* (1993): 204–220; Jeremy Sarkin, "The Trials and Tribulations of South Africa's Truth and Reconciliation Commission," *South African Journal of Human Rights* XII (1996): 617–640; R. Scott, "Procedures at Inquiries—the Duty to be Fair," *Law Quarterly Review* CXI (1995): 596–616; and Sanford Levinson, "Trials, Commissions, and Investigating Committees," in this book.

24. See the "Findings and Conclusions" of the TRC, *Final Report*, V, chap. 6, 196–258.

25. See *Final Report*, I, chap. 4, 65–78.

26. Ibid., I, appendix, on apartheid as a crime against humanity, 94–102. See also Mary Burton, "Making Moral Judgements," and Kader Asmal et al., "When the Assassin Cries Foul: The Modern Just War Doctrine," in Charles Villa-Vicencio and Wilhelm Verwoerd (eds.), *Looking Back, Reaching Forward* (Cape Town, 2000).

27. See *Final Report*, V, chap. 6. A notable exception is Anthea Jeffery's *The Truth about the Truth Commission* (Johannesburg, 1999).

28. From Lord Acton's Inaugural Lecture, quoted by Brian Tierney, "Religious Rights: An Historical Perspective," in John Witte and Johan van der Vyver (eds.), *Religious Rights in Global Perspective* (The Hague, 1996), 33.

29. Section 3(1), the Act.

30. This task is explicitly addressed in *Final Report*, V, chap. 7, 259–303. The tale told in this chapter on "causes, motives and perspectives of perpetrators" is incomplete and in some respects premature since the bulk of the material dealing with perpetrators will only be available for analysis once the Amnesty Committee has completed its task. Drawing on a wide-ranging literature from local and international sources, this chapter

provides an initial framework for understanding. It is an agenda for further research and verification.

31. Albert Camus, *Neither Victims nor Executioners* (Chicago, 1972).

32. See also Aronson's notion of a "spiral of responsibility" underlying large-scale human rights violations by modern states. Ronald Aronson, "Responsibility and Complicity," *Philosophical Papers* XIX (1990): 62.

33. Section 3(1)(a), Promotion of National Unity and Reconciliation Act, no. 34, 1995.

34. See *Final Report*, II, chap. 6, 537–548.

35. Ibid., I, chap. 8.

36. Mahmood Mamdani, "Reconciliation without Justice," *Southern African Review of Books* (November/December 1996): 3–5.

37. See *Final Report*, I, chap. 2, 24–43; chap. 4, 58–65, 78–86.

38. Ibid., I, chap. 1, 1–4.

39. André du Toit, "Philosophical Perspectives on the Truth Commission. Some Preliminary Notes & Fragments," *Comment* (Rhodes University, Grahamstown) XX (Summer 1996): 2–14.

40. Michael Ignatieff, "Articles of Faith," *Index on Censorship* V (1996): 113.

41. William S. Merwin, *The Miner's Pale Children* (New York, 1970), 85–88.

42. Submission to the TRC health sector hearing (Cape Town, 18 June 1997) by Michael Simpson, a psychiatrist specialising in post-traumatic stress disorder.

The Contributors

Rajeev Bhargava teaches at the Centre for Political Studies, Jawaharlal Nehru University, New Delhi. He wrote *Individualism in Social Science* (Oxford, 1992) and edited *Secularism and Its Critics* (New Delhi, 1998) and (with Amiya Bagchi and R. Sudarshan) *Multiculturalism, Liberalism and Democracy* (forthcoming). Bhargava was Fellow in Ethics at the Program in Ethics and the Professions and Visiting Lecturer, Harvard University, 1995–1996; Visiting Senior Fellow at the Centre for the Study of Developing Societies, New Delhi, 1998–1999; and Visiting Fellow of the British Academy, 1999.

Alex Boraine, former President of the Methodist Church of Southern Africa, was an opposition Member of Parliament in South Africa from 1974 to 1986. He resigned from Parliament and, together with the former leader of the opposition, founded the Institute for Democracy in South Africa (IDASA). In 1994, he resigned from IDASA to start another nongovernmental organization, Justice in Transition. In 1995, he was appointed by the President of South Africa as Deputy Chairperson of the South African Truth and Reconciliation Commission.

David A. Crocker is Senior Research Scholar in the Institute for Philosophy and Public Policy and the School of Public Affairs at the University of Maryland. A former visiting professor at the Universities of Munich and Costa Rica, he specializes in sociopolitical philosophy, international development ethics, and transitional justice. Crocker's writings include *Praxis and Democratic Socialism: The Critical Social Theory of Markovic and Stojanovic* (Atlantic Highlands, N.J., 1983) and *Florecimiento humano y desarrollo internacional: La nueva ética de capacidades humanas* (San José, 1998). He co-edited (with Toby Linden) *Ethics of Consumption: The Good Life, Justice, and Global Stewardship* (Lanham, Md., 1998). He is president of the International Development Ethics Association (IDEA).

André du Toit is Professor of Political Studies, University of Cape Town. From 1969 to 1986, he was a professor of political philosophy at Stellenbosch University, and he has been a fellow or visiting professor at Yale University; Harvard University; Free University, Amsterdam; Aarhus University, Denmark; and Princeton University. He edited *Towards Democracy: Public Accountability in South Africa* (Cape Town, 1991) and (with Chabani Manganyi) *Political Violence and the Struggle in South Africa* (Basingstoke, England, 1990).

Kent Greenawalt is University Professor at Columbia University School of Law. He was a law clerk to Supreme Court Justice John M. Harlan, and a special assistant at the Agency for International Development. He was Benjamin N. Cardozo Professor of Jurisprudence at Columbia Law School before being appointed University Professor. He served as Deputy Solicitor General in 1972–1973, is a past president of the American Society for Political and Legal Philosophy, and is a fellow of the American Academy of Arts and Sciences and a member of the American Philosophical Society. He is the author of seven books, including *Fighting Words* (Princeton, 1995), *Law and Objectivity* (New York, 1992), and *Conflicts of Law and Morality* (New York, 1987).

Amy Gutmann is Laurance S. Rockefeller University Professor of Politics and Director of the University Center for Human Values at Princeton University. Her most recent books include (with Dennis Thompson) *Democracy and Disagreement* (Cambridge, Mass., 1998) and (with Anthony Appiah) *Color Consciousness* (Princeton, 1997), which was the winner of the American Political Science Association's Ralph J. Bunche Award for "the best scholarly work in political science that explores the phenomenon of ethnic and cultural pluralism" and the North American Society for Social Philosophy Book Award for "the book that makes the most significant contribution to social philosophy."

Elizabeth Kiss is Director of the Kenan Ethics Program and Associate Professor of the Practice of Political Science and Philosophy at Duke University. She has written on human rights, feminist theory, and issues of nationalism, group rights, and democracy in Central Europe.

Sanford Levinson is the W. St. John Garwood and W. St. John Garwood Jr. Regents Chair in Law at the University of Texas Law School. He is the author of *Constitutional Faith* (Princeton, 1988) and *Written in Stone* (Durham, N.C., 1998), as well as the editor of *Responding to Imperfection: The Theory and Practice of Constitutional Amendment* (Princeton, 1995). He is also co-editor of *Processes of Constitutional Decisionmaking* (Gaithersburg, 2000; 4th edition), and *Constitutional Stupidities/Constitutional Tragedies* (New York, 1998). He has taught at Princeton University, the Hebrew University, and the Harvard, Boston University, and New York University law schools, as well as the Central European University in Budapest and the Institute of United States Studies in London. He was a fellow of the Institute for Advanced Study (1986–1987) and the Program in Ethics and the Professions at Harvard (1991–1992).

Charles S. Maier teaches history and is the Director of the Center for European Studies at Harvard University. He has taught at the University of Bielefeld and at Duke University. He wrote *Recasting Bourgeois Europe*

(Princeton, 1975); *In Search of Stability* (New York, 1987); *The Unmasterable Past: History, Holocaust and German National Identity* (Cambridge, Mass., 1988); and *Dissolution: The Crisis of Communism and the End of East Germany* (Princeton, 1997).

Martha Minow is a professor at Harvard Law School. She has also taught at Harvard College, the Harvard Graduate School of Education, Boston College Law School, and the University of Toronto Faculty of Law. Her books include *Between Vengeance and Forgiveness: Facing History after Genocide and Mass Violence* (Boston, 1998); *Not Only for Myself: Identity Politics and Law* (New York, 1997); and *Making All the Difference: Inclusion, Exclusion, and American Law* (Ithaca, N.Y., 1990). She co-edited with (Gary Bellow) *Law Stories* (Ann Arbor, Mich., 1996), and she has also co-edited casebooks on civil procedure, women and the law, and family law.

Dumisa Buhle Ntsebeza is a South African human rights lawyer. He headed the South African Truth and Reconciliation Commission's Investigative Unit. In 1982, Ntsebeza joined the Sangoni Partnership, then the largest black African law firm in South Africa. He became well known for his defense of the politically persecuted. He served as President of the National Association of Democratic Lawyers. A former schoolteacher, he has lectured on human rights law, criminal law, and evidence at the University of Transkei.

Robert I. Rotberg is President, World Peace Foundation, and Director, WPF Program on Intrastate Conflict, Conflict Prevention, and Conflict Resolution in the Belfer Center of the Kennedy School of Government, Harvard University. He was Professor of Political Science and History, MIT; Academic Vice President, Tufts University; and President, Lafayette College. He is a Presidential appointee to the Council of the National Endowment for the Humanities and a Trustee of Oberlin College. He is the author and editor of numerous books and articles on U.S. foreign policy, Africa, Asia, and the Caribbean, most recently *Creating Peace in Sri Lanka: Civil War and Reconciliation* (Washington, D.C., 1999); *Burma: Prospects for a Democratic Future* (Washington, D.C., 1998); *War and Peace in Southern Africa: Crime, Drugs, Armies, and Trade* (Washington, D.C., 1998), *Haiti Renewed: Political and Economic Prospects* (Washington, D.C., 1997); *Vigilance and Vengeance: NGOs Preventing Ethnic Conflict in Divided Societies* (Washington, D.C., 1996); *From Massacres to Genocide: The Media, Public Policy and Humanitarian Crises* (Washingto, D.C., 1996); *The Founder: Cecil Rhodes and the Pursuit of Power* (New York, 1988); and *Suffer the Future: Policy Options in Southern Africa* (Cambridge, Mass., 1980).

Ronald C. Slye is an assistant professor of law at Seattle University. From 1996 to 1997, he was a visiting professor at the Community Law Centre of the University of the Western Cape, South Africa, and from 1996 to 1998, he was a consultant in international law to the research department of South Africa's Truth and Reconciliation Commission. From 1993 to 1996, he was Associate Director of the Orville H. Schell Jr. Center for International Human Rights at Yale Law School.

Dennis F. Thompson is Associate Provost, Harvard University; the Alfred North Whitehead Professor of Political Philosophy at Harvard University; and the founding director of the university's Center for Ethics and the Professions. His most recent book (jointly authored with Amy Gutmann) is *Democracy and Disagreement* (Cambridge, Mass., 1998). He has also published numerous other works on democratic theory and practice, including *Ethics in Congress: From Individual to Institutional Corruption* (Washington, D.C., 1995), *Political Ethics and Public Office* (Cambridge, Mass., 1987), *John Stuart Mill and Representative Government* (Princeton, 1976), and *The Democratic Citizen: Social Science and Democratic Theory in the 20th Century* (London, 1970).

Wilhelm Verwoerd is a lecturer in political philosophy and applied ethics in the Department of Philosophy, University of Stellenbosch, South Africa. From June 1996 until June 1998 he worked as a researcher for the TRC. He helped to draft those sections of the *Final Report* dealing with the mandate of the TRC, the concepts and principles underlying the TRC process, and reconciliation. He is the co-editor and co-author of two books on the TRC: *Truths Drawn in Jest: An Analysis of TRC Cartoons* (forthcoming) and *Looking Back, Reaching Forward: Reflections on the South African Truth and Reconciliation Commission* (London, 2000).

Charles Villa-Vicencio was National Director of the Research Department of the South African Truth and Reconciliation Commission. He had responsibility for overseeing the drafting of the TRC's *Final Report*. During his time in the TRC he was on leave of absence from the University of Cape Town, where he is Professor of Religion and Society. The author of several books and articles on the South African situation, he heads the Institute for Justice and Reconciliation in Africa.

Index

A. C. Nielsen-Market Research Africa survey report, 19
accountability: exposure as tool of, 16; justice and, 74–79; the law and, 179–182; as reconciliation requirement, 15, 170–171; transitional justice and, 102–105; in TRC amnesty process, 180–182
Ackerman, Bruce, 125, 211, 262
acknowledgment: described, 65n.25; healing as knowledge with, 152–153; as healing requirement, 245–246; of historical interpretation of other's suffering, 267–268; knowledge vs., 94n.19, 132–134, 221–222; lack of U.S. official, 92–93; need in democratic society of, 268, 278n.18; as operative act, 57–58; of others' legitimate pain, 90; by perpetrators and bystanders, 56, 247–250; public, 101, 238–239; regarding apartheid, 65n.26; remembrance as, 54–56; TRC model of, 92; truth as, 128, 132–135
the Act. *See* Promotion of National Unity and Reconciliation Bill (South Africa)
adversarial public action, 111–112
African National Congress (ANC): amnesty guarantees agreement by, 68–69, 172, 192, 217; *Final Report* on violations by, 287; human rights inquiries by, 239; human rights violations by, 6, 9, 41; political settlement between NP and, 122; reconciliation facilitated by, 81; TRC origins in, 143, 144
Afrikanerdom (South Africa), 5
Alfonsin, Raúl, 70, 115
amnesties: defining, 189; due process for, 202–203; identified as perpetrators, 196–197; justice and consequences issues for, 191–194; justified, 194–198; political nature of, 196; relations between truth commissions and, 190–191; seven dimensions of, 195. *See also* human rights perpetrators
amnesty: blanket, rejection of, 164–165; comparison of amnesty with disclosure and, 264; as controversial mechanism, 170–171; due process for offenders with, 202–203; granted in South America, 182, 184n.6; historic use in U.S. of, 189–190; human rights culture created through, 170–171, 182–184; as in-

justice, 194; justice and problem of, 74–79; justice as served by, 15–16; old and new regime issues regarding, 192–193; as plea bargain, 17; reconciliation and, 177–179; TRC rejection of general, 65n.53; U.S. studies on tax, 183, 188n.39. *See also* TRC truth for amnesty provision
Amnesty International, 89, 116
Anglo-Boer War (1899–1902), 72
Angola, 167
antigovernmental transitional justice model, 109, 110
apartheid, 141–142; acknowledge regarding, 65n.26; defining victims of, 250; injustice of, 64n.11; understanding perspective of, 74. *See also* South Africa
Arendt, Hannah, 39, 87
Argentina: amnesties granted in, 182; criminal proceedings in, 104; influence of truth commission of, 143; public revelation of truth in, 151–152; response to victims in, 262
Argentine "mothers of the disappeared," 262
Ash, Timothy Garton, 84, 87, 216, 217, 222
Asmal, Kader, 144
Aspen Institute, 115
Assembly of Civil Society (ACS), 110
associational transitional justice model, 109–110
asymmetrically barbaric society. *See* barbaric society
authority/authorities, 222, 223. *See also* due process of law
Aylwin, Patricio, 151
Azanian Peoples Organization (AZAPO) and Others v. President of the Republic of South Africa and Others, 159, 161, 162, 281

Bantu education, 127, 128
barbaric society: descent into asymmetrically, 58–60; lack of reconciliation in, 45; moral restoration of, 48–50; prevented by basic procedural justice, 47; restoring minimal decency into symmetrically, 58–60; symmetrically vs. asymmetrically, 45
Barbie, Klaus, 265
Barnard, Ferdi, 165

Die Rapport newspaper, 284
"A Different Kind of Justice" (Villa-Vicencio), 164
dishistoricization, 53–54. *See also* memory
Doctors Without Borders, 114
Douglas, Justice William O., 16, 214
due process of law: "American Dilemma" over, 212–216; for amnesties, 202–203; importance of adherence to, 226–227; moral consensus and, 220; plea bargaining and, 220; right to counsel/habeas corpus and, 224–225; ruinous cost of, 225–226; truth commissions as replacement for, 211, 217–220, 228n.2; truth/political justice and, 216–227; in United States, 218. *See also* criminal trials; government; law

Eastern Europe, 142
economy of moral disagreement, 38–42
Eichmann, Adolf, 219, 265
El Salvador, 117, 250, 257n.39
Elon, Amos, 71
emotional truth, 100
English rule of civil litigation, 225
Enquete-Commission (Germany), 263, 265
evil: basic procedural justice to control, 46, 47; defining, 64n.5; moral response and aftermath of, 49

Facing the Truth (documentary film), 236
Faulkner, William, 215
Fifteenth Amendment (U.S. Constitution), 212
Fifth Amendment (U.S. Constitution), 213
Final Report (TRC). *See* TRC *Final Report*
Ford, President Gerald, 190
forensic/factual truth, 70, 100, 102, 151
forgetting, collective, 53
forgiveness: Christian morality and, 29–33, 61–62, 85, 199; confusion between mercy and, 62–63, 209n.54; individual reconciliation level and, 181; link between results and, 209n.48; moral hatred and, 84; moral objection to, 9; moral responsibility and, 60–61; national healing and, 250–251; restorative justice and, 199; truth for amnesty provision and, 29–33; truth commission as mechanism of, 45; *ubuntu* (humanness) and, 81, 86, 87; as value shared by citizens, 40
former Yugoslavia, 91, 114, 116, 147
Foucault, Michel, 33

Framework Agreement (1994), 110
France, W.W. II collaboration of Vichy, 177–178, 263
Fraser, Nancy, 73
Freedom Front (South Africa), 168
Friedrich, Carl J., 222
Friedrich Ebert Foundation (Germany), 115

Gandhi, Indira, 55
Gandhi, Mohandas K., 48
Gauck Authority (East Germany), 263
GDR (German Democratic Republic), 262, 263
Geneva Conventions and Protocols, 287
Genocide Convention, 105
Germany: Enquete-Commission of, 263, 265; experiences of united, 262–263; inquiries into collaboration with Nazi, 177–178, 263; Nazi regime of, 46, 219; opening of Stasi files in, 273, 278n.28. *See also* Gauck Authority (East Germany); Holocaust (World War II)
Gobodo-Madikizela, Pumla, 73, 243, 285
Goldstone, Justice Richard, 16, 80, 88, 91, 143
Goniwe, Matthew, 161, 162
Goniwe, Mbulelo, 162
government: amnesty and old/new regime issues for, 192–193, 217; discretion regarding prosecution by, 208n.38; nonprosecution by, 206n.24. *See also* due process of law; political compromise
Greenawalt, Kent, 15
"Guatemala: Nunca Mas" report (REMHI), 111
Guatemala: Alliance against Impunity of, 110; CEH (Historical Clarification Commission), 104, 111; Historical Clarification Commission (CEH) of, 104, 111; National Commission for Truth and Reconciliation of, 111; National Reconciliation Law (NRL) of, 104–105, 110; National Revolutionary Union (URNG) of, 110; Project for the Recovery of Historical Memory (REMHI) of, 111; public actions by NGOs of, 112; public sphere enlarged by newspapers in, 113
Guguletu Seven, 250
Gutmann, Amy, 8, 9, 14, 107, 108, 123

habeas corpus, 224–225
The Hague war crimes tribunal, 159